Studies in African American History and Culture

Edited by

Graham Russell Hodges
Colgate University

A Routledge Series

Jesuit Slaveholding in Maryland, 1717–1838

Thomas Murphy, S.J.

NEW YORK AND LONDON

Published in 2001 by
Routledge
711 Third Avenue, New York, NY 10017, USA
2 Park Square, Milton Park, Abingdon, Oxfordshire OX14 4RN

First issued in paperback 2016

Routledge is an imprint of the Taylor and Francis Group, an informa business

Library of Congress Cataloging-in-Publication Data
Cataloging-in-Publication Data is available from the Library of Congress.

ISBN 13: 978–1–138–97377–0 (pbk)
ISBN 13: 978–0–8153–4052–2 (hbk)

For my Aunt,
Marian Cashman
and for my friend,
Scott Brodeur, S.J.

Contents

Acknowledgments

I BEGIN WITH MY FAMILY. IT WAS MY GOOD FORTUNE TO GROW UP IN Massachusetts, near Boston, an area so permeated with history that it was an ingredient of the atmosphere. My parents, John and Betty Murphy, my stepmother, Norma Murphy, my grandparents, my aunts, uncles and cousins have always encouraged me to exploit my birth in this setting. My mother, Betty, made me into the reader that I am today, and from an early age I enjoyed having the newspapers read to me with an ear to history by my paternal grandparents, John and Agnes Murphy. My father, John, my aunt, Margaret Murphy, and my maternal grandmother, Marion G. Daley, spent many hours walking me around Boston or driving me through the New England countryside. My deep thanks go to all—both those still in the space and time that is accessible to the historian and those who have gone ahead to God. During the final stages of preparation of my dissertation, my Aunt, Marian Cashman, passed on suddenly. I dedicate this book to her with fond memories of her loving encouragement over so many years.

The Society of Jesus, which I joined in 1987, has likewise fostered my interest in history. Three provincial superiors of the New England Province have propelled me along the way—Bob Manning, Bill Barry and Bob Levens. Bob Manning also later became my local superior at Jesuit School of Theology at Berkeley in Berkeley, California, joining Michael Boughton at Fairfield University, Connecticut and Charlie Moutenout at Berkeley in the same role of coaxing me to fulfill my mission to produce this dissertation. I also recall with thanks the interest of two formation directors, Jim Gillon and Jim Lafontaine. All of these men have listened to my struggles, celebrated my successes with me, and shown a great deal of conviction that I could accomplish this project.

I have lived in four Jesuit communities during the research and writing of my dissertation and now this book —the Fairfield Jesuit community, Leonard Neale House in Washington, D.C., the Jesuit Community at the Jesuit School of Theology in Berkeley, California and the Seattle University Jesuit Community. All the Jesuits whom I have lived with during this process have shown great support and affection throughout. In the climactic months of the dissertation, especially, when I was also preparing for M.Div. comprehensive examination, my fifteen companions at Chardin House in Berkeley kept me going with their prayers and warmth. There are a few individual Jesuits, however, whom I wish to single out for special thanks. First of all, there is Scott Brodeur, who shares the dedication of the dissertation, and whose enthusiasm for the idea has persisted from the beginning. Gary Menard's computer skills have been indispensable to putting the dissertation in final form. Mark Bosco and Chris Weekly have also been good friends in the Lord, listening to my discouragement and helping me to place setbacks in perspective against the opportunities and the achievements. Joining them as good Jesuit companions have been Joe Wagner and Jim Prehn, whose invitations to dinner or a movie usually came along at just the moment that I needed a break. Steve Maekawa, O.P., who has a lively interest in history himself, has always been willing to listen to my tales of the Jesuit slaves. Brian Dumont of Boston has likewise been a willing listener and confidant, going back to the early writing days at Fairfield.

The History Department at Fairfield University fostered me as a fledgling instructor of undergraduate students and cheered me through my comprehensive exams in 1992. They have been willing to examine my proposals and drafts for the dissertation, and I recall with appreciation all their interest in my career over the years. Particular thanks go to Richard De Angelis, William Abbott and Patricia Behre.

At the University of Connecticut, I am grateful for the help I received from two dissertation directors, Karen Kupperman and Larry Goodheart. Allen Ward has been a good friend ever since I began as a teaching assistant at Storrs in 1983. I thank, too, the other members of my committee—Kent Newmyer and Altina Waller. I am also grateful to Ron Coons for his help, particularly during my return to the doctoral program after several years away.

Tom Buckley, S.J. of the JSTB faculty deserves special gratitude. He read my dissertation manuscript in its later form, and has offered many helpful suggestions about writing for publication. I am grateful for Tom's permission for me to participate in his Church History seminar in the spring semester of 1997, and for his friendly suggestions about various professional opportunities.

Since the fall quarter of 1999, I have been a member of the History Department faculty at Seattle University. There I have received unstinting encouragement from Tom Taylor, the Chair, Dave Madsen, Jacquelyn Miller, Kan Liang, Danny Bernstein and Theresa Earenfight. I am particularly grateful to Arthur Fisher and Patrick O'Leary, S.J., for inviting me to guest-lecture in their Jesuit History course during the winter quarter of 2000.

So many people have been so good to me that these acknowledgements are the hardest part of this book to write. I fear that many have been left out, but

I know that the Lord has a better memory than I do, and will smile upon the kindness of one and all. As I come to the end of this challenging enterprise, so soon after grace-filled ordinations to the diaconate and priesthood, I am aware of what a lucky and blessed man I am.

Introduction

On October 16, 1771, Father Joseph Mosley, S.J. made the following entry in the baptismal register of St. Joseph's Church, Talbot County, Maryland: "Matthew, negro of ours, Talbot. Godparents were Thom., Negro of ours, and Peg, Negro of Chas. Blake."[1]

Mosley's use of the phrase "negro of ours," referred to the slaves owned by the religious order to which he belonged, the Society of Jesus, or Jesuits. To this day, "ours" is a Jesuit expression referring to whatever things that this Roman Catholic religious order of men hold in common. It can refer to the membership which unites Jesuits into the Society—it is quite common for a Jesuit to refer to another Jesuit as "one of ours." The expression may also refer to material possessions, which the Society holds collectively rather than individually. For approximately the first two centuries of Jesuit presence in Maryland, those possessions included other human beings. By 1838, the year that they decided to hold a mass sale of their slaves, the Jesuits owned 272 slaves on six plantations totalling 11,607 acres in the state. This study is an attempt to measure the ties which bound the Jesuits to their slaves, as well as the events which finally led the Jesuits to loosen those ties.

Despite clear evidence that their management of plantations was a fiscal and economic failure, Jesuits remained entrenched slaveholders for political, theological, intellectual reasons and social reasons. In the last quarter of the eighteenth century, the twin shocks of the Church's temporary suppression of the Jesuit order and the American Revolution's achievement of religious liberty essentially ended the political motivation for Catholic clergymen to own slaves in what had become the United States, inducing some discussion among the priests of Maryland about ending the practice. However, no drastic change took place until the 1830's, when the Society of Jesus, now restored and anticipating that American Catholicism would urbanize under the influence of massive European immigration, decided to sell its slaves in order to devote more energy to ministry in the cities. The expectation that large numbers of white Europeans would need priests triumphed over any thought that the Jesuits' slaves and plantations had a premier claim to their owners' ministry. Jesuits thus ignored Catholic abolitionists like the Irish politician Daniel O'Connell, opting instead to dispose of their slaves in a mass sale.

I began thinking about a dissertation on slaveholding by Jesuits in Maryland during my two years in Jesuit philosophy studies at Loyola University of Chicago (1989–1991). I was sent from my native Boston to study with some two dozen other young Jesuits drawn from several sections of the United States. The American Assistancy of the Society of Jesus is currently divided into ten provinces, and these provinces have all the distinct identities and friendly rivalries of the "several states" of the nation. It was not unusual for classmates to tease each other about the backgrounds of each other's provinces. When the target of a barb was a member of the Maryland Province, it was almost certain that the man would be joshed about the fact that his ancestors in the religious life had once owned slaves. It seemed like a perfect opportunity to portray a young Maryland Jesuit as the heir to a system of oppression and reaction. I myself participated in this ribbing; it seemed like a good way for a northerner to score some points against southerners. As time wore on and the jokes grew stale, however, I began to wonder about the real story of Maryland Jesuit slaveholding. By the time my religious superiors asked me to follow my philosophy studies with the pursuit of a doctorate in history, I knew what topic I wished to write about: What was the real story behind the stereotyping?

Early in my research, I discovered that the basic narrative of Jesuit slaveholding has already been reconstructed over the past generation by four fine historical studies. The first was "The Slaves of the Jesuits in Maryland," a master's thesis written at Georgetown University in 1974 by Peter C. Finn, S.J. in an effort to reconstruct the rise, daily proceedings, and termination of the slaveholding. Two other studies were written by Robert Emmett Curran, S.J. In an article published in 1983, "'Splendid Poverty:' The Slaves of the Jesuits in Maryland, 1805–1838," Curran concentrated on the decline of the Jesuit slave system during the decades just before their final, mass sale of slaves in 1838. A decade later, in *The Bicentennial History of Georgetown University: Volume I, from Academy to University 1789–1889*, Curran placed the continuation and eventual termination of the slave system within the context of the founding and solidification of that Jesuit school in Washington, D.C. Curran believed that the desire of the Jesuits to provide a sound financial foundation for that school and open further ones had a major role in the decision to sell the slaves.[2] Like Finn, Curran worked to recapture a tale that had been in some danger of being lost or ignored. Finally, in 1996, Edward F. Beckett, S.J. published "Listening to our History: Inculturation and Jesuit Slaveholding." Intended as an internal reflection for members of the Jesuit order, Beckett's work argues that the facts of Jesuit slaveholding show that these men were overly influenced by the environment of British North America. Rather than challenge its ethos, the Jesuits succumbed to their eagerness to demonstrate that Catholics could be loyal Englishmen and embraced values they should have challenged.[3]

The facts uncovered by Finn, Curran and Beckett make several things clear. Jesuit slaveholding began subtly; the earliest documented record of its existence dates only to 1717.[4] It seems likely that the Jesuits, like other landowners in the Chesapeake colonies, turned to slaveholding as the supply of indentured servants immigrating from the British Isles grew smaller during the second half of the seventeenth century.[5] There is also the strong possibility that many, if not most, of their slaves came to them as gifts from lay people eager to serve as benefactors of the Church. If so, the fact that the official teaching of the Roman Catholic Church condemned the African slave trade while presenting slave labor itself as a natural proceeding of human society would have allowed the recipients of these second-hand slaves to gloss the question of how the slaves had reached the United States. In any case, there is no record whatsoever of colonial Jesuits deliberating whether to turn to slaveholding; we simply know that they did.[6] It is also probable that the Jesuits of colonial Maryland worried about the possibility that the government might confiscate property belonging to Catholics, and so tended to avoid documentation of their possessions.

Beginning in the late eighteenth century, however, there is evidence that, while still proceeding within the context of their Church's doctrinal and philosophical approbation of slavery, the Jesuits conducted a long and painful debate over whether and how to end their personal participation in slaveholding. Paradoxically, the quantities of Jesuit slaves grew even as the Society hesitated over the matter. There were 192 slaves in 1765, and 272 just before abandonment of the practice in 1838.

The reconstruction of the narrative of Jesuit slaveholding has not completed the story, however. What is needed still is a reconstruction of the moral universe of these Jesuits—-the ideological paradigms and experiential biases through which they analyzed the world they lived in and through which they approached the moral decisions they had to make. It is impossible to complete the study of Jesuit acculturation in British North America and the United States without addressing this broader question. It is reasonably clear that there were three overriding patterns of thought that influenced the conduct of Jesuit slaveholding—a feeling that slaveholding was politically advantageous for Catholic planters whose civil liberties were insecure in a predominantly Protestant colony, a fear that profit and the acquisition of wealth were goals that would separate Christians from God, which led to consistent financial maladministration of the farms, and a theological conviction that members of the superior white race were called to exercise paternal care over members of the inferior black race. The Jesuits' decision to abandon the practice of slaveholding was delayed by their insistence on reconciling any change with these traditional ideals. It was not inevitable, however, that these ideals should have become the principle means through which they analyzed their dilemma. How did those attitudes originate and strengthen in the Jesuit mind to the point of making it very difficult for these men to dispose of their slaves?

Furthermore, when the Jesuits did cease their slaveholding, they made the significant decision to sell their slaves en masse instead of setting them all free. How did their traditional attitudes influence this decision to sell rather than manumit? These questions can only be answered if we engage the Maryland Jesuits on their own terms, approaching their world through the eyes with which they themselves saw it.

Furthermore, the tone of general American Catholic historiography suggests a prodigious need for greater objectivity in evaluating the slave question. Before the decrees of the Second Vatican Council (1962–1965) urged Catholic scholars to undertake a more impartial study of Church history, the tone of Catholic historiography, on almost any topic, was usually apologetic. An occasional historian like Theodore Maynard (*The Story of American Catholicism*, 1941) attempted to be more objective, only to be ostracized by opposition from powerful bishops.[7] More typically, if errors and embarrassments could not be hidden, they were glossed over. An example of that style was the article "The Survival of the Catholic Faith in Southern Maryland, " by John LaFarge, S.J., which appeared in 1935 during the tricentennial celebrations of the founding of the colony. Lafarge openly regretted that Jesuits had owned slaves in the United States, but argued that at least they had a benevolent style of governing which set a humane example for other slaveholders. Lafarge felt that while they failed to change the system, the Jesuits at least showed the least offensive means of proceeding within it.[8]

The Council's call for less defensiveness in the Church's interactions with the rest of the world created a greater openness to critical analysis of the Catholic past by Catholics themselves. A new tendency to look unabashedly at problematic aspects of the Church's past meant that Jesuit slaveholding received due mention in two general histories of the American Church which appeared during the 1980's. These were *American Catholics: A History of the Roman Catholic Community in the United States* (1981), by James Hennesey, S.J., and *The American Catholic Experience: From Colonial Times to the Present* (1985), by Jay Dolan. Both were objective scholars who focused on narrative reconstruction, and their impartiality was a departure from the apologetic LaFarge approach. The nature of their comprehensive studies prevented Hennesey and Dolan from giving slavery more than passing attention in their books, however. Ultimately, when it comes to their treatment of Jesuit slaveholding, Hennesey and Dolan must be identified with the Finn-Curran approach of reconstructing the basics of a long glossed over narrative as evenhandedly as possible. They did not treat thoroughly the moral paradigms that determined the manner in which the Jesuits functioned as slaveholders.

Other pressures than historiographical objectivity were exerting themselves on Catholic scholarship concerning slavery, however. The Council's call for greater objectivity coincided with the height of the civil rights movement in the United States—-the year of the Council's close, 1965, was the same year that saw Martin Luther King's march on Selma, Alabama, and the enactment of the Voting Rights Act. Many Catholics reacted to this combination of events by making a collective examination of conscience on the race question. It was natural that when some Catholic historians considered their Church's slaveholding, they showed a direct moral outrage that reacted sharply against the LaFarge approach. A typical expression of this righteous anger may be found in Cyprian Davis' book *The History of Black Catholics in the United States* (1990). Davis' theme was not so much an objective study of African American Catholics as it was a celebration of the faith of a community who never ceased claiming as their own a Church which historically treated them with a mixture of outright injustice and unthinking neglect, both before and after abolition. Davis concluded that

> The story of African American Catholicism is the story of a people who obstinately clung to a faith that gave them sustenance, even when it did not always make them welcome. Like many others, blacks had to fight for their faith; but their fight was often with members of their own household. Too long have black Catholics been anonymous. It is now clear that they can be identified, that their presence has made an impact, and that their contributions have made Catholicism a unique and stronger religious body.9

There is a major theological place for such a meditation within the Church, but Davis' approach has serious historiographical limits. Is it fair to evaluate the moral decisions of the antebellum Jesuits according to the ethical standards of the late twentieth century, when slavery is universally condemned? There is a clear need to try to see the world as these men themselves saw it at the time they made their decisions.

The moral outrage epitomized by Davis has been accompanied by the rise of still another method of pondering Catholic slaveholding, the effort to use the Church's eventual turnabout on the issue as a historical precedent for those seeking reform in today's Catholic Church. The issue of whether and how the Church can change its doctrines has been a great preoccupation of the post-Counciliar Church, which has been marked by a tension between great demands for vast reforms and vast institutional resistance to further reform. One key query that has emerged has been this: how can an institution that proclaims itself incapable of error adapt itself to social and doctrinal change? Slaveholding, one issue on which the Church clearly changed its teaching late in the nineteenth century after hundreds of years of defending the practice, has attracted attention from theologians who wonder whether and how the Church can accommodate its moral theology to such matters as changing views on human sexuality, the status of women, and the structure of the priesthood.

Two examples of this use of the slaveholding issue may be found in the article "Development in Moral Doctrine," by John T. Noonan, Jr. (1993) once presented as part of the Warren Lecture Series on Catholic Studies at the University of Oklahoma, and the book *Infallibility on Trial: Church, Conciliarity and Communion* by Luis M. Bermejo (1992). These types of studies collect much historical information of great value, taking great care to trace the legislation of popes and councils, but do so primarily to make a broader theological point. The objective reconstruction of the past is not their priority; they are more interested in the fact of that the theology of slaveholding was destroyed by a Church of reform than they are in what that theology actually said to a Church of tradition. Ultimately, therefore, these studies also do not fill the gap in our objective understanding of the moral universe of the Jesuit slaveholders.

Ironically, the increased attention to Catholic slaveholding within the Church itself has not been paralled by all that much interest in Catholic slaveholding by mainstream historians. That is regrettable, for the record of the Maryland Jesuits as slaveholders shows that they were exceptions to many of the general theses about the typical motives and conduct of American slaveholders that historians have offered recently.

Just as there has been a revolution in Catholic historiography since the 1950's, so there has also been a revolution in the general historiography of slaveholding. Furthermore, in comparing these two subsets of the historiographical discipline, the similarities of transition from apologetic to critical to moralistic approaches has been striking. Eric Foner has described the old apologetic approach to slaveholding, with its thesis that it was a civilizing masters devised a benevolent institution to deal with the natural backwardness of the enslaved. Apologists argued that plantation life was marked by good standards of living for the slaves, gentle punishments, and true reciprocity between masters and slaves.[10] This thesis is a good description of the ideals that the Jesuits, at least, said they had for their slaves. Neither in the case of the Jesuits or any other masters, however, did it fit reality.

Revision began in 1956, when Kenneth Stampp's *The Peculiar Institution: Slavery in the Ante-Bellum South* reconstructed plantations as places of persistent conflict between masters and slaves, a conflict caused by the clash between the master's desire to earn the greatest possible income and the slaves' constant efforts to undermine the slaveholding institution through both direct and passive aggression.[11]

Whatever the general accuracy of Stampp's thesis, it does not fit the Jesuit picture very neatly. The accurate model of a Jesuit plantation is a place where there was a clash between masters ambivalent about profit and slaves eager to undermine the institution through direct and passive aggression. So, the

Stampp thesis only half fits the Jesuit situation. The slave resistance on the Jesuit plantations may have been as motivated as much by resistance to the control the masters tried to exert over the religious lives of the slaves as it was by resistance to efforts to get the slaves to work harder.

Stampp's thought began a discussion which eventuall produced a thesis of slavery as a ruthless engine of economic prosperity that was practiced with capitalistic efficiency and prodigious profit. This analysis reached its culmination with the work of Robert William Fogel and Stanley L. Engermann, first writing together in *Time on the Cross: The Economics of American Negro Slavery* (1974) and later by Fogel writing alone in *Without Consent or Contract: The Rise and Fall of American Slavery* (1989).

In their joint work, Fogel and Engermann focused in a provocative way on the accomplishments that slaves themselves were able to make during their bondage, to the point where some critics wondered whether their thesis to left room to question why slavery had ever been abolished. They responded:

> We have attacked the traditional interpretation of the economics of slavery not in order to resurrect a defunct system, but in order to correct the perversion of the history of blacks—in order to strike down the view that black Americans were without culture, without achievement, and without development

for their first two hundred and fifty years on American soil. . . . One of the worst consequences of the traditional interpretation of slavery is that is has diverted attention from the attack on the material conditions of black people that took place during the decades following the end of the Civil War. By exaggerating the severity of slavery, all that has come after it has been made to appear as an improvement over previous conditions.[12]

The view that the slaves made an indispensable contribution to the early American economy through their work for the welfare of their masters would have startled the Jesuits, who constantly stressed in their writings the burden of governing and caring for these resistant people. Furthermore, the Jesuit record modifies the idea that the living standards of slaves should only be measured materially. For example, living conditions for the Jesuits' slaves declined sharply once they were sold to new masters in Louisiana in 1838, and this decline was spiritual as well as material.

Jesuits were self-consciously moral men, well versed in centuries of theology and ethics, who attempted to conduct slaveholding in a manner which they hoped would be pleasing to God. They were, however, resistant to the abolitionist agenda.

In addition, major writers on the connection between slaveholding and organized religion have had little to say about the Jesuits. Albert J. Raboteau and Eugene Genovese both overlooked the slaveholding experiences of the

Jesuits in their books. Raboteau's *Slave Religion: The 'Invisible Institution' in the Antebellum South* (1978) focused almost exclusively on the experience of Protestant slaves.[13] His more recent study, *A Fire in the Bones: Reflections on African American Religious History* (1995) does contain a chapter on black Catholics, but the emphasis is on the experience and reflection of slaves rather than their masters, despite a passing reference to the Jesuits.[14] While Raboteau's approach is in laudable accordance with the recent historiographical trend of concentrating on the experiences of "outsider" groups whose perspectives have traditionally been neglected in mainstream American historiography, it leaves a gap in our understanding of how Jesuit slaveholders justified their practice to themselves.

Genovese had little to say about American Catholic slaveowners or slaves in *Roll, Jordan, Roll* (1974), despite his strong interest in how slaveholders tried to manipulate religion to hold slaves in obedience, in how slaves, in their turn, tried to manipulate religion as a tool in their struggle for freedom, and in how slaveholding in Protestant North America compared with the more Catholic derivatives in Latin America.[15] His more recent study of slaveholders' religion, *The Slaveholder's Dilemma: Freedom and Progress in Southern Conservative Thought, 1820–1860* (1992) focused on what Protestant slaveholders thought about medieval Catholicism rather than on what they thought of the Catholic Church in their own time in the South.[16] Genovese thus missed an opportunity to study some key differences between other slaveholders and Jesuits, most notably the fact that when Jesuits defended slavery, they tended to regarded it as a necessary evil rather than a positive good.

While zeal for profit may have characterized the general class of American slaveholders, the Jesuits were too ambivalent about profit to fit into such a category. Their unease about wealth had direct consequences: their farms were disastrously unproductive until the sale of their last slaves. Moreover, far from having an uncomplicated determination to wring as much sweat out of their slaves as they could, the Jesuits seem to have come to regard slaveholding as a cross they had to endure for the sake of the religious salvation of their slaves. They persisted in a belief that the slaves constituted a trust given to them by God, and that the success of their supervision of them would be measured by whether or not the slaves were received into Heaven. At the very least, Jesuit slaveholders were an exception to the general rule of slaveholding in the United States. It is just possible that their experience bids us to revise our analysis of that general rule.

Jesuits in Maryland may also have been the exception to the general manner with which slaveholding was conducted within the Roman Catholic Church. When Stanley Elkins wrote *Slavery: A Problem in American Institutional and Intellectual Life* (1959), he believed that slavery in the United States was a far more rigid, racist and inhumane institution than its counterpart in Latin America. Elkins credited this difference, in part, to the Roman

Catholicism of the Latin Americans, which he saw as leading to a more benevolent approach to slaves and slaveholding than the British Protestantism that dominated slaveholders in North America. Elkins found a flexibility in Latin American practices that led to quick and flexible manumissions as well as social mobility for freed slaves.[17] The Jesuits of Maryland may have been Catholic, but their lives and those of their slaves unfolded in a vastly different way from Elkins' scenario, showing that Catholicism itself could produce pluralistic methods of slaveholding.

Maryland Jesuits departed from Elkins' reconstruction in almost every particular. They were cautious about manumissions, often changing their minds after deciding to carry them out. They did little to challenge the inhospitable reception generally given to free blacks in Maryland, in fact keeping blacks in bondage rather than sending them forth as small businessmen in a prophetic challenge to the Maryland marginalization of the free African American. In *Slavery and Freedom on the Middle Ground: Maryland during the Nineteenth Century*, Barbara Jeanne Fields described this hostility of Maryland society to manumission.[18] Comparison of her findings with the reluctance of the Maryland Jesuits to manumit their slaves helps to confirm her perspective that Maryland was not a place where a freed slave could easily prosper. Their record shows that the Maryland Jesuits did little to challenge that moral climate of opposition to freed blacks. Interestingly, Fields never mentioned the Jesuit slaveholders in her book, despite its exclusive focus on a state where they owned so many, and where their record had so much to add to her thesis.

Finally, a study of the thought of the Maryland Jesuits offers a chance to expand our understanding of why Catholics in the United States generally resented the abolitionist movement. Various explanations have been advanced for this hostility. In *American Catholics*, James Hennesey emphasized how white Catholic immigrants feared competing for bottom-level jobs with freed slaves. Also, Hennesey stressed how much those immigrants saw the concern of abolitionists for Blacks in the distant South as hypocritical, given that such reformers were simultaneously exploiting and discriminating against the white poor in their own Northern cities while proclaiming a nativist hostility to Catholicism.[19]

The Maryland Jesuits were resistant to abolitionism, however, long before immigration and nativism became vivid issues in the 1830's. Their opposition was based on abolitionism's origins in Protestantism, which Jesuits saw as a heresy, all of whose manifestations and derivatives must be resisted. The writings of Brother Joseph Mobberly, S.J. (1783–1827), the most prolific Jesuit author on the slavery issue, show a resistance to private interpretation of the Bible and the idea that anyone other than pope, bishops and priests could exercise authority in the Church. Mobberly saw abolitionism as both a consequence and a proponent of these two heresies, either of which he feared would lead to religious and social anarchy. Slavery became for him a necessary, pater-

nalistic evil for the preservation of order: he said he regretted that it had been introduced into the United States, but he knew not how Americans, let alone Jesuits, could rid themselves of that institution.[20]

How the Jesuits of Maryland came by, treated and finally disposed of the "Negroes of Ours" is the topic of this book. The first question, how they originally acquired slaves, is addressed in Chapter One, "Property and Religious Liberty: The Emergence of Jesuit Slaveholding," which demonstrates why Jesuits found the owning of chattel to be indispensable to the Catholic struggle for civil liberty under English rule. These political factors overruled even the compelling economic and social forces which pushed Maryland as a whole to become a slaveholding society during those years.

Chapter Two is entitled "Real Poverty and Apparent Wealth on the Jesuit Farms," and argues that the fragmentary and chaotic nature of the surviving financial records indicates that the Maryland Jesuits had an ingrained financial carelessness which resulted in a chronic indebtedness to their London superiors of the English Province of the Society of Jesus. This disregard was partly due to the Jesuits' greater professional interest in ministry than farm management, but it was also made possible by the generosity of lay Catholic planters in Maryland, whose benefactions to the Jesuits allowed the order to escape the worst consequences of their fiscal mismanagement. Another matter that was given priority over the general administration of the plantations was the pastoral care which the Jesuits felt they owed their slaves, which was caught up in the ineradicable mixture of social paternalism and racism with which the Jesuits regarded their chattel.

Chapter Three, "Doubt and Debate: Jesuit Questions about Slaveholding," demonstrates how events such as the suppression of the Jesuit order by the Church between 1773 and 1814, the American Revolution, the emergence of the early American republic, and the arrival of refugee priests from the French Revolution stimulated some argument among clergy in Maryland as to whether slaveholding by priests should continue. These discussions actually led to the adoption of a gradual manumission policy in 1814, but it was repealed six years later without having been implemented. Chapter Four, "Preaching versus Practice: Jesuit Theory and Conduct of Slaveholding" offers an explanation for this failure to change, showing that even while talking of about ideals of mildly conducted slaveholding and possible manumission the Jesuits continued to govern their slaves harshly even amid changing times.

A major cause of the impulse to retain slaveholding is traced in Chapter Five, "Brother Joseph Mobberly and the Intellectual Antecedents of Jesuit Antiabolitionism." The Jesuits' conviction that abolitionism was a derivative of Protestant heresy blinded them to the valid arguments of the anti-slavery movements of the early nineteenth century. A counterweight to this bias toward keeping the slaves is explored in Chapter Six, "To Serve the Slave or the Immigrant?" As the Jesuits foresaw the coming massive migration of white

European Catholics into the seaports of the East Coast, some grew increasingly inclined to view their black slaves as an impediment to ministry with Catholics of sounder moral character, greater religious promise, and white race.

Chapter Seven, "The End of Jesuit Slaveholding, 1838," ponders the climactic events that brought the Jesuits' to their decision finally to sell all their chattel. In context, the decision to sell rather than free the slaves can be seen as a compromise among the various positions that Jesuits took on the question of slaveholding in general. By selling instead of freeing their slaves, the Jesuits remained consistent with their heritage of antiabolitionism and their sense of official Church teaching. That they disposed of their personal slaves, however, gave the Jesuits their desired availability to the white urban Catholic immigrant. An epilogue, "A Slaveholding Both Anglo-American and Catholic," assesses the lessons of the Jesuit experience.

Underlying all these chapters is a broad thesis that the Jesuits always had their unique motives for slaveholding. It is tempting to classify them as typical Maryland slaveholders. They began the practice around the same time as it generally emerged in the colony, and they abandoned it as it was in overall decline throughout the state. All the social and economic factors that influenced other slaveholders influenced them. However, the Jesuits always had their own reasons, springing from their status as professional, Catholic men of God and participants in the Anglo-American culture that produced the United States.

Historiography has passed through several phases in evaluating slaveholding: championing it, measuring its efficiency, condemning it, reconstructing its narrative and using its example to shed light on pressing issues of today. Slaveholding has received enough attention that we are no longer shocked by its existence or its extent. It is timely, therefore, to look beyond the basic tale of Jesuit slaveholding and study the moral assumptions upon which its conduct and termination were based. A belief system which was initally based upon the political expediency of holding black Catholics in bondage so that all Catholics might have religious liberty combined with ambivalence about profit and a theological justification of moral, social, and racial paternalism of betters toward their lessers to create the network of Jesuit slaveholdings. In the later decades of the eighteenth century, this practice survived ecclesiastical suppression and political revolution to endure a climate of antiabolitionism in the early nineteenth century. Finally, however, it gave way to the demands of immigration. In reconstructing how the moral sensibility of the Jesuits gave meaning to these events, this dissertation proposes to offer a greater understanding of the elaborate historical experience of Jesuit slaveholding in the colony and state of Maryland.

NOTES

1. "Father Joseph Mosley's Baptismal and Marriage Records, 1763–1787," Item #103.5X1, Archives of the Maryland Province (MPA), Box 31, Folder 4, Special Collections Division, Lauinger Library, Georgetown University, Washington, D.C.

2. Robert Emmett Curran, S.J., *The Bicentennial History of Georgetown University, I: From Academy to University, 1789–1889* (Washington, D.C.: Georgetown University Press, 1993), p.119.

3. Edward F. Beckett, S.J., "Listening to Our History: Inculturation and Jesuit Slaveholding," *Studies in the Spirituality of Jesuits* 28, #5 (November, 1996).

4. "Deed of the chattel of Newtown from Father William Hunter, S.J. to Thomas Jameson, Senior, January 30, 1717," in Thomas Hughes, S.J., *History of the Society of Jesus in North America, Colonial and Federal, Documents: I, Part I, 1605–1838* (New York: Longmans, Green and Co., 1908), #40, p. 222.

5. Allan Kulikoff, *Tobacco and Slaves: The Development of Southern Cultures in the Chesapeake, 1680–1800* (Chapel Hill: The University of North Carolina Press, Published for the Institute of Early American History and Culture, Williamsburg, Virginia, 1986), pp. 37–43; Gary B. Nash, *Red, White & Black: The Peoples of Early North America* (Englewood Cliffs, N.J.: Prentice Hall, 1992), pp. 154–161.

6. See "Part One: The Catholic Tradition on Slavery," in Kenneth J. Zanca, editor, *American Catholics and Slavery, 1789–1866: An Anthology of Primary Documents* (Lanham, Md.: University Press of America, 1994), pp. xxvii-29.

7. John Tracy Ellis, *Catholic Bishops: A Memoir* (Wilmington, Del.: Michael Glazier, Inc., 1983), p. 70.

8. John LaFarge, S.J., "Survival of the Catholic Faith in Southern Maryland," *The Catholic Historical Review* XXI, 1 (April, 1935), pp. 1–20.

9. Cyprian Davis, *The History of Black Catholics in the United States* (New York: Crossroad, 1990), p. 259.

10. Eric Foner, "Slavery, the Civil War and Reconstruction," in Eric Foner, editor, *The New American History* (Philadelphia: Temple University Press, 1990), p.74.

11. Kenneth Stampp, *The Peculiar Institution: Slavery in the Antebellum South* (New York: Random House, Vintage Books Edition, 1989), p. 399.

12. Robert William Fogel and Stanley L. Engerman, *Time on the Cross: The Economics of American Negro Slavery* (New York: W. W. Norton edition, 1989), p. 258, p. 260.

13. Albert J. Raboteau, *Slave Religion: The 'Invisible Institution' in the Antebellum South* (New York: Oxford University Press, 1978), p. 381. This index reference to Roman Catholicism shows that only eleven pages in a text of 321 pages was devoted to that Church.

14. Albert J. Raboteau, "Minority within a Minority: The History of Black Catholics in America," in his book, *A Fire in the Bones: Reflections on African*

American Religious History (Boston: Beacon Press, 1995), pp. 117–137.

15. Eugene D. Genovese, "Slave Religion in Hemispheric Perspective," in his book *Roll, Jordan, Roll: The World the Slaves Made* (New York: Random House, Vintage Books Edition, 1976), pp. 168–183.

16. Eugene D. Genovese, *The Slaveholders' Dilemma: Freedom and Progress in Southern Thought, 1820–1860* (Columbia: University of South Carolina Press, 1992), p. 6.

17. Stanley M. Elkins, *Slavery: A Problem in American Institutional and Intellectual Life* (Chicago: The University of Chicago Press, 1976 Edition), pp. 63–80.

18. Barbara Jeanne Fields, *Slavery and Freedom on the Middle Ground: Maryland During the Nineteenth Century* (New Haven: Yale University Press, 1985), p. 79.

19. James Hennesey, S.J., *American Catholics: A History of the Roman Catholic Community in the United States* (New York: Oxford University Press, 1981), p. 145.

20. Brother Joseph Mobberly, S.J., "Diary, Part V: Fourth of July, 1826," p. 92; The Brother Joseph Mobberly, S.J. Papers (BJMSJP), Special Collections Division, Lauinger Library, Georgetown University, Washington, D.C.

Jesuit Slaveholding in Maryland, 1717–1838

CHAPTER ONE

Property and Religious Liberty: The Emergence of Jesuit Slaveholding

As overseer of St. Inigoe's Plantation between 1806 and 1820, Brother Joseph Mobberly, S.J. often visited the nearby hamlet of Centreville, Maryland on business. Centreville was a Methodist stronghold, and the Roman Catholic Mobberly often found himself drawn into theological debate during his visits there. One prominent figure, whom Mobberly did not name in his diary but recorded as simultaneously holding the roles of magistrate, store-keeper and minister, "pretended to be a man of very extensive reading." He frequently challenged Mobberly's beliefs.

One day, sometime between 1815 and 1817, the storekeeper and Mobberly quarreled about whether Saint Augustine of Hippo had been a Calvinist. The storekeeper insisted that Augustine was indeed a Calvinist, probably attempting to communicate that this patristic father of the Church had at least been an intellectual forbear of John Calvin's doctrine of predestination. Mobberly relied strictly on the chronological facts for his rebuttal: "that is impossible, because Saint Augustine lived several centuries before Calvin was born." Mobberly recorded that each proponent repeated his position several times, neither yielding at all. Finally, the frustrated Jesuit turned his back and strode out of the store, chiding himself "for having indulged so long in conversation with a Methodistic Ninnyhammer."[1]

The doctrinal affinity of Augustine and Calvin is a matter for theologians to resolve. It is possible for a historian, however, to discern more subtle supporting evidence for Mobberly's claim. Jesuits had embraced enough of Augustine's social philosophy to be justified in claiming him as one of their own. Augustine's specific views on slavery influenced the Jesuit's everyday treatment of their slaves, as Chapter Three of this study will discuss more fully. However, Augustine's broader philosophy of the relationship between the church and secular society was of even greater importance in disposing Jesuits toward slaveholding in the first place. His portrayal of history as the faithful's struggle to attain the righteous "city of God" while living within the sinful "city of man" rang true for Jesuits as they tried to build the Roman Catholic Church in the unfriendly climate of predominantly Protestant Maryland. In the pursuit of their difficult task, Jesuits discerned that the possession of slaves was another means by which they could protect their Church from its enemies.

Throughout the colonial period, the Jesuits dealt with a hostile culture by establishing little "cities of God"—their own plantations—throughout Maryland's "city of man." Within these private enclaves, the exercise of the Catholic religion could proceed in relative harmony. This land had to be developed, however, for sufficient income was necessary in order to keep the plantations in Catholic hands. Jesuits could themselves not farm fulltime without neglecting their priestly duties. Therefore, servants were an important support to the Jesuit plantation apostolate from the earliest years. Eventually, the possession of slaves came to serve a wider goal, the Jesuits' assertion of their own right and the right of Catholic laymen in the colony to be accorded the full rights of English subjects.

This situation endured until the American Revolution, making it unlikely that the Jesuits would seriously consider the abandonment of their slaveholding before that time. Their struggle throughout the colonial period for religious liberty and property rights is well-known, but the utility of slaveholding in their struggle has not received adequate attention. There is a need to reexamine Jesuit colonial political philosophy in the light of its implication for the possession of slaves. So far reconstructions of the Jesuit propositions about Catholic rights to worship and property ownership have ignored the implications of these propositions for this issue.[2]

The evolution of their political philosophy took place within a context of sectarian struggle, which the Jesuits interpreted mystically, as the manifestation of a deeper conflict between good and evil. They regarded the good forces of the Catholic Church as arrayed against worldly Protestant heretics. In an effort to imbibe the mystery of this struggle, Jesuits turned to Augustine, particularly to *The City of God*, his book responding to the sack of Rome in the year 410 C.E.

To Augustine, the misfortune of Rome was another act in the constant drama of sin's mysterious power to thwart the progress of the reign of God. "I must speak also of the earthly city—of that city which lusts to dominate the world. . . . From this earthly city issue the enemies against whom the City of God must be defended."[3] He went on to speak of the spiritual challenges that faced Christians as they struggled to maintain their fidelity to God and community with one another amid the pressures of daily life. The danger was that until the second coming of Jesus Christ, the Christian would be forced to live simultaneously under the influence of both cities. The believer's challenge was to avoid overshadowing by the human dimension. Translated to the Maryland situation, this theological formula guaranteed that political imperatives would rank with spiritual, theological and intellectual influences in encouraging Jesuits to persist in slaveholding throughout the colonial era.

Study of the connection between the struggle for political liberty of Catholic colonists and their slaveholding is important, for it can augment study of a possible connection between the emergence of political liberty for all white male freeholders of the Chesapeake and the evolution of a slaveholding system. Lower class Protestant colonists did not have to deal with the burden of religious minority in pressing their case for liberty, but the upper class Catholics of Maryland, including the Jesuits, did.

According to one reconstruction, the liberties of white planters in late seventeenth century Virginia were secured through the emergence of an elaborate system of African slave labor. Social and economic tensions increased as the population of Tidewater Virginia grew; many white settlers finished their term of indenture but had little prospect of obtaining land. Bacon's Rebellion of 1676, in which planters on the western edge of the Virginia colony rose up against the largerscale owners to their east, was a symptom of this problem. The eventual replacement of a white indentured laboring force by an enslaved black labor force contributed to conditions which finally allowed poor whites to develop modest prosperity they might not otherwise have obtained, to own small amounts of land, and to share a modicum of the social prestige enjoyed by largescale, slaveholding planters. The result was to secure for all white male freeholders a right of participation in a republican government and a superior social status simply by the fact of their whiteness. These factors, this reconstruction concludes, greatly defused the potential for class conflict in the Chesapeake.[4]

The problem faced by the first Jesuit planters of Maryland, however, was not the pursuit of upward mobility. Most of them were of high English birth, "Popish Gentlemen of good families," according to a commentary of Peter Atwood, S.J. in 1718.[5] Indeed, in early seventeenth century England, on the eve of Maryland's colonization, only the sons of the gentry could afford to travel to the mainland of Europe for the Jesuit novitiate and subsequent clerical education that was banned in England itself. Roman Catholicism largely died out among most lower class Englishmen during the reign of Elizabeth I because they generally lacked the means to provide for a private space for the practice of the faith. Only those poor who managed to cluster near Catholic businessmen in London or around gentry estates in the countryside found havens for devotion. The result was that the first Catholic settlers of Maryland, while a small minority of the colony, were also its elite until at least the late 1640s. The large majority of the first settlers were lower class Protestants.[6] This situation of Catholic elitism was unique in "the entire history of English North America."[7]

After decades of threats and occasional repressions, Catholics were effectively eliminated from political participation in Maryland by the Glorious Revolution of 1689 and remained so until the American Revolution of 1776. The exclusion began when Maryland Protestants took advantage of the deposition of the Catholic James I in favor of the Protestant monarchs William and Mary to bar Catholics from government. This event was known locally as the revolt of the Protestant Associators.[8] As far as Catholics were concerned, it was no longer enough to be a propertyholder in order to vote. The exceptional impediment to Catholic civil rights thus became religious minority status rather than social class. Jesuits remained the intellectual leaders of the Catholic planters of Maryland, however, and led the way in articulating resistance to this imposed settlement. They developed a political philosophy which regarded landholding and slaveholding as avenues to the procurance of civil rights for themselves and their coreligionists. Examination of this philosophy may augment studies of white people of the Chesapeake, in general, found slavery to serve their own purposes. For Catholics, at least, more was at stake in the tradeoff between slavery and freedom than simple political participation and social prestige. They used the fact of their slaveholding to argue the case for their own religious liberty.

Much of their spiritual and intellectual formation prompted Jesuits to conduct slaveholding for what they told themselves were fundamentally altruistic reasons, as part of a paternal responsibility for the spiritual and material welfare of lower class people and people of darker color whom the Jesuits regarded as needing the direction of others. The political motivations for their slaveholding, however, revealed that this rationale of selflessness was not wholly accurate. Jesuits, like their peers, thought of their self-interest when they practiced politics. Moreover, the self-interest they pursued in this matter resulted in a Church which accorded spiritual freedom to slaves even while holding them in material bondage. Jesuits' theological, political, and social activities thus intermingled generosity and repression in a paradoxical way.

It is not possible to understand the weight the Jesuits attached to land ownership in the Maryland colony unless one comprehends their experience as fugitive, landless priests in Elizabethan and Jacobean England. The English government feared that the Jesuits were agents of the papacy and Catholic Spain in a conspiracy to overthrow the Protestant settlement. From 1585, it was high treason for a Jesuit even to be present in England. This policy was reinforced after Jesuits were implicated in the so-called "Gunpowder Plot" to blow up the houses of Parliament in 1605.[9] While many Jesuits continued to enter the country secretly, they fell dependent on the willingness of sympathetic householders to conceal them.

This dependence on the English gentry lessened Jesuit freedom to choose and conduct their own apostolates. Their occupations became chaplaincy and tutoring behind the doors of manor households rather than open proclamation of the Gospel.[10] This was a frustrating situation for most Jesuits, whose spiritual heritage and personal dispositions inclined them toward a bold public evangelization of the English nation. They were restless at the gentry's willingness to privatize religious practice in return for the government's tacit consent to leave upperclass Catholics alone. An open break with the gentry, however, would have cost the Jesuits not only financial support, but also possibly their lives.

On balance, therefore, life in England was disappointing to many Jesuits by the middle third of the seventeenth century. Those who traveled to Maryland from 1634 were responding to this frustration, and to the hope that in the New World they might be able to proceed more freely.[11] This hope was not to be fulfilled entirely, but from the start of the colony Jesuits fully shared in the typical desire of colonists to seek their own land rather than dwell perpetually on estates belonging to others.

Their eagerness to leave England led to Jesuit acquiescence in the conditions which the first proprietor of the colony, Lord Baltimore, imposed on all Catholic settlers proceeding to Maryland. In the interests of domestic peace within the settlement, and in hopes that the Protestant colonists would refrain from sending complaints to the government in London, Baltimore directed Catholics to keep their religious observance private and not engage in polemics with their neighbors.[12] Baltimore may have devised this strategy following his failure to secure a colony at Avalon in Newfoundland, where sectarian bitterness was a major impediment to success. This experience made him all the more determined to promote Catholic discretion from the outset of Maryland.[13] The result was that the Jesuits were impelled to seek a zone of privacy for Catholic practice immediately—their own landholdings.

Jesuits joined Lord Baltimore in articulating an important paradigm for the new colony. Baltimore's promotional literature for his settlement envisioned Maryland landholdings as analogous to the medieval manors of England—not only in terms of their legal classification, but also in terms of their social structure. They would be class-based, with landlords, tenants and servants in descending order.[14] Thus was devised a patriarchal order that would provide an important context for the emergence of slaveholding.

Most importantly, there was an aspect of Catholic life on the gentry estates of England that the Jesuits were determined to continue on their own farms. Back home, lower class Catholics who went to work for the gentry as servants found, on these large estates, a private space in which to carry out religious devotions that the penal laws denied them a public right to perform. In the gentry homes, domestics and estate workers could attend the liturgies at which Jesuits and other priest chaplains presided. Thus, gentry estates became the nuclei of what small pockets of Catholic population survived in the English countryside.[15] If there was indeed to be no public promotion of religion in

Maryland, in accordance with Lord Baltimore's wishes, this model appeared to be the best alternative for Catholic proceeding there as well.

A slight revision of this model, in which the Jesuits joined the laity as estate owners, became the paradigm for Catholic community among the English settlers of Maryland. This model regarded the farms as fundamentally conducted for the good of the upper and lower classes living together in a unity of soul. Catholics who came to a Jesuit estate in Maryland were drawn first of all by their common religion, and only secondarily by their diverse social roles.

The early Maryland manor is believed to have fulfilled three main functions. First, it provided an overwhelmingly male population with a community to live in until they could afford their own households. While working for the manorial lord, they could learn the skills of farming tobacco and maize, as well as accumulate equipment for their eventual own farms.[16] To these reasons, we may add the thought that a Jesuit manor, in particular, provided a safe place for the practice of Catholicism. For Protestants, the manor rather quickly fulfilled its function and passed from the scene toward the end of the seventeenth century.[17] However, for Jesuits, the manor remained a key ideal. They continued to regard the colony itself a "manor writ large" until the Revolutionary War.[18]

Important theological and historical currents within Counter-Reformation Catholicism encouraged this persistence in manorialism. The Church of this era envisioned itself as a "perfect society." This expression did not signify a morally flawless Church, but a Church in accordance with a definition of perfection found in medieval scholastic philosophy—a self-sufficiency in every respect, "a society having all the means at its disposal to reach its own end."[19] The Jesuits hoped that their Maryland manors would become such entities, places where Catholics could gather for prayer because economic productivity had made them places where the Church would be free to pursue its goal of union with God through Catholic practice.

Following the Council of Trent (1545–1563), the "perfect society" paradigm also came to be understood as involving a parallelism between church and state. Each should have its own sphere, within which each would have all the means at its disposal for the work proper to its own sphere. In Catholic countries, this meant that the Church developed its own parallels of several governmental institutions ordinarily associated with secular rule, such as law courts and administrative agencies, but to handle the business of the Church rather than that of the state.[20] The Jesuits of England and Maryland were not in a position to create parallel secular government, but they could and did develop attempt to develop parallels of secular *social* institutions, such as manorial estates and, in Maryland, plantations.

Under the pressure of the persecutions which Jesuits faced in Elizabethan England during the years immediately following Trent, they altered church-state parallelism into the proposition that the world was divided into rigid spheres of influence for church and state, with each having all the means to function autonomously within its own sphere, but also with neither having any right to intrude on the specific business of the other. Fatefully, the Jesuits would accept parallels for the regulations for slaveholding according to this model. The state would codify it as a social institution, while the Church would limit itself with the spiritual lives of slaves.

The influence of this parallelism on the English Catholicism that would give birth to the Maryland Jesuit manors can be measured by examining two sets of comments made forty six years apart during the sixteenth century. At his execution in 1535 for failing to acknowledge the royal supremacy over the English Church, the former lord chancellor Thomas More (1478–1535) remarked that he died "the king's good servant—but God's first."[21] The logical implication of More's declaration was that the good English Catholic would obey the papacy before the Crown. This was characteristic of a medieval outlook that the Church enjoyed supremacy over the state in every particular. In 1570, this belief seemed to be reaffirmed when Pope Pius V excommunicated Elizabeth I and exhorted English Catholics to work for her deposition, violently if need be.[22]

A Jesuit who reentered England after this decree, Edmund Campion (1542–1581) realized that he would only be able to do priestly work there if he could convince the authorities that Jesuits sincerely held the belief that it was wrong for priests to interfere in the business of the state. Therefore, Campion took More's thesis and revised it, making church and state parallel—equal but separate entities. He informed the Privy Council that he had never intended, and in any case was strictly forbidden by his religious superiors, to deal with the political issues facing the English crown. These were not part of his vocation, so Campion claimed that he had been trained to keep himself away from them.[23]

At his trial for treason, Campion emphasized that Jesuits were "dead men to the world; we only traveled for souls; we touched neither state nor policy; we had no such commission."[24] Campion concluded his defense with an emphasis on the obedience due to Elizabeth I in all temporal matters.

Some have equated Campion's thought with More's identification of himself as a loyal servant of the King.[25] The truth, however, is that Campion was much more willing than More to give the state autonomy within its proper sphere. Campion wanted the government to abstain from ecclesiastical interference in return for Jesuit abstinence from politics, so his only disagreement with the Elizabethan state was to deny its right to regulate religious practice.

Campion's successors on the Jesuit mission to England matured his philosophy of political reticence. Robert Southwell, S.J. (1561–1595), for example, addressed "An Humble Supplication to Her Majiestie" in 1593. In this treatise, Southwell tried, once again, to convince Elizabeth I that the Jesuits were prepared to be docile on other political questions in exchange for their religious liberty:

> Disloyalty shall never be found the sequell of any Article of our Religion; which more than any other tieth vs to a most exact submission to your temporall authority, and to all points of allegiance, that either now in Catholique cuntries, or ever before in Catholique times, were acknowledged to be due any Christian prince. . . . It is a point of the Catholique faith (defended by vs against the Sectaries of these dayes) that Subiects are bound in Conscience, vnder pain of forfeitting their right in heaven, and incurring the guilt of eternal torments, to obey the iust lawes of their princes . . . in all . . . civil and temporall respects, we are as submitted and pliable as any of your Maiesties best beloved subiects.[26]

There are two reasons why this rigid division of church and state was important for the emergence of Maryland Jesuit slaveholding. First, it encouraged the Jesuits to establish small private enclaves, their manors, where they attempted to function as unobtrusively and self-sufficiently as possible and thereby ensure the survival of their faith. The means to religious liberty was always discretion. Therefore, Jesuits and other Catholic elites resorted to a policy of regarding Maryland as "the manor writ large" in lieu of formal laws protecting Catholic rights.[27] In their attempt to make their enclaves self-contained, Jesuits would accept whatever labor they needed—indentured servants at first, slaves when the supply of indentured laborers began to run low.

Second, their theory of church-state separation adversely affected the Jesuits' ability to participate in the debate over how the colonial government should regulate the emerging institution of slavery. Significantly, this result came about because the Jesuits, pursuing their ideal of temporal abstinence to a logical conclusion, demanded exemption from service in the Maryland Assembly.

The Maryland Assembly was an important institution in colonial America—the first such body to be established in a North American English colony from the settlement's founding.[28] At least three of the first seven Assemblies were general meetings. All freemen, including the Jesuits, were summoned to participate.[29] Had this tradition continued, the Jesuits would have been drawn more deeply into the political process than they wished to be.

The issue of the Jesuit presence in Maryland became an important means for acting out a struggle between the proprietor and the assembly to determine who would have the greater law-making power. Lord Baltimore believed that the assembly's role should be subordinate to his own decisions; the legislature was to advise and consent but not initiate policy on its own. A strict interpretation of the colonial charter supported Baltimore's opinion: it spoke of a unitary process in which the proprietor would propose and enact laws with "the advice assent and approbation of the Free-men of the said Province."[30] From the beginning, however, the Assembly wished to devise laws on its own.[31] Since Baltimore was inclined to regulate Jesuit activity and the assemblymen were not, during the first decade of the colony defenders of the Jesuits were usually also advocates of legislative supremacy.[32]

The conventional interpretation of the Jesuits' own role in this controversy is that they wanted to establish a Catholic ascendancy in Maryland and actively lobbied Catholic assemblymen to vote accordingly.[33] There were three Jesuit activities that convinced Baltimore of Jesuit aspirations for a Catholic ascendancy—their desire to have their manors exempted from political, military and financial obligations, their willingness to accept gifts of land from native Americans without seeking proprietary permission, and their evangelization among both the indigenous peoples and the Protestant settlers.[34] However, what the Jesuits really wanted was recognition of their right to live without interference on their manors.

The Jesuits envisioned each of these goals as only pursuing and expressing their deeper desire for a more secure network of private manors. They wanted to exempt the land from secular obligations so that it might be more fully private and private in its Catholicism. Jesuits were willing to accept land from the natives because they were eager to establish their private manors as quickly as possible. Even the evangelization of the Protestants was to be done passively: the Jesuits hoped that Protestants would be drawn by the word and example of the priests to visit the manors and so be converted. The annual letter of the missionaries to the English Provincial in 1639 said:

> To the hope of the Indian harvest, are to be added also no mean fruits reaped from the colony and its inhabitants, to whom, on the principal feast days of the year, sermons are preached, and the expositions of the catechism given on the Lord's Day. Not only Catholics come in crowds, but very many heretics. . . . Our people cease not daily to engage in their divine employment, and to dispense the sacraments to those that come, as often as circumstances demand.[35]

An important reason that the evangelization of the Protestants was envisioned so passively was that the Jesuit mission to Maryland, in its earliest years, regarded itself as primarily directed to the conversion of the native Americans. Work among the English settlers was secondary to the prospect of winning natives to Christ. Many Jesuits who volunteered for the Maryland mission spoke of the chance to work among the native peoples as their primary motivation in migrating.[36]

Had they really been as politically ambitious for a role among the English settlers as Baltimore regarded them, the Jesuits would not have persistently claimed an exemption from service in the Assembly throughout the sessions that debated Baltimore's wish to limit their role within the colony. They sent proxies named Thomas Cornwaleys, Cuthbert Fenwick and Robert Clarke to the Assembly of 1637–38, which refused to accept their votes.[37] The Jesuits did not really believe they should sit in the assembly; they sent the proxies because the law required them to do so. They did not fight the dismissal of the proxies, a telling sign that representation in the colonial government was repugnant to their doctrine of abstinence from temporal affairs.

In fact, negotiations between Baltimore and the English Province of the Society of Jesus in 1642 resulted in a compromise in which the exemption of Jesuits from further summons to the Assembly represented their side of the bargain. Baltimore wanted them to abandon the land claims they had received from native Americans without the proprietor's permission; the Jesuits demanded the exemption from officeholding in return. This result was due to the negotiating tactics of the English provincial, Henry More (1587–1661), a great-grandson of Thomas.[38] His demand for the exemption shows that he leaned closer to the theory of Campion regarding church-state relations than to those of his own ancestor.

This accommodation, coming just eight years after the founding of the colony, set up one of the most important reasons why the Maryland Jesuits acquiesced in the later emergence of slaveholding in the colony. It ensured that the Jesuits would not be party to the process that began in the Maryland Assembly as early as the 1660s, the statuatory definition and regulation of slavery. The Assembly early adjudicated such issues as enslavement of negroes for life and a ban on interracial marriages.[39]

This situation was acceptable to the Jesuits because the writings of a premier English Jesuit political philosopher, Robert Persons, assigned the regulation of slavery to the temporal realm as early as 1606. Parsons believed that the temporal order "helps to gouerne well the Commowealth, in peace, aboundance, order and prosperitie . . . handleth the Ciuill affaires of the Realme, and Commonwealth, as they apertaine to the temporall good, and prosperitie thereof."[40] The regulation of property, both landed and chatteled, was what determined "the temporall good and prosperitie" of Maryland with its planting-based economy. Jesuits found it entirely natural that the Assembly should be the party to regulate slavery.

Henry More's decision of 1642 gave the theories of Campion and Parsons about church-state separation formal recognition among the Jesuits in Maryland. This decision provided an unappreciatedly early beginning to a theme often regarded as appearing in American Catholic history only during the Revolutionary War, the idea that priests should remain aloof from politics while only the Catholic laity pursued the full rights of citizenship.[41]

Because Campion's theory of parallelism between church and state and Person's division of labor between the two were both embraced by Henry More in his settlement with Baltimore, the legislature's assumption of jurisdiction over slaveholding signified for the Jesuits of a generation later the end of their eligibility to comment on the future of slavery. Publicly, they could neither advocate its adoption nor advocate its abolition; the only role left to them was to set examples of good moral conduct for masters through the treatment of their own slaves.

When slavery was discussed within the Assembly, records of the proceedings indicate that the debates were brief and superficial. Decisions were reached quickly, with little dissent.[42] The presence of the Jesuits might have at least extended this process. There is no evidence that they would have sought to abolish slavery, but their thought regarding the spiritual lives of slaves and the religious liberty of all was different enough from Protestant conceptions of the same issues to suggest that Jesuits might have at least sought to place some Catholic influence upon the slave codes. It would have been particularly intriguing had they contributed to the debate on the relationship between baptism and temporal status as a slave. The latter seventeenth century was a time when several colonial legislatures, including Maryland's, passed laws denying the proposition that Christian conversion would necessitate the manumission of a slave.[43] Jesuits embraced this proposition willingly, raising their chattel as both Catholics and slaves from birth. Had Jesuits been in the legislature, they might have championed the perspective that these slaves had a right to their Catholicism, thus upholding the proposition that the basic human right to religious freedom extended even to people without any other civil rights.

There was a deeper level on which the absence of the Jesuits from the Assembly after 1642 hurt the Maryland colony itself. Seventeenth century Maryland was a place of great political immaturity and instability. Settlers proved unable to express and resolve philosophical differences within stable political institutions, instead resorting to violence, uprisings, and manipulation. One reason for this situation was the prolonged political ascendancy of recent immigrants in political office due to high mortality rates and the general failure of the colony's population to reproduce itself naturally during the early decades of settlement.[44]

The Jesuits might have contributed to an earlier stabilization of this situation had they remained active in officeholding. Their experience in accommodating themselves to a difficult political situation in England, combined with their extensive intellectual formation, especially in philosophy, and their tendency to value social stability, all qualified them to make public policy. They exerted indirect influence on the process through the Catholic lay planters whom they educated and ministered to. In fact, until the revolution of 1689, a disproportionate number of the Catholic laity served in elective office.[45] The Protestant majority's resentment of the predominance of the Catholic minority was a major cause of the revolution of 1689.[46]

The fact that there was a Catholic ascendancy makes the Jesuits' abstinence from it between 1642 and 1689 all the more striking. It is a powerful indication of the depth of their desire to live in privacy on their landholdings. It is possible that their theory of the "manor writ large" emerged only after, and in response to, the 1689 Revolution. The Jesuits were characteristically English in that they devised political theory only in response to actual events, and shunned *a priori* reasoning. This underlying point is true, but the Maryland Jesuits took their underlying philosophy from thought shaped long before 1689, in response to events in Elizabethan England.

There were deeper, more human reasons why the Jesuits came to regard landholding as so important. There were three criteria by which to measure the full integration of new arrivals into Chesapeake society. These were to become a planter, to marry and raise children, and to participate in the political decisions of the community.[47] The Jesuit vow of chastity barred them from the second criteria, while the crucial decision of Henry More in 1642 barred them from the third. Thereafter, the Jesuits were left with only the first goal, the pursuit of planting. From the beginning, they pursued the accumulation of land with great zeal—perhaps because it was the one outward sign of success they could demonstrate to the rest of the colony.

Jesuits first exploited the proprietor's policy of awarding land to gentlemen settlers who paid for the transportation of indentured servants from England in 1634. 400 acres were to be granted for each servant thus imported.[48] One Jesuit alone, Thomas Copley, earned entitlement to 28,000 acres through his diligent response to this offer.[49] Copley, therefore, must have imported sixty-five servants. However, the Jesuits only took possession of 8000 of the acres they thus earned.[50]

Therefore, the missionaries decided to press for the restoration in Maryland of the medieval English law of mortmain, by which the Church would receive the right as an institution to hold its own land in perpetuity, able neither to transfer or sell it. Recognizing the medieval origins of mortmain, some historians have concluded that their advocacy of it meant that Maryland Jesuits desired to return to a medieval English conception of the church-state relationship. Some believe that the Jesuits regressed to this position after arriving in the Cheasapeake.[51] This argument is echoed by those who stress the importance of medieval papal bulls to the Maryland Jesuits.[52] However, to focus only on the Jesuit desire for mortmain is to take a narrow view of their wider goal. They wanted to use mortmain as part of a creative synthesis of the best of medieval philosophy and the Campion-Persons theory of church autonomy in its own sphere. This desire is best illustrated by their nuanced approach to the colonial charter. They championed the charter's provision supporting mortmain, and ignored the provision that only the proprietor could dispose of native American land.

The Charter granted to the first Lord Baltimore by King Charles I indeed provided that mortmain be secured in Maryland. However, within England there was considerable doubt that the monarch had the arbitrary perogative to overrule the Parliamentary statutes that had ended the practice a century earlier. The struggle between Crown and Parliament for supremacy added spice to this uncertainty. Another complication was a further act of Parliament, passed in 1585 and amended in 1604, which made it a capital felony to "wittingly and willingly receive, comfort, and/or maintain any . . . Jesuit." Lord Baltimore, anticipating the victory of the Puritan party in the English Civil War, refused to concede mortmain in Maryland for fear that a strict interpretation of this later legislation might then cost him his life.[53]

Henry More apparently recognized Baltimore's dilemma and sympathized with it. As part of the compromise of 1642, More agreed to an arrangement whereby the Jesuits would own land as individuals rather than as a corporate body. In effect, colonial Maryland law would not recognize the corporate existence of the Society of Jesus, but it would treat individual Jesuits like any other Englishmen in their personal right to own property.[54] While this was not what the Jesuits had initially wanted, it was an advance over the situation in England itself, where they could not own property under any conditions, either corporately or individually. At least an important individual right of Englishmen had been guaranteed to them by the proprietor, and the Jesuits defended his guarantee for the remainder of the colonial period.

After 1642, the only ways left for individual Jesuits to obtain land was either to buy it outright or receive it as a gift from other English settlers. This simple fact suddenly made the system of indentured servitude much more important to the Jesuits. Who would be willing to sell or give them land? An obvious source was the Catholic lay planter elite, including those who emerged as landholders after initial service as indentured servants. Having their own indentured servants became a way for the Jesuits to assure the emergence of a class of benefactors in later years, donors who would provide them with both land and chattel in gratitude for Jesuit assistance to their passage to the colony.

The Jesuits quickly proved willing to assist indentured servants to Maryland for reasons that went far deeper than the practical need for assistance in the working of the land. Unlike Massachusetts Bay, where most of the migration from England took place during the first decade of settlement, Maryland continued to absorb large numbers of immigrants for most of the seventeenth century. These immigrants fulfilled two crucial economic functions, providing a supply of labor for the tobacco crop and the replenishment of a population as yet unable to reproduce itself naturally due to high and youthful mortality rates.[55]

For the Jesuits, however, these new arrivals served two additional functions: the chance to exercise their project of converting lower class Englishmen to and upholding them in Catholicism, as well as a chance to increase the number of Catholics in the Maryland colony itself. The Jesuits regarded this as an important proactive task for themselves because they did not trust the English Catholic gentry's enthusiasm for Catholic colonization. As early as 1605, Robert Persons, S.J. felt that odds were against the project of "transferring Englishe Catholiques to the Northen partes of Americe" because the rich would not wish anyone to go and the poor would follow their advice.[56] Thus the Jesuits came to regard themselves as the only trustworthy champions of Catholic immigration to Maryland. Underscoring this fact is the discovery that they never completely abandoned the practice of sponsoring Catholic servants who wished to immigrate to Maryland, owning indentures well into the nineteenth century.[57]

Religion has been an overlooked motivation for migration to Maryland, at least when it comes to people who were recruited to the Jesuit manors. In general, people who emigrated from England to the Chesapeake were people of little wealth, low social standing—illustrative of those Englishfolk who were obliged to work with their hands for a living, either in agriculture or the craft trades. They came from a broad geographical cross section of English society.[58] Many factors impelled people to emigrate, but unemployment was probably the strongest one. Few left their homes in the English countryside with the intention of proceeding overseas, but ventured on to the Chesapeake as an expediency when they could not find work in English cities and seaports.[59] It is probable, however, that Catholic emigrants were more likely than others to have known from the beginning that Maryland was their goal, due to its reputation as a haven for Catholicism.

The eighteenth century was a time when the slave trade was more important than the recruitment of indentured servants in meeting labor needs in Maryland. The importation of some indentures continued, however, and its probable that slaves were reserved for work in the fields while the indentures received the skilled work of the plantation—clerkships, carpentry, masonry, housekeeping and, tutoring for the planter's children.[60] These were skills that pointed to upward mobility once the indenture expired. It was in the Jesuits' interest to cultivate Catholic laymen of such skills, since they could go on to become important benefactors of Church activities.

In 1729, a wealthy planter named James Carroll left "all my servants . . . and chattels" to some Jesuits.[61] This was the type of gifts that Jesuits counted on receiving from their lay neighbors. Such bequests vindicated the policy that the Jesuits had begun, long before the eighteenth century, of nurturing Catholic indentured servants. As early as 1638, the annual report of mission activity sent to superiors back in England recorded the Jesuits' interest in engaging indentured servants primarily as a means of protecting the faith of those servants:

> We bought the contracts of two Catholic indentured servants in Virginia. Nor was the money ill-spent, for both showed themselves good Christians; one, indeed, is extraordinary. Some others have performed the same charitable act in buying from that place Catholic servants, of whom there are a great number. For every year a great many sell themselves into bondage for Virginia, and, as they live among persons of the worst example and are utterly deprived of any spiritual means, they generally make shipwrecks of their souls.[62]

There is no indication here that the Jesuits placed their practical economic need for these servants first. What was important to them was that Catholic servants be brought to the Jesuit plantations so that they could practice the faith in a protective and encouraging environment. It seems likely that servants were encouraged to stay on the farms whether they were needed or not as long as those farms were the safest place for their Catholic devotional practice.

This prioritization of religious over economic need would eventually become a motive for the acquisition of slaves as well. Just as they initially saw an opportunity to salvage the faith of indigent Catholic immigrants from the British Isles by bringing them to the Jesuit manors, the Jesuits later saw the need to protect slaves from assertions by some Protestants that slaves were not worthy of Baptism. In 1749, George Hunter, S.J. affirmed that the "greater glory of God" demanded that all slaves be recognized by their masters as "members of Jesus Christ, redeemed by his precious blood."[63] The one way to illustrate this point was for the Jesuits to obtain slaves and treat them according to Hunter's affirmation of their humanity and Christianity. Keeping them in Jesuit hands was one way to make sure that such slaves received catechesis and the opportunity to persevere as Catholics. Jesuits like Hunter saw the desirability of financial self-support for the plantations as a means of serving the deeper goal of establishing the plantations as such havens of religious liberty that even slaves could be spiritually free there. The plantations' importance as a place of refuge for the reign of the Catholic God took priority.

The idea that the Jesuits may have initially seen little to distinguish the status of indentured servants and African slaves is encouraged by a list of Jesuit indentures from 1638. In an attempt to claim reward under Baltimore's conditions of plantations, which promised land for each servant sponsored on the journey to Maryland, the Jesuits submitted this list to officials of the colony. It included "Matthias Sousa, Molato . . . Francisco, a Molato . . . black John Price." These servants were imported in the same manner as "white John Price" and "Charles the Welshmen."[64] It may be presumed that they were worked in a similar manner, too.

Jesuit political philosophy indicates that what ultimately distinguished white from black labor for them was the equation of the right to purchase one's own property with Englishness. What separated "white John Price" from "black John Price" was that the former, as a British subject, could go on to buy his own land once his indenture expired.

Robert Persons, S.J. made this Jesuit identification of property rights with Englishness in a written rebuttal to some opinions of Justice Edward Coke in 1606. As a Catholic dissenter, the basic issue for Persons was, what made a man English? Coke had argued that an indispensable component of Englishness was membership in the established Church. Persons answered, fatefully for the future emergence of slaveholding among his confreres in Maryland, that religious liberty transcended nationality but that what really set apart an Englishman was his right to buy, own and sell property. It was this equation of Englishness with property-holding that motivated Maryland's Catholics to join the patriot cause during the American Revolution; they fully agreed that taxation without representation was an affront to English liberty.[65]

Persons argued that the right to worship God preceded the establishment of the English state or any other state; it was a birthright for all human beings due to the universal or "generall large commission" of Jesus Christ to the apostles to spread the faith throughout the world and govern the Church everywhere.[66] Persons noted, "That is Catholic, and undoubtedly trew, which everywhere, is one and the same. And this both in tyme, place, and substance."[67] Therefore, religious affiliation lay outside the regulation of the secular state of one mere nation.

The state emerged much later in history; Persons liked to point out that nearly half a millenium separated the conversion of England to Catholicism under Pope Gregory the Great and the Norman Conquest, which he took as the beginning of the modern English state.[68] The state emerged at that much later time to protect the rights of property owners.[69] Persons pointed out, however, that property owners were relatively few and far between; "a good patrimony . . . is not every man's case." He asked, "what riches, or inheritance have those men . . . which are born without landes or liuings?"[70]

Parsons' answer to this question, that the rights left to the propertyless were spiritual and therefore placed under the protection of the Church, pointed to the Jesuit regard for the spiritual lives of their slaves. Slaves were, by definition, people who could not own property. Jesuits, however, also stressed constantly that these same slaves, eligible as they were to receive the Gospel, were as human as any English people who lacked land. Therefore, slaves were as free religiously as anyone else.

Jesuits, therefore, developed a consistent record in Maryland of guaranteeing the rights of slaves to worship as Catholics. They always allowed them to be baptized and married, and to receive the Eucharist. Having Catholic slaves on hand, moreover, also proved to be a convenient way of demonstrating Person's point that the right to religious liberty was separate from, and prior to, superior to and more universal than the rights of being English.

While the Jesuits thus based the right to religious liberty on an encompassing humanity, they based the right to own property on narrow nationality. It was Englishness that awarded the right to own land. Furthermore, this right to own land was not in the gift of the state. In 1642, the Jesuits denounced as unjust "laws, formerly passed in England and unjustly observed there . . . that it shall not be lawful for any person or community, even ecclesiastical, in any wise, even by gift, to acquire or possess any land, unless the permission of the civil magistrate first be obtained."[71] It would be a mistake to overemphasize the appearance of the words "community" and "ecclesiastical" within this passage, which broadly claims a clear right for every English individual to own land. Again, the presence of African bondsmen in Maryland dramatized this point. Who could be less English than an African without land? His skin color dramatized the race and nationality that English Catholics and Protestants shared rather than the religious issues that divided them, and his landlessness suggested that only people of color should be landless.

The emergence of slaveholding and the inferiorization of blacks were entangled parts of a systemic process, and it is impossible to designate one of these two factors as taking priority over the other.[72] The Persons philosophy, however, suggests that this debate could be settled more clearly by imagining the English perspective as nationalistic as well as racial. For Catholics, at least, "English over Black" was as important an expression than "White over Black."

There are indications that just as the Jesuits initially provided little sense of a division of labor between white and black servants, so too they did not always clearly divide labor between masters and slaves either. Jesuits were quite willing to join in manual tasks when the occasion demanded it. This willingness to humble themselves may be traced to an important book of the English Catholic heritage, Thomas More's *Utopia*. This work provided many models for the conduct of the Jesuit manors in Maryland.

Thomas More became a hero to all Catholics of English heritage after his execution in 1535.[73] For Jesuits, this tie assumed a more personal aspect through the connection of Thomas' great-grandson Henry More, whose role in securing their manors and political philosophy in Maryland was so decisive. Two themes of the fictional country of Utopia—rejection of religious coercion and the proposition that civic peace was more important than doctrinal conformity—formed ideals of conduct for Maryland Catholics.[74] To them, these fictional ideals of Catholic discretion became more important than what More said about the supremacy of church over state on the scaffold in real life.

It is, therefore, pertinent to examine the models of servitude that More constructed in the same book, and compare them to what little we know of Maryland Jesuit proceeding.

An important justification for Utopian slaveholding helps to explain complaints by Maryland Jesuits that they experienced a conflict between their vocation to apostolic labor and the demands of plantation work. More's Utopians believed that certain low, material tasks hindered the educated elite from contemplation of higher, more spiritual matters. Hunting and the slaughter of livestock were believed to make the person performing them act less humane, so such tasks were to be left to the less educated.[75] Compare this insight with the conviction of Maryland Jesuits that they must be as free as possible from the day to day activities of their plantations so that they might pursue priestly work—the preparation of homilies, the riding of the circuit to celebrate the sacraments for the laity, and the tutoring of children from upper class Catholic families. Jesuits often complained that the assignment to do both the tasks of plantation management and clerical duties ensured that neither was performed well.[76]

Utopians strove to make any worker above the level of slave as "free from physical drudgery as the needs of the community will allow." That would free him for the cultivation of his mind,"the secret of a happy life."[77] This was an obvious incentive for Jesuits, with their intellectual heritage and theological interests, to leave the mundane needs of their plantations to servants.

Utopians also stressed, however, that there should not be too sharp a division of labor between upper class people and servants; they should work together on important projects. For example, the preparation of meals should be done together. The creative side of cooking was left to the ruling class, who devised the menus and planned the courses while the slaves pursued "all the rough and dirty work."[78]

When Father Joseph Mosley was assigned as the lone Jesuit at a mission station in Tuckahoe, Maryland, from 1765–1787, he honored this Utopian insight by joining his slaves in work. The only difference between them was that Mosley lived in a "miserable dwelling house" while the slaves had "a much worse." In 1766, the slaves accomplished the messy task of plastering the priest's house for Mosley, but he himself built a brick chimney after choosing the type of bricks he wanted and hauling them five miles from market. In a letter to his sister, Mosley noted "I have my own grain, and make my own bread."[79] Eighteen years later, when Mosley was able to resume correspondence with his sister after the long hiatus of the Revolutionary War, he noted that "Since the commencement of the War, I've built on my farm a brick chapel and dwelling house." Concerning this latter accomplishment, Mosley noted how difficult it was to do under wartime conditions, when nails, in particular, were in very short supply.[80]

This comment echoes the flexibility shown by the Utopians in time of war. Officers in the Utopian army were often put to work usually done by slaves, such as digging fortifications in the interest of quick completion by many hands.[81]

As the Jesuits grew more and more preoccupied with securing their landholdings as enclaves for the protection of Catholic religious observance, simultaneously noticing more and more the difficulties involved in making a living with these landholdings, More's insight about the desirability of the upper class pursuing manual labor in emergencies came to have a greater and greater influence on Jesuits management of their plantations. Jesuits showed a similar openness to manual labor in emergencies, even carrying it further than the Utopian soldiers by working alongside rather than replacing the slaves. Their willingness to do so was in the spirit of this passage from *Utopia*:

> they believe that the only way to earn happiness after death is to spend one's life doing good works. . . . In short, they behave like servants, and work hard-

er than slaves, not only for the community, but also for private individuals . . . the more they make slaves of themselves, the more everybody respects them.[82]

In Utopia, "The normal penalty for being too aggressive in religious controversy is either exile or slavery."[83] That was certainly not the explicit reason why any individual was enslaved by the Jesuits. However, the deeper insight of this statement was that the institution of slaveholding was somehow linked to the price that society had to pay for a climate of religious toleration. This was certainly a proposition that the Jesuits in Maryland accepted by treating their slaveholding plantations as devices for the protection of religious liberty.

Utopian slaves were often used as tools to teach moral lessons to the whole country. Slaves were chained in gold as part of a didactic effort to persuade Utopian freemen not to covet that metal.[84] The Jesuits hoped that the kind treatment of their slaves would serve as a didactic reminder to other masters that they should not view their pursuit of riches as the most important thing in their lives, and that they should concentrate on the just governance of the less fortunate committed to their care. George Hunter's observations of 1749 that Jesuits were called to set a charitable example of the treatment of slaves was made in that spirit. Jesuits sought to teach by clothing the slaves in kindness rather than gold.

More portrayed the Stywards, supervisors of servants in Utopia, as officials responsible for striking a balance between mandating the laborers to work all the time and leaving them completely idle. The result was to be time balanced between work and leisure.[85] Regulations devised by the Jesuits in 1722 for the observance of holydays by slaves in Maryland show the influence of this balanced philosophy. Despite pressures to make the slaves work every day of the planting season, they were given five holydays completely off during the summer, including Ascension, Whit Monday, Whit Tuesday, Corpus Christi, and Assumption. On other important feast days of the summer, they were to be allowed to attend Mass or a prayer service before proceeding to the fields. However, those servants who worked within the household were to take all the holydays completely off from work.[86]

The Jesuits thus entered the eighteenth century with their unique way of governing their slaves and operating their plantations. The task that remained to them was to defend this right, and they produced two important political philosophers, Peter Attwood, S.J. (1682–1734) and George Hunter (1713–1779) who brought their case to a maturity of political expression.

Attwood's contribution was composed in 1718 and was called "Liberty and Property: or, the Beauty of Maryland Displayed, Being a Brief and Candid Search and Inquiry into her Charter, Fundamental Laws and Constitution, by a Lover of his Country." It was written in response to the crisis of the Old Pretender's Rebellion.

The German princes of the Hanoverian dynasty had just succeeded to the British throne in preference to the Catholic members of the House of Stuart, who had the better hereditary claim but the inferior political one. A Protestant Parliament had enacted the Act of Settlement, limiting the crown to professed Anglicans. Jesuits and the Catholic laity were suspected of plotting to aid the "king across the water" in France, the Stuart pretender, James Edward, in his efforts to overthrow George I. Within the Britain itself, there was an outburst of fear that absolute monarchy was about to be restored under "papist" influence.[87]

This apprehension spread to Maryland. In 1715, the Maryland Assembly imposed an importation tax "on all Irish Papist Servants imported into the Province." An additional levy of twenty shillings was imposed "on all Irish Servants being Papists" through an act of May 28, 1717.[88] There were indications that the Assembly might proceed further, stripping the Jesuits of all their property. As a precaution, the Jesuit owner of the Newtown plantation, William Hunter, temporarily signed his land, slaves and other effects over to a sympathetic lay friend, Thomas Jameson, for ten shillings[89]. The deed of this transfer provided what is now the earliest known surviving legal documentation of Jesuit ownership of slaves in Maryland.

The issue of Irish indentured servants is important to understanding the emergence of slaveholding in in the Chesapeake. The major social difficulty of the indenture system was that each year it graduated into the Chespeake economy numerous young settlers with limited prospects for prosperity. Fearing the potential of such frustrated young men for violence, planters often welcomed the importation of African slaves as an alternative to further white immigration.[90]

Imagine, however, the special Jesuit and Catholic predicament in this situation. Given the continuing Protestant tendency to portray the Jesuits as plotters against the political and social order of both England and Maryland, Jesuits were particularly vulnerable to charges that they were behind any revolt of the restless freedmen. This suspicion was probably a factor in the denial of political rights to Catholics at the time of the 1689 Revolution. The Irish, with their record of hostility to the British Crown, were a particularly provocative group to have present as indentured servants in such an atmosphere. Other planters may have turned to slave labor out of economic motivations, but the Jesuits had the extra pressure of finding a labor pool whose composition would not arouse the hostility of suspicious neighbors.

The year 1715 may have been the crucial moment in the general transition from indentured to slave labor. After this date, the number of servants no longer kept pace with the number of slaves entering the colony.[91] Not coincidentally, this was the very same year that the Assembly cracked down on the importation of Catholic indentured servants. This evidence suggests that the special circumstances of religious intolerance forced the Jesuits to rely even more on slave labor than the typical Marylander came to.

Whatever circumstances forced them to do, however, Jesuits like Attwood clung to the argument that any subject of the Crown had inalienable rights that should be unaffected by religious affiliation. It was Attwood's understanding that *any* English subject who settled in Maryland was to be granted a free tract of land, on which they could live according to all the rights and privileges of Englishmen.[92]

As Englishmen, Jesuits like Attwood felt that they shared an ancient right to buy, own and sell property. As far as they were concerned, this was a right based on Englishness alone, and not on whether one was a *Protestant* Englishmen. Moreover, this right was not dependent on the crown; the king could neither grant nor deny this right. He had only the duty to recognize it and guarantee it. As George Hunter put it, Catholics desired "that they may be assured they shall not at any time be molested or affected by any law touching their Religion or Property uncommon to their fellow subjects."[93] Efforts by Parliament to take away these rights from English Catholics struck the Jesuits as violations of the true spirit of the Constitution.[94]

When the Jesuits decided that property ownership was a function of English nationality, they produced the side effect of neglecting the civil rights of people who did not happen to be English subjects. Had they based the claim to property ownership on humanity, as they did in the case of religious liberty, they would have found it difficult indeed to justify holding other human beings as property. But since Jesuits decided to limit land ownership to a right of Englishness, they missed an opportunity to affirm a universal right to economic liberty.

It was the Jesuit view of religious liberty that was exceptional. The idea that property was an English right made the Jesuits reflective of conventional political thought. Their only quarrel with the Bill of Rights passed by Parliament in 1689 was that it limited the ancient property rights of the English to Protestants. Jesuits quite agreed with John Locke when he wrote that political power is delegated by the people who happen to own property for the protection of their property.[95]

The theory that Maryland Jesuit thought was characteristically English is instructive here, especially as regards the notion that such thought flowed from experience rather than theory.[96] Jesuits made no attempt to impose an *a priori* political philosophy upon their conduct in Maryland. Rather, they adapted a pragmatic approach in reaction to events. They affirmed the universality of religious liberty and the particularity of property ownership because developments in Maryland suggested to them that such a combination of policies would be the best way for the Catholic Church to survive there.

A crucial consequence of their political theory was that Jesuits developed a great sensitivity to exercising all the same property rights as their fellow English colonists. They also realized early on that to claim such a right was not enough; one had to also exercise it. In fact, one also had to be **seen** to exercise this right. If their Protestant neighbors had property, Catholics not only had to have it, too, but they also had to prompt Protestants to see that they had it. In that spirit, as mission superior, Attwood was willing to make the first public concession that Jesuits actually owned slaves in 1718. In doing so, he explicitly laid claim to a right to do so.[97]

Attwood combined a lengthy documentation of the colony's founding and its early legislation regarding religious liberty and property rights with a protest over the more recent denial of those freedoms to Catholics. Everything he wrote was designed to demonstrate his case that Maryland was meant to be religiously blind. All Englishmen who came to Maryland had the same rights:

> All Christians enjoyed not only ye free use of their religion, but an equal share, in all their Rights, Places, and Privileges . . . there was also an entire liberty and full enjoyment of all other rights, privileges and immunities for all subjects of Great Britain, as to buy and sell, to take profits and enjoy,to transmit to their heirs, or to convey and bequeath unto anyother wt goods or chattles, lands or hereditaments, and in a word, all their estates, or any part there of, whatever, real or personal . . . both Clergy and Laity of all persuasions, and consequently of ye Roman Catholics among ye rest, were ever deemed to be qualified to purchase, buy, sell, or possess any lands or estates in Maryland.[98]

Attwood protested the injustice and inconvenience of taking these rights away from Catholics, noting that the Jesuits had a great practical need for this land, their only potential source of subsistence. To deprive them of this means of livelihood on account of their religion would be a form of molestation.[99]

Here Attwood made a remarkable statement: it was wrong to take away his right to own a slave just because the master was Catholic. This treatise had the effect of definitively incorporating Robert Persons' political philosophy within Maryland Jesuit thought.

The second important Jesuit document in support of property holding in colonial Maryland came four decades later. In 1757, George Hunter, S.J. (1713–1779) produced "A Short Account of the State and Conditions of the Roman Catholics in the Province of Maryland, Collected from Authentic Copies of the Provincial Records and Other Undoubted Testimonies."

Protestant Maryland experienced a renewed anti-Catholic panic in the 1750s, as the French began infiltrating the neighboring Ohio Valley and allying themselves with the native Americans there. French Jesuits had a historical presence among the indigenous peoples of Canada, and it was suspected that their English confreres in Maryland would collude with them in stirring up transAppalachian peoples against the British Crown. Meanwhile, the English Jesuits might also assist the enemy by inciting slave revolts in the Chesapeake itself. These suspicions were not true, but they led to further threats to Catholic religious liberty and property rights that Hunter felt obliged to respond to.[100]

Forty years earlier, the object had been to strip the Jesuits of their indentured servants. Now there was much agitation to take away their slaves. In 1753, the General Assembly formed a "Committee on Grievances" to investigate "the growth of Popery within this province." Its report showed signs of paranoia concerning the Jesuit custom of allowing white people and slaves to worship together: "Their public preaching is so notorious and unreserved, that there are known instances of their Preaching publicly to large mixed congregations." Another suspicion was that the Jesuit custom of hearing the confessions of Catholic slaves might become the means by which to issue secret orders for revolt. The Committee also blamed the Jesuits for a supposed increase in the rate of Catholic conversions among slaves owned by Protestants.[101]

In 1756, these Protestant suspicions prompted a new law, which doubled the property tax for Catholics. It was this measure that drew George Hunter's protest. He worried that the double tax would prove to be an underhanded way of driving Catholics off their land. Rather than ban them from it outright, it would simply make it financially impossible for them to remain.

Hunter began his commentary with two essential claims. The first was that the penal laws of England did not extend to Maryland, thanks to an exemption granted by Queen Anne in 1705. The second was that Roman Catholics in Maryland had committed no acts which warranted any punishment, let alone a double tax.

Thus far, Hunter had made a conventional Jesuit defense of Catholic civil rights. What set his appeal apart from Attwood's was Hunter's threat that Catholic planters would leave the colony unless their just rights were restored and honored. Not only should the offensive tax be repealed, but "such an order be given as that they may be assured they shall not at any time be molested or affected by any law touching their Religion or Property uncommon to their fellow subjects." Only the Crown and the Proprietor could change that situation, and Hunter trusted their "justice and clemency" toward contemporary Catholics and their posterity.

Hunter concluded his demand with this emphatic assertion to the Lord Proprietor:

> This is the humble petition of the Roman Catholic gentlemen, merchants, planters and others, Inhabitants of the Province of Maryland, as a necessary encouragement to the people of that persuasion to continue to cultivate and improve that Province. They, on assurances of this sort, contributed chiefly to the first settling of it, and to the bringing of it to that flourishing condition in which we now behold it under your Lordship's wise government and administration.[102]

This assertion showed a new measure of self-confidence in Jesuit political thought. For the first time, there was an awareness that their property was an economic weapon which they could use to their advantage. Hunter believed that the colony's economy and culture would be hurt if Jesuits and other Catholics left Maryland, and that his political enemies knew that to be the case. Hunter's boldness foretold the coming participation of Catholics in the American Revolution, but it also showed that the possession of slaves and other attributes of Catholic wealth would also make that participation effective. This was a clear example of a Jesuit using his slaves in pursuit of political self-interest. It also foreshadowed that many participants in the American Revolution would regard a right to slaveholding as one of the "liberties" they were fighting for.

That the new value which Hunter accorded to the Jesuit properties was shared by other Jesuits is shown by a series of new "ordinations and regulations" for the Maryland Mission, promulgated on April 2, 1759. These rules took elaborate steps to protect the plantations. The eighth of the new rules acknowledged the danger facing "our lands and settlements," and ordered each individual Jesuit holding the title to a plantation to make a will, leaving the property to whatever Jesuit was designated to inherit it. The willmaker also had to sign a bond, holding his estate liable for 40,000 pounds if he should ever change the inheritance to favor someone other than the Jesuit selected. Copies of both the will and the bond had to be deposited at two Jesuit plantations other than the one which was their subject, and placed in the possession of a Jesuit not mentioned in either. While the designees of wills were customarily selected by the Provincial in England, the mission superior or his consultors on the scene in Maryland could make the choice in urgent cases.[103] While it had been the custom for Jesuits to make wills from the time it became clear that there would be no mortmain in Maryland, the tightened procedures of 1759 showed a new awareness of how important land and slaves were in the struggle for Catholic civil liberties.

The evidence presented in this chapter shows that slaveholding emerged among the Jesuits for reasons peculiar to their status as English Catholics. Their exceptional motivations for slaveholding have been overlooked. Since the Jesuits emerged as slaveholders at about the same time as everyone else in Maryland, it has been taken for granted that they shared the general motivations. They no doubt did, but they also had special reasons of their own. Quite simply, the Jesuits found in slaveholding a special way to illlustrate their belief that anyone could be Catholic but only Englishmen in Maryland could own property.

In 1995, Martin E. Marty published *A Short History of American Catholicism*. In the introduction to this work, Marty called it "the first extended historical essay on American Catholic history by a non-Catholic."[104] Catholic slaveholding, however, is very poorly covered in this book. The index only contains one reference to it, a brief discussion of the enslavement of native Americans in Latin America in the sixteenth century.[105] Remarkably, Marty's only reference to the Civil War does not mention slavery at all, instead stressing that Catholics identified with whatever part of the country they found themselves dwelling in during that struggle.[106]

Marty made a serious omission in not exploring Jesuit slaveholding. It resembled general slaveholding in many respects, but it was conducted for additional reasons and according to additional norms than other variations of the practice. The spirituality, the intellectual life, and the economic sensibilites of the Jesuits also contributed to their unique variation of a peculiar institution. To these factors this study will now turn.

NOTES

1. Brother Joseph Mobberly, S.J., "Diary, Part One: Breadth of a Methodist's Conscience," p. 115; The Brother Joseph Mobberly, S.J. Papers (BJMSJP), Special Collections, Lauinger Library, Georgetown University, Washington, D.C.

2. Gerald Fogarty, S.J., "Property and Religious Liberty in Colonial Maryland Catholic Thought," *Catholic Historical Review* 71 (1986), pp. 573–600.

3. Augustine, *The City of God* (New York: Doubleday, Image Books Edition, 1958), p. 40.

4. See Edmund S. Morgan, "Slavery and Freedom: The American Paradox," in Stanley N. Katz and John M. Murrin, editors, *Colonial America: Essays in Political and Social Development* (New York: Alfred A. Knopf, 1983), pp. 572–596.

5. Peter Attwood, S.J., "Liberty and Property, or, the Beauty of Maryland Displayed," 1718, *United States Catholic Historical Magazine* III (New York: Press of the Society, 1890), p. 239.

6. John D. Krugler, "'With Promise of Liberty in Religion:' The Catholic Lords Baltimore and Toleration in Seventeenth Century Maryland, 1634–1692," *Maryland Historical Magazine* 79, no. 1 (Spring, 1984), pp. 26–27.

7. James Hennesey, S.J., "Roman Catholicism: The Maryland Tradition," *Thought* 51, no. 202 (September, 1976), p. 284.

8. David W. Jordan, "Political Stability and the Emergence of a Native Elite in Maryland," in Thad W. Tate and David L Ammerman, editors, *The Chesapeake in the Seventeenth Century: Essays on Anglo American Society* (New York: Norton, 1979), p. 249.

9. Francis Edwards, S.J., *The Jesuits in England: From 1580 to the Present Day* (Tunbridge Wells, England: Burns and Oates, 1985), p. 24, p. 43.

10. For a summary of Jesuit status in England, see John Bossy, *The English Catholic Community, 1570–1850* (New York: Oxford University Press, 1976), especially Chapter 7, "Congregation: The Role of the Gentry," pp. 149–181, and Chapter 11, "The Priest in the Community," pp. 250–277.

11. John Bossy, "Reluctant Colonists: The English Catholics Confront the Atlantic," in David B. Quinn, editor, *Early Maryland in a Wider World* (Detroit: Wayne State University Press, 1982), pp. 155–156.

12. Hennesey, *op. cit.*, p. 284.

13. R.J. Lahey, "The Role of Religion in Lord Baltimore's Colonial Enterprise," *Maryland Historical Magazine* 72 (Winter, 1977), pp. 492–511.

14. Aubrey C. Land, *Colonial Maryland: A History* (Millwood, N.Y.: KTO Press, 1981), pp. 23–24.

15. Bossy, *English Catholic Community*, p. 168.

16. Land, *op. cit.*, pp. 23–24.

17. *Ibid.*, p. 24.

18. John S. Krugler, "Lord Baltimore, Roman Catholics, and Toleration: Religious Policy in Maryland During the Early Catholic Years, 1634–1649," *Catholic Historical Review*, LXV (January, 1979), p. 74; Fogarty, *op. cit.*, p. 573.

19. Ladislas Orsy, S.J., "The Meaning of *Novus Habitus Mentis:* The Search for New Horizons," *The Jurist* 48, no. 2 (1988), p. 437.

20. *Ibid.*

21. Henry Sebastian Bowden, *Mementoes of the Martyrs and Confessors of England and Wales* (Wheathampstead, Eng.: Burns and Oates, 1962), p. 171.

22. G. R. Elton, editor, *The Tudor Constitution: Documents and Commentary* (Cambridge, Eng.: Cambridge University Press, 1975 Reprint), p. 418.

23. Edmund Campion, S.J., "Campion's Brag," reproduced in Evelyn Waugh, *Edmund Campion* (London: Longmans, Green, and Co., 1935), pp. 220.

24. Bowden, *op. cit.*, pp. 17–18.

25. Thomas O'Brien Hanley, S.J., *Their Rights and Liberties: The Beginnings of Religious and Political Freedom in Maryland* (Chicago: Loyola University Press, 1984), p. 38.

26. Robert Southwell, S.J., *An Humble Supplication to her Maiestie*, edited by R.C. Bald (Cambridge, England: At the University Press, 1953), pp. 15–16.

27. Krugler, "Lord Baltimore, Roman Catholics, and Toleration," p. 74.

28. David W. Jordan, *Foundations of Representative Government in Maryland, 1632–1715* (Cambridge: Cambridge University Press, 1987), p. 1.

29. *Ibid.*, p. 19.

30. "The Charter of Mary Land," in Clayton Colman Hall, editor, *Narratives of Early Maryland, 1633–1684* (New York: Scribners, 1910), p. 104.

31. David W. Jordan, *Foundations of Representative Government*, pp. 1–5.

32. *Ibid.*, pp. 36–42.

33. *Ibid.*, p. 40.

34. *Ibid.*, p.37.

35. "Extract from the Annual Letter of the English Province of the Society of Jesus, 1639," in Hall, editor, *op. cit.*, p. 130.

36. "Letters of English Jesuits Volunteering for Maryland," in Robert Emmett Curran, S.J., *American Jesuit Spirituality: The Maryland Tradition, 1634–1900* (Mahwah, N.J.: Paulist Press, 1988), pp. 55–61.

37. Jordan, *Foundations of Representative Government*, p. 40.

38. Geoffrey Holt, *St. Omer's and Bruge's Colleges, 1593–1773: A Biographical Dictionary*, p. 183.

39. Winthrop D. Jordan, *White Over Black: American Attitudes Toward the Negro, 1550–1812* (Chapel Hill: University of North Carolina Press, 1968), pp. 79–82.

40. Robert Persons, S.J, "An Answere to the Fifth Part of Reportes, 1606," in D.M. Rogers, editor, *English Recusant Literature, 1558–1640,* no. 245 (London: Scolar Press, 1975), p. 24.

41. David J. O'Brien, *Public Catholicism* (Maryknoll, N.Y.: Orbis Books, 1996), p. 17.

42. David W. Jordan, *Foundation of Representative Government*, p. 102.

43. Winthrop Jordan, *op. cit.*, p. 92.

44. David W. Jordan, "Political Stability and the Emergence of a Native Elite in Maryland," pp. 244–246.

45. *Ibid.*, p. 249.

46. Lois Green Carr and David William Jordan, *Maryland's Revolution of Government, 1689–1692* (Ithaca, N.Y.: Cornell University Press, 1974), p. 1.

47. Lois Green Carr and Russell R. Menard, "Immigration and Opportunity: The Freedman in Early Colonial Maryland," in Tate and Ammerman, editors, *op. cit.*, p. 207.

48. No. 30, "The Claims for land by Conditions of Plantation," in Thomas Hughes, S.J., editor, *History of the Society of Jesus in North America, Colonial and Federal: Text, I: From the First Colonization Till 1645* (New York: Longmans, Green and Co., 1908), p. 212.

49. Attwood, *op. cit.*, p. 250.

50. John LaFarge, S.J., "The Jesuit-Baltimore Controversy," unpublished manuscript, The John LaFarge, S.J. Papers, Special Collections Division, Lauinger Library, Georgetown University, Washington, D.C.

51. Fogarty, *op. cit.*, p. 579.

52. David W. Jordan, *Foundations of Representative Government*, p. 40.

53. LaFarge, *op. cit.*

54. Fogarty, *op. cit.*, p. 580.

55. James Horn, "Servant Emigration to the Chesapeake in the Seventeenth Century," in Tate and Ammerman, editors, *op. cit.*, p. 51.

56. No. 1, "Father Robert Parsons, S.J. to Mr. Winslade, March 18, 1605;" in Hughes, editor, *op. cit.*, pp. 3–4.

57. Robert Emmett Curran, S.J., " 'Splendid Poverty':Jesuit Slaveholding in Maryland, 1805–1838," in Randall M. Miller and Jon L. Wakelyn, editors,

Catholics in the Old South: Essays on Church and Culture (Macon, Ga.: Mercer University Press, 1983), p. 126.

58. Horn, *op. cit.*, page 65.

59. *Ibid.*, pp. 94–95.

60. Land, *op. cit.*, p. 281.

61. No. 62, "White Marsh: devise of James Carroll," in Hughes, editor, *op. cit.*, pp. 248–251.

62. "Excerpt from the Annual Letter Concerning the Jesuit Mission in Maryland for 1638," in Curran, S.J., editor, *American Jesuit Spirituality*, p. 63.

63. George Hunter, S.J., "Notes on his Spiritual Retreat at Port Tobacco, December 20, 1749," Item no. 202A7, Archives of the Maryland Province (MPA), Special Collections Division, Lauinger Library, Georgetown University, Washington, D.C.

64. No. 30, "The Claims for Land by Conditions of Plantation," in Hughes, editor, *op. cit.*, p. 213.

65. Gerald Fogarty, S.J., "The Origins of the Mission, 1634–1773," in R. Emmett Curran, S.J., Gerald Fogarty, S.J. and Joseph T.
Durkin, S.J., *The Maryland Jesuits, 1634–1833* (Baltimore: Maryland Province of the Society of Jesus, 1976), p. 26.

66. Persons, *op. cit.*, p. 26.

67. *Ibid.*, p. 10.

68. *Ibid.*, pp. 12–13, p. 16.

69. Fogarty, "*Property and Religious Liberty*, p. 576.

70. Persons, *op. cit.*, p. 14.

71. "A Narrative Derived from the Letters of Ours, Out of Maryland, 1642," in Hall, editor, *op. cit.*, p. 140.

72. Winthrop Jordan, *op. cit.*, pp. 80–82.

73. David Mathew, *Catholicism in England: The Portrait of a Minority, its Culture and Tradition* (London: Eyre and Spottiswoode, 1955), pp. 7–10.

74. Hanley, *op. cit.*, p. 21.

75. Thomas More, *Utopia* (Harmondsworth, Eng.: Penguin, Classics Edition, 1965), p. 81.

76. Roy Wagner, *The History of St. Joseph's Mission, Cordova, Maryland, 1765–1965*, MPA, Box 31, Folder 5.

77. More, *op. cit.*, p. 79.

78. *Ibid.*, p. 82.

79. Joseph Mosley, S.J to Helen Dunn, October 14, 1766, in Curran, *American Jesuit Spirituality*, p. 106.

80. Joseph Mosley, S.J. to Helen Dunn, October 4, 1784, in Curran, *American Jesuit Spirituality*, p. 112.

81. More, *op. cit.*, p. 116.

82. *Ibid.*, p. 122.

83. *Ibid.*, p. 119.

84. *Ibid.*, p. 86.
85. *Ibid.*, pp. 75–76.
86. "Robert Hall to his Lordship Bonaventura, Bishop of Madura and Vicar Apostolic of London, December 21, 1722: Submitting Five Regulations About the Observance of Holydays by the Catholics of Maryland," Item no. 2T 0–4, MPA, Box 2, Folder 9.
87. J.D. Mackie, *A History of Scotland* (Harmondsworth, Eng.: Pelican Books, 1987), p. 269.
88. Father George Hunter, S.J., "A Short Account of the State and Condition of the Roman Catholics in the Province of Maryland, Collected from Authentic Copies of the Provincial Records and Other Undoubted Testimonies," *Woodstock Letters* X, no. 1 (1881), p. 9.
89. No. 40, "Specimen of Measures Taken to Save the Personal Property," in Hughes, editor, *op. cit.*, pp. 222–223.
90. Edmund S.Morgan, *American Slavery, American Freedom: The Ordeal of Colonial Virginia* (New York: Norton, 1975), p. 218.
91. Land, *op. cit.*, p. 281.
92. Attwood, *op. cit.*, p. 238.
93. Hunter, *op. cit.*, p. 21.
94. Fogarty, "Property and Religious Liberty," p. 576.
95. John Locke, "Second Treatise on Government," in Marvin Perry, Joseph R. Peden and Theodore H. Van Laue, editors, *Sources of the Western Tradition, II: From the Renaissance to the Present* (Boston, Massachusetts: Houghton Mifflin, 1991), pp. 59–60.
96. Fogarty, "Property and Religious Liberty," p. 576.
97. Attwood, *op. cit.*, p. 250.
98. *Ibid.*
99. *Ibid.*
100. Timothy W. Bosworth, "Anti-Catholicism as a Political Tool in Mid-Eighteenth Century Maryland," *Catholic Historical Review* 61 (1975), pp. 539–563.
101. J. Hall Pleasants, editor, *Archives of Maryland, L: Proceedings and Acts of the General Assembly of Maryland, 1752–1754* (Baltimore: 1933), pp. 198–199.
102. Hunter, *op. cit.*, pp. 20–21.
103. Henry Corbie, S.J., "Ordinations and Regulations for Maryland, April 2, 1759," Item no. 202 A11, MPA.
104. Martin E. Marty, *A Short History of American Catholicism* (Allen, Tex.: Thomas More, 1995), p. 7.
105 *Ibid.*, p. 37.
106. *Ibid.*, pp. 117–118.

CHAPTER TWO

Real Poverty and Apparent Wealth on the Jesuit Farms

IN 1819–1820, AN IRISH JESUIT PRIEST, PETER KENNEY (1779–1841) INSPECTED the Jesuit apostolates and plantations in Maryland on behalf of the General of the Society of Jesus in Rome. Ostensibly, Kenney was sent to Maryland in order to resolve tensions between American-born and European-born Jesuits working in the United States. More discreetly among his mandates, however, was a directive to determine why the plantations had been in perennial financial and fiscal difficulty since colonial times.

In his report to Rome, Kenney emphasized a paradox. The Jesuits in Maryland certainly had the *appearance* of wealth. Anyone who counted the thousands of acres of land and hundreds of slaves that these men owned would conclude that they were rich. In actuality, however, these Jesuits were poor. They had great resources, but had not demonstrated sufficient skill to develop them, and so were deep in debt. The result, Kenny said, was "so much apparent wealth and real poverty."[1]

Kenney thus defined a mystery that impressed observers of the Maryland Jesuit mission. How did a group of intelligent men, with impressive possessions, fail to exploit their resources? Also, if the Jesuits took so seriously their professed obligation to care for their slaves, why did they persist so long in an improvised, financially unprofitable mode of operation in which the slaves were the first to suffer the consequences of the resulting systemic poverty?

Kenney sought his own answers to this question. One of his first observations reveals why it is so difficult to trace the financial history of the Jesuit plantations. Since there was not "anywhere a regular + uniform system of keeping the books," he was forced to conclude that "he could not exactly learn the actual state of each farm."[2] These plantations had been gradually accruing to the Jesuits and expanding since the middle of the seventeenth century, but at

Kenney's inspection in 1820 no uniform system of management and accounting was in place. Instead, Kenney found "everywhere, almost" accounts of "bad management, unprofitable contracts, useless + expensive experiments and speculations."[3]

Did these dysfunctions arise simply because the Jesuits were talented professional clergymen with no particular aptitude for the very different field of finance? As early as 1789, John Carroll (1735–1815), a Jesuit who became the first Bishop of Baltimore, had noted "the mismanagement so common to men not trained to the cultivation of landed estates."[4] Or were there other factors working against efficiency, including tension between the Jesuits' ideals for governing the slaves on their plantations and the desirability of making the plantations profitable? Could the Jesuit slave system itself have played a key role in instilling the systemic chaos which so frustrated Kenney?

In fact, two attitudes which the Jesuits held toward their slaves each made it more difficult to cultivate successful plantations. Their spiritual concern to treat the slaves as equal in dignity to all other baptized Catholics restrained the Jesuits, in conscience, from material exploitation of them. John Carroll once commented that the phrase "a priest's negro" had come to be synonymous for slaves who were governed with lax discipline.[5] Jesuits continued to hold slaves who could no longer contribute to the labor of the farms, such as the elderly and the disabled. They also, tried to avoid sales which would break up married couples and their dependent children. Jesuits believed that sacrificing the slaves to self-interest would threaten their own souls as well as those of the slaves themselves. The second attitude contributing to the Jesuit propensity to keep economically useless slaves was their social and intellectual condescension. Jesuits felt both spiritually and materially responsible for a people whom they did not believe were capable of governing themselves, either in everyday life or in religious affairs.

At the same time, Jesuits did have some desire to survive economically in the emerging American system. They hoped that self-sufficient plantations would support someday the ministry of the Roman Catholic Church in the rising country. Therefore, they often expressed a wish to make the plantations more efficient and productive. Their inability to resolve the tension between humane treatment of the slaves and efficient farm production, however, ensured that the Jesuit farms would not prosper so long as they held slaves. Furthermore, a growing awareness of their dilemma seems to have led some Jesuits to act out in frustration, abusing slaves despite a stated determination to act humanely.

Both goals can be seen in the decision to sell the Jesuit slaves to plantation owners in Lousiana in 1838. The Jesuits, instructed by their superiors in Rome, insisted that the new owners must be practing Roman Catholics who would promote religious devotion among the slaves, and that slave families must be kept together in the transaction. Louisiana, with its French heritage and sugar economy, was the only place where the Jesuits could find both Catholic masters with the economic means of supporting several hundred slaves. By the 1830s, the Louisiana sugar economy was the one area of the South where the slave population had failed to reproduce itself naturally, creating a market for mass sales from the Upper South.[6] The money which Lousiana planters could offer for slaves seemed to promise a jump start for the Jesuit estates further north.

One reason that Jesuit mismanagement continued so long was that they had many generous lay benefactors, whose constant gifts rescued them from the worst consequences of their inefficiency. The oldest surviving specific reference to slaves owned by a Jesuit in Maryland came in a "deed of gift" dated January 30, 1717. Father William Hunter, a legal resident of Charles County, in exchange for ten shillings, "gave, granted, bargained and sold" to Thomas Jameson "all and every, ye goods, church stuff, platt, household stuff, negroes, horses, mares, neat, cattle, hoggs, sheep, husbandry, implements, tobacco, corn and all other things" from the plantation of Britton's Neck, more familiarly known as Newtown.[7] This was a legal maneuver, designed to save Hunter's property from possible confiscation by an anti-clerical colonial government. In fact, it is likely that Hunter continued to hold all these assets during the period that the understanding Jameson technically possessed them. The property was formally transferred back to Hunter as soon as when the immediate threat of hostile legislation receded. It was definitely in his name on August 16, 1723, when the celibate and heirless Hunter fulfilled the command of his superiors that he pass his land to another Jesuit and signed a will leaving his "temporal estate" to his brother Jesuit, George Thorold.[8]

The arrangement which Hunter made with Jameson had an importance that went beyond its temporary nature. It pointed to a tradition of intimate collaboration between Jesuits and wealthy, landed Catholic laymen that existed throughout the colonial period. These men were willing to serve as benefactors of the Society of Jesus, providing Jesuits not only with legal help, as in the case of 1717, but with considerable financial assistance as well. Through the generosity of such friends, the Jesuits were bequeathed many of their slaves and much of their land. The will of James Carroll, written in February, 1728, and executed after his death on June 13, 1729, was a major example of such munificence. It awarded the Jesuits, through the person of James' priest cousin Charles, with over five hundred acres of land in Ann Arundel County and over two thousand acres in Prince Georges County.[9] While the number of the slaves Carroll bequeathed to the Jesuits was not specified in the will itself, research two centuries later speculated that at least 100 were involved.[10] Because of this generosity, the colonial Jesuits were able to keep alive and even expand struggling farms. While the general tobacco economy of the Chesapeake passed through varying fortunes, the Jesuit plantations struggled on in a perpetual state of malaise because benefactors shielded the Jesuits from the consequences of their inepitude.

The general pattern of the Chesapeake tobacco economy was a cycle of alternating prosperity and depression through the end of the eighteenth century, followed by a gradual yet steady decline during the period between 1800 and the commencement of the Civil War. Beginning in the 1620s and continuing for about sixty years, there were was a high rate of tobacco exportation. Prices remained low, but planters still succeeded as long they could raise more harvests without increasing the amount of their laborers. Around 1680, however, exportation stagnated. Prices remained low or declining until about 1715. A short upswing faded by 1720; then depression returned for a decade as overproduction failed to accommodate a sagging demand. It was the general pattern of Chesapeake planters to overproduce each time demand reappeared, bringing swift stagnation of demand. However, by mid-century the tobacco planters had learned shrewder financial skills and were able to ride a fairly long boom amid gradually rising prices. During this phase, depressions were less marked and recoveries sharper and more sustained than earlier. The struggle for independence from Britain hurt the tobacco market so severely during the 1770s and early 1780s, however, that many planters shifted to raising grain and herding animals in order to survive. A brief revival after the peace of 1783 failed to coax many planters toward exclusive tobacco cultivation—luckily so, for there soon came another depression amid the wars of the French Revolution. The result was that, by 1800, tobacco cultivation had been reduced to a few isolated areas of the Chesapeake, including the counties of southern Maryland.[11]

This pattern then leveled off into permanent decline during the nineteenth century. Tobacco lost its dominant niche in the Maryland economy: it fell from 90% of the overall agricultural production of the colony in 1747 to 14% of the overall agricultural production of the state in 1860. Cereal crops, especially wheat, came to the fore instead. This change had great implications for slaveholding, since slaves were needed year round for the cultivation of tobacco but only seasonally for the production of cereals. The problem of what to do with slaves during the fallow seasons of the year simply made the possession of slaves unprofitable for cereal farmers. Therefore, slaveholding declined in the Upper South even as it flourished anew amid the cotton economy of the Deep South.[12]

The Jesuit plantations remained anchored in scarcity no matter what the general economic picture was. The testimony of Brother Joseph Mobberly (1779–1827), the manager of St. Inigoe's plantation from 1806–1820, provides an important clue as to why: the Jesuits were locked into tobacco cultivation by their need to both employ and feed their slaves. Mobberly stated that since the slaves needed constant work, the Jesuits had to cultivate extensive tobacco fields which were much too large for their available stock of manure. This practice soon led to soil exhaustion, but rather than turn to grain cultivation instead, the Jesuits resorted to corn. A single acre that could produce five bushels of wheat could produce 7.5 bushels of corn, significantly increasing rations for the slaves.[13] Mobberly's comments demonstrated that the Jesuits were sacrificing economic advantage for the sake of feeding their slaves. Mobberly himself deplored this policy and advocated disposing of the slaves instead.

A strong connection with trade was a major factor which distinguished Old World from New World forms of slavery. In more traditional forms of slaveholding, the household economy rather than the marketplace was the key factor. Slaves produced goods and services which were consumed mainly by themselves, their masters, and the other members of the masters' household. New World slavery, by contrast sought markets in Europe, exploiting the zeal of buyers to smoke tobacco, dress in cotton cloth, or spoil a sweet tooth.[14] While the records of the Jesuit plantations are scanty, what we do know about their proceeding suggests that they were not market-oriented slaveholders. They sought to be self-supporting in their ecclesiastical work through their planting, so what they produced was used to pay the expenses of ministries like Georgetown College rather than increase Jesuit investments overseas. Mobberly's ruminations suggests that food raised on Jesuit farms was used to feed the slaves themselves, Jesuits in their ministries,and students at tuition-free Georgetown before it was ever sent to market. Jesuits were bound by what may have been a characteristic tension of the South—the juxtaposition of commerce with an economy based on non-captalist productive relationships.[15]

It was the benefactors of the Society of Jesus, men like James Carroll, who allowed this situation to continue as long as it did. In the parlance of today's twelve-step "recovery movements," the benefactors served as "enablers" who allowed the Jesuits to continue unhealthy financial practices without undue fear of the consequences.[16] This enabling allowed the Jesuits to remain immersed in a contradictory array of concerns: the spiritual care and paternalistic direction of their slaves and the attainment of full civil rights for Catholic planters. Against these values, the plantations' financial health remained a weak fourth priority. Jesuits could so arrange their goals because they knew they could depend on friends like Carroll.

Thus another member of the Carroll clan, the future bishop John, accorded the traditional priority to spiritual considerations in plantation management in his memorandum "Plan of Clergy Organization" of 1782. Carroll rejoiced that the lack of Church government in the United States at the time of the suppression of the Jesuits in 1773 had spared Jesuit estates in Maryland from the confiscation that befell Jesuit landholdings in Europe and Latin America at that time. This was a special blessing , an exemption from misfortune not shared by former Jesuits anywhere else. Carroll saw in this unique situation God's will that the Maryland clergy perpetuate the traditional ministry of its plantations. It was a duty, "to do this good work." It involved the obligation of justice to the benefactors, who had given or willed these estates for "pious uses." Carroll believed that estates designated for these purposes acquired a kind of consecration, and that the clergy would sin if it neglected them. There was also the duty of charity to the Catholic laity of the present and the future, who would always need the priestly ministry which the plantations had so long supported.. When he finally turned to economic considerations in his memorandum, Carroll stressed only that the clergy had a common ownership of this land and deserved equal enjoyment of it, which should be attained through a "due and equitable administration of it."[17]

A list of grants, deeds, bequests and benefactions that came to the Jesuits in Maryland between their arrival in Maryland in 1634 and the Suppression of the Society of Jesus in 1773, compiled in 1908, extended for over sixty pages.[18] Such manuscripts tended to be much more specific about amounts of money and acreages of land than they were about quantities of slaves. The result was that the financial origin of slavery on the Jesuit farms was hazy, but seemed to have resulted from a combination of bequest and purchase.[19] It is also easy to see how gifts of land might have prompted the Jesuits to purchase still more land, thus creating a need for more people to work it all.

In determining why planters left slaves to the Jesuits, it is helpful to examine a statement in John Carroll's will which indicates that he shared much of the Jesuit philosophy of the master's moral obligation to care for their material and spiritual needs. Concerned for the dignity of his slaves, Carroll directed that "such of my apparel as may be still not indecent" should be given to certain of his slaves who had manifested such attributes as "honesty and a sense of Christian duties." He named some of them: Tomboy, Jack and Jerry. He also willed that they be provided with instruction in the Catholic catechism.[20] Carroll may have felt that the Jesuits were the most likely and qualified people to carry out these wishes.

Carroll also had a family motive, however. Two nephews were attending Jesuit schools. Both of them, in fact, would enter the Jesuit order in later life. It is possible that Carroll felt that the Jesuits would be better able to carry out these educational tasks if they enjoyed the firmer basis of income that slave labor could help to build. Certainly Jesuit schools needed the income benefactors could provide so long as their Constitutions forbad them to require tuition form their students.[21] The attempt to sustain upper class education through slave labor would reach its culmination with the opening of Georgetown College in 1789. The Jesuits' decision in 1832–1833 that they could no longer conduct Georgetown without charging tuition removed one of the last major justifications for the possession of the slaveholding plantations.[22]

Another factor in prompting gifts of slaves to the Jesuits, particularly influential when pious people were writing their wills, was the hope that the Jesuits would celebrate Mass for the eternal repose of those who remembered them with a bequest. Material generosity to the Church at the time of death might then ease the spiritual process of purgation of sin which followed death, a doctrine in which the Catholic laity of the eighteenth century devoutedly believed.[23]

It is also likely, especially in colonial times, that clergy and laity were bound in Catholic community by a common experience of frontier hardships. Struggling to prosper in a sickly climate and in an underdeveloped area, they missed ties of fellowship they had taken as given in England and took great care to build new ones, which they centered around their priests and their gatherings for worship. The Catholic dissenters of early Maryland, therefore, manifested a sense of community that was based on religion as well as geographical patterns of settlement. They sought social, political and economic exchanges with which to enhance this mutual support.

Chapels became centers of socialization in an area where such meeting halls were otherwise scarce, and settlers took their obligation to provide the Church with material support quite seriously. Some Jesuit benefactors were likely former indentured servants of theirs who were grateful that the Jesuits had brought them to the colony and set them on the arduous road to success.[24]

Had these donors not supported the Society as it did, the Jesuits could neither have obtained nor preserved the slave system that they had for as long as they did. The impact of the lay gifts and bequests was felt by the middle decades of the eighteenth century, when the first surviving lists of substantial numbers of slaves made their appearance in the Jesuit records. On June 17, 1734, Father Arnold Livers, S.J. entered an inventory of the slaves at Newtown and St. Inigoe's plantations onto the blank page opposite the title page of his copy of Rider's Almanac for the year 1734 (printed in London by R. Nutt for the Company of Stationers). Livers counted forty-seven slaves altogether, twenty-seven at Newtown and twenty at St. Inigoe's. Those at Newtown were named Andrew, Peg, Jane, Ben, Sam, Jenny, Harry, James, Benj., Clare, Nel, Teresa, July, Clem, Ann, Fletcher, Jess, Suckey, Henry, Peggy, Rody, Betty, Josey, Mary, Monica, Beckly and Sally. Those at St. Inigoe's were Matthew and Betty, Thomas, Nacy, Will, Susan, Abraham and Briget, Peter and Bess, James, Abram, Charles, two Walters, Ann, Suckey, Mary, Martha and Henry.[25]

Livers listed slave couples together in response to the Church teaching that partners in a slave marriage be considered as a unity. There were strict sanctions against breaking up a married slave couple through sale. As early as the thirteenth century, Thomas Aquinas taught that marriage lay outside the direction of the master. Legislation by Catholic powers, notably in French Louisiana, provided that the master could prevent matrimony from taking place.[26] However, there remained a Catholic consensus that once marriage took place, the couple could not be disturbed. Since Livers did not provide any details beyond the names of these slaves, we know nothing about their ages, nor of their state of health, nor of their specific assignments, nor which were capable of working and which were not.

By the second quarter of the eighteenth century, when Livers compiled his record of Newtown and St. Inigoes', there was an emerging structure to African American culture. The growth of the slave population was occurring through natural increase rather than importation. There was a better balance between the sexes, and more slave marriages resulted. [27] The data assembled by Livers tends to confirm this scenario. It should be added that Catholics had an extra incentive to encourage marriage—unlike Protestants, they regarded matrimony as a sacrament. Thus Jesuits like Livers were not newcomers to the encouragement of slave marriage.

This early record was much more focused on documentation of slaves than it was on any other aspects of the two plantations. As little as Livers recorded about the slaves, it was much more than he recorded about the accounting and management of the two farms. Thus, even at this early date, there was evidence that the Jesuits tended to worry more about their slaves than their other properties. It was a foreshadowing that the care of the slaves would impede the prosperity of the farms.

There is some feeling that New World slaveholding of Livers' era generally succeeded at obtaining timely results with slaves. Especially with regard to sugar planting, most masters fostered stricter forms of agricultural discipline. Emphasis was placed on regimentation and efficiency. This new method of plantation management contrasted with the emphasis on custom that had dominated the regulation of serfs during the Middle Ages. Medieval lords of the manor did not set exact hours of labor, nor did they strictly supervise the quality of work that was done. The rhythm of work developed slowly, was gradual and variable in the manner of its unfolding, and was quite individualistic in mode.[28] Modern agriculture sought a fast evolving rhythm, a swift and regular manner of unfolding, and a standardized mode.

When European society first attempted to industrialize, one of the greatest obstacles to the process was persuading peasants to value industrial methods of work. Britain and New England during the Industrial Revolution, and later the Stalinist Soviet Union, all showed the difficulty of converting workers to new procedures. By contrast, many slaveholders in the New World, especially but not exclusively sugar planters, are said to have had a much higher degree of success at procuring efficient results from slaves, who came to the New World with no familiarity with European custom.[29] In considering the tendency of the eighteenth century Maryland Jesuits not to keep careful business records, however, it seems plausible that in their special case it was the Jesuits themselves, as slaveowners, who resisted or ignored the new methods of plantation management. They seem to have conducted themselves according to the medieval method of governing serfs—managing relatively lightly and according to long established customs. There is no evidence that Maryland Jesuits sought a fast evolving rhythm, a swift and regular unfolding and a standardized mode.

This theory acquires even more plausibility when it is recalled that all the traditional moral teachings of the Catholic Church regarding slaveholding were in place well before the end of the Middle Ages. The sources of these teachings were not modern economic theory but venerable manuscripts from the Scriptures, the early Church Fathers, Thomas Aquinas, and medieval Church councils. The last of these formative influences appeared in the year 1272. Pope Pius II's condemnation of Portugal's African slave trading in 1482 seems to have been uninfluential in British North America three centuries later.[30] There was a condemnation of the enslavement of native Americans in Spanish America by Pope Paul III in 1537, but this legislation said nothing explicit against enslaving Africans.[31] Paul's teaching set off a chain of papal condemnations of international slavery and slave trading, but this emerging tradition was expanded to include specific reference to the trading of Africans only in 1839 by Pope Gregory XVI. That was not only too late to influence the eighteenth century Jesuits, but even too late to affect the mass sale of 1838.[32] It seems clear, then, that the eighteenth century Jesuits were left to rely on a series of moral formulations and business ethics that were devised in the eras of small-scale, household slavery and European serfdom, not in the eras of Atlantic slave trading and plantation systems.

Despite his clerical celibacy, Livers was a Jesuit who thought of himself in patriarchal terms, as head of a household in which the slaves were among his children. He made no attempt to situate himself or them within the overall economic system in which both he and they were ensnared. He does seem to have known his slaves personally, however. In this combination of economic neglect and personal interest, Livers would have only half matched the so-called "resident mentality" that characterized Southern slaveholding. Masters were interested in the personal lives as well as the labors of their people, this theory claims.[33] Livers only showed the first of these interests. Yet, he shared a debilitating form of control in which plantation owners smothered their slaves with a malignant brew of overpowering love and protection on the one hand and constant direction and correction on the other.[34] The Livers case suggests that it is only half right to say that this system debilitated Jesuits slaves. It also drained masters of many resources and personal energy.

The extent of the burden which Jesuit masters imposed upon themselves is clearer from the records of the latter half of the eighteenth century. Financial record keeping on the Jesuit plantations became somewhat more exact under pressure from the offices of the Jesuits' English province in London, which governed the Maryland Mission. Each year, the Maryland Mission was expected to help support its mother province in Britain through payment of a tax. Consistently, Maryland Jesuits failed to meet this obligation. In 1728 and again in 1738, however, the accumulated debts were forgiven by the English Provincial. Despite these steps, by 1754 a further debt of nearly 1575 pounds had accumulated.[35] As attempts were made to deal with this problem, pressure mounted to inventory exactly what assets the Jesuits possessed in Maryland. As late as 1789 and 1811, however, there were still outstanding debts owed to

London.[36]

The need for such inventories was given impetus by a series of ordinations and regulations for the conduct of the Maryland Mission, which were issued from the London office of the English Province on April 2, 1759. The preamble to this document stressed that a conflict had arisen between the ideal that the mission maintain "all independence upon seculars" and the "highly unreasonable" proposition that "ye Province, as it has done, sh. d continue to run itself into great inconvenience to support ye said independence" of the Marylanders. The London superiors affirmed that the only way to resolve this conflict was for the mission to become self-supporting as soon as possible, lest it "run to decay for want of fresh supplies" or be forced "to levy charitable contributions upon those, for whose help + existence they are procur'd."

The regulations of 1759 revealed a fear that the unity of Jesuits in Maryland was fragile. This anxiety manifested itself in the admonition that next to God, Jesuits must search for their happiness "in mutual union and concord amongst themselves, and to the Sup r. of ye Mission: a thing . . . to be purchased and maintained at any rate." This need was augmented, the document declared, by the fact that the Maryland Mission was so geographically remote from the remainder of the English Province. "Strict uniformity" was therefore proclaimed as desirable in all "ministries + functions." Disagreement in opinions and in methods of acting were to be considered as "destructive to ye desired fruit of the mission." This emphasis suggests that the Jesuits in London were more inclined to attribute the financial difficulties of the Maryland Mission to quarrels among its members rather than the financial structure of its plantations or the organic nature of their slaveholding.

The bias against public expression of dissent revealed by this manuscript likely inhibited individual Jesuits from expressing any reservations they may have had about the financial conduct of the Mission during subsequent decades. The sixth regulation of 1759 itself, however, did offer one concrete proposal to deal with the financial difficulties. Since all the plantations of Maryland were canonically considered one Jesuit community under a common mission superior, the needier farms were to be entitled to provision from the surpluses of the more successful ones. The goal was that all Jesuits, no matter what the status of the farm they dwelt on, should be able to proceed in the "ordinary way of living," according to the Society's rules for fulfilling out the vows of religious poverty. In pursuit of this ideal, "all must study economy as much as possible, retrench unnecessary expenses."

As a business practice, however, this regulation was dubious, since it burdened the prosperous plantations with the problems of the struggling ones and thus minimized overall profits. It also allowed an ailing plantation to escape the full consequences of its failure to organize properly.

The eighth regulation addressed the issue of wills. Since the Society's existence was not recognized in Maryland's civil law during colonial times, the only way for Jesuits to possess property was as individuals rather than as a corporation. The only way to hand on this property was by bequest. Thus it was specified that each Jesuit was to will the land he was responsible for only to the individual designated to receive it by the Mission Superior.

A variety of safeguards were constructed in order to enforce this provision. The Jesuit drafting his will also had to sign a bond for 40,000 pounds, the fee which would be levied upon his entire estate if he should ever make a will in favor of anyone else. Copies of both his will and his bond had to be deposited in two separate Jesuit residences other than his own. This provision was a reminder that the Jesuit in residence and management at any given plantation had no autonomy in running the place. Everything he might decide was subject to review by the mission superior. Even the selection of the Jesuit to be designated in the will was left to the Superior.

The eleventh regulation offered the principle that "ye hoped for fruit of their labours, must chiefly proceed from the interior." Missionary work, however worthy in the sight of God, was not to take the place of prayer and contemplation. For this reason, each Jesuit was reminded of the solemn obligation to make an annual retreat of at least eight days in length.[37] This duty was to take priority over everything else they did, including their priestly work and their management of the farms. It was a reasonable reflection of the low priority of plantation administration in the annual Jesuit priorities. First came their prayer, then their pastoral and educational work, then their plantation management.

The regulations of 1759 demonstrate the nuances that distinguished the Jesuit notion of freedom from the pursuit of "hegemonic liberty" that may have characterized other Chesapeake settlers, especially in Virginia. Hegemonic liberty was an ideal which envisioned freedom as something possessed by individuals who were capable of dominion over others because they had achieved dominion over self.[38] This was a motif which contributed much to the ethos of the secular slavemaster: someone fit to rule over unruly Africans because he had achieved mastery over himself by exploiting his superiority as a white person. The difference between superiority and inferiority of two races lay in the degree of capacity for self-control, this philosophy argued. To some extent, the Jesuits did agree. Consider Joseph Mosley's observation that the Jesuits' slaves were a stubborn, dull set of people who did nothing unless driven to do so by their masters.[39] However, the Jesuits did not think in terms of a hegmony of individuals over individuals, but of the hegemony of a community over a community. They subordinated themselves to the group that was their religious order, and then attempted to subordinate their slaves to that same group. This process must have created an odd sort of affinity between the slaves and the Jesuit novices, men in the first stage of training as Jesuits. Both groups were called to overcome self-identity in order to identify with the Society of Jesus. While the correspondence was not exact—novices voluntarily identified with the Society and the slaves did not—Jesuit novices were often assigned to nurse ill slaves as a lesson in humility.

The Jesuits brought an English Catholic folkway to Maryland that has received much less attention than the Anglican folkway that was based in Virginia. Numerically, this omission may be justified. The English Catholic folkway was small, had little influence on its Protestant neighbors, and was eventually deluged, even within the American Catholic Church, by massive Catholic immigration from other parts of Europe during the nineteenth and early twentieth centuries. A consideration of this folkway, however, is essential for understanding the Jesuit way of doing business on their plantations. Since whatever sense of hegemony they possessed was expressed as the hegemony of a group, the Society of Jesus, this hegemony involved conceptualizing the estates as a single cooperative unit.

This form of imagining can be seen in the next major fragmentary record of a plantation, which dates from 1764, when Father John Lewis composed a memorandum about the farm at White Marsh. He took particular care to list the slaves who were too elderly or too young to work. Lewis' report also implied how easily slave women could be lost to work for long periods of time through the demands of childbearing and childrearing. "At the lower quarters," for example, Nanny was preoccupied with "Kate, her child. Fanny born 1762, and Samuel, 1764."[40]

Lewis' reconstruction of slave status and occupations is an interesting point of reference with the data concerning the life of Chesapeake slaves as the eighteenth century advanced. As the tobacco economy diversified to include production of wheat and iron, more slaves received training in artisanry beginning in the 1740s.[41] At White Marsh, Issac the carpenter and Robert and Tom the shoemakers seem to have fit this pattern. The fact that they were too old to work by 1764 suggests that they received their training during the earlier period of diversification. The lack of active artisans in Lewis' list suggests another observation, however. Slave life remained tenuous, many were left in field work and all slaves remained subject to the economic fortunes of their masters. Considering the outstanding debts owed to the Jesuits in England in the 1760s, it is plausible that the Jesuits tried to step up agricultural production in Maryland during that decade at the cost of foregoing further training of young male slaves as artisans.[42]

Lewis showed a great deal of concern for women who had reached childbearing years and for their offspring. When the different fates of the artisan males and the women Lewis surveyed are compared, there is support for speculation that within the institution of racial slavery there were two systems, one for the men and one for the women, with different expectations and responsibilities for each.[43] Slaveowners may have gradually perceived the unique potential benefits which could be obtained from a situation in which slaves in North America, in contrast to their counterparts in Latin America, achieved an even sex ratio. This fact meant that the reproductive capacities of female slaves could be manipulated to bring about profits.[44]

Did this emphasis on reproductive capacity prevent masters from putting their female slaves to work in the fields? Some scholars feel that there was a tension between treating the slaves as equal workers and treating them as unequal reproducers. Slaves reacted against the reluctance of masters to acknowledge gender differences in field assignments by making their own strict divisions of labor within their own households and communities.[45] There is not enough testimony from either the Jesuits or their slaves to test their own experiences regarding these issues. It is plausible, however, to think that the Jesuits, with their traditional view of social relationships and their medieval sense of patriarchy, may have been less willing than other slaveowners to put slave wives and mothers into field work. It is significant to note, in this regard, that Lewis described childbearing as a preoccupation. This reluctance to pull a mother away from her child could have helped to keep the debt to London as high as it was.

On July 23, 1765 the first surviving "Full Account of the Plantations of Maryland" was submitted to the offices of the English Provincial in London. This report listed eight plantations, totalling 12,677 acres. Total income for that year was estimated as 696 pounds sterling. There were 192 slaves altogether, just eighty short of the number that would be sold in the final sale of 1838. The statistics for the individual plantations were kept separate from each other in the manuscript of 1765.

St. Inigoe's, whose official name was the Mission of the Holy Assumption of the Virgin Mary, had an annual income of ninety pounds. Fifty-four pounds of that income were traced to the work of the slaves, and the remaining thirty-six pounds were attributed to nine tenants. There was one Jesuit missionary in residence, and twenty slaves. Twelve of the slaves were able to work; three of those worked in the Jesuit residence while the other nine worked in the fields. The eight inactive slaves were described as "children or past their labour," but no exact breakdown of the ratio of children to elderly was provided.

The Newtown mission, officially dedicated to St. Francis Xavier, the first Jesuit missionary to East Asia, had three Jesuits in residence. There were 650 acres on the main plantation, with some distant tracts adding 900 more to the total. Of twenty-nine slaves, fifteen were workers. Twelve were in the field, and three in the Jesuit house. The remaining fourteen were children or elderly. The total annual income was eighty-eight pounds, of which twelve slaves produced six pounds apiece for a total of seventy-two pounds. Four tenants produced four pounds apiece for the remaining sixteen pounds. Newtown thus joined St. Inigoe's in producing more income through slave labor than tenant labor.

The mission at Portobacco was named for St. Ignatius of Loyola, the founder of the Jesuits, and had three Jesuits in residence. The immediate plantation was 900 acres, but there was also a distant, noncontiguous tract of 3500 acres. There were thirty eight slaves, twenty one of them at work: three indoors, and eighteen in the fields. The rest were sickly or superannuated. The total annual income was 188 pounds; eighteen slaves produced six pounds apiece for a total of 108 pounds. There were twenty tenants, whose four pounds produced 80 pounds of the total.

The Whitemarsh mission was named for St. Francis Borgia, the third general superior of the Society of Jesus. Two Jesuits were in residence. The main plantation contained 1900 acres, with adjoining tracts of 700 acres and non-contiguous tracts of another 700. There were sixty-five slaves at Whitemarsh, of whom only twenty-nine were able to work. Whitemarsh thus became the first plantation listed in the survey with a majority of inactive slaves. Three were assigned indoors, twenty-six worked in the fields. The rest were children or superannuated. The annual income was 180 pounds. Twenty-Six slaves produced six pounds apiece, for a total of 156 pounds. Six tenants produced four pounds apiece, for the remaining twenty-four pounds.

The Deer Creek Mission was named for St. Joseph, the husband of Mary, the Mother of Jesus. Only one Jesuit lived on its 127 acres. There were seven slaves, one in the house, four in the fields, and two children. There were no tenants. The annual income was 24 pounds, produced by four slaves at six pounds apiece.

The Mission of St. Stanislaus Kostka, patron of Jesuit novices, was situated at Fredericktown. There was one Jesuit stationed there. The order owned three lots of land in the town, all of them still undeveloped in 1765. The annual allowance was a mere thirty pounds, but the mere existence of this mission in a town was an important sign that the Jesuit presence in Maryland would move in a more urban direction in the future, with important consequences for their continuation as rural slaveholders.

The Mission of St. Mary's was located at Queenstown. One Jesuit was assigned to live on its 200 acres. Seven slaves were classified as follows: one worked indoors, three worked in the fields, two were children, and one was elderly. The annual income was eighteen pounds, produced by three slaves working at six pounds apiece.

Bohemia, also known as St Francis Xavier's, had one Jesuit on its 1500 acres. There were twenty-six slaves, of whom three worked indoors and twelve in the worked in the fields. The remaining eleven were children or antediluvian. There were no tenants. The annual income was 108 pounds, generated by twelve slaves producing nine pounds apiece.

These statistics concerning the plantations reveal several essential attributes of Jesuit interaction with their slaves in the late colonial period. The first was their diligence in taking care of the very young and the very old. The second, which can be deduced from the first, was that such care must have been very costly. As Thomas Hughes, S.J. noted from the perspective of the early twentieth century, "The finding of these in food, clothing, habitation and doctor's care, though so beneficial to the negro in his home life, was nowise conducive to economy in the management of a plantation."[46]

The final section of the report of 1765, entitled "Notanda," made some further observations about Jesuit life in Maryland. Each plantation was required, at its own expense, to keep a chapel on the premises. Also, out of the income of each plantation, the Jesuits had to buy all housekeeping articles, clothing for both masters and slaves, building materials, reparations in addition to taxes, quit rents, medical expenses, etc.."in short everything exclusive of bread, meat, and firing." The anonymous compiler believed that about 10,000 adult Catholics in Maryland and an equivalent number of children relied on Jesuit ministry. Each Jesuit priest was expected to keep two Sundays of the month on his own plantation, and to spend the rest riding a circuit of plantations owned by lay Catholics. "Our Gentlemen are dispersed all over the Province," the report accurately concluded.[47] It is difficult to imagine that such busy men had much time to devote to plantation management.

It has been pointed out that while the accounting of 1765 claimed that the estimated income of all the plantations together was 696 pounds sterling, this figure ignored some important expenses: building repairs, clothes for both Jesuits and the slaves, medical bills, quit rents and taxes. Perhaps as a consequence of this inexact accounting, the mission debt was still 1400 pounds sterling when the Jesuit order was dissolved eight years later.[48]

Buried in the report of 1765 was some data which pointed to the eventual ending of Jesuit slaveholding. That was the revelation that four of their plantations had tenant farmers. The Jesuits, in fact, never completely abandoned the use of indentured servants on their land.[49] Like most planters in Maryland, Jesuits did turn to slavery when the supply of indentured servants began to run low in the latter seventeenth century. However, Jesuits continued to seek indentured servants and tenants when possible. The likely reason for that preference is that they wanted to increase the white Catholic population of Maryland, and saw encouragement of Europeans immigration as the best means to do so. Also, the Jesuits may have felt obliged to provide such opportunities for their coreligionists during an era when Catholics were harassed throughout the British Isles. Indentures granted by the the Jesuits not only allowed Catholic immigrants to Maryland to earn a living. They also accorded servants a chance to practice their faith in close proximity to priests at a time when the Catholic Church's organizational structure in British North America was almost entirely rural.

This Catholic practice was common enough to draw opposition from Protestants. During colonial times, as late as the 1750s, the Maryland Assembly tried several times to level draconian fees and duties on the importation of Irish Catholic servants.[50] The Jesuits, however, basically persisted in importing enough such people that in 1772 Joseph Mosley, S.J. identified a major problem on Catholic farms as the abuse of the indentured servants by overseers whose supervision of slaves had accustomed them to harshness. Mosley also fretted that Catholic indentured servants could not find jobs once their contracts had expired. Other planters in the Chesapeake wanted to use only slave labor, which was cheaper, and many did not want to employ Catholics. Therefore, Mosley discouraged his relatives in England from contemplating indentures in Maryland.[51]

A year after Mosley wrote, a new reason to avoid indentures in Maryland seemed to arise when the suppression of the Society of Jesus occurred. However, when Pope Clement XIV's call that landholdings of the Jesuits be confiscated proved to be unenforceable in Maryland, the Jesuit estates remained very much in the conditions described in the report of 1765. The only other place in the world where Jesuit estates remained intact was Russia, where the Orthodox Empress Catherine the Great refused to honor Clement's decree because she valued the educational work of the Jesuits in a country she was anxious to modernize.[52] Meanwhile, Jesuits who were ordained priests before the suppression retained their priesthood, and continued to dwell on the Maryland estates as Roman Catholic clergymen.

By 1782, however, concern had again developed about the future of the plantations. There was no longer any legal way to bind their individual owners to one another. While ties had remained unusually strong and cooperative during the nine years since the suppression, there was no way to guarantee their endurance once those who had once been Jesuits were dead. It was an individual priest, John Carroll, who pressed for a resolution to this problem—a decision which led to the next major effort to deal with the poor financial management of the plantations.

It was Carroll's presence in Europe at the time of the suppression that convinced him that the clergy in Maryland had a unique opportunity to preserve a threatened heritage. Born in Upper Marlboro, Maryland on January 8, 1735, Carroll was the scion of a prominent Catholic planter family. After two years of education at a small school operated by the Jesuits on their Bohemia plantation, Carroll sailed to Flanders in 1748 to attend the Jesuits' St. Omer College. He was to stay in Europe for a quarter century, entering the Jesuit novitiate in 1753 and working at the Jesuit College in Bruges after ordination in 1769. As such, he was a witness to the swift seizure of the college from the Jesuits once the Pope issued the suppression —an event which Carroll interpreted as testimony to the damage that was done to religion when church and state were too closely united. Only then did he return to Maryland, arriving in the spring of 1774.

During the Revolutionary War, Carroll quickly embraced the patriotic rather than the Tory faction, feeling that it offered greater opportunities for religious liberty for Catholics. He accompanied Benjamin Franklin on an unsuccessful mission to Quebec in 1776 to persuade French Canadian Catholics to join the struggle against England. Then Carroll settled into pastoral work at St. John's Chapel in Forest Glen, Maryland, where he reflected on ways to preserve the plantations as means of support for the education of future clergy.[53]

Carroll felt that Jesuit traditions served as checks on abuse of power and financial scandal. He worried about what would happen once clergymen emerged who had not been formed in that heritage. Carroll warned against trusting that such men would use power moderately or money fairly. Provision must be made for the future while the old generation still lived. Carroll went on to justify his proposal for incorporation of the land by stating his belief that the spiritual authority of the Church, which had ordered the suppression of the Jesuits, was separate from "the common rights of the missioners to their temporal possessions, to which as the Bishop, or Pope himself have no just claim." To Carroll, the emerging American law of religious liberty was one of the most important signs that God willed the clergy in Maryland to own plantations.[54]

Carroll therefore proposed that representatives of the Maryland Catholic clergy meet together in convention and devise a plan of administration to insure "the preservation of the Catholick clergy's estates from alienation, waste and misapplication." He emphasized the importance of "common consent" if any such plan were to work. Government by "a junto of three or four" would only breed dissent and further chaos.[55]

The plan that emerged from the meetings called by Carroll was the "Constitution of the Clergy," drafted at Whitemarsh plantation between June, 1783 and October, 1784. It was a sincere effort to bring rational management to the plantations. A chapter, or representative body of the clergy, was set up to make common decisions. The clergymen were grouped into geographical districts—Eastern Shore, Western Shore, Charles and St. Mary's Counties—each of which could elect a designated number of representatives to the chapter. There were also two representatives from some Jesuit farms in neighboring Pennsylvania. The chapter, which was required to meet at least once every three years, was authorized to elect a Procurator General from the ranks of the clergy. This official served as overall administrator of all the estates, but could not sell real property without the permission of the general chapter.

The final section of the constitution was entitled "Regulations respecting the management of Plantations." It outlined the responsibilities of the manager of an individual estate. He was to raise, dispose and receive the profits from crops, rents and emoluments, keeping careful written records of credits and debts. Interestingly, his first responsibility in the use of these profits was "the providing of necessaries for house-keeping & Servants." At the transition from one manager to another, an inventory must be made, signed by both the incoming and outgoing officials, and then transmitted to the Procurator General for safekeeping.[56]

The clerical constitution was enacted at the very end of the Revolutionary War. It is instructive to recall that this conflict had caused a steep depression in the tobacco market.[57] The constitution attempted to deal with this depression, but Mobberly's testimony that tobacco was still the chief crop of the Jesuit plantations in the first decade of the nineteenth century shows that the new procedures did not result in major changes of proceeding on the farms. The strategies of Carroll did not dwell much on finances. His preoccupation was on using the estates to maintain the unity of the clergy amid an adverse ecclesiastical climate.

It was not an aberration that Carroll downplayed economic matters. The complaints which Peter Kenney made about financial records in 1820 indicates that, in general, the goal of the clerical constitution to provide orderly administration was not kept. From the years between its establishment and Kenney's visit, financial records continued to survive in only fragmentary and chaotic fashion. However, there does survive an inventory from 1803 of the property and stock of St. Joseph's Farm, Talbot County, Maryland. This was taken by Father Ambrose Souge, a French secular priest who had arrived in the United States as a refugee during the French Revolution, just before he completed his pastorate at St. Joseph's. After noting that the buildings were in poor condition, and that the farm itself was run down, Souge recorded that there were twenty-five head of cattle, four horses, twenty-four sheep, and twenty six hogs. Before his departure, Souge repaired most of the buildings, put a new roof on the chapel, built new fences and raised a new garden.[58]

To each of the eleven slaves he left behind at St. Joseph's, Souge assigned a number—but with no explicit indication as to how it was determined, or as to what it meant.[59] One slave had been rented out to an unreliable leaser and another had run away; it would be up to Souge's successor to deal with these problematic cases. [60]

Souge wanted even his rented-out slaves to remain in the immediate neighborhood under the watch of himself or his successor, lest the renters abuse them. In the United States, Catholic slaves were in a situation where the Church had to care for them alone, without help from the state, so priests were very conscious of their responsibilities. The Catholic Church in Latin America had a deliberate and proactive policy of trying to preserve the legal rights of slaves: to personal security, to private property, and to the purchase of their own freedom. While it could not remove all harshness from the treatment of slaves in that region, the Church did succeed somewhat in influencing the Spanish crown to restrict the growth of large scale plantations.[61] The Latin American strategy, however, depended on an alliance of church and state. It was unavailable to Jesuits in Maryland, where there was no such correspondence between the two.

That fact is an opportunity to think beyond legal categorizations of masters and slaves. It is possible to think of slavery as a relationship of domination rather than a legal category. An ideal term for describing slavery is parasitism. According to this model, the master is the parasite, depending on the slave for his status—an illustration of "the distinctively human technique of camouflaging a relationship by defining it as the opposite of what it really is."[62] Souge was but one of many priests in Maryland who tied his ministerial identity to his ability to keep track of his slaves in a paternalistic manner—hence, the numbering of his chattel and the insistence on keeping all his slaves nearby. This practice made it more difficult to construct a priestly identity independent of his ownership of slaves.

By the time of Souge, it was clear that the clerical constitution had both succeeded and failed. Its great success was to preserve a spiritual bond among the Maryland clergy and former Jesuits until the Society of Jesus could be restored in the United States in 1805. However, the secondary intention of the plan, to provide more rational and efficient financial management of the plantations, clearly failed, as reflected in Souge's last-minute efforts to restore his physical plant as he was about to leave his farm.

The best evidence for the constitution's financial failure comes from the writings of Brother Mobberly. Mobberly ranks alongside Carroll as someone who thought extensively about the plantations and what needed to be done with and for them. Unlike Carroll, however, whose major concern was that disunity among the former Jesuits would undermine the plantations, Mobberly was convinced that the unprofitability of slavery was the major reason why the plantations were floundering.

As Mobberly began to articulate his thoughts, the War of 1812 provided a major blow to St. Inigoe's plantation. In the autumn of 1814, during the same invasion of the Chesapeake that featured their capture of Washington and assault on Baltimore, the British occupied St. George's Island, a portion of St. Inigoe's plantations near the mouth of the Potomac River, claiming that the Jesuits there were inciting the American militia. While Mobberly's denial of the accusation was sufficient to deter a threat to burn the farm's buildings, the invaders did ransack the chapel and seized many provisions. The British then offered liberty to any slave who might wish to depart with them, but Mobberly reported that the slaves instead hid until the island was clear again. Mobberly bragged that the slaves thus showed their essential loyalty to their Jesuit masters. In this, he reflected the "Sambo myth" that arose among slaveholders: the idea that for all their infantile behavior, slaves had at bottom a childlike attachment to their masters.[63] In the absence of surviving testimony from any of the slaves who were there that day, it is hard to know why, in fact, they stayed. However, since the British had threatened to burn all the buildings on the island, including the slaves' quarters, the slaves may have actually seen the British as threats to homes they regarded as their own.

Even as he celebrated his sense of the slaves' fidelity, however, Mobberly wanted to exploit the turmoil of the British invasion and withdrawal as a chance to reorganize the estates.[64] In fact, the occupation seems to have pushed Mobberly into outright advocacy of disposing of the slaves. Throughout the ensuing winter, Mobberly compiled an array of facts to support his case, which he finally stated in a letter to Fr. Giovanni Grassi, S.J. (1775–1849), the President of Georgetown College, on February 5, 1815. Writing from St. Inigoe's, Mobberly detailed how "we shall make more and more to our satisfaction without slaves."

This he sought to do by computing the actual cost of outfitting the forty-three slaves at St. Inigoe's for a single year and comparing that expense with his estimate of how much it might cost to employ fourteen hired hands for a year instead. He believed that only about a third as many tenants as slaves would be required.

In order to provide the slaves with enough bread, 630 bushels of "corn" (in the British sense of corn as a cereal product or grain) were set aside at St. Inigoe's in 1814. At $.80 a bushel, this was an expense of $504.00. The slaves' meat was obtained through the slaughter of 3468 pounds of bacon at $.17 per pound, for a total of $589.56. Sixty-eight pounds of hogs lard at $.15 per pound was an added expense of $10.20.

Forty-three pairs of new shoes, which cost $1.10 each, cost the Society $43.30, although Mobberly miscounted this expense as $47.60. Meanwhile, thirty-four pairs of old shoes were mended at a figure of $17.00. To make enough clothing for the slaves, 206 yards of material had to be bought at $.40 per yard. A further $34.00 was paid to the laborers who sewed the clothes, for a total clothing expenditure of $116.40.

"Medicine and contingent expenses" for the St. Inigoes's slaves cost the Jesuits $20.00 in 1814. One hundred and twenty cords of wood were provided to warm the slaves through the winter; at $2.00 per cord, the expense to the Society was $240.00. An extra expense was incurred when Mobberly rented three male slaves from a laywoman in the neighborhood, Mrs. Fenwick, for $40.00 apiece, a total of $120.00.

Mobberly thus recorded that the grand total of all money spent on outfitting slaves at St. Inigoes' during the year 1814 was $1834.26.

The Brother proposed to replace this system with a contingent of fourteen hired hands. Ten would work in the fields, each receiving a salary of $80.00 per year, while the other four would work around the house for various salaries. As freemen, these laborers would be responsible for providing their own clothing, and they would only receive one meal a day at Jesuit expense, luncheon. To prepare this meal, Mobberly would set aside 190 bushels of corn; at $.80 per bushel, this would amount to a cost of $152.00. The meat for this meal would be supplied through the purchase of 1340 pounds of bacon at $.17 per pound, an expenditure of $227.80.

The four household jobs would be broken down as follows: A gardener would be paid $80.00 a year, a milk maid $40.00, a cook for the priests $40.00, and a cook for the workmen $40.00. Thus Mobberly planned to spend a total of $1000 a year on salaries. He would also provide his employees with sixty cords of wood at $2.00 per cord, a total of $120.00.

Mobberly estimated that the total cost of supporting the hired hands would be $1499.80. Compared with the $1834.26 spent on the slaves, this would be a savings of $334.46. However, Mobberly stressed to Grassi that he felt this to be a low estimate of the potential savings. Additional costs would be cut through the elimination of the county and district taxes on slaves, and also through the simple fact that more of the crop and livestock would be available for sale off the plantation, especially corn and pork. Furthermore, there would no longer be need to procure and burn wood around the clock for slave dwellings in the winter—fuel would only be needed in the Jesuit residence and in certain work areas during the day. Rather than spend all winter gathering timber, the hired hands could manure the land and perform needed construction and repair tasks.[65] Mobberly, in short, believed that he had only begun to estimate the possible savings from a switch from slave to free labor at St. Inigoes.

Mobberly did not succeed in influencing Grassi, but he kept up his own reflections into the decade of the 1820s. In Part I of his Diary, in an essay entitled "Systems," Mobberly discussed the "poverty of the land" in St. Mary's County. He felt that deficient soil had never been improved, and that superior soil had been "greatly injured by improper modes of cultivation." Mobberly traced this double problem, "in part," to the fact that "the inhabitants are generally slaveholders." Slaves had to be kept employed all year, and they had to be supported by their masters; the result was that the soil was used too much.

Mobberly wanted to cultivate wheat alone, and disliked having to grow the corn and tobacco crops that he felt the slave system made necessary. Wheat could not adequately feed large numbers of slaves; the same land that produced only five bushels of wheat to the acre could yield 7.5 bushels of corn. Yet wheat was easier to harvest—plow a field twice, roll it once, and then the third ploughing would bring in the crop. Corn required six plowings for the same result, and tobacco even more. Confronted by his superiors with the question of why corn and tobacco required so many more hands for cultivation than wheat, Mobberly felt that "Any planter in Maryland can answer this question."[66]

Mobberly then contrasted the lot of the Maryland planter unfavorably with the lot of the planter in the neighboring free state of Pennsylvania. The Marylander was always "reducing his land and bringing it down to zero," while the Pennsylvanian was constantly "improving his land and putting it in the highest state of cultivation." He praised the Quakers, in particular: after a tour of their farms in Pennsylvania, Mobberly concluded that they were united in an "unchanging . . . simple, uniform system." Although Mobberly was ordinarily not ecumenical, he made an eloquent confession that Quaker ways of doing business were superior to Jesuit ways: "They will not have slaves, and in this they are very wise . . . (Luc. 16:8). May it not be lawful for the children of light to learn wisdom from the children of this world with respect to temporal concerns?"[67]

When Mobberly compiled a litany of the problems facing the slaveowner, he began with the familiar observation that the need to feed, clothe, and house the elderly and the children was a prodigious burden. There was also a county tax on every slave between eighteen and forty-five years of age. Physicians and midwives demanded "handsome sums" for their treatment of slaves. What really raised Mobberly's concern, however, were the demands of his overseers.

One of Mobberly's overseers expected to be provided with 300 pounds of pork and three barrels of corn each year. Each overseer had to be provided with living quarters and a garden of his own to cultivate; he had a right to have firewood cut and hauled to his door by the slaves all winter. He also received the privilege of raising and marketing his own poultry, and was paid between $150 and $200 in cash each year. A more basic burden, however, was that the master constantly "must overlook his overlooker" and monitor for dishonesty. Occasionally, Mobberly would quarrel with his overseers about management decisions.

Then Mobberly turned to what he considered to be his slaves' dishonesty, thereby providing significant evidence of their many ways of subverting an oppressive system. Despite the many admonitions he had given to the slaves to be truthful, Mobberly noted "now and again" the theft of "a pig, a sheep, a goose, a turkey, some tobacco, some corn from the field, and perhaps a little wheat from his granary with a long list of et ceteras." Mobberly also discovered that his horses were "ridden to death at night" while he slept. Objecting to such subversions was futile, for public sympathy lay with the slaves: "Master will complain, but he must bear with the times . . . he will not be a good man if he complains of such troubles."[68]

When Mobberly contemplated whipping in order to punish these transgressions, he encountered growing concerns about the morality of that practice.. The whipping marked him among the slaves, too, as "a very *bad man*." In retaliation, his plantation utensils were frequently shattered, or else spoiled from either careless lack of maintenance or, more accurately, "malice." Mobberly rejected the idea that masters should meet these small daily uprisings with "Christian patience," for he was beginning to fear for his personal safety. "In fine, his negroes may rise, and put an end to his life."

One reason that Mobberly feared death at the hands of his slaves was his apprehension that African culture encouraged violent disposal of one's enemies. Mobberly believed that "about 35 years" earlier, that is to say around 1785, it was "very common" for murders to be committed by blacks in Maryland. He felt that that phenomenon had been due to the majority of slaves at that time being "chiefly Africans, or those immediately descended from them."

To Mobberly, African culture encouraged skill at the manufacture of poison, and produced people "malicious to a high degree." While American-born slaves were less familiar with this heritage, they might committ instead "the rising *en masse*," Mobberly felt that an attack on the general store at St. Inigoe's Village around 1815 was an inciting precedent, even though the raid had failed and its perpetrators had ended up in the Baltimore penitentiary.[69] Jesuits now had to spend too much money on security for their plantations.

Mobberly saw still another expense in the high birth rates among his slaves. Some plantations saw five or six births annually, more than the number of slave deaths, prompting Mobberly to raise some vexing questions about possible consequences. Either the adjoining forest would have to be cut down to house the extra slaves, or the slaves would have to be sold to plantations in Georgia or the Carolinas. If the latter course was pursued, Mobberly feared that slaves might grow blind through the cultivation of rice. They would surely lose the Christian principles which the Jesuits had struggled for so long to teach them, and families would be separated. Mobberly did not want the Jesuits to have such unchristian consequences on their consciences.[70] His Catholicism forbad him from teaching contraceptive techniques to the slaves, so Mobberly anticipated the social doctrine of twentieth century popes by proposing that a new and more efficient economic system be found to feed the extra mouths.[71] He did not suggest what that new system might entail, and his subsequent emphasis on slave-free plantations suggests that he did not pursue the problem of what to do with the slaves once disposed of. Nonetheless, he was the first Maryland Jesuit to join other Southern intellectuals in even touching upon the desirability of incremental, structural economic change.

Mobberly failed to become an outright abolitionist out of his uncertainty as to what to do with freed slaves. He commented, "I sincerely regret that slaves were ever introduced into the United States, but as we have them, we know not how to get rid of them."[72] Still bitter at the raid and occupation of St. Inigoe's, Mobberly declaimed that the English, not the Americans, were responsible for introducing slavery into Maryland. This was a dubious alibi, for it disregarded the fact that the Jesuits themselves had once been English. It echoed, however, Thomas Jefferson's denunciation of George III for the slave trade in the first draft of the Declaration of Independence.[73]

The tone of Mobberly's writings is that of a man who was generally aware of the different forms of agricultural labor in the United States of the early nineteenth century. He saw that some were inclined to bring their practioners prosperity, others were not. He saw no reason that the Jesuits could not be prosperous themselves if they made a prudent choice of their own form. Beneath his sense of crisis on the Jesuit farms lay a confidence that the general Southern economy was not only capable of success, but was already achieving it. In this confidence, Mobberly's writings tend to confirm observations that the antebellum Southern economy was a flourishing one. Mobberly wished to correct the problem that the Jesuits were caught in a backwater of that economy, the tobacco system of southern Maryland.

Mobberly's proposals were slow to be heard. The reports from Father Kenney's visitation of 1820 provide some indication as to why. One of Kenny's discoveries was the low regard in which Mobberly was held by the slaves he was then overseeing at St. Inigoes: "they are furious against Brother Mobberly, nor can it be hoped, that he can do good by remaining with them." In response, Kenney ordered a uniform policy on the treatment of slaves, one from which local managers were forbidden to depart. The existing policy of arbitrary regulation, not only from farm to farm but often from manager to manager, played into the hands of the slaves. "This gives these creatures cause to complain, even when they are not ill-used."[74]

Kenney hoped to raise profits by making the slaves healthier and readier to work. Their rations should be fixed, and made adequate. He particularly deplored the unsound habit of only giving them a pound and a quarter of meal, and wanted them to be allowed to eat pork and poultry. Conscious that tired slaves could not be productive, Kenney desired that they be given Saturday afternoons off. Despite all these measures to make them more content and efficient, Kenney still preferred that they be gotten rid of. It was an evil system by nature, one which could be mitigated only through zeal, piety, prudence and charity. Even these, furthermore, would not be enough to eliminate iniquity and disorder. Therefore, Kenney favored seeking opportunities to employ whites, or engage reputable tenants, or any other method that could be implemented without damaging the property. If this happened, the Mission would be spared a great burden and a painful responsibility, and the whole Society of Jesus would be spared odium from people who spoke out of ignorance of the actual situation in the United States.[75]

The Cavalier settlers of Virginia rejected manual labor as part of their ethos of the idle gentleman: one showed upper class status by living leisurely and avoiding manual labor.[76] This ideal does not describe the lifestyle choice of the Maryland Jesuits, who worked prodigiously at their apostolic labors of riding the circuit of Catholic plantations to preach and celebrate the Sacraments. However, Virginians had some other characteristics that the Jesuits do appear to have shared: an ambivalence toward commerce and a discomfort at handling money.[77]

Both the Virginians and the Maryland Jesuits were chronic debtors, although the causes for that were different. Virginians used their wealth as a means to display gentlemanly status and the pleasurable consumption that was one of the principle marks of that status.[78] Jesuits, by contrast, used their wealth to display their priestly status and to pursue the ministerial labor that was one of the principle marks of that status. Like the Virginia planters, they used wealth to display values that were more important than the mere accumulation of money. And so, they ended up with the appearance of wealth but the possession of poverty.

Why were the Jesuits so content with the mere appearance of wealth? One explanation is that they were more anxious for the recognition of their political rights than the acquisition of possesssions. Their political rights, however, were triumphantly vindicated long before 1820, the date when Peter Kenney made the complaint that began this chapter. There had to have been other forces that locked the Jesuits in an unprofitable practice of slaveholding. It was the unresolved conflict between Catholic values for the conduct of slaveholding and the American system of profit-earning plantations that completed the sorry picture which Peter Kenney discovered upon his visit in 1820.

NOTES

1. Peter Kenney, S.J., "Statement of Religious Discipline, 1820," Item no. XT1–2, Box 126, Folder 7, Archives of the Maryland Province (MPA), Special Collections Division, Lauinger Library, Georgetown University, Washington, D.C.
2. *Ibid.*
3. *Ibid.*
4. John Carroll, "Response to Patrick Smyth," in Thomas O'Brien Hanley, S.J., editor, *The John Carroll Papers (JCP)*, I (Notre Dame, Ind.: University of Notre Dame Press, 1976), p. 338.
5. *Ibid.*, p. 343.
6. Alfred H. Conrad and John R. Meyer, *The Economics of Slavery and Other Studies in Econometric History* (Chicag: Aldine, 1964), p. 68.
7. "Deed of Gift between William Hunter and Thomas Jameson," January 30, 1717, Item no. 100 1/2 Z5, Box 27, Folder 2, MPA.
8. "Will of William Hunter," August 16, 1723, Item no. 96 HI, Box 25, Folder 10, MPA.
9. "Will of James Carroll," February, 1728, Item no. 95 C2, Box 25, Folder 6, MPA.
10. "Oldest Church at Whitemarsh," Newspaper Clipping Dated September 22, 1930 (Newspaper of Issue not Given), Box 4, Folder 6, Maryland Province Collection (MPC), Special Collections Division, Lauinger Library, Georgetown University, Washington, D.C.
11. See Allan Kulikoff, *Tobacco and Slaves: The Development of Southern Cultures in the Chesapeake, 1680–1800* (Chapel Hill: University of North Carolina Press, Published for the Institute of Early American History and Culture, 1986), p. 31, p. 79, p 119, pp. 157–158.
12. Barbara Jeanne Fields, *Slavery and Freedom on the Middle Ground: Maryland During the Nineteenth Century* (New Haven: Yale University Press, 1985), p. 5.
13. Brother Joseph Mobberly, S.J., "Diary, Part I: Systems," Brother Joseph Mobberly, S.J. Papers (BJMSJP), Special Collections Division, Lauinger Library, Georgetown University, Washington, D.C.
14. Robert William Fogel, *Without Consent or Contract: The Rise and Fall of*

American Slavery (New York: W. W. Norton, 1989), pp. 21–22.

15. Peter Kolchin, *American Slavery, 1619–1877* (New York: Hill and Wang, 1993), p. 173.

16. For a definition of "enabling," see the following publication of Al-Anon Family Groups for Families and Friends of Alcoholics: . . . *In All Our Affairs: Making Crises Work for You* (New York, New York: Al-Anon Family Group Headquarters, 1990), especially Pages 73, 76, 82, 99, 102, and 163. The definition provided on Page 73 is an especially apt description of the role played by the lay benefactors of the Jesuits: "Some of us become enablers, doing for others what they should be permitted to do for themselves."

17. John Carroll, "Plan of Clergy Organization," in Hanley, editor, *JCP*, I, pp. 59–60.

18. Thomas Hughes, S.J., editor, *History of the Society of Jesus In North America, Colonial and Federal: Documents, I, Part I, Nos. 1–140* (New York: Longmans, Green and Company, 1908), pp. 201–266.

19. Edward F. Beckett, S.J., "Listening to our History: Inculturation and Jesuit Slaveholding," *Studies in the Spirituality of Jesuits* 28, no. 5 (November, 1996), p. 7.

20. Will of James Carroll, MPA.

21. John Padberg, S.J., editor, *The Constitutions of the Society of Jesus and their Complementary Norms* (St. Louis: The Institute of Jesuit Sources, 1996), no. 565, p. 234.

22. Father Peter Kenney, S.J, "Minutes of the Extraordinary Consultation at Georgetown College, August 2, 1832," Box 126, Folder 2, MPA.

23. For summaries of the Catholic teaching on purgatory, see *Catechism of the Catholic Church* (New York, New York: Doubleday, Image Books Edition, 1995), Article Twelve, "I Believe in Life Everlasting," no. III, "The Final Purification, or Purgatory," p. 291. Also, see Zachary Hayes, O.F.M., "Purgatory," in Joseph A. Komonchak, Mary Collins and Dermot A. Lane, editors, *The New Dictionary of Theology* (Wilmington, Del.: Michael Glazier, Inc., 1987), pp. 823–825.

24. Michael Graham, S.J., "Meetinghouse and Chapel: Religion and Community in Seventeenth-Century Maryland," in Lois Green Carr, Philip D. Morgan and Jean B. Russo, editors, *Colonial Chesapeake Society* (Chapel Hill: The University of North Carolina Press for the Institute of Early American History and Culture, Williamsburg, Virginia, 1988), p. 245, p. 253.

25. Fr. Arnold Livers, S.J., "Almanac and Notebook," 1734, Item no. 6 2.5, Box 3, Folder 15, MPA.

26. Kenneth J. Zanca, *American Catholics and Slavery, 1789–1866: An Anthology of Primary Documents* (Lanham, Md.: University Press of America, 1994), p. 18, p. 24.

27. Russell R. Menard "The Maryland Slave Population, 1658–1730: A Demographic Profile of Blacks in Four Counties," in Stanley N. Katz and John M. Murrin, editors, *Colonial America: Essays in Politics and Social Development*

(New York: Alfred A. Knopf, Third Edition 1983), pp. 290–313.

28. Fogel, *op.cit.*, p. 25.

29. *Ibid.*

30. Zanca, *op cit.*, pp. 1–21, p. 37.

31. Luis N. Rivera, *A Violent Evangelism: The Political and Religious Conquest of the the Americas* (Louisville, Ky.: John Knox/Westminster Press, 1992), p. 133.

32. Gustavo Gutierrez, *Las Casas: In Search of the Poor of Jesus Christ* (Maryknoll, N.Y.: Orbis, 1993), p. 312.

33. Peter Kolchin, *Unfree Labor: American Slavery and Russian Serfdom* (Cambridge: The Belknap Press of Harvard University Press, 1987), pp. 132–133.

34. *Ibid.*, p. 134.

35. Hughes, editor, *Documents, I, Part 1*, Nos 51, 52, 53, pp. 237–239.

36. *Ibid.*, p. 239.

37. Henry Corbie, S.J., "Ordinations and Regulations for Maryland," April 2, 1759, Item no. 202 A11, MPA.

38. David Hackett Fischer, *Albion's Seed: Four British Folkways in North America* (New York: Oxford University Press, 1989), p. 411.

39. Joseph Mosley, S.J. to Helen Dunn, June 5, 1772, in "Letters of Father Joseph Mosley, 1757–1806," *Woodstock Letters* XXXV, 1906.

40. Father John Lewis, S.J., "Inventory of the Slaves at White Marsh, 1764," in Hughes, S.J., editor, *Documents, I*, no. 46, pp. 230–231. Other slaves at the lower quarters of White Marsh were Ruth, Terry, Regis, Sampson and Jenny. There were also "Frank and his children, Lucy, Davi, Nancy, Paul, and Henrietta, "born May, 1763." At Fingal, another quarter of the plantation, Lewis recorded that there were fifteen children incapable of work. These included the three children of of Nanny Cooper—Mina, Simon and Henry; the four children of Sarah—Doll, Dick, and James; the four children of Phyllis—Mary, Peggy, Sall and Winifred; the four children of Mary—Nancy, Cate, Rachel and Priscilla. Nanny Cooper and Phyllis were described by Lewis as "far advanced in age and the mothers of many children." Also past service at Fingal were a married couple, Tom and Susanna, as well as Betty, Sarah and Doll. On the main farm of White Marsh, there were twenty-two children who could not labor. These included the six children of Charity—Monica, Ambrose, Ned, William, Nancy and Basil; the five children of Nelly's—Jack, Charles, James, Patric and Anastasia; the five children of Franc—Lucy, David, Nancy, Tual and Henny; the three children of Henny—Harry, Mary and Lucy; the unnamed only children of three mothers, Mary Susan, Ned Phyllis and Fanny Cate. There were thirteen people at the main farm who were too old to work. John, Nell, Samson, Jenny and Nanny were all aged around seventy. Exact ages were not listed for a number of people. It is interesting that there were two sets of fathers and sons who were both past laboring age, Isaac and son and Robert and son; that fact suggests that extreme old age was attainable by some slaves under the conditions that the Jesuits' treatment accorded them. In a few cases, the former occupations of the elderly were mentioned: Isaac the carpenter; Robert and Tom the shoemakers;

Nelly the cook. There was finally Priscilla, whose inability to work was the result of her being crippled. Her disability also left her a spinster.

41. Gary B. Nash, *Red, White & Black: The Peoples of Early North America* (Englewood Cliffs, N.J.: Prentice Hall, 1992 Edition), p. 176.

42. *Ibid.*

43. Deborah Gray White, *Ar'n't I a Woman?: Female Slaves in the Plantation South* (New York: W.W. Norton, 1985), p. 62.

44. *Ibid.*, pp. 64–68.

45. Jacqueline Jones, *Labor of Love, Labor of Sorrow: Black Women, Work and the Family, from Slavery to the Present* (New York: Random House, Vintage Books Edition, 1986), pp. 12–13.

46. Hughes,editor, *Documents, I,* "Notes Introducing "Father John Lewis, S.J.'s Inventory of White Marsh, 1764," p. 230.

47. "Full Account of the Plantations of Maryland, July 23, 1765," Item no. 202 A12, Box 57, Folder 1, MPA.

48. Peter C. Finn, "The Slaves of the Jesuits in Maryland," (master's dissertation, Georgetown University, 1974), pp. 93–94.

49. Robert Emmett Curran, S.J., "'Splendid Poverty': Jesuit Slaveholding in Maryland, 1805–1838," in Randal M. Miller and Jon L. Wakelyn, editors, *Catholics in the Old South: Essays on Church and Culture* (Macon, Ga.: Mercer University Press, 1983), p. 126.

50. Timothy W. Bosworth, "Anti-Catholicism as a Political Tool in Mid-Eighteenth Century Maryland," *The Catholic Historical Review*, LXI, no. 4 (October, 1975), p. 555.

51. Joseph Mosley, S.J. to Helen Dunn, June 5, 1772, *Woodstock Letters* XXXV (1906).

52. William V. Bangert, S.J., *A History of the Society of Jesus* (St. Louis: The Institute of Jesuit Sources, 1986), pp. 413–419.

53. "Chronological Table," in Hanley, editor, *JCP*, I, p. xli; Robert Emmett Curran, S.J, *The Bicentennial History of Georgetown University: I, From Academy to University, 1789–1889* (Washington, D.C.: Georgetown University Press, 1993), pp. 7–9.

54. John Carroll, "Plan of Clergy Organization," in Hanley, editor, *JCP*, I, pp. 59–63.

55. *Ibid.*

56. "Constitution of the Clergy," in Hanley, editor, *JCP*, I, pp. 75–76.

57. Kulikoff, *op. cit.*, p. 157.

58. "Roy Wagner's Notes on Fr. John Ambrose Souge's Pastorate at St. Joseph's Mission, 1801–1803," Box 31, Folder 5, MPA.

59. "Inventory of the Property and Stock on St. Joseph's Farm, Talbot County, Maryland, April 28, 1803, MPA. In general, however, the numbers appear to have reflected descending age. No. One was Nan, aged forty-five. No. Two, Paul, was aged forty-three. No. Three, Mary, was thirty-eight. No. Four, Matt, was thirty-

two. No. Five, Sam, was aged thirty. No. Six, Hannah, was aged twenty-two. No. Seven, John, was aged eighteen. No. Eight, Maria, was five. No. Nine, Ned, was two. Then came two extraordinary cases whose listing broke the order of descending age. No. Ten, Tilly, twenty years old, was being rented by Mrs. Sarah Price, who had "carried her over" to Baltimore in February, 1803, without the consent of Father Souge to take Tilly out of the immediate neighborhood. No. Eleven, Thorn, was aged twenty four and had run away on Friday, April 8, 1803. He had not been recovered as of the date that Souge compiled his inventory.

60. "Inventory of the Property and Stock on St. Joseph's Farm. Talbot County, Maryland, April 28, 1803," MPA.

61. Fogel, *op.cit.*, p. 38.

62. Orlando Patterson, *Slavery and Social Death: A Comparative Study* (Cambridge: Harvard University Press, 1982), pp. 334–337.

63. Stanley M. Elkins, *Slavery: A Problem in American Institutional and Intellectual Life* (Chicago: The University of Chicago Press, Third Edition Revised, 1976), p. 82.

64. Brother Joseph Mobberly, S.J. to Archbishop John Carroll, November 1, 1814, Item #204 M7, Box 58, Folder 8, MPA.

65. Brother Joseph Mobberly, S.J. to Father Giovanni Grassi, S.J., February 5, 1815, Item no. 204K3, MPA, Box 58, Folder 6; Brother Joseph Mobberly, S.J. to Reverend Giovanni Antonio Grassi, S.J., November 5, 1814, Item no. 204 M8, Box 58, Folder 8, MPA.

66. Brother Joseph Mobberly, S.J. "Diary: Part I, Systems," BJMSJ.

67. *Ibid.* According to *The New Jersusalem Bible*, the verse which Mobberly quoted from St. Luke's Gospel reads "For the children of this world are more astute in dealing with their own kind than are the children of light."

68. *Ibid.*

69. *Ibid.*

70. *Ibid.*

71. Consider *Rerum Novarum*, by Pope Leo XIII (1891), *Quadragesimo Anno*, by Pope Pius XI (1931), *Mater et Magistra*, by Pope John XXIII (1961), *Popularum Progresso*, by Pope Paul VI (1967). All may be found in David J. O'Brien and Thomas Shannon, editors, *Catholic Social Thought: The Documentary Heritage* (Maryknoll, N.Y.: Orbis, Second Edition 1995).

72. Mobberly, "Diary," BJMSJ.

73. Willard Sterne Randall, *Thomas Jefferson: A Life* (New York: Harper Perennial, 1994), pp. 276–277.

74. Peter Kenney, S.J., "Statement of Religious Discipline," 1820, MPA.

75. *Ibid.*

76. Fischer, *op. cit.*, p. 366.

77. *Ibid.*, pp. 366–367.

78. *Ibid.*, p. 367.

CHAPTER THREE

Doubt and Debate: Jesuit Questions about Slaveholding

On September 11, 1773, John Carroll, hitherto a prefect at the Jesuit College in Bruges, Belgium, wrote sadly to his mother, Eleanor Darnall Carroll, at her home in Maryland to announce the suppression of the Society of Jesus by Pope Clement XIV on the preceding July 21. "Our so long persecuted, and I must add, holy society is no more," Carroll reported. While he lamented its demise deeply and eloquently throughout the letter, Carroll still found a note of hope for his own ministry in what had happened: "You see that I am now my own master, and left to my own direction." Carroll concluded the letter by announcing plans to return to Maryland the following spring and take up ministry there as a secular priest.[1]

Eleven years later, on October 4, 1784, another former Jesuit who chose to work in Maryland after the suppression of the Society, Joseph Mosley, wrote to his sister, Mrs. Helen Dunn, in England. It was their first correspondence since August, 1775; the Revolutionary War had disrupted communications between them for nine years. Despite the hardships of a "tedious and calamitous war," and the great poverty Mosley had experienced at St. Joseph's Farm in Talbot County on Maryland's Eastern Shore, there was one great success to report: there had been a tremendous increase in the number of Catholic conversions in his neighborhood in recent years. Mosley had one explanation for this: "The toleration here granted by the Bill of Rights has put us all on the same footing, and has been of great service to us."[2]

These letters speak of two, nearly simultaneous turning points in American Jesuit history. The suppression of the Jesuit order by the Roman Catholic Church and the radical changes in civil liberties for Catholics introduced into Maryland by the American Revolution just three years later thrust the Jesuits into new religious and political worlds. Ecclesiastically, the forty-seven years between 1773 and 1820 saw the dissolution of the Society of Jesus, the founding of a Roman Catholic hierarchy for the United States in 1789, the reconstitution of the Society of Jesus in the United States in 1805 and worldwide in 1814, and the decision of the Jesuit General in Rome to intervene in the intramural disputes of American Jesuits in 1820. Secularly, these same years saw the United States win its independence from Britain, establish a federal constitution and bill of rights, and begin a long course of radical economic and technological transformation. Together, all these events posed opportunities to reinvent the manner in which Jesuits lived and worshipped in Maryland. No aspect of their lives together escaped reassessment, including their slaveholding. This was a reassessment that went beyond the practical business reasons that Brother Joseph Mobberly offered for discarding the Jesuit slaves. There was philosophical introspection going on, too. Eventually and remarkably, however, these clergymen reaffirmed and continued almost every aspect of their life together, including slaveholding. The outcome of these years is that little changed amid so much external pressure to change. Jesuits doubted the wisdom of their slaveholding, and moved toward selling off all their slaves, but they did not do so. Still sorting out what it meant to be fully Catholic and fully American all at once, still insecure about their acceptance by the Protestant majority, Jesuits found that the best way to handle an uncertain situation was to make no change for the time being. For thirty-two years after 1773 the sometime Jesuits were secular priests, subject to the governance of a diocese rather than a religious superior. However, the clergy of Maryland had little contact with their nominal bishop, the vicar apostolic of London, once the Revolutionary War began. Furthermore, no resident bishop was appointed in the United States until 1789, when the former Jesuits' own John Carroll was named Bishop of Baltimore after his election by his fellow clergymen was confirmed by Pope Pius VI.[3]

The suppression was a European event which took place for reasons that had nothing to do with the lives of Jesuits in British North America. The leading Catholic powers of Europe, especially Spain, France and Austria, each increasingly nationalistic in their thinking, tired of what they saw as interference in their internal affairs and economies by a wealthy supranational body. Therefore, they exploited the financial dependence of the papacy on their largess to force Pope Clement XIV to dissolve the order. The papacy also had a political and military reliance on the Catholic monarchs that gave Clement little choice in the matter.[4] Jesuits in England and Maryland, who had long since worked out tense if working relationships with Protestant-dominated governments, found this subversion by Catholic rulers ironic.

The American Revolution partially compensated for the Jesuit suppression by according legal recognition to the religious liberty of Maryland Catholics. A law of 1776 recognized a Catholic right to public worship.[5] The old law that Mass could only be celebrated on private property—a major incentive for colonial Jesuits to hold title to their own plantations—was repealed. For the first time since the Protestant supremacy set up by the Glorious Revolution of 1689, Catholics in Maryland could be open in the practice of their faith. The former Jesuits no longer needed to retain slaves and other property as security for their religious liberty, but they were left with a some sense of obligation toward these servants and the question of whether slave labor might yet foster plantations that would support the ministries of the Catholic clergy.

If these clergymen wished to make changes, this was their chance. Why, then, did dramatic reform fail to materialize? There are three explanations: the former and restored Jesuits' wish to preserve as much as possible of their heritage from the years before 1773, their wish to embrace the political system of the new United States without demanding parallel radical social change; their desire to remain faithful to Roman Catholic moral theology. Each explanation deserves study.

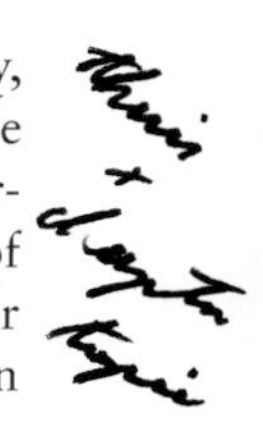

The former Jesuits believed that the way of life they had led in the Society of Jesus had been good, effective, and above all holy. They felt profoundly that the suppression was unjust and would not last. Carroll boasted to his mother in 1773 that the Society had been devoted to both the spiritual and material needs of its neighbors, never thinking of itself.[6] Such defiant pride gave these clergymen little wish to make drastic changes in the way they conducted their lives as priests.

Politically, the Revolution simply affirmed what the former Jesuits had asserted as their rights since the inception of the colony. The event looked to them like a vindication rather than an innovation. Furthermore, the suppression transformed the Jesuits' seventeenth-century failure to revive in Maryland the medieval English law allowing the Church to own property corporately into an advantage. Since they had legally held property in the colony as individuals rather than a religious order, there was neither reason nor ability to enforce in Protestant Maryland the papal decree that property formerly belonging to the Society be confiscated by the institutional Church. Carroll saw in this development a signal that it was God's will that the former Jesuits keep and protect their land.[7]

Therefore, the former Jesuits first determined that whatever else might happen ecclesiastically or politically, they ought to remain in some formal communion with one another pending the appointment of a bishop or the hoped for restoration of their religious order. They hoped that the Maryland Assembly would recognize their right to incorporate as a rural landholder. If they could no longer receive recognition of their association from the Church, former Jesuits would obtain it from the state.

Their aspirations saw fruition in four key steps. Between June 27, 1783, and October 11, 1784, the Maryland clergy met at the White Marsh plantation on three occasions to draw up a "Constitution of the Clergy," which sketched a practical plan for their continued association.[8] In 1789, they finally received their first bishop in the person of John Carroll. On December 23, 1792, the priests at last persuaded the Maryland legislature to pass an act granting them formal incorporation as the "Roman Catholic Gentlemen of Maryland," a move which made their association and the constitution of 1784 legally binding rather than entirely informal.[9] Finally, on September 20, 1805, Archbishop Carroll communicated with those of his clergymen about to join the reestablished Society of Jesus, whose refounding in the United States had just been allowed by decree of Pope Pius VII, nine years prior to its reconstitution in Europe.[10]

This pattern of events is important for its demonstration of how strong Jesuit identity remained in Maryland despite the long decades of suppression. They saw the continued possession of their land as key to maintaining that identity, and were inclined to hold the operation of that land to traditional means.

The solidity of this identity was manifested by the Jesuit-like character of the "Corporation of Roman Catholic Clergy of Maryland," or RCCC. Consider this resolution, passed on October 4, 1793:

> The Trustees are required to have particular attention to the interests of the former members of the Society of Jesus, and in case of its future reestablishment in this state, to use their best endeavours to restore the estates to its numbers; and they shall elect them into the select body in preference to all others.[11]

Therefore, it is appropriate to assume that there was a Jesuit identity in Maryland throughout the suppression even though, from a strictly ecclesiastical and canonical perspective, the order did not formally exist there during the period 1773–1805.

Another factor that influenced the clergy's discernment was the nature of Roman Catholic moral theology. There is a longstanding, four part process whereby the Catholic Church evaluates the morality of an issue. Four sources of Christian ethics are taken into consideration—scripture, heritage, philosophical reflection, and experience.[12] Does the Bible seem to take a clear position on the issue? Does the Church have a consistent history of taking a stand on a certain side of the problem, or does the heritage show a history of disagreement? Do philosophers and church fathers show a consensus in favor of a specific position? Has the Church's attempt to live out a certain understanding of an issue worked effectively? Historically, all four of these queries have had to begin pointing in a single direction before the Church would contemplate any manifest change of moral doctrine. In the particular case of slaveholding, in late eighteenth century Maryland, only the last of these four, the Jesuits' actual experience of holding slaves, prompted any reflection that the Church should change its longstanding evaluation that slavery was an ethical practice. However, experience in this case was ambivalent. The case against slaveholding was based largely on two propositions, the first that there was a link between the financial problems of the plantations and slaveholding and, second, that it was difficult to form slaves into people of reliable character. The first proposition had to fly against evidence that many other slaveholders prospered, and the second could be blamed as much on the Jesuits' poor catechetical skills with African Americans as any deliberate unwillingness of the slaves to learn Catholic moral principles. Some Jesuits who wanted to sell the slaves felt that some other Catholic owners might prove to be more effective with the slaves in this regard.

The first three quadrants of Catholic social ethics—the scriptures, church heritage, and the philosophers whose reasoning most influenced Church teaching and policy—all remained strongly supportive of slavery as late as 1800. As yet, no scripture scholar reputable among Catholics had challenged the assumption that the Bible could only be read as supportive of slavery. The Church's history showed a resistance to slavetrading, but not to slaveholding itself. The philosophers and moral theologians most read by Catholics all embraced a theory that slaveholding was a natural part of the divinely shaped order of human life.

Catholic moral theologians argue that a sound Catholic moral evaluation can only be conducted through equal attention to each quadrant. Wariness is in order when any one of the four quadrants is accorded precedence over the others.[13] This was how Jesuits in Maryland evaluated early proposals to abolish slaveholding. At the same time, they were attracted to the alternative of selling the slaves as a means of leaving the institution of itself intact, thereby honoring tradition. It would not be a statement that slaveholding was wrong, only a declaration that the Jesuits themselves no longer wished to conduct it. Joseph Mobberly commented, "God . . . himself has always prescribed this method of serving him, and has never left it to men to prescribe it for him."[14] At a time when many planters sold slaves to meet the demands of the market, Jesuits had the additional motivation that sales would uphold an ancient heritage.

But what of other possible motives for slave sales? About half the slave sales in Maryland between 1830 and 1840—the very decade that the Jesuits finally sold their slaves—resulted from the breakup of the estates of deceased planters. Other motives may have included financial distress in a small number of cases; the refusal of various slaves to adjust to plantation routine; the desire of certain slaves to be reunited with family members; the fact that some slaves may have been motivated to work harder for one master than another; the requirement of the government that slaves convicted of crimes be sold to other counties or states.[15] In general, slaveholders made shrewd decisions about selling and buying based on the needs of the emerging capitalist market.[16] Slaveholders in border states like Maryland used the prospect of sale to the Deep South as an incentive to frighten their slaves into better behavior. Incorrigible slaves were often passed among several masters for this reason.[17] .

While financial distress was a major factor in the Jesuits' ultimate decision to sell, sometimes the punitive motive was a more comfortable reason for them to contemplate. The thought of selling slaves in hopes of developing their moral characters fit more more comfortably into Jesuit theology than the idea of selling them to make money. Many Jesuits thus persuaded themselves that the selling of offensive slaves would lead to improved behavior. Joseph Mobberly mentioned in his diary for 1815 that Father John Henry, an estate manager at Bohemia, who wanted to sell some ungovernable and morally corrupt slaves to the Deep South, was "probably supposing that a change of climate, place etc. would produce a change in their morals."[18]

In classic Catholic fashion, Jesuits like Henry sought a way by which any new proceeding regarding slavery would grow out of tradition rather than negate it.[19] The idea that some other Catholic master might succeed in helping the slaves where Jesuits could not seemed to offer the Jesuits promise of both freedom from the burden of parenting slaves and a sense that they were actually fulfilling that parenting by selling.

Interestingly, such reflections showed no awareness that the slaves' bad behavior may have reflected their own decision to resist oppression. Slaves' determination not to cooperate with the institution that bound them had much to do with its inefficiencies and contributed to its ultimate downfall.[20] Jesuits saw in this behavior not systemic protest against an injustice, but only individually wicked people, whose resistance and passive aggression they usually attributed to a slothful and deceitful nature rather than a justified yearning for freedom. The Jesuits, seeking an explanation for the ineffectiveness of their paternalism, found it in a racist view of the behavior of black people.

The RCCC was the group whose business meetings provided the setting in which a discussion of the future course of slaveholding by Catholic clergy began. Within this context, priests struggled to reconcile attention to the growing financial difficulties of the farms with the moral problems of the slaves. The record indicates a group which oscillated between a defense of tradition and demands for reform, making few concrete changes but acting as a forum for venting a growing unease about slaveholding.

In the Constitution of the Clergy that was drafted in 1783 and 1784, there was only one specific, very traditional provision for the slaves. It made each estate manager responsible for "the providing of necessaries for house-keeping & Servants."[21] This was a classic restatement of the longtime Jesuit sense of responsibility toward those who worked under them. The civilization of the white South was based upon "religions that profoundly deepened whatever sense of guilt may be inherent in human experience."[22] The Catholicism of the Jesuits certainly stood in that heritage. Guilt concerning their sense that the slaves were a moral responsibility whose care had been given them by God influenced the Jesuit sense that they must hang on to them and produced such periodic resolutions to care for them more adequately.

However, by its November meeting in 1786, the RCCC's honoring of tradition was balanced by a suggestion to use the slaves in retiring plantation debt. A proposal was adopted that urgent expenses be partially met through the renting out of some slaves from Bohemia plantation. This decision showed the Jesuits' entry into an aspect of American slaveholding that has been neglected by historians.[23]

Father Joseph Mosley, Bohemia's manager, had borrowed a large sum of money to purchase some additional land for that estate. To pay back the loan, it was suggested that Mosley temporarily rent out Crosley's Quarters, a section of the plantation, along with everything on it. The provisions thus leased would include "negroes, stock, grain sowed, and a proportionate part of this year's salt provision and corn." The resolution quickly added, however, that all these items, including the slaves, would revert to the care of the Bohemia plantation manager as soon as rent receipts were equivalent to the amount that had been borrowed.[24] Mosley was only to pay off his debt, nothing more. Paying what one owed was a moral duty; making a profit with slaves was not.

The resolution said nothing specific about finding a renter who would be kindly disposed toward the Catholicism of the slaves. However, the provision that the rental be ended as soon as possible suggests that the spiritual welfare of the slaves remained a Jesuit concern. Later such resolutions often called explicitly for the selection of renters and buyers who would treat slaves in "a humane and Christian way," suggesting that Jesuit reflection on the initial results of such transactions convinced them of a need to provide for the slaves' religion more carefully. The minority status of Catholic planters within Maryland was no doubt a factor here; the prospect of finding a Catholic renter was small. While there were about 9000 adult Catholics in Maryland in the mid-1780s, most were poor farmers—probably unable to afford a rented slave. The few wealthy Catholic planters already had more than enough of their own slaves.[25] They preferred to give slaves away to the Jesuits rather than rent some from them.

Rental transactions were probably over five times as frequent as sale transactions of slaves in antebellum America. Many people needed slave labor for only small intervals at a time, and saw no need to burden themselves with the permament maintenance of chattel.[26] The likelihood with the Jesuits, however, is that they foreswore a potentially lucractive market for essentially religious reasons. They did not want to rent to Protestants. While specific data from the Jesuit rentals is lacking, when they did sell slaves, they made the religious credentials of potential buyers a far greater concern than their business abilities. It is unlikely that they behaved any differently with regard to rentals.

Masters often found it convenient for business purposes to rent out slaves but disliked the practice personally, worrying about what kind of treatment the slaves would receive from their temporary masters and what their condition would be like upon their return home.[27] In most cases, however, these scruples were not sufficient to prevent masters from renting slaves anyway. The Jesuits seem to have differed from their brother masters in attempting not to rent unless they could guarantee good religious treatment first.

Unfortunately, no record of the RCCC's actual debates during these early years survives; only their resolutions do. There was no James Madison present to keep detailed notes of the proceedings as there was at the convention that drafted the Constitution of the United States, so we only have the actual legislation of the Maryland clerical corporation to read. The reconstruction of what happened is therefore difficult, although not impossible. Some events that took place outside their official proceedings suggest some division over the care of slaves.

For example, on April 25, 1788, a group of priests who did not like the church government provided by the new system circulated an open letter among all former Jesuits complaining that "this established form had not produced that harmony and regularity, without which all is thrown into confusion." Therefore, they advocated that the clergy should be governed in the closest possible manner to the suppressed Jesuit constitutions that had been in effect before 1773, and proposed a meeting at St. Thomas Manor for July 21 to carry out their resolve.[28]

While nothing came of this proposal, so that the arrangements of 1783–1784 remained in effect, it will be noted that one of the innovations about the new manner of proceeding was that its openness to the rental of slaves. To traditionalists, this may have seemed to place clerical financial difficulties ahead of the personal needs of the slaves. It is a reasonable guess that this was one of the matters which distressed the disgruntled priests who produced the St. Thomas petition. During the same year, the Reverend Patrick Smyth, an Irish priest who had briefly and unhappily worked in Maryland, published *The Present State of the Catholic Missions Conducted by the Ex-Jesuits in North America*. Smyth accused the Maryland clergy of mistreating their slaves. John Carroll's indignation at Smyth's attack led to the drafting of a detailed public rebuttal.[29] While Smyth's specific charges about such beatings may have been exaggerated, the decision to rent their slaves out did make the clergy vulnerable to his broader charge that they were treating the slaves out of self-interest rather than altruism.

More change was in store, however. On May 15, 1789, the RCCC passed a much more drastic proposal which concerned all their plantations, not just Bohemia, and which advocated outright sale rather than mere rental. Recognizing "the great danger of our estates suffering from keeping supernumerary slaves," the clergymen now resolved for the first time that they must reduce permanently the quantity of such servants.

An elaborate procedure for reduction was adopted. The "procurator general," the clergyman who exercised the general supervision of all the estates on behalf of the entire corporation, was directed to consult with the manager of each local estate and one or two clergymen who lived nearby. Together, they were to determine the number of slaves adequate to run the plantation. They were then to sell "to the best advantage" all that would exceed that figure, keeping only those needed for the work to be done.

Careful directions were drawn up regarding how to use money from these sales. It was to be applied first to the retirement of any debts from the specific plantation from which the slaves had come. After that, was be applied to the debts of whichever of the corporation's three districts contained the plantation in question. The third priority was to apply the funds toward any maintenance needs or improvements on the original plantation. If anything was left after that, it was to go to the fund of the general corporation for the same purposes and priorities—retirement of debt of local and general debt, followed by repairs. Care was to be taken not to profit from the sale of slaves, and no thought was given to use the money to create more personal wealth or more luxurious living quarters for individual priests.

Finally, this resolution required that the procurator general and the other officials were to complete a new census and subsequent sale of superfluous slaves every three years, reporting to the trustees on their findings and on the allocation of the money thus raised.[30]

Implementation of the 1789 resolution was never completed. The resolution was passed at the end of a decade in which the abolitionists of the Upper South began to organize themselves more tightly against slavery and white racism. The core of Southern abolitionist sentiment lay with artisans and tradesmen who did not own slaves themselves. Planters tended to resist the cause, even when they saw its worth, because they feared the economic losses and class ostracism such advocacy might cause them.[31] The fact that the planter Jesuits of Maryland did not opted for sale rather than manumission shows that they did not act uncharacteristically of their class at this time. They were definitely not attracted to the abolitionist cause.

It is revealing also to place the failure of the 1789 policy in the context of the Jesuits' struggle to obtain legal incorporation for the clergy association, a goal that they did not achieve until 1792. The Maryland legislature took an anti-abolitionist turn in 1791. It voted to condemn the state abolitionist society, fell only two votes short of declaring it subversive, and rebuffed that organization's subsequent demand for an apology. The legislature then took steps to restrict lawsuits demanding the freedom of slaves.[32] Into this climate came the former Jesuits, a group of planters who happened to be Catholic clergymen, seeking legal incorporation from an antiabolitionist, predominantly Protestant legislature. The clergy had no wish to abolish slavery, but in such a climate, even a decision to ease out of slaveholding by selling every servant might have impeded the process of obtaining legal incorporation.

The failed policy of 1789 also offers a chance to compare the Jesuits with the general disposition of American masters toward elderly slaves. Many slaveholders boasted of their concern for their old slaves, but the actions of many failed to reflect those words. Maryland saw many objections to a tendency to manumitt the elderly to fend for themselves. The overall record ranges on a spectrum from mistreatment to indifference to minimum attention to full concern. Ultimately, any slaves who did enjoy a dignified old age received it largely through the care of their own community, who honored the African custom of venerating the aged and the ancestor.[33] This veneration manifested itself in the prominent role that grandparents played in socializing and enculturating their grandchildren, continuing a West African tradition of grandparents serving as checks on the authority of parents.[34]

The Jesuits of the late eighteenth century did record any evidence of these practices which may have occurred among their own slaves, and continued to feel personally responsible for the fate of their elderly, youthful and infirm bondsfolk. Mobberly believed that slaves who came directly from Africa and their children were inclined to malice and murder by poisoning. Later generations who were raised in America, he believed, were turned away from these practices only by their slaveholders.[35] John Carroll believed that both lay masters and slave parents neglected children, handing their religious education over to priests while providing the children with very little time for catechesis.[36] Mobberly attributed the longevity of the slaves at St. Inigoe's to Jesuit care, not the support of their own family members.[37] The Jesuit sense of racial and class superiority, overlaid with their clerical sense of superiority to the laity, is the probable explanation of their failure to equate any of these behaviors with the deliberate decisions of slaves concerning how to care for one another or what was important in their lives.

Another problem for the Jesuits was the formation of a consensus concerning the definition of a supernumerary slave. The obvious answer—people whose age or health prevented them from contributing to the work of the plantation—troubled many clergy who felt that they simply could not abandon the many children, elderly, and sick who fit that description.

It is probable that unease about the prospect of selling these helpless people prompted Jesuits to seek choices of other kinds of slaves for sale when they absolutely had to meet some debt. The selection of slaves who had misbehaved became the most common alternative. Unfortunately, this option usually meant the selection for sale of those slaves who were theoretically in the best condition to work—youthful males. The Maryland clergy thus subverted the prosperity of their plantations by tending to keep the physically unfit and sell the

physically fit. What they did not address was the fact that a plantation which could not function economically would be ultimately unable to provide for frail slaves anyway. Jesuits here missed an opportunity to develop a morally strong case for making profits out of right motives. If more money were needed to care justly for the sick slaves, then it is difficult to see why reasonable profits would have been immoral in such circumstances.

The unease about profit and the preference for selling delinquents rather than supernumeraries can be traced through the manner in which the Maryland clergy policed the Sulpician Fathers, a religious congregation of seminary teachers whom they allowed to administer the Bohemia plantation during the years 1793–1799. The idea of granting the Sulpicians occupancy at Bohemia was that any profits from the sale of crops and livestock from that estate were to be applied to the construction of a seminary for the recently founded diocese of Baltimore. The RCCC soon showed alarm, however, over a Sulpician tendency to compute money from slave sales as such profits.

The corporation first manifested its concern on August 21, 1795, when it admonished the Sulpicians that neither money from the sale of slaves nor timber carried off the land should be counted as profits of the plantation.[38] Instead, the timber was to remain on the farm to warm the slave quarters during the winter. The corporation solemnly informed the president of the seminary that profits were to be understood as consisting only of "the annual crops, rents, the increase of stock, and firewood not fit for building or fence rails."[39]

There survive a few records of the sales that the Sulpicians had carried out at Bohemia before the corporation passed this resolution. They help to make comprehensible the anxiety that the corporation felt about the practice, for the Sulpicians followed the traditional definition of a superflous slave in choosing subjects to sell. Louis Caesar Delevan, the first Sulpician estate manager, sold Philis and her five week old daughter, Nell, for $35.00 to George Reece on January 8, 1794. Women of childbearing and child rearing years, as well as small children, were obvious cases of slaves who could not work much. Slightly over a year later, on February 11, 1795, Philis' other child, Clare, four years of age, was sold to Mrs. Nelly for $5.00. This decision was a clear violation of church custom that slave families were to be kept together, but much in keeping with the literal wording of the Chapter's resolution of 1789 that those incapable of working were to be disposed of.

In two other sales, Delevan did keep some families intact. On February 13, 1795, Bob and his daughter, Lucy, were sold to John Çainan for $80.00; on February 28, Ralph and Jenny were sold, along with their daughter, to Robert Hodgson for $70.00. In selling so many children, however, Delevan continued to rid the farm of slaves unable to work but in need of care. Delevan did modify his conduct slightly after receiving the Corporation's clarification about profit. In April, 1796, eight months later, Delevan sold an ill former runaway slave named Henry for $15.00 to an unspecified buyer.[40] While Henry's illness may have fit him into the technical definition of a supernumerary, the overriding factor in his sale seems likely to have been the rebellion of this captured fugitive. The illness might have been considered a consequence of his absconding. The comparatively low price received for Henry suggested the high risk of purchasing such an unreliable character. The payment for Henry, compared with the money received for other adult slaves, matches general research that slaves known to be unhealthy or ill-behaved sold at substantial discounts.[41] Delevan's decision to sell Henry showed that the focus in selecting subjects for sale was shifting from those who *could* not to those who *would* not work.

That the 1790s were a decade of transition in the clergy's approach to slaveholding is demonstrated by some correspondence which Bishop Carroll had with one of his priests, John Thayer, in 1794. Carroll's episcopal jurisdiction then included the entire United States, and he had transferred Thayer from Boston to a rural posting in Prince George's County, Maryland. Thayer wrote to Carroll of his unease at the slaveholding practices he witnessed in the new assignment.

On January 13, 1794, Carroll raised with Thayer the old Jesuit custom of providing an example which might inspire modification of the conduct of other, less generous slaveholders:

> I am sorry to hear of the negligence of masters with respect to their servants. Instead of it being motive for you to leave them, it ought, in my opinion, be one to remain with them. Mr. Roger, who amongst those belonging to yr. care, has much the largest number of slaves, kept a priest many years in his family for their sake; who was assiduous in instructing them.[42]

The following July, Thayer requested permission to leave the assignment because of "difficulties concerning Negroes;" he felt that both he and his predecessors had failed to improve the moral character of the slaves in his parish. Carroll did not see this assertion as a legitimate excuse. To him, clergymen were not justified in leaving their posts simply because the sins they preached against endured. Instead, the bishop was anxious that Thayer remain and bear in mind that the Church had an ancient and tested set of principles for dealing with the slaveholding question. As long as he acted within the bounds of official Catholic teaching, Carroll promised Thayer that he could remedy the abuses of slavery without interference.

However, Carroll conceded that his reliance on tradition was due, at least in part, to his genuine uncertainty about what to do in this troublesome situation:

> I am as far, as you, from being easy in my mind at many things I see, and know, relating to the treatment & manners of the Negroes. I do the best, I can to correct the evils I see: and then recur to those principles, which, I suppose, influenced the many eminent & holy missioners in S. America & Asia, where slavery equally exists.

In a passage which he seems to have deleted from the dispatched version of his letter to Thayer, Carroll added his resentment of the claim that clergy could not control the irregularities of the slaves. This was an unfair indictment of the many skilled priests, not only in the United States but throughout the Americas and Asia, who had succeeded in governing slaves effectively over the years.[43] However, Thayer's contrary opinion of the failure of the clergy to manage slaves morally was an idea that would continue to greatly influence the unfolding discernment.

On May 5, 1801, when the RCC convened at Newtown, there was concern about the plans of a Father Brasuis to free a slave named Peter. The corporation informed Brasuis that such a step would harm "that sublimation, which ought to be preserved among the other slaves." Therefore, they advised that Peter be required to purchase his own freedom by providing security equal to the amount for which he might otherwise have been sold. [44] The clergy felt that if Peter managed to fulfill these conditions, he would thereby demonstrate that he had earned slavery freedom a demonstration of his moral character rather than received it as a right.

This advice to Brasuis evolved into a policy proposal that slaves of the clergy be set free only after a specified number of years following their sale to some new Catholic master who would agree to direct their final preparations for freedom. During that interval, the slaves would hopefully develop the moral sensibility and the practical skills needed to function as freemen. This policy signified that in negotiations with potential buyers, the priests would need to evaluate much more than the simple ability of the buyers to pay for their purchases. They would also have to evaluate these buyer's qualifications to prepare the slaves for personal freedom.

In the case of Peter in 1801, the priests showed a conviction that if Peter could manage to purchase his liberty, he would thereby witness to the remaining slaves that freedom had its patient price. Hopefully, his example then would guard against slave revolts and the temptation to believe that freedom could be claimed on demand. Like many whites, Jesuits feared the associations that might take place between free blacks and those remaining enslaved. This might implant the idea of freedom for all, leading the remaining slaves to run away or rebel.[45]

The decision that Peter must earn his freedom shows that the Jesuit practice had coincidences with a strain of Southern thought which repudiated the idea of natural rights. John C. Calhoun, among others, attempted to demonstrate that freedom had no meaning apart from participation in and acceptance of the restraints of society.[46] By asking Peter to accept their conditions for his manumission, the Jesuits demonstrated their wish that he participate in society according to their definition and their restraints.

In 1803, the action which had been followed in Peter's specific case became general policy. The procurator general of the RCCC was ordered to ensure that in any case in which a slave might be either sold or freed, his proper value would be obtained, whether from a new owner or a freed individual himself.

Steps were also taken in 1803 to clarify whether local managers had the autonomy to dispose of "unruly slaves" without having to await the action of the whole Corporation at is semi-annual meeting. They could indeed so proceed, but only in emergencies, so long as the local trustees and representatives of the particular district where the plantation was located were consulted and consented in writing.[47]

This policy illustrates a key difference between the clerical slaveholder and the typical slaveholder: lack of autonomy. Most plantation owners could make their own decisions in business matters, but Jesuits were part of a religious community and had to rely on a combination of communal consensus and the direction of superiors.

During the decade between 1803 and 1813, a period which saw the formal restoration of the Society of Jesus in the United States in 1805, the fragmentary records of the corporation continued to record various individual cases of manumission and sale. For example, in 1804 it was authorized that the supernumerary slaves at Deer Creek plantation be sold to "humane and Christian masters" in disposition of some lawsuits that had been brought against that farm. The corporation, at that same meeting, also reviewed two proposed sales, and approved the terms of each because it was believed that in each case, the priests involved had applied the money to the plantations' needs rather than their own profits.[48]

In the meeting of July 9–11, 1805, at Whitemarsh, managers of "the several estates" were asked to sell "superflous slaves, stock or any other means within their power" to pay off a loan owed by the whole Corporation.[49]

The years around 1805 also offered further evidence of John Carroll's own wrenching discernment. On November 12, just a few weeks after the Jesuit restoration in Maryland, the Bishop wrote to Father Francis Neale, S.J., manager of St. Inigoe's plantation, with instructions concerning a deficit for that farm. "The sale of a few unnecessary Negroes, three or four, and stock, would replace the money."[50] Note that Carroll did not state that he would sell these slaves for the outright enrichment of St. Inigoe's. Instead, he ascribed a negative motive in the retirement of debt. Carroll found it more comfortable to talk in the language of frugality than in the language of profit. Ordinarily a Federalist in his politics, Carroll here demonstrated the Jeffersonian party's abhorrence of debt, which it held despite Jefferson's personal persistent debts at his Monticello plantation.

A little over eight months later, on July 21, 1806, Carroll described the very different sale of one of his personal slaves, an active alcoholic named Alexis who had functioned as the Bishop's valet. Lacking the modern understanding of alcoholism as a disease, Carroll saw the drinking as a moral flaw. He therefore sought a lay buyer who might have more leisure than a busy prelate to tutor the slave in right behavior. In effect, Carroll here conceded the observation of John Thayer a dozen years earlier, that priests had been utter failures as moral teachers of slaves.

At first it seemed that Carroll had found a buyer for Alexis in a Mr. Stenson, a wealthy Baltimore gentleman who agreed to purchase the slave even after hearing Carroll's frank description of his shortcomings. Stenson, however. turned out to be "not the most patient man in the world." The very next day he sold Alexis yet again, this time to someone outside Carroll's purview, because the slave had failed to attend some call of his new master quickly enough. When the Bishop heard of his sometime valet's fate, he commented: "So much for this depraved young man who has banished from himself happiness & comfort."[51] Impatience was an improbable motive for Stenson, howeve. Instead, it seems likely that he sold Alexis for much more than he had paid for him, swiftly exploiting the financial naivete of Bishop Carroll.

The only noble moral goal was for a Catholic master to guide the slave toward eternal salvation; becoming a slaveowner meant assuming responsibility for a slave's soul. Alexis was sold to Stenson because Carroll convinced himself that it would enhance the black man's prospects for reaching heaven if he were placed under the direction of a new master, not because Carroll was thinking of his own needs for money. (He did not even record how much money he received for Alexis.)

Carroll's treatment of Alexis refutes a thesis that, as the Jesuit farms deteriorated, the Jesuits became more singlemindedly concerned with the monetary value of those plantations.[52] The fact is that while they did worry constantly about their financial problems, they continued to worry more about the character and fate of the slaves. Carroll's treatment of Alexis, coming just a few months after his concern about Whitemarsh, also suggests that the Jesuits ultimately had a different motive for their paternalism than those slaveowners who sought to control slaves in order to make plantations more efficient at making money[53] Some masters believed that paternalism was necessary if plantations were to attain productivity. The Jesuits, however, primarily saw paternalism as an essential tool for teaching the slaves to be good Catholics who might ultimately join their masters in heaven.

Meanwhile, the RCCC continued its discernment. At both the spring and fall meetings of the year 1808, the sale of supernumeraries was again encouraged. This time, it was proposed that the money be deposited in a fund whose future disposition would be determined only by the trustees themselves.[54] However, the actual determination of which slaves were actually supernumerary was left to each local manager. The corporation itself was now content not only to leave the conundrum of definining superfluity to others, but also to the possibility that there might be more than one definition from estate to estate.

The subsequent decisions of local managers show that different answers were indeed provided, and sometimes by the same people acting from case to case. The records of the spring meeting of 1809 suggested some reversion to the literal definition of a supernumerary, with many children and elderly being designated for sale. At St. Thomas' Manor, "one boy named George" had been sold for $300. At St. Inigoes, a family of eight people, both children and elderly, had been sold for $1300; an elderly couple had also been sold for $350, with interest payable within eighteen months.

The same meeting showed, however, that the plight of the orphans of Sarah, from the farm of Arabia Petrea, moved the trustees to delay their sale. The trustees authorized their sale only "to humane and Christian masters," and specified that the low funds of the corporation that year were not to deter the manager from applying benefactions first to the clothing, lodging and nourishment of Sarah's children. If all else failed, they were to be sent to St. Inigoe's via Baltimore at the expense of that comparatively more prosperous estate. Meanwhile, Corporation promised that anyone who might recover Tom, a runaway from White Marsh, would receive a reward from the corporation.[55] When these several resolutions are compared, it is clear that a consistent approach to the slavery question continued to elude Jesuits.

Thus far any manumissions and sales had been carried out only in these select cases. The War of 1812, however, brought hard economic times to the Chesapeake. On May 17, 1813, at Georgetown, the corporation faced for the first time a resolution to lease "the whole or greatest part of the slaves" for a number of years, after which they would all be granted freedom. This was the first occasion on which the Jesuits deliberated disposing of every last slave, not just the superannuated ones.

After some discussion, the details of which are unfortunately unavailable, it was decided that this new proposal was too serious a matter to be voted upon immediately. Action was deferred until the next regular RCCC meeting the following autumn. Meanwhile, the trustees were directed to study the question carefully themselves, and also to take careful soundings of opinion from the priests in their districts.[56]

When the Chapter reconvened at Georgetown on September 14, 1813, it was reported that a majority of the clergy in the state had expressed their support of the May proposal. However, consensus, not majority, was what the corporation sought. Therefore, the trustees remained reluctant to vote. They postponed action yet again, and meanwhile solicited suggestions about how the proposal might be implemented. While a general decision was awaited, case-by-case sales continued. Carroll, now an Archbishop, was directed to dispose of a woman and child from the Bohemia Estate.[57]

In testimony to the controversy which the proposal for a general Jesuit manumission had awakened, the Congregation met twice that autumn, reconvening on October 26, 1813. Ordinarily, there were just two meetings a year, one in the spring and one in fall. The extraordinary October meeting resulted in yet another delay and calls for further investigation.[58]

The proposal was finally adopted at the regular spring meeting of June 14, 1814, at Georgetown. However, the final form of the resolution was ambivalent. On the one hand, the Jesuits provided that the text be sent to each district representative quickly, "to urge their constant attention to it so that it may not suffer by unnecessary delay." On the other, the resolution concluded that "this resolve, is not made obligatory in such manner, as to compel the representatives and managers to make sale of all the blacks; some may be reserved for domestic and necessary uses." These contradictions were similar to the "all deliberate speed" with which the Supreme Court would seek to desegregate American schools over a century later.

In the text of this resolution, Jesuit managers were ordered by the General Corporation to act slowly, pay close attention to the law, and not offer a large number for sale at any one time. It was still left to the individual managers and their district representatives to choose how many should be sold, which should be sold, and for what number of years before manumission. Money received from the sales was to be first applied to the plantation from which the slaves came and then invested in a safe fund subject to review by the procurator general.[59]

For all the hedging in this resolution, it constituted a historic step. For the first time, the Jesuits had committed themselves in principle to the specific goal of ending their slaveholding and eventually setting their slaves free. To be sure, they set no schedule for achieving this goal and had devised plenty of loopholes in its implementation. Overall, however, they were finally nudging in the direction of a great reform. Had they carried out the intentions of 1814, the calamitous general sale that eventually occurred in 1838 would have been avoided.

This scheme of gradual manumission was prophetic; it would become the Catholic Church's preferred means of ending slaveholding in the United States. As late as 1866, they year after slavery had been abolished by the Thirteenth Amendment to the Constitution, the American bishops expressed regret at the abruptness of Lincoln's general emancipation:

> We could have wished, that in accordance with the action of the Catholic Church in past ages, in regard to the serfs of Europe, a more gradual system of emancipation could have been adopted, so that they might have been in some measure prepared to make a better use of their freedom, than they are likely to do now. Still,the evils which must attend upon the sudden liberation of so large a multitude, with their peculiar disciplines and habits, only make the appeal to our Christian charity and zeal, presented by their forlorn condition, the more forcible and imperative.[60]

The 1814 resolution did not succeed because its ambivalent language was followed by an ambivalent implementation. Jesuits still disagreed as to whether slaves had the moral character to live on their own, as is shown by the contrasting views of Father Antonio Grassi (1775–1849) and Father Peter Kenney (1779–1841).

Grassi, a native Italian, served from 1812 to 1817 both as superior of the Jesuits in Maryland and as President of Georgetown College. Upon his return to Rome, Grassi was requested not only to describe the state of the American nation and church to his superiors, but to take particular care to discuss the institution of slavery.

On the one hand, Grassi grasped the fundamental incompatibility between slavery and the American way of life, calling it an "apparent contradiction to one of the first articles of the Constitution which proclaims liberty an inalienable right inherent in man." He therefore lamented the fact that "the sad clang of servile chains may yet often be heard beneath the sun of liberty." Grassi expected that slaveholding would eventually die out completely in the United States because it was already abolished in many northern states. Meanwhile, the slave trade had been banned nationwide in 1808. However, Grassi also felt that there were good practical reasons not to set the slaves free, either immediately or all at once.

A great many slaves were still uncivilized, Grassi reported—lost in superstition, witchcraft, and lecherous conduct. Some had a complete ignorance of Christian religion, and were neither baptized nor validly married. Grassi expressed particular scorn for the "avaricious master" who "counts it enough that they labor," leaving them only "to follow like animals the dark impulses of their passions." That was what happened when masters were too concerned about profit and not enough about the character of their slaves. Grassi saw a need for Jesuit masters to remain as slaveholders to set an example against such neglect. If there were no Catholic slaveowners, Grassi feared, the slaves would be left to "follow like animals the dark impulses of their passions."

When slaves were in Catholic hands, Grassi felt, the results were already often good. They were usually better treated and fed than European peasants whom Grassi had observed in his home continent.[61] This last conviction was also held by Peter Kenney, Rome's official visitor to the Jesuits of the United States in 1820 and again in 1830, who felt that Americans treated their slaves much better than the British treated the Irish peasantry.[62] These observations of Grassi and Kenney were not meant so much to belittle the severity of bondage in the United States as to express a conviction that Catholic slaveholding still had a role to play in mitigating the generally bad effects of slavery.

Unlike many Jesuits, including Kenney, Grassi had some good things to say about the character of slaves who lived under their direction. Kenney believed that the slaves neglected "duties the most sacred to a Christian," in a manner that reproached the Society's teaching of sanctity to savages and created special scandal when they occurred on the threshold of the sanctuary.[63] Grassi, by contrast, admired the slaves' ability to grasp God's love for them despite the contempt they received from the world. Their resulting piety was so great as to inspire the Jesuit himself to pursue God's glory more ardently. He declared that they offered their work to the Lord, bore ill-treatment with patience, and often recited the Rosary with great devotion. Grassi's conclusion was that "Catholic slaves are to be preferred to all others, because they are more docile and faithful to their masters."[64] This was a great contrast to Kenney's conclusion was that the goal of raising godly Catholic slaves was impossible. However, it is also true that Grassi did not attribute these good qualities to any inherent goodness in the slaves. He believed that they held taught rather than innate virtues—virtues conveyed to them by Jesuit teachers.

The different comments of Grassi and Kenney cast interesting light on American slaveholders' ambivalent attitude toward progress in the early nineteenth century. Even the most sophisticated Southern intellectuals refused to define progress too closely, although they did tend to distinguish material and moral progress.[65] To many, the new American Republic looked like a place of both moral and material progress where the Christian Gospel was spreading more widely than ever before, where republican values were in ascendancy, and where technological and industrial progress was unprecedented. How were these three forces linked, if they were at all? Some said that no aspect of this progress would have been possible without slavery, while others feared that these same trends doomed slavery to a gradual but natural death.[66] The comments of Grassi and Kenney, both foreign observers of the emerging American milieu, demonstrated that Catholic theology, with its pessimism that sin could be overcome by human initiative, was skeptical of the concept of moral progress and actually regarded material progress as a temptation to further moral regression. This attitude created a major psychological barrier to ending Jesuit slaveholding. In the end, each of these two Jesuits found it philosophically impossible to imagine any better system. Their only disagreement, in fact, was whether masters or slaves were more in need of moral direction.

At least as concerns material progress, Joseph Mobberly was a prophetic but unheard exception to the philosophical pessimism of most Jesuits. He constantly urged that the implementation of the 1814 policy be speeded up: "The sooner that resolution is executed, the better it will be." Mobberly harped on the theme that the plantations would lose money until the disposition was complete, but portrayed a future of prosperous farms once it was.[67]

Mobberly failed to sway enough votes, however, for the new policy was repealed at the Chapter meeting of August 22, 1820. There was a bare notice in the minutes of that day's meeting that upon "mature reflection" it was now considered "prejudicial."[68] This economy of words is another reminder that it is unfortunate that only resolutions, not debates, from proceedings of the Jesuit corporation have survived. However, when this repeal is placed in the context of certain contemporary events in Maryland, both secular and religious, plausible motivations for this "mature reflection" emerge.

The lives of freed and free blacks in nineteenth century Maryland gave the Jesuits considerable reasons to doubt that their slaves would be able to prosper in freedom. United States census records reveal that between 1810 and 1865, Maryland had the largest free black population of any state. By the census of 1840, slightly over 40% of Marylanders were free blacks. The white population remained large enough, however, to absorb virtually all jobs of the "petite bourgeoisie." It was virtually impossible for freed slaves to become artisans, shopkeepers, clerks and small holding farmers. This was a sharp contrast to the situation in certain parts of Latin America and the Caribbean, where white people were such a small proportion of the population that the free blacks became essential performers of these important tasks. In Maryland, however, the unhappy result of a population nearly evenly divided between whites and blacks was that there was no really socially acceptable role for free blacks. Not only were freed black Marylanders unlikely to rise much higher than manual laboring, they were still regarded with constant suspicion by the remaining slaveowners. Their very presence was taken as an incitement for slaves to revolt, and slaveowners therefore put constant pressure on the free blacks to either leave the state or make themselves as unobstrusive as possible. Thus, the manumitted were even deprived of any role in keeping peace among the slave population, a role often assigned to their counterparts in the Caribbean and Latin America.[69] Virtually all white Marylanders looked with alarm upon all who freed their slaves, and made life difficult for both former masters and their former slaves.[70]

When the Jesuits of 1820 debated their future course, they must have had some conception of this situation. Six years of struggle to implement their manumission resolution of 1814 had likely shown them the difficulties involved in helping an emancipated slave to prosper in Maryland. Given the continuing sense of paternal responsibility for the slaves embodied by Jesuits like Grassi, it is reasonable to surmise that Jesuits feared the consequences of setting them free in a society which had no real social place for free blacks.

The discouragement of manumission, often by law, was not unique to Maryland. The Deep South restricted the process much more extensively than the border states.[71] It is never enough, however, to measure the Jesuits' decisions against whatever legal situation they found themselves in. They always added consideration of the religious situation. If temporal advantages for freed slaves were to be few and far between, their Catholicism would surely suffer, too, in a predominantly Protestant culture. That is why John Carroll, when setting his slave Charles free in his will in 1815, specified that Charles should remain in or near the city of Washington and remain closely associated with the Catholic friends Carroll had introduced him to.[72]

The modern reader might wonder whether any Jesuits took prophetic initiative and tried to set up their freed slaves in petite bourgeoisie jobs despite Maryland's cultural resistance to that idea. The likely answer is that the Jesuits' bias against business, their fear that financial gain meant moral retardation, prevented them from seeing that possibility as an opportunity. Such jobs were based on profit-making, a concept which the Jesuits clearly regarded with great ambivalence. It is revealing that one of the Jesuits most interested in setting up manumitted slaves in jobs, Joseph Carberry, wanted those so set free to rent farmland from the Society of Jesus as tenants, rather than set themselves up as independent small businessmen.[73]

In 1820, internal circumstances within the Jesuit order in the United States worked against the setting of firm policies regarding slaveholding. There remained much division over such questions as how far the Jesuits should go in embracing American values. Generally, American-born Jesuits and those from the British Isles were great advocates of republicanism. Those born on the continent of Europe, many of them refugees from the French Revolution, favored a more authoritarian approach. The dispute became so severe that in 1820 the Jesuit general in Rome sent Peter Kenney to try to restore order. In one of his reports, Kenney commented that "should the day ever come" that the slaves could be gotten rid of, a great burden and painful responsibility would fall from the shoulders of the Maryland Mission. Also, an odium would fall from the whole Society, since people outside the United States would no longer be able to hold it against Jesuits for holding slaves in that country. However, Kenney doubted that this could happen until a way could be found to find reputable tenants and avoid injury to the landed property.[74] Kenney knew what he wanted done, but did not know how to go about it. Kenney's observations gave no relief to the paralysis, for he basically left it up to the local Jesuits to determine the best time manner of meeting his condition.

The repeal is also explicable because by 1820 the Jesuits suddenly faced a new threat to their landholdings from the Church itself. John Carroll and his Jesuit successor as Archbishop of Baltimore, Leonard Neale, were both dead. The new and third Archbishop of Baltimore, who had taken office in 1818, was a Sulpician, Ambrose Marechal. Marechal took a dim view of the notion that the clergy estates in Maryland were all Jesuit property alone, and claimed legal title to on behalf of the entire Catholic Church in the state.[75] Only with difficulty was Rome persuaded away from the Marechal position a few years later. Some of the profits from the slave sale of 1838 had to be devoted to buying out the Archdiocese's claim to the land.[76]

In the midst of this dispute between the Jesuits and Marechal over land, there was also tension between them over slaves. There is evidence that Marechal believed the Jesuits were too partial to their slaves. In 1819, he notified a Jesuit priest, Leonard Edelin, that he had overreacted in confiscating some Bibles from Protestant preachers who were attempting to evangelize Catholic slaves and other poor folks.[77] Eight years later, Marechal reprimanded another Jesuit pastor, Peter DeVos, for acting too hastily in excommunicating a woman whose who had broken up a slave marriage by selling off the wife.[78] Marechal did not wish to see the slaves become a reason for sectarian tension between white Protestants and Catholics, and he wished to avoid personal distress for a wealthy contributor to the Church.

Thus continued the tension between Jesuits and Sulpicians which had manifested itself at Bohemia during the 1790s, a pattern in which the Jesuits resisted what they felt were the efforts of Sulpicians to sacrifice slaves for the expediency of white people. First, they resisted the Sulpician idea that profits from slave sales should benefit seminaries. Next, they fought the Sulpician practices of subordinating slaves to the resolution of Protestant Catholic tensions and the feelings of lay Catholic slaveowners. This analysis suggests that for all its limitations, the paternalistic attitude of the Jesuits allowed them to side with their slaves in some significant situations. The Jesuit-Sulpician tension also shows that the Catholic position on slaveholding was not monolithic, and that the Jesuits' ambivalence concerning financial profit may have been unusually strong even for the Catholic tradition.

There is a darker explanation for the Jesuits' partiality toward the slaves in this episode, however. What was really at stake between Marechal and the Jesuits in their wrangling was neither land nor slaves, but the question of who would hold effective power over the Archdiocese of Baltimore: its bishop, the nominal head, or the Jesuit order, which controlled most of its missions and much of its wealth.[79] In this sense, the Marechal-Jesuit controversy was a major step in the transition from an American Church governed basically by religious orders, the case since colonial times, to an American Church directed by its own secular clergy. The slaves may have been pawns in this struggle for control, just as in secular affairs they were pawns in the struggle at the Constitutional Convention of 1787 to find a formula for federal government acceptable to the states of both the North and the South.[80]

In sum, the situation around the year 1820 was one of Jesuit irresolution on the slavery issue. Mobberly's comment, "I sincerely regret that slaves were ever introduced into the United States, but as we have them we know not how to get rid of them," summed up the ambivalence of his order quite well.[81] They professed to dislike the manner in which the practice had evolved within the United States, and said that they wished for a way out of so conducting it. However, their actual acts revealed little serious effort to find such a way. In this, they resembled the pardoxical approach that Thomas Jefferson took to the slavery question—saying they disliked the institution while remaining locked in the conduct of it.[82] Is it merely a coincidence that the Jesuit farm system and Monticello were both perennially in debt? Or is it possible that both Jefferson and the Jesuits were so ambivalent about the "peculiar institution" as to stymie their attempts to earn a living through it?

One thing is indeed clear. The Jesuit practice of slaveholding in Maryland had become, by 1820, far less resolute than the practice of their confreres in Latin America. Evidence from Latin American often prompts scholars to argue that Catholic slaveholding was universally and inherently more benevolent than Protestant slaveholding, and designed to be so. In particular, some feel that the Catholic slaveholding practiced in Latin America showed a flexibility and fluidity that stood in sharp comparison to the rigid attitudes displayed in the Protestant culture of British North America and later in the United States. In Latin America there was apparently a much greater openness to manumission, a determination to develop the slaves to the point where they could handle freedom, and a receptivity to the part that could be played in society by free blacks. These convictions led the Catholic Church in Latin America to pursue proactive work to mitigate the evil of slavery, work which had some positive effects.[83] By contrast, the Maryland Jesuits of 1820 continued to practice slavery by inertia— seeing it as more an inherited burden than a positive practice on behalf of the poor. They had little vision as to what they would do with the practice while they continued to engage in it, and remained so engaged due to habit.

That force of habit raised a protective wall around the practice of Maryland Jesuit slaveholding. There were many stones in this wall—the Jesuit sense of self-preservation during the long suppression of their order, the Jesuit desire to celebrate the religious liberty of the new American republic while avoiding drastic social change, Catholic moral theology, and fears that moral progress was difficult for slaves and material progress a temptation for slaveowners. One remaining stone, however, was significant enough to deserve a chapter in its own right. This was Jesuit antiabolitionism, an important fruit of their opposition to the Reformation and their ambivalence about the Enlightenment. Antiabolitionism was a particularly important factor in this story because it essentially reduced the Jesuits' options to two: keep the slaves or sell them. Yet another issue, the Jesuit sense of responsibility to European immigrants, would emerge to nudge the eventual choice between these two options toward selling the slaves rather than keeping them. Each of these issues, anti-abolitionism and openness to immigration, deserve chapters in their own right—the first because it made the slaveholding last so long, the second because it detonated the final disposition of the slaves after so many decades of indecision.

NOTES

1. John Carroll to Eleanor Darnall Carroll, September 11, 1773; Thomas O'Brien Hanley, S.J., editor, *The John Carroll Papers (JCP)* I (Notre Dame, Ind.: University of Notre Dame Press, 1976), pp. 31–32.

2. Joseph Mosley, S.J. to Mrs. Helen Dunn, October 4, 1784, in Robert Emmett Curran, S.J., editor, *American Jesuit Spirituality: The Maryland Tradition, 1634–1900* (New York.: Paulist Press, 1988), pp. 112–113.

3. Thomas W. Spalding, *The Premier See: A History of the Archdiocese of Baltimore, 1789–1989* (Baltimore: The Johns Hopkins University Press, 1989), pp. 13–14; p. 21.

4. For a basic discussion of the period of the suppression of the Society of Jesus, see Chapter Six, "Exile, Suppression and Restoration," in William V. Bangert, S.J., *A History of the Society of Jesus* (St. Louis: The Institute of Jesuit Sources, Second Edition, 1986), pp. 363–430.

5. Maryland Declaration of Rights, November 11, 1776, in John Tracy Ellis, editor, *Documents of American Catholic History,* I (Wilmington, Del.: Michael

Glazier, Inc., 1986), pp. 137–138.

6. John Carroll to Eleanor Darnall Carroll, in Hanley, editor, *JCP*, I, pp. 31–32.

7. John Carroll, "Plan of Clergy Organization," 1782, in Hanley, editor, *JCP*, I, pp. 59–63.

8. "Constitution of the Clergy," in Hanley, editor, *JCP*, I, pp. 71–77.

9. Spalding, *op. cit.*, pp. 8–9.

10. John Carroll, "Agreement with the Jesuits," September 20, 1805, in Hanley, S.J., editor, *JCP*, II, pp. 489–490.

11. Corporation of Roman Catholic Clergymen of Maryland (RCC), Proceedings of the General Congregation, October 4, 1793, Resolution no. 16, Item no. 91.1, Box 24, Folder 1, Archives of the Maryland Province (MPA), Special Collections Division, Lauinger Library, Georgetown University, Washington, D.C.

12. "New Trends in Moral Theology," lecture delivered by James T. Bretzke, S.J., Jesuit School of Theology at Berkeley, Berkeley, California, October 10, 1995.

13. *Ibid.*

14. Brother Joseph Mobberly, S.J., "Slavery or Cham," p. 8, Brother Joseph Mobberly, S.J. Papers (BJMSJP), Special Collections Division, Lauinger Library, Georgetown University, Washington, D.C.

15. Robert William Fogel and Stanley L. Engerman, *Time on the Cross: The Economics of American Negro Slavery* (New York: W. W. Norton, 1974), pp. 53–55.

16. Robert William Fogel, *Without Consent or Contract: The Rise and Fall of American Slavery* (New York: W. W. Norton, 1989), pp. 67–68.

17. Kenneth Stampp, *The Peculiar Insitution: Slavery in the Antebellum South* (New York: Random House, Vintage Books Edition, 1989), pp. 154–155.

18. Mobberly, "Diary, Part I: Negroes Taken out of Prison," BJMSJP.

19. In changing the Church's teaching on religious liberty in civil society at Vatican Council II, the decree *Dignitatis Humanae* noted "This Vatican Synod . . . searches into the sacred tradition and doctrine of the Church—the treasury out of which the Church continually brings forth new things that are in harmony with the things that are old." See Walter M. Abbott, S.J., editor, *The Documents of Vatican II* (New York: America Press, 1966), p. 676.

20. See Eric Foner, "Slavery, the Civil War, and Reconstruction," in Eric Foner, editor, *The New American History* (Philadelphia: Temple University Press, 1990), pp. 73–92.

21. "Constitution of the Clergy, Whitemarsh, June 27, 1783 to October 11, 1784," in Hanley, editor, *JCP*, I, p. 75.

22. Eugene D. Genovese, *Roll, Jordan, Roll: The World the Slaves Made* (New York: Random House, Vintage Books Edition, 1976), p. 120.

23. Fogel and Engermann, *op. cit.*, pp. 55–56.

24. Proceedings of the Roman Catholic Clergy Corporation of Maryland (RCC), Resolution no. 3, November 13, 1786; Item no. 2N 7–10, Box 2, Folder 6, MPA.

25. James Hennesey, S.J., *American Catholics: A History of the Roman Catholic*

Community in the United States (New York,: Oxford University Press, 1981), p. 73.

26. Fogel and Engermann, *op.cit.*, pp. 52–57.

27. Genovese, *op.cit.*, p. 391.

28. Letter of certain members of the Catholic Clergy in Maryland, April 25, 1788, Item no. 2 KO 4, MPA, Box 2, Folder 4.

29. John Carroll, "Response to Patrick Smyth," in Hanley, editor, *JCP*, I, pp. 337–346.

30. Proceedings of the RCC, May 15, 1789, Item no. 2N 7–10, Box 2, Folder 6, MPA.

31. Ira Berlin, *Slaves Without Masters: The Free Negro in the Antebellum South* (New York: The New Press, 1974), pp. 80–81.

32. *Ibid.*, p. 81.

33. Genovese, *op.cit.*, pp. 519–523.

34. Herbert G. Gutman, *The Black Family in Slavery and Freedom, 1750–1925* (New York: Random House, Vintage Books Edition, 1976), pp. 198–199.

35. Mobberly, "Diary, Part I: Systems," BJMSJP.

36. John Carroll to Leonard Antonelli, March 1, 1785, in Hanley, editor, *JCP*, I, pp. 180–181

37. Brother Joseph Mobberly, S.J. to Father Giovanni Grassi, S.J., Summer 1812, Item no. 203 C12, Box 57.5, Folder 3, MPA.

38. Records of Bohemia Plantation, 1790–1799, Box 1, Folder 1, Maryland Province Collection (MPC), Special Collections Division, Lauinger Library, Georgetown University, Washington, D.C. Note that this is a different collection from the MPA.

39. *Ibid.*

40. *Ibid.*

41. Fogel, *op.cit.*, p. 68.

42. John Carroll to John Thayer, January 13, 1794, in Hanley, editor, *JCP*, II, pp. 108–109.

43. John Carroll to John Thayer, July 15, 1794, in Hanley, editor, *JCP*, II, pp. 122–123.

44. Proceedings of the RCC, May 5, 1801, Item no. 91.1, Box 24, Folder 1, MPA.

45. Berlin, *op.cit.*, p. 95.

46. Eugene D. Genovese, *The Slaveholders' Dilemma; Freedom and Progress in Southern Conservative Thought, 1820–1860* (Columbia: University of South Carolina Press, 1992), p. 49.

47. Proceedings of the RCC, Whitemarsh, May 23, 1803, Item no. 91.1, Box 24, Folder 1, MPA.

48. Proceedings of the RCC, April 25, 1804, Item no. 91.1, Box 24, Folder 1, MPA.

49. Proceedings of the RCC, Whitemarsh, July 9–11, 1805, Item no. 91.1, Box

24, Folder1, MPA.

50. John Carroll to Francis Neale, November 12, 1805, in Hanley, editor, *JCP*, II, p. 497.

51. John Carroll to James Barry, July 21, 1806, in Hanley, editor, *JCP*, II, p. 521.

52. Jay P. Dolan, *The American Catholic Experience: A History from Colonial Times to the Present* (Garden City, N.Y.: Doubleday, 1985), p. 123.

53. Genovese, *Roll, Jordan, Roll*, p. 4.

54. Proceedings of the RCC, Georgetown, May 12 and October 4, 1808, Item #91.1, Box 24, Folder 1, MPA.

55. Proceeding of the RCC, Georgetown, June 26, 1809, Item no. 91.1, Box 24, Folder 1, MPA.

56. Proceedings of the RCC, Georgetown, May 17, 1813, Item no. 91.1, Box 24, Folder 1, MPA.

57. Proceedings of the RCC, Georgetown, September 14, 1813, Item no. 91.1,Box 24, Folder 1, MPA.

58. Proceedings of the RCC, Georgetown, October 26, 1813, Item no. 91.1, Box 24, Folder 1, MPA.

59. Proceedings of the RCC, Georgetown, June 14, 1814, Item no. 91.2, Box 24, Folder 2, MPA Folder 2.

60. Catholic Bishops of the United States, "Pastoral Letter of the Second Plenary Council of Baltimore," 1866, in Hugh J. Nolan, editor, *Pastoral Letters of the American Hierarchy, 1792–1870* (Huntington, Ind.: Our Sunday Visitor, Inc., 1971), p. 157.

61. "39., From the Letters of Father Giovanni Grassi, S.J. to the Vatican on Slavery in the American South, 1818," in Kenneth J. Zanca, editor, *American Catholics and Slavery, 1789–1866: An Anthology of Primary Documents* (Lanham, Md.: University Press of America, 1994), pp. 114–115.

62. Father Peter Kenney, S.J. to Father John McElroy, S.J., March 30, 1822, Item no. 205 Z10a, Box 60, Folder 17, MPA.

63. Father Peter Kenney, S.J., "Statement of Religious Discipline," 1820, Item no. XT1–2, Box 126, Folder 7, MPA.

64. "39. From the Letters of Father Antonio Grassi, S.J., to the Vatican on Slavery in the American South, 1818," in Zanca, editor, *American Catholics and Slavery*, pp. 114–115.

65. Genovese, *The Slaveholders' Dilemma: Freedom and Progress in Southern Conservative Thought 1820–1860* (Columbia: University of South Carolina Press, 1992), pp. 3–4.

66. *Ibid.*

67. Brother Joseph Mobberly, S.J., to Father Giovanni Antonio Grassi, S.J., February 5, 1815; Box 58, Folder 7, MPA.

68. Proceedings of the RCC, St. Thomas' Manor, August 22, 1820, Item no. 91.2, Box 24, Folder 2, MPA.

69. Barbara Jeanne Fields, *Slavery and Freedom on the Middle Ground:*

Maryland During the Nineteenth Century (New Haven: Yale University Press, 1985), pp. 1–4.

70. Berlin, *op.cit.*, p. 101.

71. Stampp, *op.cit.*, pp. 232–235.

72. John Carroll, "Last Will and Testament, November 22, 1815," in Hanley, editor, *JCP*, III, p. 371.

73. Robert Emmett Curran, S.J., *The Bicentennial History of Georgetown University, I: From Academy to University, 1789–1889* (Washington, D.C.: Georgetown University Press, 1993), p. 119.

74. Peter Kenney, S.J., Statement of Religious Discipline," 1820, Item no. XTI-2, Box 126, Folder 7, MPA.

75. Curran, *Bicentennial History*, p. 100.

76. Robert Emmett Curran, S.J., " 'Spendid Poverty': Jesuit Slaveholding in Maryland, 1805–1838," in Randall M. Miller and Jon L. Wakelyn, editors, *Catholics in the Old South: Essays on Church and Culture* (Macon, Ga.: Mercer University Press, 1983), p. 142.

77. Archbishop Ambrose Marechal to Leonard Edelin, S.J., June 8 and June 22, 1819, Box 59, Folder 10, MPA.

78. Archbishop Ambrose Marechal to Peter DeVos, S.J., January 15, 1827, Catholic Historical Manuscripts Collection (CHMC), Box 2, Folder 8, Special Collections Division, Lauinger Library, Georgetown University, Washington, D.C.

79. Spalding, *op. cit.*,p. 84.

80. William Lee Miller, *Arguing About Slavery: The Great Battle in the United States Congress* (New York: Alfred A. Knopf, 1996), p.14.

81. Mobberly, "Diary, Part I: Systems," BJMSJP.

82. John Chester Miller, *The Wolf by the Ears: Thomas Jefferson and Slavery* (Charlottesville: The University Press of Virginia, 1991 Edition), pp. 277–278.

83. Stanley Elkins, *Slavery: A Problem in American Institutional and Intellectual Life* (Chicago: The University of Chicago Press, Third Edition, 1976), pp. 52–80.

CHAPTER FOUR

Preaching versus Practice: Jesuit Theory and Conduct of Slaveholding

On Christmas Day, 1750, Father John Lewis, S.J. (1721–1788) celebrated the Lord's Nativity in Maryland for the first time since arriving from England to serve as a missionary in the Chesapeake—an occupation that would fill the remainder of his life. Lewis' sermon that day revealed one of his strong first impressions of the Maryland colony and its Catholic planter community. The young priest declared that the poverty of Christ in the manger was a rebuke to their status seeking. He urged them to "learn a true + real contempt for all ye goods of ye world, since he who is ye wisdom of God has rejected and despised them as false and counterfeit."[1]

However, this rebuke to the slaveowning class did not make Lewis an abolitionist. Rather, he advocated that masters retain their slaves but treat them more charitably. In another homily, delivered in "preparing you for the coming celebration of ye forming of J. XT. in human flesh" during Advent, 1761, Lewis admonished masters to conform themselves more fully to the humanity of Jesus by treating slaves like members of their families. "Abhor ye unchristian practice of treating them with contempt and loading them with injurious language."[2]

Lewis' sermon pointed to a problem in which Jesuits themselves shared. Their rhetoric constantly promoted moderate and kind treatment for slaves, yet their own slaveholding was as harsh as any other form of the practice. Were there aspects of Jesuit spirituality that gave rise to such an inconsistency? The answer is that in their preoccupation to balance their Catholic and Anglo-American identities, the Jesuits ignored aspects of their own spirituality which could have been developed into support for abolition.

This question takes on pertinence when the spirituality and practice of people like John Lewis is compared with those of his near contemporary, the

Quaker theologian John Woolman (1720–1772).[3] Woolman both practiced and preached a spirituality that called for the abolition of slaveholding.

As a similar encounter did for Lewis in Maryland, Woolman's first experience of the slaveholding South on a trip through Maryland, Virginia and North Carolina in 1746 instilled a conviction that riches were corrupting. Woolman subsequently reflected that "wise instructions, a good example, and a knowledge of some honest employment" were better legacies than the snare of material treasures, "especially to them who, instead of being exampaled to temperance, are in all things taught to prefer the getting of riches and to eye the temporal distinctions they give as the principal business of this life."[4]

Yet, Woolman reached an entirely different conclusion than Lewis did as to the morality of slaveholding. Woolman concluded that it violated the golden rule, that it did unto others what slaveholders would surely not want done to themselves. Speaking of "the general disadvantage which these poor Africans lie under in an enlightened Christian country," Woolman declared that "To seek a remedy by continuing the oppression . . . will, I apprehend, not be doing as we would be done by."[5] Thus Woolman became an early advocate of abolition. Jesuits upheld slaveholding, while Quakers did not.

The spirituality and theology of the Jesuits is, in fact, a much neglected key to their decision to uphold slaveholding in Maryland. These men viewed the management of their plantations and the treatment of their slaves through a prism of presuppositions and imperatives that cultivated conflicting virtues: detachment from the material world and suspicion of the acquisition of wealth on the one hand, cultivation of the vocation of slaveholders to perpetual care of their slaves on the other. The result was a unique form of slaveholding, one that centered around the good of the slave rather than the use of slaves as in the pursuit of wealth.

Jesuit slaveholding had its exceptional features: unique in its origins, unique in its conduct, and unique in its termination. This exceptionalism was anchored in the spiritual inspirations for Jesuit slaveholding, which set them apart not only from Christian abolitionists like Woolman but also from Protestant proslavery theologians. Jesuits were the only Christian masters in colonial Maryland who drew primarily on the *Spiritual Exercises* of Saint Ignatius of Loyola (1491–1556) for justification and guidance regarding slaveholding. This sixteenth century manual for the direction of prayer, written and refined by the founder of their religious order between 1522 and 1548, was the prism through which Jesuits interpreted scriptural passages regarding slavery, and the lens through which they reconstructed the moral example and pronouncements of Jesus Christ concerning the same question.

As Catholics, Jesuits disagreed with the Protestant theology of *sola scriptura*. Jesuits certainly read the Bible, but rather than feeling free to make personal interpretation of the scriptures, they relied upon books of theological and devotional commentary to provide analysis of what was found in the sacred writings. The *Spiritual Exercises* was, for all Jesuits in colonial Maryland, a major source of meditation on the tales and principles of salvation history, since they lacked the resources and the circumstances to purchase large numbers of books.[6]

Students of the Jesuit way of prayer, sometimes called Ignatian spirituality after its founder, are familiar with such thematic constructions of the *Spiritual Exercises* as the "Call of the Temporal King," the "Principle and Foundation," the "Contemplation of the Incarnation," the grace of being placed with Christ on the cross, the meditation on "The Two Standards," the "Three Degrees of Humility" and the *Suscipe* Prayer. The various scripture texts proposed for consideration during the thirty-day retreat are classified according to their pertinence to one or another of these themes.

What united these individual exercises was what Ignatius regarded as the basic spiritual principle: that growth of the soul could only occur in proportion to conversion from self-love, self-will, and self-concern.[7] In other words, the golden rule was as important to Ignatius as it was to John Woolman. This fact only increases the fascination that Maryland Jesuits and Woolman made different applications of that precept when it came to slaveholding.

A major reason that the *Spiritual Exercises* became important for Jesuit slaveholding was that Ignatius regarded his book as a manual for making practical daily decisions as well as momentous and longterm ones. His "rules for perceiving and knowing in some manner the different movements which are caused in the soul" were designed for communal as well as individual decision making.[8] The ideal was to reassess constantly whether or not a particular habit brought the Society of Jesus and all its members closer to God. Under these norms, colonial Jesuits discerned their belief that slaveholding led both its practicioners and its objects to the Lord.

From these principles of discernment came not only the Jesuit rhetoric that slavery must be conducted with moderation, but also their rationalizations concerning the less edifying tasks of the slaveowner. The best manner to approach Jesuit thought about slaveholding, therefore, is to begin with their sermons, later augmenting this testimony with data from Jesuits' private correspondence and papers and some oral testimony recorded in the early twentieth century.[9] Overall, these records reveal a public emphasis on kind governance that masked a private harshness.

An instructive way to study the typical setting of Jesuit sermons is to compare the circumstances of their preparation and delivery with parallel data concerning Puritan sermons in colonial New England. Maryland was a religiously diverse colony whose Catholic priests maintained political discretion for the sake of sustaining religious toleration. Massachusetts was a theocracy under the Puritans; its Congregational ministers were expected to speak on public policy in the pulpit. On any particular Sunday, Jesuits spoke on texts mandated for all priests in the world for that week by the papacy. The Roman Catholic

Church had an international common lectionary for each Sunday of the liturgical year that remained constant from 1570 to 1970, only to be supplanted then by a new common lectionary. Puritan ministers, enjoying a much greater degree of local autonomy, were able to choose their own texts of scripture, and often devoted considerable care to choosing a particular book of the Bible, whose exegesis they developed verse-by-verse and week-by-week over an extended series of sermons.[10] The Catholic sermon structure lent itself to the preservation of tradition, while the Puritan sermon structure was more likely to encourage radical social reform like the abolition of slavery.

The contrast between Jesuit and Puritan sermons also reveals that the Jesuits spoke to congregations accustomed to regarding religion as a matter of discreet private devotion to be separated from public political questions, while the Puritans spoke to a culture which regarded the Congregational Church as the cornerstone of both private and public life. In 1705, Maryland Jesuits were pleased when Queen Anne recognized the right of Catholics to hold Mass in private, giving them an exemption from English penal law.[11] The Queen's condescension was a further incentive for Jesuits to internalize the political philosophy of Robert Persons and Edmund Campion that there should be a strict division of function between church and state, with slavery assigned to the state's sphere. The implication of this policy for Jesuit sermons on slaveholding was that these manuscripts ignored the issues of whether to establish or abolish slavery. Instead, they took the existence of the practice for granted and concentrated on morally acceptable ways to conduct or live under the practice.

There were different atmospheres in the private Catholic chapels on the Maryland manors and the public Puritan churches on the New England village commons. "Occasional sermons" addressed every significant social, political and religious issue facing New England on such important occasions of state as fast days, election days and mustering days.[12] In Maryland, Jesuits spoke only on Sundays and the ancient feast days of the Church and confined themselves to the Church's theme of the day. They were silent regarding the great questions of state.

When slavery was mentioned in a Jesuit sermon, it was because it was pertinent to the scripture text assigned to the occasion by the Roman Missal. Puritans interpreted Scripture according to a theology of covenant, in which individuals and nations were called to transform the world according to God's will.[13] Maryland Jesuits had a less ambitious goal, the survival of their Church and its practices in a hostile environment. They had no wish to transform Maryland if that were to generate a backlash against Catholicism.

These differences highlighted the Jesuits' loyalty to the Catholic hierarchy. Just as they would not defy the Church by displacing its common lectionary, so too they would not challenge it by dissenting from the universal teaching that slaveholding, in itself, was morally acceptable.

Bennett Neale, S.J. (1709–1787), writing sometime after his arrival in

Maryland in 1742, showed just how deeply Jesuits internalized their discretion. Neale reminded his congregations that all political ambitions must be subordinated to the spiritual: "God has not called us to ye government of kingdoms and empires: he has quite other designs upon us, and tho he had charged us with state affairs . . . yet this were only a vain and empty and accidental employ, a trivial affair if compared with our own salvation."[14] In other words, Catholics should stay out of great political controversies not only because of the risk of alienating their Protestant neighbors, but also because such preoccupation would mean separation from God himself. In this way, a practical necessity was converted into a spiritual virtue.

The typical Jesuit-written sermon was redelivered often, in many different places throughout the widely scattered farms of rural Maryland. Jesuits of the colonial period combined two activities, working as priest planters on their own farms and as circuit riding priests throughout the countryside. Catholics who lived in the immediate neighborhood of a Jesuit plantation would visit it for confessions and Sunday Mass, at the conclusion of which service a sermon would always serve the ongoing instruction of Christian doctrine.[15] Many Catholics lived too far away to make that journey themselves, however, so Jesuits subsequently rode to those distant outposts on horseback, pursuing an apostolic goal that each Catholic in the colony should have access to the ministry of a priest at least once a month. Moreover, the legal situation from 1705 to 1776 required that Catholic worship be held on private property only, confining the delivery of these sermons to the chapels and fields of Catholic-owned plantations.[16]

Besides the structure of the lectionary and the taboo on discussion of public events, another incentive for Jesuits to recyle these sermons was that they had little access to theology books for fresh research. There was no Catholic printing press in British North America; books could only be imported from Europe at great expense. A further barrier was that it was difficult to obtain Catholic books through Protestant England. The correspondence of Joseph Mosley, S.J. (1731–1787; in Maryland from 1758) indicates that he relied on the generosity of his sister in Bladon, near Newcastle-upon-Tyne, England, Mrs. Helen Dunn, to purchase an occasional text for him. Once he received any book it was shared among the Catholic community, passing from household to household.[17]

Whenever a Jesuit sermon is mentioned, the date or dates for delivery of a specific sermon manuscript are noted, if available. Otherwise, the dates that an individual Jesuit lived or was active in Maryland are noted as the next best approximations of when they composed and spoke.

The most basic and distinctive tenet of Jesuit spirituality is found at the very beginning of the *Spiritual Exercises*. It is the conviction that God is somehow present in all things.[18] Ignatius' expression of this conviction is called the "Principle and Foundation."

core tenet of Jesuit theology

> Man is created to . . . serve God our Lord. . . . And the other things on the face of the earth are created for man and that they may help him in prosecuting the end for which he is created. From this it follows that man is to use them as much as they help him on to his end, and ought to rid himself of them so far as they hinder him as to it.[19]

A good example of the "Principle and Foundation" at work in the lives of Maryland Jesuits was their speedy ability to abandon their aspirations to build a model Christian society among the Indians of the colony in favor of the discreet, privatized practice of Catholicism among white planters and African slaves. The desire to create a transformed, fully Christian society motivated the very first Jesuits who volunteered to go to Maryland.[20] Yet they quicky abandoned such Utopian schemes in order to accommodate themselves to the political reality of the new colony, in which the Proestant majority constantly watched for the slightest hint of a Catholic ascendancy.[21] An English willingness to govern through compromise and broad consensus combined with the adaptability Ignatius urged upon all Christians in the "Principle and Foundation" to create a pronounced practicality in Jesuits who actually made it to Maryland.

What the "Principle and Foundation" meant was that every material good at a Christian's disposal, every circumstance in which he had a choice of how to act, had to be reassessed constantly for its utility in drawing its possessor or actor closer to salvation. If a practice was not specifically banned in scripture, then Jesuits were free to pick it up or discard it according to their ongoing sense of whether it was practically helpful at the moment or not. Slavery was such a practice: it was mentioned many times in Scripture without an explicit condemnation of any kind. Instead, the emphasis of the Biblical author who most influenced the Jesuits on the subject, Paul, was on how to construct a just relationship between master and slave. Since the question was the salvation of the masters as well as that of the slaves, the focus was on the totality of the relationship, not just on the status of the slave.

In using some object according to the "Principle and Foundation," the goal for the Jesuit was to use it as Jesus would have used it. The way to achieve salvation was to become Christlike in behavior. This interpretation of the "Principle and Foundation" led the Maryland Jesuits, in their search for paradigms of Christ-like behavior, to the two Scriptural passages which most influenced their sense of the master-slave relationship. Both were from Paul: Philippians 2: 5–11 and Ephesians 5:21–6: 12. Philippians taught that the way to imitate Jesus was to make oneself a slave to God the Father as he had done. Ephesians discussed various ways to apply this goal through one's conduct within the relationships one found oneself in in life, whether that be husband-wife, parent-child, ruler-subject, master-slave, etc. Both passages mentioned slavery explicitly and approvingly, so Jesuits felt that here was explicit divine sanction for slaveholding.

The preeminence of this Pauline theology in Jesuit proslavery thought contrasts with the scriptural passages chosen by John Woolman to develop his abolitionist theology. For Woolman, the central opponent of slavery among the authors of scripture was the evangelist Matthew. He cited Matthew 12: 48–50, in which Jesus stressed that his family was formed of all who did his will rather than his biological relatives. He also reflected on Matthew 6:33, in which Jesus elevated the pursuit of the kingdom and its justice above pursuing a material security that God alone should be trusted to provide. Woolman felt that masters would be especially subject to the measure of the last judgment in Matthew 25, that whatever they did or did not do for the slaves would be regarded as if it were treatment of Christ himself. For Woolman, the epitome of Matthew's moral theology was the golden rule in Chapter 7:12: "Do unto others as you would have them do unto you."

Woolman also cited two passages from the Hebrew Scriptures. One was Genesis 3:20, that Eve became the mother of all the living. He interpreted this as a radical statement of the fundamental equality of peoples, a dignity which the practice of some people holding others in bondage denied. There was also Leviticus 19: 33–34, a passage which called for hospitality to the alien.[22]

For Woolman, these verses basically formed a "canon within a canon." They were standards against which he measured and subordinated all the remaining scriptures. In these explicit calls for universal brotherhood, he found implicit condemnations of slavery. Thus Woolman used his favorite verses to overrule those passages elsewhere in Scripture which seemed to to approve slavery explicitly.

In Woolman's text, he also developed a comparison between African slaves and the role of the Gentiles in the book of Acts. A central theme in Acts was the conversion of Jewish Christians, especially the apostle Peter, to the idea that God wished to include non-Jews in his kingdom. He wanted to extend the same inclusivity to African slaves.[23] In all these instances, Woolman worked according to the Protestant principle of the individual Christian's right to private interpretation of the Bible. Ironically, it was the Jesuits who were the Biblical fundamentalists by comparison, for they refused to abandon slaveholding due to its apparent direct sanction in the Bible. Not all advocates of *sola scriptura* were Protestant.

Against Woolman's broad range of texts, the Jesuit focus on Paul looks narrow indeed—but also more obvious. The Jesuit approach may also be compared with a much later Protestant treatise, written in 1841 as a typical example of antebellum proslavery theology. This was Thornton Stringfellow's "A Brief Examination of Scripture Testimony on the Institution of Slavery." About half of the thirty pages of this manuscript were devoted to a discussion of Old Testament sanctions of slavery. When he did discuss Paul, Stringfellow accorded nearly equal treatment to Peter, in this case in order to prove that the same teachings favoring slavery were preached to both Gentiles and Jews. Stringfellow also considered Jesus' own attitudes concerning slavery, arguing that his silence on the subject showed that he accepted the existence of slavery in the Roman Empire.[24]

In contrast to Stringfellow's reflection on the silence of Jesus, the Jesuits concentrated on some words of Paul. While they ignored the letter to Philemon, they particularly emphasized the letters to the Philippians, Ephesians and the Colossians.

In the brief, one-chapter letter to Philemon, Paul's major concern is a runaway slave named Onesimus whom he apparently desires to see set free. This is the only book in the Bible whose principle topic is the social institutions of slaveholding and slavery, which makes it astonishing that the Maryland Jesuits paid it little mind. It is also one of Paul's letters which is addressed to an individual rather than a community, and is personally addressed to a slaveholder. Onesimus, who seeks refuge with Paul after escaping from Philemon, is now being returned by Paul to his owner. A recent scriptural commentary notes that the letter is valuable because its demonstration of how Paul applied his views about slaveholding to a particular case.[25]

Paul decides not to order Philemon what to do with Onesimus, but to rely on Philemon's own free will and disposition to love in the spirit of Christ to guide his treatment of the returned runaway. Paul argues that Onesimus was taken from Philemon for a time so that he might return not as his slave but as his brother. The implication is that Paul wants them to renew their relationship so that Philemon and Onesimus will be essentially equal to one another, two brothers united in the same Christ. Strikingly, there is no reference to Philemon in the texts of the Jesuit sermon collection.

Philippians is placed after Ephesians in the Catholic arrangement of the New Testament, but it is good to consider it first in an analysis of Jesuit slaveholding. This letter is a summary of the character of Jesus, which is significant because of the extremely Christological nature of Ignatian spirituality. Three of the four weeks of the *Spiritual Exercises* are devoted to intense contemplation of the nature of Jesus—Jesus as minister in the second week, Jesus as crucified in the third week, Jesus as risen in the fourth. Always, the retreatant seeks to become Jesus' companion and to become as much like him as possible. The question therefore becomes urgent: Who was—and is—this person?

Philippians provides the significant answer that the Jesus of history was a slave—moreover, a slave who freely chose his bondage. Sacrificing his godliness, he became human and died for the rescue of sinners. His subsequent exaltation was not only the Father's ratification of this sacrifice, but also a call to all Christians to act similarly. Therefore, Peter Attwood, S.J. (1682–1734), who lived in Maryland from 1712, chastised masters because "you know not how to look but with horror on those who are in humility." He also pointed out the contrast between the conduct of Jesus and the conduct of Marylanders: "it is quite the form of God to take up that of a slave, and you think on nothing, but raising yourself to something great." To make oneself "the slave of the world," Attwood concluded, was to set one's life in "strange opposition" to that of Jesus Christ. "To what purpose is J. C. annihilated so low, if you yet wake in pride and arrogance of before?"[26] It was much better to make oneself the slave of God the Father, as Jesus had done, than to make oneself the slave of the world.

This theology points to the Jesuits' own answer to "the slaveholder's dilemma," the problem of determining the connections among the concepts of freedom, slaveholding and progress. The most common proposed solution was the formula that slavery grounded the social order necessary to support the freedom required for progress.[27] This concept was also expressed by the formula "progress through freedom based on slavery."[28] For the Jesuits, the only progress that was worthwhile was spiritual and depended on both owners and slaves making of their lives a self-donation.

Attwood showed that Philippians gave the Jesuits their variation of the formula. For them, "progress through freedom based on slavery" occured through growth in the spiritual life. Spiritual freedom came about through a paradox, the decision to enslave oneself for Christ. His own liberty, the resurrection, came about only through the bondage of the cross. What resulted from cross and resurrection was the ultimate progression of the spiritual life, reconciliation with God. So, the frustrations of life were to be embraced joyously as paradoxical events leading to progress.

In searching for practical advice with which to fulfill this formula, Jesuits turned to Ephesians and Colossians. Ephesians shows two ways in which to make oneself the slave of God, through the two verses which bracket the passage which discusses slavery. The first is to enter into relationships of mutual fidelity with other Christians—"Be subordinate to one another out of reverence for Christ." (Chapter 5:21) The second is to remember the admonition of 6:12—"For our struggle is not with flesh and blood but with the principalities, with the powers, with the world rulers of this present darkness, with the evil spirits in the heavens." In other words, the essential struggle is spiritual, not material. Material bondage is of less concern to Paul in Ephesians than the possibility of spiritual bondage to sin.

Consider Paul's sense of subordinate relationships. While Paul, in Ephesians and Colossians, did assign superior and inferior roles within such relationships, making the husband superior to the wife, the parent superior to the child, and the master superior to the slave, he also emphasized that each party had to self-sacrifice in order for any such relationship to work. Whether one had the superior or inferior role, the relationship was mutally *binding* and thus a form of spiritual slavery for both parties. So, while husbands were clearly to be superior to their wives, the husband was still to love his wife with the same self-giving that Jesus gave to the Church in dying on the cross. Masters and slaves were likewise to regard service to each other as imitation of Jesus on the cross. This created a sense of ordered stewardship over slaves.

This construction might become clearer if one were to reserve the term "slavery" to the spiritual bond between the inferior and inferior parties of any relationship and reserve the word "servant" to describe someone who worked for a temporal master. Jesuits seemed to have used the words "slave" and "servant" interchangably, however, so the distinction they were making has not always been communicated clearly.

Colossians 3:22–4:1 offers a theology of slaveholding quite similar to Ephesians. Slaves are admonished to remember that in serving their temporal master, they serve Christ. The orders of the master are to be followed as if they had come directly from God. Further, these orders must be carried out even when the master is absent, for slaves have a duty to internalize their service of the Lord. Meanwhile, masters must treat the slaves uprightly and fairly. The Master of Heaven watches all and treats all fairly. There is no divine favoritism, just the expectation that each party in the master-slave relationship will do what they are called to do.

Covenant theology was important to the Puritans, covenant in the Old Testament sense of an agreement between God and an entire nation.[29] For the Maryland Jesuits, their interpretation of Ephesians set up "covenants writ small." Deprived of the chance to think nationally by their status as members of a religious minority within the colony, the Jesuits instead focused on the interpersonal relationships within the small Catholic community. Masters and servants were enslaved to each other in the sense that their service to each other created the community called Church.

When John Lewis gave a sermon that was influenced by Ephesians in 1761, he prefaced his remarks with a quotation from John 1:19—"Who are you?" In its original context, this was the question that the Jewish priests asked John the Baptist as they tried to determine if he was the Messiah. John denied that he was. Lewis, however, pointed out that for the Christian, the proper answer to this question would be not to deny being the Christ but to declare that he was Christ-like. Therefore, Lewis asked his listeners to consider how they might become like the generous Christ described in Philippians and so "be guided entirely according to ye sacred self-denying principles of the Gospel." Each state of life, Lewis argued, had its particular obligations; "tis upon a faithful compliance with these, that each one's salvation and perfection in a special manner depends."

The rich, in fact, were in a state of "formidable danger." They had better means of doing good at their disposal. Therefore, they would be judged more strictly. They had particular obligations to guard the poor and the oppressed. They were only stewards of their riches, which really belonged to God. But their servants, for their parts, owed the rich three things: faithfulness to the responsibilities placed in their hands, prompt obedience to new commands, and peace among each other.[30]

Richard Molyneux (1696–1766) served in Maryland for nearly two decades, from 1730 to 1749. He discussed the principles of Ephesians in a pre-Lenten discourse entitled "On Hearing Sermons Diligently." He admonished masters that their obligations to their charges included the duty to "be not a tyrant in your house ruining your domestics and oppressing your servants." Meanwhile, servants must remember that in serving the master they were really serving God. Then Molyneux cited an important contemporary reason why these commands must be obeyed. The Catholic Church in England's kingdom, which for Molyneux included Maryland, had fallen to small membership and the true Word of God was in danger of being lost. In such circumstances, it was crucial for the remaining Catholics to set a good moral example, which they could only do by first hearing the word preached. It would be "barbourous to ye common cause of our nation's conversion as to aggravate ys. calamity by our neglect of God's word and slight ye opportunities of hearing it."[31] Since the Jesuits had abandoned the effort to work actively for conversion, example was all they had left to spread the Church.

This emphasis on Ephesians and its evangelization by example instilled among the Jesuits an ideology of slaveholding subtly different from that fostered by other slaveholders. For many, a "self-serving designation of the slaves as a duty and a burden" combined with a philosophy of slavery as a "natural condition of labor" to become the "core of the slaveholders' self-image." [32] While the Jesuits accepted the idea that slavery was a natural condition of life, they always took a broader view of the master-slave relationship than merely the duty of the master. It was one of mutual fidelity, with rights and obligations for both parties. Furthermore, it was not a negative task for the master but a means of procuring his own salvation through paternalistic care of the souls entrusted to him. To be a master was a cross, but every cross had a resurrection.

The spirit of enslavement to God in Philippians influenced the whole Christology of the Jesuit sermons. This can be seen not only in their applications of the "Principle and Foundation," but also in their applications of another section of the *Spiritual Exercises*, the contemplation of the Incarnation. This passage makes it clear that Jesuits were to worship a God of cross and loss—not a God of gain. In this contemplation, the retreatant is asked to imagine how the divine persons of the Trinity looked over the world and saw how desperately all who lived in it needed redemption. Thus, they decided that the second person of the Trinity, the Son, must put aside his godliness to become human and subject himself to death on the cross.[33] To Ignatius, it was this self-effacing act of God's that all Christians were called to imitate.

One can never grasp the Jesuit inertia about addressing the problematic economic situation of their farms unless one understands this Ignatian attraction to the humility of Jesus Christ, the circumstances of whose birth in the poverty of the Bethlehem stable so impressed John Lewis on his first Christmas in Maryland. Chapter Two of this book has demonstrated the consistent mismanagement of the Jesuit farms. That the governance of their slaves made them poor struck Jesuits as a grace to be cherished rather than an obstacle to be overcome, for it imitated the sacrifice and suffering that Christ made by becoming human. As Peter Atwood, S.J. (1682–1734) commented, sometime during a ministry to Maryland that extended from 1712, "if you don't annihilate yourselves, you are not truly Christians."[34] This was spirituality which sought to enter into material failure rather than avoid it.

It was not just through the cross and the manner in which his life ended that Jesus was humiliated. Atwood stressed that humiliation began in the instant God became human and extended throughout his life. How debasing for the creator to take on the form of the created! Yet this event, the Incarnation, was described by Atwood as "the foundation of our religion."

Honoring Ignatius' instruction that the contemplation of the Trinity's action at the Incarnation be accompanied by a simultaneous contemplation of a maiden's consent to become the Mother of God, Atwood graphically proclaimed that the miracle of God's becoming man occurred "in the bowels of the Virgin Mary." Atwood noted that at that moment, "he who enjoyed all the treasures of the wisdom, knowledge and power of God" became instead "ignorant, poor, and weak." After quoting directly from Philippians, Atwood went on to praise God for the graciousness of that exchange. Therefore, he deplored the habit so many nominal Christians had of making themselves "slaves of the world" in "strange opposition of your life with that of J.C."[35]

Atwood's last point is telling. In his spiritual paradigm, all human destiny lay in some kind of enslavement. The question was whether it would be enslavement to God or enslavement to evil. The only choice before the human heart was what kind of master it would serve, not whether it would be slave or free. This was a perspective that made the existence of slaveholding seem like the most natural thing in the world. As long as this paradigm persisted, the issue for Jesuits was not whether slaves should be set free or not. The issue, instead, was two-fold: whether the slaves would serve God through the obedient acceptance of their bondage and, even more importantly, whether the slaves would find God through the manner in which they were treated by their masters.

The annual celebration of the birth of Jesus Christ was an opportunity to renew this understanding of slaveholding. The image of the child in the manger, bound in swaddle, was meaningful in the rural culture of colonial Maryland. Joseph Greaton, S.J. (1679–1753), writing around 1730, urged that the proud man "who exalts himself above others, who hunts worldly grandeur, who hunts after honours, dignities, and preferments" should fight these traits with a "step to Bethlee." There he could "seriously contemplate ye profound humility and contempt of ye world of our Blessed Lord." In Bethlehem, Jesus had revealed himself in debasement so far as "to assume the form of a slave, nay become a worm."[36] In 1750, John Lewis, too, urged Maryland congregations to "see and do according to ye pattern which is shown you in ye manger."[37] It was a pattern which had messages for both the poor and the wealthy.

Pragmatism may well have been the original reason for the Jesuits' decision to become discreet and private subjects in Maryland, but this move was supported by their interpretation of a contemplation of the second week of the *Spiritual Exercises* called the "Call of the Temporal King."

This exercise showed the respect Ignatius had for legitimate secular authority. Retreatants making his *Spiritual Exercises* are asked to imagine "a human king chosen by God our Lord, whom all Christian princes and men reverence and obey." This king invites all to share with him in a project "to conquer all the lands of unbelievers," stressing that those who join in his cause must share in his portion, eating, drinking, dressing, laboring and watching with him. Those who did not join in such a cause would be deservedly censured by "all the world, and held for a mean spirited knight." Ignatius then went on to remind his retreatants that if such a king was so worthy of service, Jesus Christ was even worthier of being followed.[38]

Ignatius' temporal king is pursuing a goal completely compatible with Christianity, the conquest of unbelievers. So the call for the retreatant here is not that he repudiate the temporal king but that he realize the subtle role of Christ in motivating what is good in the intentions of this king. This "conquest" need not be taken literally, as a strictly military exercise. Ignatius was a soldier prior to his religious conversion, and he continued to use martial imagery throughout his theological writing. The use of the concept "conquest" here was symbolic of the winning over of hearts to Christ. In the ideal of Lord Baltimore—that there be a society where all might privately practice their religion—the Jesuits saw some possiblity of achieving such a conquest through setting an example of Catholic docility and cooperation with the temporal order. Thus, they were willing to privatize religion and emphasize obedience to the state so long as the state left Catholic religious practice alone.

In the Catholic heritage, the opening of the liturgical year on the First Sunday of Advent is an annual reminder of the Last Judgment and how they will be held accountable for the various tasks they were called to perform in life. James Ashby, S.J. (1714–1767) declared on one such occasion that "We are all accountable for others in some sort as well as ourselves." Thus, the magistrate would have to answer for "ye power put into his hands for the administration of justice" while the subject would have to answer for "his behaviour to those in authority."[39] This was a classic example of the Jesuit sense that unequal social relationships were still ones of mutual obligations.

The consequences for slaveholding are obvious. Not only would the slave be expected to be obedient to the master, but the master would be expected to be loyal to the slave. One can never grasp why the Jesuits found it difficult to end their slaveholding unless one grasps this point: this loyalty meant strong paternal care over their slaves. In this, they were like many other slaveowners, both Catholic and Protestant. However, unlike most slaveowners, the Jesuits themselves had no personal autonomy. Even as they governed their slaves, they had to answer to authorities in the form of the rulers of the Catholic Church. Since popes, bishops and generals of the Society of Jesus all sanctioned slaveholding, the Jesuits felt obliged by their own betters to continue the practice.

In this hierarchical view of the Church, there was always someone for the Jesuit slaveowner to submit to himself. A Christmas sermon prepared by John Lewis in 1767, used the Nativity to make this point. He began by asking "Has Jesus Christ laid himself low enough for your example?" He then acknowledged that Christ indeed enjoyed a choice in this matter: he could have freely entered the world "all in glory and majesty" if he had so wished. This raised a conundrum which Lewis believed that Saint Bernard had first identified during the Middle Ages: either Christ was mistaken in his choice of poverty over riches or the world was mistaken in *its* choice of riches over poverty. To Lewis, the drama of moral life was the imperative that one take a stand either against or for Christ. He believed that many people preferred to admire Christ only at a distance, drawing away in fear when he came near in dread of the prospect that his approach might introduce material poverty into their households.[40] So, Lewis found in the example and mandate of Christ ample discouragement from the pursuit of profit.

At Christmas, 1771, Matthias Manners, S.J. (1719–1775) marveled that "the angels of Heaven sing glory to God" at the poverty and misery of the newborn Savior. That paradox, however, was "ye mystery of this day: a poor infant destitute of all human means and forsaken by all replenishes the heavenly quires of angels with joy." This was an "opposite way of seeking glory" from that customarily sought by men, who liked "such supports of their vanity and misery" as numerous attendants. By his birth, in contrast, Jesus "most powerfully triumphs over those vices, which keep men slaves to ye devil." He concluded, significantly, that "what Jesus did to save us we must do to be saved by Jesus."[41]

Matthias' mockery of men who liked the prestige of numerous attendants was not a call for manumission. Rather, it was a call to greater social responsibility toward the slaves. To Jesuits, slaves were possessed not for the good of the master, but for the good of the slave. God had given the slaves to the master because these people needed to be governed by someone of higher wisdom and social status if they were to achieve eternal salvation. The master was required to govern them in the spirit of that realization. It was an example of what Ignatius called a "right intention": to do a good thing for a proper reason rather than a good thing for a wrong reason.

The minority of Catholic priests in Maryland who did not belong to the

Society of Jesus were influenced by the Jesuit admiration for enslavement to God. Germain Barnabas Bitouzey, whose birth and death dates are unknown, was a diocesan priest who fled the French Revolution to work in Maryland from 1794 to 1815. A sermon possibly written for New Year's Day, 1798, featured Bitouzey's praise for an event of Christ's infancy, his circumcision. The humility which Jesus showed in submitting himself "to so painful and ignominious a ceremony" was an antidote to the pride of those who aspired to wealth and power. Bitouzey believed that Christ was eager that the example set by this submission to the law of Moses would inspire all to further their own salvation by fostering similar humility in their own lives.

To Bitouzey, each deed of Christ was designed to destroy some vice in the human soul. Christians were to watch what Jesus did in each instance, record how opposite to his their own behavior typically was, and then proceed to convert themselves to Christ's pattern.[42] Bitouzey and the Jesuits were impressed that the circumcision of Christ showed his obedience to the old covenant. As God, Jesus certainly could have set aside the Jewish law, but he did not. Furthermore, as a subject of the Roman Empire, Jesus obeyed the temporal order in which he found himself living. All this obedience was an example to those who might have wished to change the laws and customs of Maryland.

The Jesuits believed that one of the best ways to develop fidelity to the example of Jesus was through the frequent reception of Holy Communion. Praise for this practice was a frequent theme of their sermons.[43] How did frequent Communion affect Jesuit slaveholding? Bernard Diderich (1726–1773), in a sermon prepared most likely between 1775 and 1787, stated that "Crimes multiply, in ye same proportion that Communions diminish." Significantly, he recounted that one such crime was abuse of slaves. "A child, a servant has committed a small oversight, and presently the parents or master puts all ye house into an uproar and ferment . . . tremble . . . ye unhappy victims thereof."[44]

Diderich believed that Communion's grace would soften a master's personality so that he became docile like Christ, and would therefore look upon the poor as benevolently as Christ had. That he saw physical abuse of slaves as a danger suggests that perhaps Diderich or some other Jesuits struggled against such tendencies themselves.

It was not an accident that Diderich equated slaves with children. Jesuits believed that the two groups shared an intrinsic need for care by others. The point of Diderich's sermon, however, was that the masters had an obligation to be humane in their proceeding. Jesuits could set an example in this regard.

At the opposite end of Christ's life from his Incarnation was his cross. Contemplation of the crucifixion played just as large a role in the *Spiritual Exercises* as contemplation of the Incarnation did. In the third week, the retreatant was invited to join in the sufferings of Christ, to feel the same sorrow and bondage and helplessness that the Lord himself felt during the Passion.[45] This attitude, that it is a grace to join Christ in chains, is an intriguing clue as to why the Jesuits remained dutifully chained to their unprofitable plantations and slaveholdings for so long.

Joseph Greaton (1679–1753) delivered a sermon in 1728 entitled "Whipps and Thorns," in which he praised the example of Jesus' willingness to accept an unjust and unreasonable sentence of death. Furthermore, the mode of his death was "ye common punishment of ye vilest of slaves, yet Christ joyfully accepted it." Because Jesus shared their condition by sharing it, even to the point of being flogged, the condition of slavery was given a new dignity.

Greaton favorably contrasted the behavior of Christ with that of Samson in the Old Testament, who broke out of his cords to kill his oppressors. Christ certainly had the power to do the same, "but his hands were faster bound with fetters of love."[46]

This was a lesson to slaves. Greaton wanted them to act more like Christ than like Samson, and thereby abandon any thought of an uprising. Moreover, rumors frequently swept British America that Catholics incited slave revolts.[47] Greaton's sermon may have been a public attempt to remind both slaves and Protestant neighbors that the Jesuits were not subversives.

Greaton's message, however, was for masters as well. Love may have been the virtue that bound slaves to their masters, but it was also the virtue that chained masters to their slaves. Masters had the freedom of Samson, and could rid themselves of slaves if they so desired. If they wished to be more like Christ, however, they would accept their obligations to their slaves in the spirit with which Christ born the cross.

James Farrar, S.J. (1707–1763) saw the annual season of Lent as an opportunity to remind his congregation to unite themselves to Jesus' sacrifice. In doing so, he recalled for them the one form of slavery that the Church of the eighteenth century unequivocally regarded as evil, spiritual bondage to Satan. Farrar hoped that all would reform their lives once they had pondered the "memory of our Savior's sufferings . . . what . . . he underwent to redeem us from sin and the slavery of the Devil."[48]

Farrar believed that people's social condition would not count when they came before God for judgment. Only the resemblance of one's behavior to Christ would count. Farrar emphasized that all were "all equally sharers of the sacrifice and merits of his death." Thus all were also "equally in power to benefit ourselves and apply those, his merits, to our own advantage."[49] This was an argument against an egalitarian society. Why bother to right inequalities of material status when everyone already had equality where it really counted, in spiritual matters?

This was a subtle difference from Calvinist theologies of predestination, which led many people to attempt to sort out just who was saved. John Calvin himself recognized the danger of people thinking that they themselves, and not God alone, could distinguish the saved from the damned.[50] Such a mindset encouraged the drawing of sharp distinctions between various peoples at every level of life. Such an attitude influenced many English settlers in their dealings with other races.[51] English Jesuits, however, were more Catholic than English on this question. They believed that there was a radical egalitarianism before the fall of Adam which was marred by his sin but never completely destroyed, remaining latently in force at the spiritual level and awaiting its renewed manifestation at the Second Coming of Christ. Thus the slaves had a dignity that their servile status could not mar.

However, their theology required Jesuits to address parts of scripture that could be interpreted as teaching that material bondage was evil. On such book was Exodus, an enormous source of hope for slaves.[52] James Farrar showed that Jesuits were aware of Exodus' implications. During Lent, 1743, Farrar dismissed the abolitionist interpretation of Israel's flight from Egypyt. Farrar's response was to explain that at a deeper level, Passover actually prefigured the Eucharist and its remembrance "of that never to be forgotten redemption from a worse than Egyptian slavery, the sin and eternal misery which the Son of God . . . delivered us from."[53] Farrar thus denied any suggestion that the story of Moses was in any way a universal condemnation of material bondage. Rather, it was an allegory of the deliverance of the soul from spiritual slavery.

Farrar's message was also a reminder to masters, however, that the cruelty of the Egyptians was not an example for Christian slaveholders. The cross called them to paternal responsibility, but underneath lay an essential sameness of soul before the Lord. The devotion of "creeping to the cross" symbolized this spiritual equality of rulers and ruled. Leonard Neale, S.J. (1747–1817), described this practice. Each member of the congregation crawled before the crucifix on hands and knees, offering in one hand a representation of the serpent which had tempted Adam and Eve at the fall. In offering this symbol of sinfulness to Christ, the pilgrim expressed gratitude for his redemption.[54] Creeping to the cross took place in congregations composed of both masters and slaves. It is striking to think of the masters crawling on the ground in the presence of their slaves.

In the *Spiritual Exercises*, a meditation called "The Two Standards" signifies the Jesuit ambivalence about wealth. Retreatants are invited to compare the ideals of Christ and those of the devil. To Ignatius, three choices were required between Christ and Lucifer: poverty against riches, contempt against worldly honor, and humility against pride. Retreatants are invited to ask for material poverty, if God's "Majesty would be served and would want to choose them."[55] These points provide one explanation as to why the Jesuits let their plantations linger in economic disarray for so many decades.

As a result of this meditation, Jesuits mistrusted the ability of anyone rich to avoid the moral dangers of wealth. However, they also mistrusted the ability of the poor to see their own state as one of blessing. It was one thing to choose to become poor out of a sense of religious conviction, quite another to have it thrust upon you by circumstance. Jesuits, therefore, spent much time trying to persuade their slaves to internalize their poverty as God's gift.

James Beadnall, S.J. (1718–1772), in a sermon delivered several times between 1755 and 1767, illustrated the similar moral challenge that faced both rich and poor despite contrasting appearances. He began by discussing the plight of a hypothetical elderly plantation owner who had made the pursuit of riches the primary aim of his life: "Behold ye old planter grown pale + wane. See his hollow eyes, sunben cheeks + shrivelled visage." This man had spent himself physically, but now had no spiritual resources to turn to for compensation in his old age. Beadnall believed that had this planter cultivated the Ignatian indifference toward wealth that was described in the two standards meditation, he would have had more serenity.

Beadnall also believed that the slave could become similarly misfocused if he counted on pleasing his master to the exclusion of working to please God. His hypothetical slave ended up "both decreped and old, maim'd in his limbs + shattered in his body" due to seeking "only a pitiful applause, the love of his master."[56] He, too, had gotten into trouble by neglecting to place God before all else. That was the ultimate lesson of the two standards meditation—that whatever one's condition in life, the moral challenge was to place God at the center of it.

To Beadnall, the slave must measure the commands of his master against the commandments—in other words, develop enough power of discernment that he could tell when the master was asking him to contradict the will of God. While the slave needed religious instruction in order to do so, Jesuits believed he would ultimately to be able to make his own choice.

Beadnall here expressed the paradox that lay at the heart of Jesuit slaveholding. On the one hand, their respect for the human dignity of the slave compelled these churchmen to portray the slave publicly as someone who should be taught, as much as was possible, to interact with God as a free spiritual and moral agent. On the other hand, this internal autonomy of the soul was not to be accompanied by any material freedom—disobeying the master regarding some specific conscience issue did not mean that the slave should go free alltogether. It is possible that some Jesuits saw the slaves as schizophrenic personalities.[57] However, it was the Jesuits themselves who may have been schizophrenic in their thinking about the slaves.

Beadnall and other Jesuits tried to resolve the tension between spiritual freedom and material bondage by calling for a cooperative interaction between master and slave. Each should understand the other's role and they should work together, but within a hierarchical relationship which would place the master in the superior role. Jesuits of Beadnall's era were willing to concede that blacks and whites were spiritually equal before God, but they saw continued social inequality as the only means by which the slaves could attain their religious potential.

Many proslavery writers did not directly challenge the philosophy of equal rights that began to emerge in late colonial America. They were either unable, unwilling, or afraid to do so, and tried to avoid the question by limiting discussion to the topic of equality among white men.[58] Beadnall's sermon demonstrates that Jesuit proslavery writers straddled rather than avoided the debate about whether Africans were humans with full rights, conceding them equality only in the spiritual sphere. It was a tactic which subtly undermined slavery by exposing the contradiction between interior liberty and exterior bondage, but only subtly, for Jesuits did not explicitly propose that slavery was inherently wrong.

Jesuits believed that masters and slaves were morally alike in their temptation to seek wealth. Bernard Diderich, S.J. (1726–1793), in a sermon prepared sometime after 1769, reproached parents who grieved excessively for dead children: "methinks to hear Almighty God reproving such mothers in these terms . . . why dost thou not thank and praise me, for having taken my child out of the wicked world before it was corrupted by it.?"[59] These children were safe because they had not lived long enough to choose the vain pursuit of wealth. Diderich embraced a theological paradigm which regarded earthly life merely as a time of testing people's suitability for salvation. Those who were lucky enough to die young thus escaped many temptations and obstacles which might have damned them later. In this perspective, the possession of plantations and slaves was a potential obstacle to attaining heaven, and needed to be regarded as, at best, a sad necessity.

Jesuits helped to design the benevolent scenario of slaveholding stressed much later by postbellum scholars, who proposed that slaves were generally treated mildly throughout the South because it was in the economic interests of the master to cultivate "propriety, proportion and cooperation" in his relationship with the slaves. A "cordial but respectful intimacy" was the goal, with severity the clear exception.[60] Diderich's funeral sermon suggests that the Jesuits had a motive other than prosperity for pursuing such relationships. They saw themselves as united with the slaves in preparation for death and a judgment in which they would all be measured by the same standard, and so they sought for all the golden mean of indifference to riches which would uphold that standard.

Diderich, like Beadnall, was impressed with the fact that both masters and slaves knew the same temptations. In an undated funeral sermon for a Mrs. Kelly, delivered sometime between 1769 and 1793, Diderich described death as "that merciless tyrant who spares . . . neither rich nor poor."[61] Such constant anticipation of death and judgment influenced choices as to whether slaves would be freed or sold. The risk of damnation might run higher if one became free than if one remained a slave. A major danger of freedom, after all, was that it might make an individual responsible for moral judgments of which he was really incapable. It was also believed that masters had to answer to God for their slaves: if the freed slave were ultimately damned, the former master would be considered partly responsible. It was easy to rationalize the continuation of slavery in this way: better to let the Jesuit govern the slave than let the slave ruin himself, and better to let the Jesuit govern the slave than lose his own soul through an inappropriate manumission.

There were many other expressions of Jesuit suspicion of riches in their sermon texts. Joseph Greaton, S.J. (1679–1753) made one in some remarks about purgatory in 1725. In Catholic doctrine, purgatory is the state in which the souls of the dead are purified of their sins before rising to heaven. Lewis reminded his congregations, through comments that were redelivered in 1729 and 1734, that material wealth would be of no good to the soul placed in purgatory following death. "Ye goods are confiscated and ye are not in a capacity of cancelling your debt." In other words, neither ownership of land nor possession of slaves would be of any practical benefit in attaining reconciliation with God. Helpless, the souls in purgatory must rely on the prayers of the living and the mercy of God for help.[62] This was the arena where class would finally fade away and egalitarianism would prevail. It was better to remain detached from one's possessions, lest they foster the illusion that one would have power over the end of one's life.

Nowhere was the Jesuit rhetoric that the choice of material wealth was the selection of the wrong standard displayed more dramatically than in the remarks of John Lewis, S.J. to slaves gathered for Mass at an Annapolis plantation on the Third Sunday of Advent, December 13, 1761. He told them that they ought to rejoice that they were not rich, for their poverty placed them "in a happy state both in order to ys. life and the next." This situation meant that they were freed from "innumerable cares of ys. world" and so lived "in an easy road to eternal felicity in ye world to come." Unlike a master, a slave had "few or none to answer for but yourself," and so "your obligations are both few in number and easily comply'd with."[63] In other words, slaves were blessed in having no underlings whose moral lives they would have to answer to God for. Thus they escaped what Lewis and other Jesuits viewed as the cross of the master—a vision which placed them squarely in the central theme of the self-image and self-respect of the master class.[64]

Sermons like this one sound very benevolent when stood alone. However, they were delivered in a specific social context. Was there as much goodwill toward the slaves behind the scenes? The answer to this question lies in the private papers of the Jesuits and in oral testimony of aged former slaves transferred to paper around 1910.

The ideal of Ignatius Loyola was for Jesuits to be "contemplatives in action," with their work leavened by prayer.[65] Because of the many priestly and plantation tasks that occupied Maryland Jesuits, it was crucial for them to make annual retreats for the replenishment of the contemplative dimension of their vocations. People often engaged in Ignatian retreats "to reform their lives within their station."[66] During the week of retreat, it was customary for Jesuits to hear exhortations from the mission superior about issues that required attending to. Significantly, in December, 1749, one such superior, George Hunter, S.J. (1713–1779) chose Jesuit attitudes toward slaves as his topic. Hunter set down three points—duties toward slaves, ministry to other planters, and the overall moral example that the operation of Jesuit plantations should set.

Masters owed their slaves charity, Hunter insisted, because both masters and slaves shared the dignity of having been redeemed by Jesus Christ. That fact made them spiritually equal, even though the master remained socially superior. The best way to teach the slaves their "duty to God," therefore, was to treat them in a "Christian and paternal manner." Hunter believed that slaves would respond to such kindness by seeing their own call to serve God. Once they served God, their salvation would be assured.

The fact that Hunter felt he had to remind Jesuits of this approach to the slaves suggests that he feared they were losing touch with the ideal. The forum of the annual retreat, during which Jesuits were customarily urged to recognize and repent of their sins, is an important clue to the motives for his talk.

Hunter was also concerned lest Jesuits speak too much in public about the administration of their "temporals," as they often called their plantations. Such preoccupation might be understandable among men faced with their severe and perennial business difficulties, but ultimately it would be "disedifying in persons of our calling." Their ministry made it imperative that Jesuits set an example of keeping wealth in perspective. Again, the choice of topic within the forum of retreat suggests that Hunter believed Jesuits were becoming too enamored of the pursuit of wealth.

Hunter listed the alternatives that Jesuits should talk about, the first being the "the progress of our missions." To better provide for sacramental ministry to Maryland's Catholics, white and black, was the only reason that plantations had been acquired by the Jesuits in the first place. The plantations were to provide the physical setting as well as the financial support for the celebration of Mass and the other sacraments.[67]

Instead of striving to make money, Jesuits on the plantations were "to serve God in a more decent, handsome, pompous manner." Thereby the proper "interior" dispositions were to be nurtured: "awe, respect, and reverence," rather than worldliness. There would then be more conversions to Catholicism, and better catechizing of children and negroes. Hunter believed that sermons should be given in a "familiar" rather than a "formal" manner: it would be easier to inspire the poor that way.[68] Hunter thus foreshadowed John Carroll's later confidential recommendation to Rome that the liturgy be celebrated in English rather than Latin so that the uneducated could better follow the Mass.[69] Carroll's suggestion was rejected by Rome, but he and Hunter had both shown a pastoral concern for slaves in making these recommendations.

Considering that the liturgy of the Roman rite was universally and strictly celebrated in Latin from the Council of Trent until the aftermath of the Second Vatican Council in the 1960s, it then becomes clear just how revolutionary a reform Carroll proposed nearly two centuries before a vernacular liturgy was finally adopted.[70] That Carroll suggested it at all is an indication that he thought that common methods of Jesuit and Catholic ministry were not completely reaching slaves.

The unity of masters and slaves in a single Christian community, Hunter and Carroll realized, was a symbolic foreshadowing of the harmonious unity of heaven. The influence of this concept on the Jesuit determination to keep their slaves must not be overlooked. To Hunter and Carroll, getting rid of the slaves *en masse* would not have witnessed to the truth that all races and classes were destined for the same God, despite their social inequalities.

Their reaffirmation of the Catholic tradition of racially mixed congregations opens an opportunity to compare and contrast Catholic and Protestant practices in this matter. A seventeenth century French historian, Jean-Baptiste Du Tertre, believed that a fundamental difference between the Protestant and Catholic treatment of slaves was the greater spiritual inclusivity of the Catholics. Where the Protestants emphasized individuality and self-responsibility, the Catholics emphasized universality, human community, and unskeptical loyalty to the precepts of a hierarchical church. In the long run, Du Tertre believed, the Catholic approach was the more likely to admit slaves to full communion with their denomination.[71]

Hunter's reflections confirm Du Tertre's observations, but they show another consequence of Catholic slaveholding. Catholicism was much more likely than Protestantism to promote the idea that there was mutual bondage between master and slave. Chains had links tieing both ends together in the Jesuit imagination. This conception is interesting to compare with a reconstruction of the emergence of slaveholding, in which the binding of black people is portrayed as a self-centered move to ease colonial society's burden of dealing with landless freed white servants.[72] The Jesuits, however, were not inclined to see slavery as a protector of their self-interest once they had attained religious freedom in 1776.

The idea that each Christian must choose between two standards, one good and the other evil, remains a graphic meditation form the second week of the *Spiritual Exercises*.[73] This imagery haunted Jesuits whenever they contemplated the manumission of a single slave. In 1815, a dying John Carroll drafted a will in which he provided for the freedom of his valet, "my black servant Charles." Carroll was torn, however, between setting Charles free immediately or first leaving him to a nephew, Daniel Brent, during a twelve month preparatory period for emancipation. Carroll finally declared to convey Charles to Brent for that interim period only in the event that he had not been freed by the time of the Archbishop's death.

The reason for Carroll's hesitation concerning Charles' manumission became clear when the will went on to make specific directives for how Charles should lead his life once ostensibly set free. Carroll wanted him to stay in the area of Washington, D.C., near the friends he had made as a slave. The Archbishop expressly hoped that thereby Charles would "make a prudent use of his emancipation."[74] Clearly, the paternalistic side of Carroll made him fear that a free Charles would make the wrong choices in life. In this regard, Carroll lived up to a conviction which shared by many masters: "The planters had a saying . . . that a negro was what a white man made him."[75]

Other points from the second week of the *Spiritual Exercises*, the "Three Manners of Humility," also affected the attitudes that the Jesuits revealed toward their slaves in private references. The first manner of humility was the minimum that the Christian had to do to be saved: obey the law of God rather than his own impulses. The second manner went a little further: the Christian reached the point where he was indifferent as to whether he had riches or poverty, honor or dishonor. In the third and deepest manner of humility, the Christian moved beyond that indifference to freely choose poverty and dishonor, so as to more closely correspond himself to Christ on the cross.[76] Only when a Christian reached this third manner was he capable of self-governance.

Some Jesuits believed that an unusally high degree of lust made blacks incapable of reaching this third manner of humility. This perception made them doubt that blacks had the inherent self-control to reach the deepest level of abnegation, for the Jesuits had a long tradition of distrusting sensual drives.

John Digges, S.J. (1712–1746) praised fasting during the brief years he spent in Maryland beginning in 1742. For Digges, the greatest utility of self-mortification was that it let reason prevail over passion. Passion, Digges felt, deluded people into believing that the indulgence of one's appetites for pleasure and riches was the way to permanent happiness. Deliberately denying oneself the satiation of bodily desires, on the other hand, would make way for reason to convey its insight that no material thing was permanent. The result would be that people would act rationally rather than beastly, recognizing that their bliss was postponed until they reached heaven.[77] There is testimony that Jesuits' slaves were given sparse diets. While this deprivation may have simply reflected the economic depression on the plantations, it may also have involved some attempt to quence their passions and promote their reason.

To Jesuits, reason was an antidote to lust, but white people were believed to have more of this antidote than black people. This feeling contributed heavily to the Jesuit sense that that Africans were savages who needed the continued guidance of white priests. Father Joseph Mosley (1730–1787) described "the Negroes that do belong to the Gentlemen of our Persuasion" in a letter to his sister, Mrs. Helen Dunn. in England in 1773. Mosley asserted that "They are naturally inclined to thieving, lying and much lechery . . . the innate heat of the climate of Africa and their natural temper of constitution gives them a great bent to lechery." However, Mosley also conceded to Mrs. Dunn that he could see how the slaves' poverty aggravated their thefts and lies—an unusual admission by a Jesuit that the material conditions the slaves had to face might influence their behavior as much as their nature did.[78]

There was disagreement in English America as to whether the characteristics of the Negro were innate or acquired.[79] Mosley's comments indicate a Jesuits capable of believing that both heredity and environment might play a role in shaping the behavior of their slaves. In his own thoughts, Mosley reflected the tension between the two theories.

In a later sentence of the same letter to Helen, in an attempt to discourage their brother from immigrating to Maryland, Mosley distinguished the words "negro" and "servant" in saying, "He is too old to work, day by day, with our negroes here, so he surely never intendes to indult himself for a servant."[80]

The candor of Mosley's remarks, especially his use of the word "Negro," are an opportunity to compare his private words with declarations that Jesuits often called their slaves "servants" in public.[81] The contrast suggests that the Jesuits sometimes found it more polite to refer to their slaves in terms of class. In private, however, they were much more likely to distinguish their workers by race, as Mosley did.[82] This practice points to the sharp distinction drawn by colonial Americans between indentured and involuntary servitude.

That the Jesuits shared this distinction raises the question of whether the Jesuits allowed their slaves to collaborate in the ministry of the Church to any degree. In most premoderen chattel systems, there was an important role for so-called "elite slaves." These were "persons who were at once slaves and figures of high political and adminstrative importance."[83] It might seem that such slaves would have had no place in the Jesuit system in Maryland, not only because of the more repressive nature of modern slave systems but also because the Jesuits themselves abstained from political participation for most of the period that they owned slaves. However, as far as the religious function of the slaves is concerned, it is possible to explore whether or not the Jesuits gave at least some of their chattel important roles in preaching the Gospel.

Jesuits apologists have customarily believed that this was the case. Beginning in the 1930s, there was an argument that slave women who functioned as nursemaids in plantation houses were intimately involved in teaching the catechism to their masters' children. Apparently relying on oral traditions that had been passed along for several generations, this theory asserted that the nursemaids issued warnings against sin, taught children how to recite their prayers and Catholic devotions, gave reminders to frequent the Sacraments, and admonished the practice of virtue.[84] These were tasks which could rely on rote memorization, and so could have been fitted within the apparent determination of the Jesuits not to teach the slaves reading and writing. However, as was the case with the assertion that other owners' slaves envied the Jesuits' slaves, there was not contemporary evidence for this claim. There is also a theory that the Jesuits' own slaves were taught to regard themselves as co-laborers in the mission of the Society. This sense of identity with the Jesuit apostolate may eventually led to catechesis of slaves by one another in the absence of a priest.[85] Much of the case for this theory rests on a certain interpretation of some rhetoric in the petition for manumission of Thomas Brown in 1833. Brown referred to himself as "a faithful servant in the Society going on 38 years," and said that his wife, Molly, "has been borned and raised in the Society."[86]

Brown's comments may reveal that there arose some sense of identification with the Jesuits among their slaves. However, there is no evidence that Brown himself had been a teacher of catechesis. His petition for freedom was in fact occasioned by the Browns' sense that they had been mistreated by the Society of Jesus—they wished to sever themselves from Jesuits who had provided them with cold accomodations in the winter and even suggested that they move to the loft of an outhouse with no fireplace.[87] If there were elite Jesuit slaves, Brown and his wife were apparently not treated as such. They seem to have been disregarded because of their old age and decline in productivity. Their rhetoric of identification with the Society in their petition may well have been due to their desperate wish to strike a chord of compassion in their neglectful owners.

There survives somewhat stronger evidence of slave participation in Jesuit aposotolic labors when in the chronicle of a baptism at Cornwallis Neck, Maryland, in 1851. The Jesuits who performed this ceremony found "Negroes well instructed by their fellow slaves,."said a near-contemporary observer.[88] If so, this was indeed an example of slaves exercising among themselves a ministry more typically exercised by actual Jesuits.[89] However, this evidence comes from a date thirteen years after the sale of the Jesuits' own slaves. The blacks involved in this episode may not have received their initial spiritual training from Jesuit priests, and both parties may have begun by then to feel more comfortable collaborating together outside the grip of a master-slave relationship.

Anecdotal evidence suggests that the slaves owned by the Jesuits worked rather ingeniously to annoy their masters. An elderly white woman who had lived on a Jesuit farm remembered that "the black people were always so courteous that they would always answer what they thought would please you." If a Jesuit approaching a farm on horseback would ask a slave how far the manor house was, the slave would say a mile or two. When the real distance turned out to be closer to three or four miles, the horse felt its rider's rising fury.[90] The woman who related this recurring episode described rather well a form of passive aggression which hints that there was not much friendliness in the Jesuit-slave relationship.

Even if there was some ministerial collaboration, it is doubtful that the slaves were allowed to determine what to do or say themselves. Jesuits made sharp distinctions between whites and blacks, with the blacks always regarded as inferior. A white woman, a descendent of the first English settlers to live near

St. Thomas' Manor, was described as "an old lady of as many summers as the negroes' winters."[91] This comment reveals a pronounced sense of distinction between white and black—so sharp that even time was reckoned differently for the two races. The white women was conceived in terms of many fruitful summers, the blacks in terms of many barren winters. Little creativity or imagination was expected from the African. This sense of white racial superiority was augmented by the Jesuits' sense of clericalism—a conviction that priests were unique representatives of Christ, superior members of the Church to laymen. The Catholic Church of the post-Reformation was characterized by a hierarchical theology that every precept descended from on high—God handed the truth to the popes, who handed it to the bishops, who handed it to the priests, who handed it to the laity.[92] The slaves were at the bottom of the lowest of these groups. Speaking of the Incarnation, Peter Atwood said "It is an indispensable obligation for me to speak of so great a mystery: it is an indispensable obligation for you to hear because it is the foundation of our religion."[93] The slaves were distinctly among those meant to hear.

Finally, there is a most compelling case to be made from inference against any thesis that Jesuits regularly entered apostolic collaboration with their own slaves. This argument involves the Jesuits' fear of miscegenation. Father James Walton went on a witchhunt at Newtown in 1774 to punish slaves who had copulated with whites, selling ten mulattoes. Some of these were women suspected of relationships with white men. Walton recorded that a suspiciouis number of young slaves looked light skinned or bore white facial characteristics.[94] Walton echoed a later comment that "blacks and whites were not free to love one another without considerable emotional confusion, marked in part by a self-contempt projected onto the other."[95]

If the white men involved with these women were Jesuits, specific evidence for such relationships has not survived. A concern for scandal no doubt would have inhibited Jesuits from saving any such testimony. However, the possibility of sexual relationships between Jesuits and slave women must be considered.

The fact is that Jesuits often expressed fear of the sexual drives of blacks. Mosley's comments of 1774 were a perfect example.[96] Mosley's reflections on a virulent form of lechery which he linked to the African climate reflected a constant English attitude of Africans as "a particularly libidinous sort of people."[97] Declaration of a link between heat and lust was a constant theme of English observers after Jean Bodin first made the connection in 1566.[98]

Indeed, English of the slaveholding era dwelt on miscegenation to such an extent that some scholars believe that they had to have had both an attraction to, and an aversion from, the prospect of a sexual relationship with a black. The attraction is easily attributed to human nature, but the aversion must have had deep roots in cultural inhibitions that require more study.[99]

Jesuits had the added need to protect their vows of chastity and lifestyles of celibacy. Such must have been a difficult task, since missionaries to Maryland were so often assigned alone to their farms. Mosley wrote in 1773, "I've lived entirely alone these nine years past, not one white person with me."[100] The possibility that there were liasons between Jesuits and slaves, therefore, can not be ruled out. However, the only concrete suggestion that this was ever considered a problem comes from 1820, when Father Peter Kenney, a visitor from the Jesuit General in Rome, issued two instructions to American Jesuits.

First, Kenney ordered that pregnant slave women should no longer be whipped and that no slave women should ever be whipped in a priest's residence. Kenney found "very indecorous" the practice of tieing up disobedient women in the "priest's own parlour."[101] In many parts of the South, the domestic slaves were offspring of the masters and frankly acknowledged by many whites to be such.[102] While there is no actual surviving evidence that this was the case for any Jesuits, the fact that Kenney took these precautions suggests that he was aware, at least, of a potential for damaging rumors.

The one specific recorded case of a Jesuit whipping a female slave would seem to have had nothing to do with sex. This incident was recorded by Brother Joseph Mobberly in 1806, but had taken place many decades earlier, in the youth of Granny Sucky, the old woman who recounted the incident to him. She resolved to find out whether rumors among the slaves that her Jesuit master engaged in nightly self-flagellation were true. Therefore, she hid in the barn where he was said to come after nightfall for this practice. Upon seeing that he was indeed beating himself, she screamed at him not to be so cruel to himself. The Jesuit's response was to turn his whip on her, as punishment for disturbing his prayer.[103] The possibility exists that the Jesuit responded as he did because he feared this young woman had come to seduce him at a time when he was particulary vulnerable. If nothing else, however, this episode shows that Jesuits and slaves had little enough collaboration in prayer, let alone ministry.

That Jesuits worried somewhat about the equally intriguing possibility of homosexual relationships between Jesuits and slaves is suggested by Peter Kenney's second regulation of 1820. After stating that lay persons might be engaged to whip female slaves if physical chastisement became absolutely necessary, Kenney ordered priests not to inflict corporal punishment on male slaves, either. However, he did allow Jesuit brothers to whip male slaves, stating that it was the dignity of their ordination that made it unseemly for Jesuit priests to do so. Kenney also stressed that when priest teachers needed to discipline boys and youth under under 21 years of age, the correction must be kept slight.[104] In pondering Kenney's two sets of precautions regarding physical chastisement of slaves, it is appropriate to remember that the actions of slaveholders often refuted their own assertions that the danger to slaves lay more in sexual harassment by lower than upper class whites.[105] Kenney behaved as though the possibility of sexual assault could arise from any class.

It seems likely that for the vast majority of Jesuits, the fear of either miscegenation or homosexual liasons was probably sufficient to draw a sharp emotional distance between themselves and slaves. This would have undermined chances either that the Jesuits would befriend the slaves or that they would have used them much as collaborators in ministry. The English often saw lechery as a symptom of godlessness.[106] For English Catholics like the Maryland Jesuits, this cultural notion would have been reinforced further by the Augustinian tendency, greatly influential in Roman Catholic thought, to evaluate lust as the major consequence of original sin.[107] Jesuits like Mosley frequently cited the sexual misconduct of the Negroes as evidence that they needed the paternal care of white masters. Such remarks suggested relationships of superiors to inferiors rather than collaborations of equals. In the end, the concept of the elite slave was not applicable to the situation of the Maryland Jesuits and "their" Negroes.

Anglo-Saxon culture and the more Catholic Mediterranean cultures are said to have differed in their attitudes toward sex. Some believed that the Anglo-Saxons had the greater self-restraint, and that that this cultural distinction was growing stronger throughout the slaveholding period in North America.[108] However, Catholic clerics were always stricter than the laity in this regard, a feeling fully reflected by Jesuits, who accorded sexual self-control great importance in their own assessment of what was required of a good Catholic. The example of the Maryland Jesuits seems to alter the generalization that Catholic slaveholders were more comfortable with sex than Protestants.. However, these particular Jesuits were also English in origin, so their anxiety about sex may also reflect the Anglo-Saxon attitudes of this period.

The question of who could name a slave, and what names would be suitable to confer upon a slave, is a good issue through which to bridge the ministerial and managerial sides of Jesuit slaveholding. The naming ritual in asserting and symbolizing the master's control over the slave.[109] Illustrative of this point is the fact that Mosley always entered the Africans belonging to the Jesuits in his baptismal register as "Negroes of Ours."[110] Jesuits deeply involved themselves in the naming of their slaves' children. They wanted the slaves to bear either the names of Old Testament prophets or Christian saints. In the 1730s, they began to assign family names as well—either the name of the Jesuit plantation on which a slave family lived or the family name of some previous master.[111] Whatever the choice, Jesuits showed their control over the slaves by making it. Beneath the concern to select names of which the Church would approve, there was concern that the Jesuits assert their total control over the lives of the children they were naming.

In the early twentieth century, the last surviving former slaves of the Jesuits claimed that there had been a social hierarchy among their number, and that the Jesuits assisted particularly favored slaves to avoid transportation to Louisiana. According to "Aunt Louisa," her family hid in the woods until the slave ships had sailed. A sympathetic individual Jesuit, Father Joseph Carbery, an opponent of the sale, then made sure that the family continued to dwell undisturbed in the neighborhood. Aunt Louisa's tale is plausible because it is documented that Carbery indeed opposed the sale.[112]

Louisa also claimed that her ancestors had been owned by Jesuits since the founding of Maryland, thanks to a gift from Lord Baltimore to Father Andrew White in the 1630s. This part of her tale could not be verified by written records.[113] However, it is possible that Louisa's family ranked higher than other slaves because the women were cooks and domestics for the priests and the men served as stable boys and coachmen rather than field hands. The men had some authority over the care of the stable and the horses, and were allowed to receive tips for transporting people.[114]

Other slaves were also treated well according to their function. Blacksmiths, for example, were given summer shoes so that they would not burn their feet.[115] Midwives were allowed to pocket one dollar from each delivery.[116] Furthermore, there was one slave on each plantation designated as a "jobber," whose task was to distribute pocket money among the slaves. This was done sometimes daily, sometimes weekly.[117]

In much of the South, there was indeed a social and economic hiearchy under bondage. Fieldhands could rise to the rank of artisan, for example. Others became involved in management, as Aunt Louisa's brothers and the jobbers apparently did.[118] One of the most crucial decisions typically made by slaveholding planters was to switch from whites to blacks to fill the various craft and management slots. This move allowed the emergence of a complex and even quasi-autonomous slave society.[119] There is no indication that such a successful slave society emerged on the Jesuits' farms, but the example of Aunt Louisa's family suggests that the Jesuits initiated at least some steps toward such a goal. This was an instance of the basic humanity of their social theology besting their more racist attitudes. It suggests that that they were still racists, but racists with consciences.

Jesuits who interviewed survivors like Aunt Louisa began to claim that any Jesuit slave was the envy of the other slaves in the neighborhood, because the kindly treatment and gentle governance of their priestly masters highlighted the cruelty of other nearby slaveholders.[120] This claim was echoed during the Maryland tricentennial celebrations of 1935. [121] However, there is no empirical support whatsover for such observations besides hearsay oral testimony. There is no way either to prove or disprove their assertions.

However, what we know of Jesuit attitudes toward clothing and food for slaves tends to damn this claim. It was thought that since slaves had lived simple lives in Africa, they were entitled to no more than that in America. Content with "food as nature produced it in Africa," there was no reason for them to crave the roasts, steaks, cutlets, coffee, tea and pie Jesuit masters are said to have specifically forbad them. They rationalized that they did not wish to spoil stomachs unused to such fare.[122] Meanwhile, the diet of corn and pork that they did receive was adequate because they "grew fat upon them."[123]

There is a theory that slaves were better fed than the written records indicate they were. While corn and pork were often the only dishes mentioned in instructions from masters to overseers, other documents indicate that a variety of additional foods were offered.[124] However, this phenomenon apparently did not extend to the Jesuit farms, where there were deliberate efforts to keep the slaves' diets restricted to corn and pork, out of a sense that the Africans did not need anything more than that.

A Jesuit decision to provide the slaves with little clothing was said to be due to the realization that they were a people accustomed to nakedness in their homeland. No consideration was taken of the difference in climate between Africa and the Chesapeake. Hence, they were issued no underwear, and were only allowed to wear shoes and socks during the winter and when they went to church. They had no nightshirts, and no change of linen for their one blanket and straw-filled sack. These hardships were shrugged off because "They needed them not, yet lived a long life."[125]

Another indication of racism was the Jesuits' decision not to educate the slaves beyond their training in the catechism and such skills as were needed on the plantations. Their lifestyle included "no need for them to read the daily papers or novels, or keeping up any correspondence."[126] Thus schooling emphasized cathecism, good manners, decent behavior and some trade or agricultural skills. Father Francis Neale founded a textile school for slave girls to manufacture garments, and Father Hunter once hired two French sisters to train slave girls as seamstresses.[127]

There were many reasons to keep slaves illiterate, but three great fears predominated. The first was that literate slaves would forge passes for running away, the second was that they would produce literature inciting revolts among their peers, and the third was that they would develop ambition beyond their station. Southern intellectual defenders of slaveholding often pointed approvingly to the decision of Catholics not to educate those unsuited to grasp Scripture.[128] The Jesuits probably feared that the development of ambition beyond station was likely to be fostered by too much independent Bible-reading, which they saw as one of worst causes and consequences of the Reformation. It is likely that this worried them more than the prospect of forged passes and incendiary literature.

However, there was a final point which prevented the Jesuits from feeling undue alarm about the material deprivations of their slaves: the conviction that for those who remained faithful to Christ, suffering would end in resurrection. This was the message of the fourth and final week of the *Spiritual Exercises*: "to consider how the Divinity, which seemed to hide itself in the Passion, now appears and shows itself so marvellously in the most holy Resurrection by Its true and most holy effects."[129] Hidden within the lowliness of the slave, there already lurked his glorification.

Joseph Mosley, in a sermon of 1782, asked rhetorically where the sufferings of the early Christian martyrs had gone—the cross of Peter, the stones of Stephen, the coals of Lawrence, the arrows of Sebastian? These were the means by which these saints now shared in Christ's glory.[130] Both masters and slaves were asked to view the crosses of their complex tasks and interrelationship as spiritual equivalents of the cross, the stones, the coals and the arrows.

It has become commonplace to regard such teachings as rationalizations for slaveholding, and the concept of Christian resignation was indeed manipulated to promote docility among slaves.[131] It is, however, important to note that the Jesuit version of this doctrine also emphasized the docility of mastership. Jesuits like John Carroll and George Hunter saw their charitable duties to the slaves as parts of their own crosses: burdens they would have preferred not to have borne, but which they accepted for the sake of their own and their slaves' salvation. In carrying out each other's part in these complex relationships, masters and slaves became more like the crucified slave that was the Christ of Philippians.

Thus the Jesuits conducted their slaveholding from a hierarchical principle of understanding. Had the letter to Philemon been larger in their theological imaginations, there would have been a sense of fraternity to balance, at least, the sense of hierarchy, paternity and superiority that Jesuits derived from Philippians, Ephesians and Colossians. Philemon was not hierarchical, so their interpretation of the *Spiritual Exercises* did not program Jesuits to absorb the principles of that book.

Why? One possible explanation is that the *Spiritual Exercises*, as noted, are strongly Christological. The verses on slavery in Philippians, Ephesians and Colossians fit well with them because all three texts are strongly Christological, too. One becomes like Christ by imitating the cross; part of the body of Christ is the individual component of the master slave relationship, and so on. In Philemon, the Christology, while present, is more in the background: in the foreground is an emphasis on a direct relationship of brotherhood and equality between master and slave. This is the only discussion of slaveholding in Paul that does not conceive the master-slave relationship as hierarchical, but because the Christology is less vivid, the Jesuit spiritual antennae was less equipped to absorb it.

It is also possible that the Jesuits did not pick up Philemon because they did not want to do so. It is important to remember that the New Testament did not create the first Christians; the first Christians created the books of the New Testament after several decades in community because they felt a need to have some spiritual documents that reflected their experience of God. The same principle was reflected in the choices, by later generations, of which parts of scripture to emphasize at any one time. They took those verses which spoke most vividly to their own experiences. For the Maryland Jesuits, Ephesians and Colossians perhaps reflected what already was their world view more than

Philemon did.

Whatever the reasons, Jesuits chose to fashion their slaveholding from the hierarchical writings of Paul. The hierarchical Paul tended to take ancient society as he found it; Jesuits did the same with colonial and early federal society. Unable to fully decide how they fit into American culture, they postponed decisive action. The result was a discrepancy between benevolent rhetoric about slaveholding and harsh practical treatment of the slaves. It was this contradiction that Jesuits carried with them in the early nineteenth century as they confronted the growing power of the abolitionist movement, the great increase of European Catholic immigration to the United States, and the continuing threat that financial failure on the plantations posed to their educational apostolate. It was a contradiction that would deeply involve the fate of the slaves in the resolution of these other questions.

NOTES

1. John Lewis, S.J. (1721–1788), in Maryland 1750–1788; Sermon Le-1, 1750, American Catholic Sermon Collection (ACSC), Special Collections Division, Lauinger Library, Georgetown University, Washington, D.C.

2. John Lewis, S.J., Sermon Le-6, 1761, ACSC.

3. Phillips P. Moulton, editor, *The Journal and Major Essays of John Woolman* (New York: Oxford University Press, 1971), Introduction, p. 3.

4. John Woolman, "Some Considerations on the Keeping of Negroes," in Moulton, editor, *op. cit.*, p. 205.

5. *Ibid.*, p. 200, p. 204.

6. Since a study of the *Exercises* and their application in Maryland yields so much insight into Jesuit slaveholding practices, a brief note on their construction is in order. Ignatius devised them with the idea of guiding the spiritual director of a thirty-day retreat in the assignment of Scriptural texts and other points of consideration to the retreatant. He divided the retreat into four phases, which were called "weeks" even though they did not have to correspond exactly to seven calendar days.

In the first week, the retreatant reflects that the purpose of human life is to come to know God personally and follow the divine will more closely. This insight is completed by a meditation on the perversity that prevents any Christians from fulfilling these two goals without redeeming divine assistance. The retreatant thereby comes to see himself as "a sinner loved by God."

The remaining three weeks of the Exercises are dominated by the effort to get to know and follow the example and will of Jesus Christ. Throughout the second week, the focus is on the deeds of Jesus' public ministry. In the third week, the emphasis changes to companionship with Christ in his suffering and death. In the fourth and final week, the retreatant reflects on his ultimate calling, to share in the resurrection of Jesus Christ. Ignatius hoped that by the end of the thirty day retreat, the retreatant would be ready to follow God with a total consecration of the will.

See William V. Bangert, S.J., *A History of the Society of Jesus* (St. Louis: The Institute of Jesuit Sources, Revised Edition 1986, pp. 8–11.

7. *Ibid.*, p. 9.

8. David L. Fleming, S.J. *The Spiritual Exercises of St. Ignatius: A Literal Translation and a Contemporary Reading* (St. Louis: The Institute of Jesuit Sources, 1978), pp. 204–219.

9. The task of examining how the Maryland Jesuits' approach to slaveholding was rooted in the *Spiritual Exercises* may be approached in several steps. First, there are the sermons which the Jesuits delivered in early Maryland. The largest single block of these sermons is contained in the 462 manuscripts of the American Catholic Sermon Collection (ACSC), an acquisition of the Lauinger Library at Georgetown University, Washington, D.C. Most of the sermons in the ACSC date from before 1800. The Archives of the Maryland Province (MPA), another holding of Lauinger, contain a few nineteenth century sermons, usually as parts of the papers of individual Jesuits. Through a persual of these sermons, some aspects of the spriituality of Jesuit slaveholding can be reconstructed.

There is, however, a serious limitation to the manuscripts in the American Catholic Sermon Collection, as well as to the sermons in the Province Archives. None of them have explicitly racial comments. This omission makes it necessary to augment their study through a comparison with the surviving private correspondence of the Jesuits, which does show candid signs of racism. When the public sermons of the Jesuits are compared with their more confidential communications, a clear implication emerges that the Jesuits considered it indiscreet to mention race in public but felt free to vent base opinions of blacks among themselves.

However, there is a serious limitation to this private correspondence, too. Relatively few letters have survived. There is, however, a source from the early twentieth century in the writings of Father Joseph Zwinge, S.J. (1855–1921). Between 1911 and 1914, Zwinge published an ongoing series on the history of the Jesuit estates in Maryland in the *Woodstock Letters*, a journal named for a Jesuit school of theology in Maryland. A source from so long after the event in question must be approached with appropriate caution, but Zwinge did put in written form for the first time many oral accounts of the slaveholding days. He also interviewed a few antedeluvians who been alive during the slaveholding era. *Woodstock Letters* was a publication for Jesuits only, often serving as a vehicle for addressing divisive issues among themselves in such a way that their disagreements would not become known to the general public. That a writing on slaveholding was published so discreetly shows that the Jesuits were aware that their conduct of slaveholding was still controversial three quarters of a century after its abandonment.

Zwinge was a northerner, born on March 28, 1855 in Melrose, New York, a village now part of the Bronx. He attended St. John's College, now Fordham University, before entering the Jesuits in 1873. His training was international in scope. Novitiate occurred in Montreal; special studies in Roehampton, England and Louvain, Belgium. In the states, Zwinge's teaching assignments included Fordham,

Georgetown, St. Peter's in Jersey City, and Holy Cross College in Worcester, Massachusetts. In 1904, however, Zwinge was reassigned from teaching to the post of procurator of what was then called the New York-Maryland Province of the Society of Jesus. He remained in this accounting job, responsible for finances, until his death at Poughkeepsie, New York, on August 6, 1921. It was apparently the fact that he had to account for the Province farms that interested him in their history and ultimately their slaveholding. See "Obituary of Father Joseph Zwinge," *Woodstock Letters* 51, no. 1 (1922), pp. 111–112.

10. Harry S. Stout, *The New England Soul: Preaching and Religious Culture in Colonial New England* (New York: Oxford University Press, 1986), pp. 33–35.

11. Gerald P. Fogarty, S.J., "The Origins of the Mission, 1634–1773," in Gerald P. Fogarty, S.J., Joseph T. Durkin, S.J., and R. Emmett Curran, S.J., editors, *The Maryland Jesuits, 1634–1833* (Baltimore: Maryland Province of the Society of Jesus, 1976), p. 22.

12. Stout, *op.cit.*, pp. 27–31.

13. *Ibid.*, p. 17.

14. Bennett Neale, S.J. (1709–1787), in Maryland 1742–1787; Sermon Ne-3, ACSC.

15. Raymond J. Kupke, "Dearest Christians: A Study of Eighteenth Century Anglo-American Catholic Ecclesiology," in Raymond J. Kupke, editor, *American Catholic Preaching and Piety in the Age of John Carroll* (Lanham, Md.: University Press of America, 1991), pp. 57–58.

16. Robert Emmett Curran, S.J., editor, *American Jesuit Spirituality: the Maryland Tradition, 1634–1900.* Sources of American Spirituality Series. (Mahwah, N.J.: Paulist Press, 1988), pp. 11–12.

17. *Ibid.*, p. 113.

18. Joseph de Guibert, S.J., *The Jesuits: Their Spiritual Doctrine and Practice: A Historical Study*, translated by William J. Young, S.J. and edited by George Ganss, S.J. (Chicago: Loyola University Press, on behalf of the Insitute of Jesuit Sources, 1964), p. 45, p. 88.

19. Fleming, *op. cit.*, p. 22.

20. John Bossy, "Reluctant Colonists: The English Colonists Confront the Atlantic," in David. B. Quinn, editor, *Early Maryland in a Wider World* (Detroit: Wayne State University Press, 1982), pp. 155–156.

21. Curran, *American Jesuit Spirituality*, pp. 8–15.

22. Philip L. Boroughs, S.J., "John Woolman (1720–1772): Spirituality and Social Transformation in Colonial America" (Ph.D. dissertation, University of California, Berkele,: May, 1989), p. 58–59.

23. Woolman, in Moulton, *op. cit.*, p. 205.

24. Thornton Stringfellow, "A Brief Examination of Scripture Testimony on the Institution of Slavery," in Drew Gilpin Faust, editor, *The Ideology of Slavery: Proslavery Thought in the Antebellum South, 1830–1860* (Baton Rouge: Louisiana State University Press, 1981), pp. 136–137.

25. "Introduction to Paul," in *The New Jerusalem Bible* (Garden City, N.Y.: Doubleday, 1985), p. 1862.

26. Peter Attwood, S.J. (1682–1734), in Maryland, 1712–1734: Sermon At-1, ACSC.

27. Eugene D. Genovese, *The Slaveholders' Dilemma: Freedom and Progress in Southern Conservative Thought, 1820–1860* (Columbia: University of South Carolina Press, 1992), pp. 12–13.

28. *Ibid.*, p. 76.

29. Stout, *op.cit.*, p. 17.

30. John Lewis, Sermon Le-6, ACSC.

31. Richard Molyneux (1696–1766), in Maryland, 1730–1749; Sermon Mo-1, ACSC.

32. Eugene D. Genovese, *Roll, Jordan Roll: the World the Slaves Made* (New York: Random House, Vintage Books Edition, 1976), pp. 85–86.

33. *Ibid*, pp. 70–72.

34. Peter Atwood, Sermon At-1, ACSC.

35. *Ibid.*

36. Joseph Greaton, S.J. (1679–1753), in Maryland and Pennsylvania, 1722–1753; Sermon Gr.-3, ACSC.

37. John Lewis, Sermon Le-1, ACSC.

38. Fleming, *op. cit.*, pp. 64–66.

39. James Ashby, S.J. (1714–1767), in Maryland 1742–1767; Sermon As-9, ACSC.

40. John Lewis, S.J., Sermon Le-10, 1767, ACSC.

41. Mathias Manners, S.J. (1719–1775), in Maryland 1752–1775; Sermon Ma-3, 1771, ACSC.

42. Germain Barnabas Bitouzey, dates unknown, in Maryland 1794–1815; Sermon Bi-2, ACSC.

43. Jay P. Dolan, *The American Catholic Experience: A History from Colonial Times to the Present* (Notre Dame, Ind.: University of Notre Dame Press, 1992 edition), p. 93; see also Joseph C. Linck, "The Eucharist as Presented in the Corpus Christi Sermons of Colonial Anglo-America," in Kupke *op. cit.*, pp. 27–53.

44. Bernard Diderich, S.J. (1726–1793), in Maryland 1769–1793; Sermon Di-11, ACSC.

45. Fleming, *op. cit.*, pp. 116–120.

46. Joseph Greaton, S.J., Sermon Gr-2, ACSC.

47. Winthrop Jordan, *White Over Black: American Attitudes toward the Negro, 1550–1812* (Chapel Hill: University of North Carolina Press, 1968), pp. 116–119; p. 121.

48. James Farrar, S.J., (1707–1763), in Maryland, 1734–1747; Sermon Fa-1, 1734, ACSC.

49. *Ibid.*

50. William J. Bouwsma, *John Calvin: A Sixteenth Century Portrait* (New York:

Oxford University Press, 1988), p. 173.

51. Gary B. Nash, *Red, White & Black: The Peoples of Early North America* (Englewood Cliffs, N.J.: Prentice Hall, 1992).

52. Albert J. Raboteau, *Slave Religion: The 'Invisible Institution' in the Antebellum South* (New York: Oxford University Press, 1978), pp. 311–312.

53. James Farrar, S.J., Sermon Fa-2, ACSC.

54. Leonard Neale, S.J. (1746–1817), in Maryland 1783–1817; Sermon Neal-11, ACSC.

55. Fleming, *op. cit.*, pp. 84–90.

56. James Beadnall, S.J. (1718–1772), in Maryland 1749–1772; Sermon Be-3, prepared sometime between 1755 and 1767, ACSC.

57. Peter C. Finn, "The Slaves of the Jesuits in Maryland," (Masters dissertation, Georgetown University,1974), p. 49.

58. Jordan, *op. cit.*, p. 304.

59. Bernard Diderich, Sermon Di-11, ACSC.

60. Ulrich B. Phillips, *American Negro Slavery: A Survey of the Supply, Employment and Control of Negro Labor as Determined by the Plantation Regime* (Baton Rouge: Louisiana State University Press, 1966 Reprint), p. 296, p. 307.

61. Bernard Diderich, Sermon Di-31, ACSC.

62. Joseph Greaton, Sermon Gr-1, ACSC.

63. John Lewis, Sermon Le-6, ACSC.

64. Genovese, *op.cit.*, p. 75.

65. Thomas H. Clancy, S.J., *An Introduction to Jesuit Life: The Constitutions and History Through 435 Years* (St. Louis: The Institute of Jesuit Sources, 1976), pp. 277–281.

66. John O'Malley, S.J., *The First Jesuits* (Cambridge: Harvard University Press, 1993), p. 131.

67. Curran, *American Jesuit Spirituality*, p. 11.

68. George Hunter, S.J. (1713–1779), in Maryland 1746–1756, 1759–1769, and 1770–1779; "Notes in his Spiritual Retreat at Port Tobacco," December 20, 1749; Item no. 202A7, Archives of the Maryland Province of the Society of Jesus (MPA), Special Collections Division, Lauinger Library, Georgetown University, Washington, D.C.

69. James Hennesey, S.J., "The Vision of John Carroll," *Thought* 54, no. 214 (September, 1979), pp. 330–331.

70. Geoffrey Wainwright, :"The Language of Worship," in Cheslyn Jones, Geoffrey Wainwright, Edward Yarnold, S.J. and Paul Bradshaw, editors, *The Study of Liturgy* (New York: Oxford University Press, Revised Edition 1992), pp. 524–525.

71. David Brion Davis, *The Problem of Slavery in Western Culture* (New York: Oxford University Press, Paperback Edition 1988), pp. 203–204.

72. Edmund S. Morgan, *American Slavery, American Freedom: The Ordeal of Colonial Virginia* (New York: W. W. Norton, 1975)

73. Fleming, *op. cit.*, pp. 84–91.

74. John Carroll, "Last Will and Testament," November 22, 1815, in Thomas O'Brien Hanley, S.J., editor, *The John Carroll Papers*, III (Notre Dame, Ind.: University of Notre Dame Press, 1976), p. 371.

75. Phillips, *op.cit.*, p. 291.

76. Fleming, *op. cit.*, p. 100.

77. John Digges, S.J. (1712–1726), in Maryland 1742–1746; Sermon Dig-3, ACSC.

78. Edward Davitt, S.J., editor, "Letters of Father Joseph Mosley, S.J, 1757–1806," *Woodstock Letters*, XXXV, 1906, pp. 235–236.

79. Jordan, *op.cit.*, p. 305.

80. Davitt, editor, *op.cit.*

81. Joseph Zwinge, S.J., "The Jesuit Farms in Maryland: Facts and Anecdotes," *Woodstock Letters* XLI, no. 2 (1912), p. 195.

82. Davitt, editor, *op.cit.*

83. Orlando Patterson, *Slavery and Social Death: A Comparative Study* (Cambridge: Harvard University Press, 1982), p. 299.

84. John LaFarge, S.J., "Survival of the Catholic Faith in Southern Maryland," *The Catholic Historical Review* XXI, no. 1 (April, 1935), p.15.

85. Edward Beckett, S.J., "Listening to our History: Inculturationa nd Jesuit Slaveholding," *Studies in the Spirituality of Jesuits* 28, no. 5 (November, 1996), pp. 14–16.

86. Thomas Brown to William McSherry, S.J., Petition for Manumission, October 21, 1833, Item no. 112 BI-P6, MPA, Box 40, Folder 5.

87. *Ibid.*

88. "Mission of the Tertians, 1851," in Curran, editor, *American Jesuit Spirituality*, p. 213.

89. Beckett, *op.cit*, p. 15.

90. Zwinge, *op. cit*, p. 185.

91. *Ibid.*

92. Richard P. McBrien, *Catholicism* (San Francisco, California: Harper Collins, 1994 edition), pp. 871–872.

93. Peter Attwood, Sermon AT-1, ACSC.

94. Zwinge, *op. cit.*, p. 203.

95. Genovese, *Roll, Jordan Roll*, p. 419.

96. Davitt, *op.cit.*

97. Jordan, *op.cit.*, p. 4.

98. *Ibid.*, p. 34.

99. *Ibid.*, pp. 137–138.

100. Joseph Mosley, S.J. to Helen Dunn, July 5, 1773, in Curran, editor, *American Jesuit Spirituality.*

101. Peter Kenney, S.J., "Statement of Religious Discipline, 1820," Item XT1–2, MPA, Box 126, Folder 7.

102. Genovese, *Roll, Jordan, Roll*, pp. 420–421.
103. Brother Joseph Mobberly, S.J., Diary, p.21, The Brother Joseph Mobberly, S.J. Papers (BJMSJP), Special Collections Division, Lauinger Library, Georgetown University, Washington, D.C.
104. Peter Kenney, S.J., "Memorial to the Missouri Mission, 1819," MPA, Box 126, Folder 6.
105. Genovese, *Roll, Jordan, Roll*, p. 419.
106. Jordan, *op.cit.*, p. 33.
107. Ian Henderson, "Original Sin," in James F. Childress and John Macquarrie, editors, *The Westminster Dictionary of Christian Ethics* (Philadelphia: The Westminster Press, 1986), pp. 443–445.
108. Genovese, *Roll, Jordan, Roll*, p. 423.
109. Patterson, *op. cit.*, pp. 54–55.
110. Baptismal Register kept by Father Joseph Mosley, S.J., 1760–1787, Item no. 103.5 XI, MPA, Box 31, Folder 4.
111. Zwinge, *op. cit.*, pp. 198–199.
112. Robert Emmett Curran, S.J., *The Bicentennial History of Georgetown University, I: From Academy to University, 1789–1889* (Washington, D.C.: Georgetown University Press, 1993), p. 119.
113. Zwinge, *op.cit.*, p. 295.
114. *Ibid.*
115. *Ibid.*, p. 206.
116. *Ibid.*, p. 208.
117. *Ibid.*, p. 205.
118. Robert William Fogel and Stanley L. Engerman, *Time on the Cross: The Economics of American Negro Slavery* (New York: W.W. Norton, 1989 Edition), pp. 149.
119. Robert William Fogel, *Without Consent or Contract: The Rise and Fall of American Slavery* (New York: W.W. Norton, 1989), pp. 58
120. Zwinge, *op.cit.*, p. 195.
121. LaFarge, *op.cit.*, p. 18.
122. Zwinge, *op.cit.*, p. 205.
123. *Ibid.*, p. 208.
124. Fogel and Engerman, *op.cit.*, pp. 109–111.
125. Zwinge, *op. cit.*, p. 205.
126. *Ibid.*, p. 217.
127. *Ibid.*, pp. 218–219.
128. Genovese, *Roll, Jordan, Roll*, pp. 561–562.
129. Fleming, *op.cit.*, p. 132.
130. Joseph Mosley, S.J. (1730–1787), in Maryland 1756–1787; Sermon Mos-5, ACSC.
131. Kenneth M. Stampp, *The Peculiar Institution: Slavery in the Antebellum South* (New York: Random House, Vintage Books Edition, 1989), pp. 156–162.

CHAPTER FIVE

Brother Joseph Mobberly and the Intellectual Antecedents of Jesuit Anti-Abolitionism

THE JESUITS OF MARYLAND DEVELOPED A THEOLOGY WHICH ATTEMPTED TO promote an ordered, restrained form of slaveholding in connection with the white Catholic slaveholder's struggle for civil and religious liberty. In daily practice, however, Jesuits often failed to apply this theology, conducting instead a disorderly and often brutal form of slaveholding as their perennially unprofitable plantations sank into ever greater disarray. In the late eighteenth century, the suppression of the Jesuit order by the Church and the effects of the American Revolution in Maryland fostered still greater disorder on the Jesuits' plantations. These events, however, did not prompt the Jesuits to seek the termination of the institution that had become so problematic in their lives. They did not change their attitude because Jesuits had a long intellectual and philosophical heritage which biased them against abolitionism, and this heritage was strong enough to survive the pressure of contrary events.

A key figure in reconstructing their anti-abolitionism is Brother Joseph Mobberly, S.J. (1779–1827). Mobberly had extensive experience in plantation administration and slave oversight, but he was removed as manager of St. Inigoe's Manor in 1820 after the Jesuit visitor from Rome, Peter Kenney, accepted the complaints of slaves that Mobberly was an overly harsh overseer.[1] In his subsequent involuntary retirement to Georgetown College, Mobberly wrote a long philosophical defense of slaveholding in his private diary called "Slavery or Cham." Yet this same man argued that it would be a practical business advantage for the Jesuits to get out of slaveholding business even as the practice remained legal. How did Mobberly reach this conclusion that slavery should continue, but without Jesuit participation?

Some of the answer may be provided by an account of Mobberly's life. Known to have been born in Montgomery County, Maryland, on January 12,

1779, the otherwise garrulous Mobberly had a reputation for refusing to discuss his parents or his childhood with other Jesuits. Many interpreted his silence on these points as an indication of illegitimate birth. Mobberly began studies for the priesthood of the diocese of Baltimore at Georgetown College in 1798, advancing far enough to receive minor orders in 1802. In 1804, he was briefly enrolled at St. Mary's Seminary in Baltimore, operated by the Sulpicians , specialists in the training of secular clergy and former renters of the Bohemia plantation. However, Jesuit records indicate that the following year Mobberly returned to Georgetown as a brother of the Society of Jesus. It is not known why Mobberly's dream of priesthood came to such an abrupt end, but his subsequent dismissal from plantation management and the tone of much of his correspondence with Jesuit superiors regarding plantation business suggests that an assertive Mobberly had trouble resigning himself to docile obedience of church authorities. In any case, Mobberly's swift change of vocation was a prelude to the fourteen years of work at St. Inigoe's that he began in 1806.[2]

His experience of operating this farm left Mobberly a staunch advocate of the idea that Jesuits should cease to use slave labor. He became convinced that the Jesuits had no chance whatsoever of using their plantations to support their apostolates unless they found a more efficient way to harvest them. He stressed this point in correspondence with the Maryland Jesuit superior, Father Giovanni Grassi, as early as 1815.[3] Frequently rebuffed when he gave such advice, Mobberly openly wondered if his status as a brother was to blame for the poor hearings his pleas received.[4]

In the privacy of his diary, however, sometime in the early 1820s, after his dismissal from St. Inigoe's, Mobberly devoted 104 pages to his passionate philosophical defense of slavery. Mobberly began "Slavery or Cham," with immediate and concise answers to two pressing questions: "Can a man serve God faithfully and possess slaves? Yes. Is it then lawful to keep men in servitude? Yes."[5]

It is crucial to note that Mobberly wrote this essay on an urban campus where he languished, sorely missing the countryside, from 1820 until his death on October 3, 1827. He frequently referred longingly to the land and people of St. Inigoe's during his self-perceived exile.[6] Even though he was now residing at a school, Mobberly continued to think in the rhythms of the agricultural year, entering his reflections on the passing year in his diary for October 20, 1824, right after the harvest season, rather than waiting for the official turn of the calendar in December or the end of the academic year in the spring. His ruminations, composed in the second person, were a reminder that suffering, both past and present, would pass and be forgotten upon the attainment of heaven.[7] It is possible that Mobberly became more rigid in his approach to slaveholding as he aged and became thus embittered.

However, "Slavery or Cham" also provides valuable evidence that even amid his personal bitterness, Mobberly drew upon a wide Jesuit heritage in forming his opposition to the abolitionist movement. "Slavery or Cham" joins sermons and letters from colonial era Jesuits to provide essential clues as to why these men were ill-disposed toward the abolitionist argument that all slavery was always and everywhere wrong.

The sermons show that Maryland Jesuits interpreted the *Spiritual Exercises* of Saint Ignatius Loyola in such a way as to justify slaveholding. Mobberly's papers demonstrate that they also interpreted the broader intellectual traditions of the Catholic Church and the Society of Jesus in favor of slavery and against abolitionism. There were several important influences on their thought. Among them was their interpretation of the life of their founder, Saint Ignatius Loyola, and his motives in founding the Jesuit order as a weapon against the susceptibility of the poor to manipulative Protestant preaching. There was also their conviction that the docility of Jesus Christ in dealing with the secular authorities of his own day was token of divine ratification of a conservative and paternalistic social order; the English Catholic tradition that a minority religion must be quiet and nonthreatening to the political and social order for the sake of its survival; the thought of the sixteenth century Jesuit social theorist, Robert Bellarmine, who mixed a clear sense of Catholic distinction from Protestantism with a philosophy, synthesizing Augustine and Thomas Aquinas, that slavery was a natural part of the created order. Other influences included the manner in which the Catholic doctrine of conscupiscence was distorted to reinforce Jesuit racism, and the nuanced Jesuit response to the Enlightenment, which led them to accept its ideals of religious liberty while simultaneously rejecting its vision of social equality. Let each of these influences on Mobberly and other Jesuits now be considered in turn.

A most important factor in the Jesuit response to the abolitionist movement was their assessment of the significance of their order's founder, Ignatius of Loyola, in the history of the Church. Religious tension was deeply rooted in eighteenth century Maryland. Protestants regarded the Reformation as a new birth of freedom, while Jesuits led Catholics in abominating it as an upwelling of heresy. Amid this context, Jesuits of the colony honored Ignatius as a mainstay of the Catholic counterattack on the Protestant reformers of the sixteenth century. They believed that he had checked a Protestant wave from rolling across all Europe and had founded the Society of Jesus for the specific purpose of ensuring that the Roman Catholic Church would always have the warriors it needed for the ongoing struggle against Protestant perfidy.[8] This interpretation of their heritage was so strong among the Jesuits of Maryland that they responded to the argument of abolitionism by looking not at the merits of the case but at its source. Jesuits ultimately regarded abolitionism as if it were just another Protestant error in three centuries of sectarian rivalry.

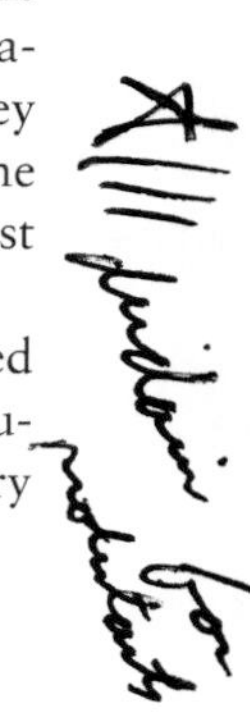

Ironically, most modern historians of the Society of Jesus have concluded that this Maryland Jesuit interpretation of their order's founding was inaccurate. In recent years a revisionist thesis has taken root, arguing that the very first Jesuits were more interested in traveling to Jerusalem to convert the Holy Land to Christianity than they were in fighting the Protestants, and that they turned their greater focus to the Reformation only after travel to Jerusalem was proven impractical. Placing themselves at the disposal of the Church, they sought to minister the spirituality of Ignatius to European Christians through such pastoral ministries as spiritual direction, confession, and presence to the sick. Only as it became clear to them that Protestantism was a pastoral problem which prevented receptivity to these ministries did Jesuits resolve to fight the reformers most vigorously.[9] Eventually, they saw in the fact that the Church found the greatest usefulness for the Jesuits in opposing Protestantism a sign that God indeed willed for them to subvert the Reformation. However, this was not a motive that the Jesuits themselves had initiated.

The goal of Christian conversion, as interpreted by Ignatian spirituality, is total assimilation of the believer to the mind and heart of Christ. Christians are called to abandon their own uncritical assessments of situations and form perspectives in the light of the scriptures, especially the Gospels. Ignatius' *Suscipe* Prayer, from the conclusion of the *Spiritual Exercises*, embodies this mandate. Retreatants offer to the Lord their liberty, their memory, their intellect—their entire will, all that they have and possess. Acknowledging that these things were gifts from God to begin with, retreatants now return them to God for disposition according to the divine will. All the retreatants ask for in return is God's love and grace, which is now enough for them.[10]

This prayer had implications for the Jesuits' acceptance of their role in the Counter-Reformation. Embracing their opposition to Protestants was the concrete way of living out Ignatius' theology that salvation was to be won not through self-initiative but through accepting the will of God as expressed by the agency of the Church. If the Church felt that the Jesuits were more needed in Europe to answer Protestants than they were needed in the Holy Land to convert Moslems, then the Jesuits would accept that opinion as God's will for them. The prayer was potentially also a device by which the Jesuits could have come to terms with abolitionism, had they made an opposite interpretation. This was because the fact that Jesuit acceptance of their role in the Counter Reformation had required adjustment, discernment, and struggling with God's will was forgotten among the Maryland Jesuits of two centuries later, who simply assumed that the task of resisting Protestantism had been the key motivating factor of their Society all along. Four sermon texts from the American Catholic Sermon collection, prepared by eighteenth century Jesuits for the feast day of Saint Ignatius (July 31) illustrate this point and show how Mobberly's hostility to abolitionists was the result of his heritage.

John Pulton (1697–1749), who worked in Maryland from 1738, delivered the earliest of these sermons. He described the conversion of Ignatius as a case of "the most accomplished youth throwing off the cavalier to become the beggar," for Ignatius renounced a lucrative career at the court of the King of Spain to seek service to God. However, the conversion of Ignatius did not fundamentally change the attributes of his character: he simply channeled a combative disposition toward a new cause.

Pulton portrayed Igantius' gifts as fundamentally martial—a "fiery and lofty genius, bred up in arms, and sensible to the least point of honor." Once Ignatius was converted, he was "transported with a holy zeal for the honour of his God." The fire that was inseparable from his "warlike genius" now blazed up in a new and more vehement flame as guardian of Catholic orthodoxy.

Pulton particularly praised Ignatius' willingness to efface himself by returning to grammar school, aged over thirty, in order to learn the Latin language that he needed for the defense of truth against heresy. Ignatius thus "became a child for the sake of Jesus Christ, and he did not blush to learn with children." This was a model of the receptivity Maryland Jesuits wished to show to the teachings of the Church, learning its doctrines by rote rather than questioning them as the Protestants were believed to do. That the example of the adult Ignatius sitting patiently in the company of schoolchildren was taken seriously by Jesuits of the Maryland Mission is shown by the fact that, when needed, Jesuits like Joseph Mosley felt no reluctance about working alongside their slaves at construction projects on the farms.[11]

Ignatius ultimately impressed John Pulton because the first Jesuit made the service of the needy his absolute priority in life. For the last 35 years of Ignatius' life, all other business gave way to the need to relieve the poor, serve the sick, instruct the ignorant, comfort the afflicted and do good to all the world.[12] This part of Pulton's sermon came closest to the work that Ignatius initially wanted to do.

Practicioners of Ignatian spirituality in the late twentieth century find it bizarre that Jesuits of the eighteenth century would have defended slaveholding as a means of being with and protecting the poor. Yet Jesuits in Maryland believed that slaves were preeminent among those poor who needed relief, those sick who needed service, those religiously ignorant who needed catechetical instruction, those afflicted who needed comfort, and those people without service to whom the task of doing good to all the world would be incomplete. To abolish slavery looked to the Maryland Jesuits like a way for the rich to abandon their responsibilities toward the poor, a renunciation Ignatius would not have tolerated.

George Hunter, writing most likely sometime between the 1750s and the 1770s, felt that Ignatius was born "for ye destruction of heresy." The order he founded had as its "sole aim" opposition to all enemies of religious truth. Like Pulton, Hunter leaned toward martial vocaculary when he described Ignatius and the Society of Jesus, stating that the vocation of the Jesuit was to extend the "conquests" of the Catholic Church and to force obedience to its laws. Hunter compared Ignatius' soldierly promptness to the Hebrew prophet Isaiah, who had answered his own divine calling with the simple declaration "Here I am; send me." Finally, Hunter praised Ignatius' realization that while the fact of human mortality would limit his personal ministry to just a few years, a religious order founded on his principles of ministry might continue his defense of the faith in perpetuity. Thus Hunter stressed that mere passive admiration of Ignatius' virtues and deeds was not enough. Latterday Jesuits were his direct heirs and must actively imitate his crusade against heretics and his championing of truth.[13]

John Bolton's sermon for Ignatius Day, July 31, 1773, was delivered amid rumors of Pope Clement XIV's imminent suppression of the Jesuit order. The Institute that George Hunter had believed would perpetuate Ignatius' work appeared to be finished after all. Bolton defied this likelihood by pointedly reminding his congregations that what really mattered was not the Jesuits' fidelity to God but God's fidelity to them. God carefully planned to raise up Ignatius, and lavished on him specific gifts for a particular hour and problem in the life of the Church. Somehow, Bolton believed, God would make new directions clear, even amid the order's suppression, for the divine will would still need the type of service that Jesuits could provide.

Bolton was convinced of the importance of the Jesuit educational apostolate, for he saw the ignorance of the Catholic laity as the major reason that the Reformation spread quickly. Was this assessment of the cause of the Reformation historically correct? At the very least, it was simplistic, attributing a complex series of events to a single overriding cause. There were causes, not a cause. A wide array of explanations for the Reformation have surfaced among historians over the last five centuries. One version emphasizes how the laity reacted against the moral laxity and pastoral neglect of the late medieval clergy. A second holds that a basically sound clergy fell victim to propaganda directed against them by reformers, and that the devotional practices of Catholicism were essentially sound rather than aimed at exploiting people for money. Still another says that the Church fell victim to undisciplined religious exuberance. There is also the thesis that the emergence of a better educated and activist laity was responsible. Many other causes have been suggested; it is likely that the actual event was somewhat influenced by all of them.[14]

Had he been more critical and historical in his approach, Bolton might have been able to see more clearly not only the complexities of the Reformation, but also the complexities of slaveholding. Meanwhile, he was confident of a continuing role for the Jesuit tradition of educating the faithful because he regarded the fundamental problem of the Church in 1773 as the same that it had been in the sixteenth century. There was still a susceptibility to heresy because of an "ignorance in matters of faith" among the lower classes, combined with poor education of all youth. Bolton thus regarded the catechesis of the poor as both a continuing urgent need and a sure way of fulfilling the wishes of Christ.[15]

Bolton, for all his myopia regarding events in sixteenth century Europe, may have been aware of how much African Americans in general favored

Protestantism by the late eighteenth century. Recent research has revealed the legacy of this preference. In 1995, only 4 out of every 100 African Americans were Catholic, and only two out of every 100 American Catholics were African American. The history of black Catholics in the United States may be summarized through the expression "minority within a minority." Many American blacks of the slaveholding era were discouraged from Catholicism by its relative lack of emotionalism in worship—its shunning of prayer meetings, shouting and spirituals in favor of a more ritualistic and formalistic spirituality.[16] It is possible that when John Bolton expressed his conviction that the attraction of the poor to Protestantism was still very much alive in the late eighteenth century, he was already aware of this trend among his slaves.

Another Jesuit who showed awareness that African Americans might be lost to Protestantism was Joseph Mosley. One of his sermonic devices for praising Ignatius was to present the model of an anti-Ignatius, indicting his congregations for following this baser example rather than the real one. The specific traits thus portrayed were models of how a plantation owner and slaveholder should **not** behave.

The anti-Ignatius neglected his family, children and servants, above all in religious matters. Seeing them misbehave, he remained, nonetheless, silent about their misdeeds. He also neglected the recitation of public prayers in his household, and failed to instruct his "ignorant children and servants." Worse, the anti-Ignatius scandalized his underlings with his "anger and passion," making "bad and indecent expressions in their presence." He approached the Sacrament of Communion without proper reverence, unfaithful to his "promise to God for humane respects" and perhaps even after having committed the sacrilege of false confession. A final bad example for his servants was his habit of spending Sundays and other holydays in revelry rather than in solitary prayer, perhaps even "singing, dancing, or something worse." In other words, the anti-Ignatius was someone who rejected his calling to offer both paternal direction and care to his family and slaves.

Mosley was confident that once his listeners searched their consciences, "Surely no one now will be surprised to find they are not Ignatius when they see their fidelity to Alm. God compared to his." Hope for them would revive, however, if only they would act upon the example and preaching of the true Ignatius and return to their call of fostering the Catholicism of their families and servants.[17]

A second Mosley sermon on Ignatius further emphasized the urgency of nourishing the spiritual lives of slaves. Mosley recommended the prayer custom of a "morning olbation": the consecration, immediately upon arising, of one's day to God. Mosley gave parents and masters the duty to check that their children and servants "performed duly this truly Christian exercise." It can not be stressed enough that Jesuits always linked parents with masters and children with slaves: this was the fundamental construct of their paternalism. Finally,

Mosley asked that whether one worked in the field or the household, one "always be mindful of ye glory of God" before all else.[18]

The legacy of this perspective on Ignatius and his heritage was a severe resistance to abolitionism by nineteenth century Jesuits. They saw it as a movement which, having originated among Protestants, was automatically heretical. Furthermore, it was a movement which seemed to propose leaving the poor to self-reliance rather than the paternalistic care of their betters. Thus Mobberly roundly denounced abolitionism in his diary.

At the beginning of "Slavery or Cham," Mobberly briefly summarized the abolitionist case, which he regarded the prevailing opinion in the United States at the time. It argued that all men were free; that it was not God's intention that one man serve another; that it was against the divine law to possess slaves; that it was even more criminal to sell them. In response, Mobberly commented:

> This Opinion is nothing less than a compound of Presbyterianism, Baptistism, Quakerism and Methodism. It is a brother to the great Protestant principle that arose out of the pretended Reformation of England, viz. 'Every man has a right to read and interpret the Scriptures, and consequently, to form his religion on them according to his own notion. Why should he be restrained by Pope or Church? Is he not free? Yes, all men are free.'[19]

The perspective expressed in the sermons of the eighteenth century Jesuits on Ignatius encouraged Mobberly's harsh judgment of abolitionism. Moreover, on this issue Jesuits were in harmony with American Catholicism in general. Traditional moral theology, the fact that many abolitionists were also anti-Catholic nativists, and the prospect of economic competition between European Catholic immigrants and freed blacks all raised Catholic barriers against the abolitionist cause.[20] Jesuits also felt increasingly that the arrival of so many Catholic immigrants in the cities demanded that they change their focus from rural to urban ministries.[21] Meanwhile, the Jesuit sermons and the writings of Mobberly showed that the Jesuits added to this assortment of reasons a deeply personal motive, their self-identity as warriors of the Counter-Reformation.

Another influence on the Maryland Jesuit rejection of abolitionism was their Christology, which stressed the docility and meekness of Jesus Christ rather than his boldness as a prophet. It was not inevitable that they should have found him to be so. Christians have found wildly different imitable traits in Christ from era-to-era, and what various generations have chosen to emphasize about him has often reflected the social needs of their particular time. Entire books have been devoted to evolving conceptions of Christ.[22] As early as the Gospels, the special needs of individual Christian communities led each of the four evangelists to present varying, sometimes even contradictory perspectives on Christ. In the passion narratives, for example, there is a contrast between Mark's account of a Jesus who went to death feeling abandoned by God and

John's account of a Jesus who went to death fully confident in the inevitability of his resurrection.

There is a theological conviction that all these portrayals of Christ must be considered together, like the various sides of a diamond, in order to form a balanced and complete sense of Christology.[23] Historians, from their perspective, note that such nuanced consideration of all sides of Christ's character and mystery has seldom occurred in fact. Each age has tended to elevate one trait over all the others. In colonial Catholic Maryland, where Jesuits found themselves forbidden the public practice of religion, the image of Jesus' submission to the Roman authorities became dominant.

Jesus was quite militant when he challenged his religious enemies, as the driving of the moneychangers from the Jerusalem temple showed. However, with regard to secular authorities, eighteenth century Jesuits believed that Jesus was more passive, urging that Caesar be rendered his due. James Ashby (1714–1767) saw the episode of Caesar's coin (Matthew 22: 15–22) as reflective of much more than Jesus' ability to elude entrapment as a seditionist. It was a reminder that no human considerations, no obligation to the "temporal master"ought to impede Christians from serving their God. The commandments could be fulfilled even while serving the lawful requirements of temporal princes.[24]

This thesis had two consequences. One, Ashby implicitly denied the notion that status as a slave need necessarily mean that the master would come between God and the slave. Therefore, there was no inherent reason to regard slavery as a danger to the souls of its subjects. Two, the sermon suggested that the temporal order had its proper place and that Christ's own wish was that it be honored and respected.

Benjamin Roels, S.J. (1732–1794) saw the admonition to render to Caesar as a warning against coveting what rightfully belonged to one's neighbor. The Jewish authorities of Jesus' day believed that it was unlawful for them to be subject to any temporal laws, but Jesus showed them that such subjection was a neighborly obligation to the Romans. Roels warned Christians that if they took a neighbor's due unjustly, they had an obligation to pay or else be eternally damned. The temporal authority to which any Christian was subject, Roels argued, was a neighbor and the obedience due that authority was part of the neighborly obligation.

This type of sermon legitimized whatever political or legal status one happened to find oneself in. If one was a slave, the duties of a slave were one's neighborly obligation. If one was a master, the duties of a master were one's neighborly obligation. These things were so because Jesus, so revolutionary in his approach to religious questions, desired to leave in place the social order he found on earth.

Joseph Mobberly personally had a limited Christology. References to Jesus Christ are surprisingly few in his writings. He mentioned the Church as his authority much more often. However, in "Slavery or Cham" he did quote the words of Jesus in Luke 18:8, "When the Son of Man comes, will he find faith on the earth?" Mobberly felt that this question was justified because of the arrogant Protestant aspiration to "ameliorate the temporal condition of the human race" now that they had accomplished their spiritual reforms. To Mobberly, this affirmed the truth that "The children of the Reformation set no bounds to their zeal."[25] In other words, they had failed to draw the distinction between the realms of God and Caesar that the Jesuits felt Jesus had clearly made. Expansive schemes for social reform, like abolitionism, were therefore wrong.

Consequently, Mobberly opposed the idea of reforming the Constitution of the United States. In his diary, he expressed the fear that an ill-educated generation, their minds improperly formed, would "see faults in the Constitution which their betters could never discover." Mobberly warned that "deigning men" desired to manipulate the deliberations of the government to foster discord among the citizenry. If unchecked, they would poison the minds of American voters against each other, violating the principle of Saint Ignatius that Christians should always assume the good faith of each other. The result would be "to impugn those principles on which the union of states is hinged." The only antidote to this dire possibility was to continue the task of teaching morality and discipline to children—they must see the unchanging principles of wisdom and truth, including especially the need to render to Caesar.[26]

Mobberly's theme came to be a common one among antiabolitionists. In 1835, Henry Clay regretted the damage that northern abolitionists were inflicting upon the harmony of the Union, which protected both master and slave.[27] However, among Catholics like Mobberly there was an added incentive to respect the Constitution beyond its maintenance of social order for master and slave: its guarantee of religious liberty to a minority denomination like theirs. John Carroll declared in 1800 that "those, who side with libertinism and irreligion, those who are not duly subordinate to the principles and laws of our federate Constitution, never can expect to enjoy true peace of mind, or to be happy here or hereafter."[28] More positively, Carroll rejoiced at "what perfect freedom Catholics enjoy nearly everywhere in these states."[29] By the time Mobberly wrote in the 1820s, Catholics had enjoyed a full generation of such liberty. They feared the notion that abolitionism might upset this freedom, and so affection for the Constitution became a new motive for opposition to setting the slaves free.

Despite their sense that the American Revolution and the Constitution had been much better for Maryland Catholicism than the English rule which they replaced, Jesuits continued to derive much of their theory of the proper relationship between the religious and the secular from English Catholic thought. They found this intellectual heritage convincing not only because of their English origins, but also because they themselves were not particularly original or innovative thinkers. Struggling to perform parochial ministry in a country of few priests, forced to travel long distances to administer the sacraments, burdened by farm management and having as yet no Catholic universities or seminaries in British North America to rely on for fresh theological research, eighteenth century Jesuits clung to conventional English Catholic ways of prayer, piety and interaction between the Church and the secular world. Not least among its legacies, English Catholic thought came from a political and social milieu still parallel enough to the situation in Maryland to be of practical use there.

This was a significant decision, for English Catholicism of the eighteenth and early nineteenth centuries displayed the defensiveness of a beleaguered and despised minority. More than anything else, English Catholics were intent on proving that they could indeed be both English and Catholic. Even after the Bill of Rights, American Catholics in Maryland felt a similar need.

The result was an approach to Catholic interaction with secular society that stressed opposition to dramatic social change and resistance to political radicalism. Religion was to be left as a private matter, not to become a device for changing the lives of one's neighbors. It was hoped that this attitude would reassure those neighbors.

In particular, two English Catholics influenced the Maryland Jesuits. They were John Gother and Richard Challoner, two secular priests, each of whom wrote manuals of prayer and moral instruction that widely circulated among Chesapeake Catholics both in colonial times and during the early republican period.[30] Although it has not been much noted, there was a connection between Gother and Challoner and Catholic slaveholding. Each man explicated social thought that encouraged the practice. They spoke for a people who sought to be bold only in the fact that they professed Catholicism.

Gother is believed to have been born in the mid-1640s. He appears to have been a native of Southampton and a convert to Catholicism from Presbyterianism by early adulthood. He began studies for priesthood at the English College in Lisbon, Portugal in 1669, during an era when Catholic seminaries were forbidden in England itself. Gother remained in Lisbon as a teacher for a few years after ordination, but he was back in England by 1682 with a specific mandate to answer attacks on Catholicism by Protestant pamphleteers. Gother combined this task with ministry to the poor of London until the Glorious Revolution of 1688 made it dangerous for a priest to remain in the capital. Following a number of years as a private chaplain to a gentry family in Hampshire, he died at sea in 1704, enroute to take up the rectorship of his old college in Lisbon.[31]

Gother strove to be more conciliatory in his writing than was typical of either Protestant or Catholic propagandists of his era. He deliberately avoided acrimony, sought to win converts by reasonable persuasion and emphasized the determination of English Catholics to live as peaceable neighbors to

Protestants. In other words, Gother did not wish to upset either the political or the social order in any way, and took great pains to show it.[32] One of his prayer manuals included a petition for the health of the English king, in which he expressed a specific wish that Catholics might bear their oppressions without ever resorting to violence.[33] Analyzing this tradition, it is reasonable to see that Gother's devotion to a noncombative and inoffensive tone of religion served well the desire of Maryland Catholics to show that they were tolerant moderates rather than religious fanatics.[34]

Gother influenced Mobberly's rejection of the disruptive political techniques of the abolitionists, whom he denounced as "ninnyhammers" for their undermining of social hierarchy.[35] The expression reflected Mobberly's belief that abolitionists were trying to impose a foolish and simplistic idea on the people of Maryland by force.

Gother was also "highly practical and ethical rather than theoretical" in his moral instructions. Evidence for this observation may be found in his concern to explicate for parents, children, masters, servants, judges, prisoners, employees and laborers, priests and laborers the specific daily demands of their state in life.[36] Gother was preoccupied with the relationship between ruler and subject. Each of the interconnections he described was a variation of such a relationship. Maryland Jesuits would later show a similar belief that at the heart of society lay the dynamic between rulers and ruled. The consequences for their slaveholding were great, for they simply could not envision a society in which the tasks of ruling might be shared among all.

When Gother was serving his stint as a household chaplain after the Glorious Revolution, he baptized the youthful son of his gentry family's housekeeper. This turned out to be a significant conversion, for Richard Challoner (1691–1781), would serve as vicar apostolic of London from 1741 to 1781 and become the second English Catholic writer to greatly influence Mobberly and other Maryland Jesuits.

During his long career, Challoner specialized in writing devotional manuals for Catholics, as well as pamphlets designed to refute Protestant positions.[37] His work quickly became widely known in Maryland.[38] Six editions of Challoner's writings were reprinted by American publishers early in the nineteenth century, shortly before Mobberly wrote. Much of Challoner's work would also have been accessible to the Jesuits in books imported from England, or in their own reading during their seminary studies in Europe.

Challoner used some important techniques and themes that were adapted by Mobberly for "Slavery or Cham." For example, both writers liked to address Protestants on scriptural grounds. Each was taken with the theme that Protestants, who frequently proclaimed their reliance on scripture alone as their source of authoritative moral teaching, actually offered teachings that contradicted scripture. One of Challoner's pamphlets, reprinted by Daniel Dougherty at Philadelphia in 1815, was entitled "The Touchstone of the New

Religion, or Sixty Assertions of Protestants Tried by Their Own Rule of Scripture Alone, and Condemned by Clear and Express Texts of Their Own Bible, to Which Is Added a Roman Catholic's Reasons Why He Can Not Conform to the Protestant Religion." On another occasion, Challoner wrote, "as the gentlemen, to whom principally I address myself this day, are of so delicate a stomach that they can digest, nothing but pure scripture, scripture I shall give them, and a bellyful of it."[39]

Mobberly copied this technique almost exactly in "Slavery or Cham" when he wrote of the abolitionists, "As they have so great a taste for Scripture, it will be well here to offer them a scriptural repast."[40]

Mobberly went on to provide over ten pages of scriptural exegesis, listing and explaining a detailed number of scriptural verses that appeared to sanction slavery. These verses extended from the book of Genesis to the letters of Paul.

Of much greater importance than technique, however, was the influence upon Mobberly of Challoner's conviction that individualism was the fruit of Protestantism to be most feared and distrusted. In particular, Challoner saw this heresy as present in Methodism—a branch of Protestantism which Mobberly frequently cited as an especially vociferous abolitionist critic of the Jesuit ministry in Maryland. Challoner believed that Methodism resulted in individual laymen seizing ecclesiastical authority that was not rightly theirs. Mobberly agreed, believing that such a practice within the Church would quickly spread to the secular realm, leading people to assume also social authority that was not rightly theirs and prompting them to put personal gain ahead of submission to the community.

In 1817, around the same time that Mobberly was feuding with a group of Methodist abolitionists in Centreville, Maryland about a proposed sale and transportation of some Jesuit slaves to planters in the Deep South, a publisher in Mount Vernon, Ohio named John P. Mardin reprinted an old Challoner pamphlet entitled "Caveat Against the Methodists." At the outset of this work, Challoner insisted that state and church were essentially similar in one important respect. Each was divided between those appointed to rule and govern and those who were appointed to be ruled and governed. Methodism, however, denied that truth through its doctrine that any baptized Christian was empowered to proclaim the word of God. The consequences of that denial were a general collapse of hierarchy. People dared "to raise the standard of rebellion against their lawful superiors; to place themselves in the chair of power, which belongs to those alone who are lawfully sent, lawfully commissioned, lawfully authorized and appointed to announce the word of God." Challoner went on to denounce this usurpation in a colorful peroration, warning about cobblers who threw away their anvils, tailors their thimbles, weavers their shuttles, schoolmasters their pins, laborers their spades, all so to jump into the pulpit with Bible in hand and begin preaching. Challoner did not mind their lowly social state, since the twelve apostles were similarly poor in origin, but he did mind their conviction that they could teach without first being taught.[41]

Mobberly, drawing from Challoner, stressed how deeply the implications of such heresy extended beyond the purely ecclesiastical. All of society would be affected by such a breakdown in respect for religious authority. This was because, to Mobberly, abolitionism was kin to "the great Protestant principle" that every man was free to interpret the Bible for himself, and did not have to yield to the interpretation favored by Pope or Church. Mobberly thus believed that abolitionism and the Protestant doctine of the priesthood of all the faithful were subversive "brothers."[42]

In order to understand Jesuit persistence in slaveholding, it is crucial to note that here Mobberly basically attacked the principle of individual autonomy, a concept seemingly in direct opposition to the Jesuit values of community and mutuality. Mobberly felt that one of two evil developments would result from this misemphasis on individual autonomy. The first would be the inappropriate manumission of slaves who were actually incapable of caring for themselves, a clear collapse of the stronger's communal obligation to provide for the weak. The second would be that masters might keep their slaves, but only for purposes of exploiting them in the pursuit of profit. To Mobberly, either consequence was evil.

Many Jesuits besides Mobberly believed that social hierarchy on the earth was divinely ordained. Influenced by Platonic philosophy, they believed that social hierarchy here below was but a reflection of a parallel hierarchy in heaven itself. When slaveholding Jesuits described paradise in their sermons, their tendency was to speak in paradigms of an ideal class society. In a sermon celebrating the Assumption of the Virgin Mary, for example, John Bolton emphasized how her high rank within the reign of God contrasted with those of lower rank in heaven. Bolton asserted that while everyone in heaven had their proper degree of bliss, the blisses were of higher and lower degrees. Below Mary were the choirs of angels, the hierarchies of blessed souls, and "all those inferior orbes of heavenly spirits." Mary, as Queen of Heaven, occupied the highest human place in heaven, alongside her Son and just below the Trinity itself. She simultaneously looked up at God and down at all the angels and saints beneath her.[43]

This theological perspective quite comfortably accommodated a division of American society into rulers and ruled, masters and slaves. It encouraged the Jesuits to think that Africans could not function as moral agents without the guidance of white Catholic slaveowners. Challoner's view also influenced the religious values that were presented to slaves at the time of their catechesis, that they had a moral obligation to accept their status and the rule of their masters.

This strong Jesuit respect for a hierarchical view of both spiritual and natural worlds is partially traceable to Robert Bellarmine, S.J. (1542–1621). This theologian of sixteenth century Catholic reform influenced both the spirit and the manner with which Jesuits responded to slaveholding and abolitonism. An

Italian, Bellarmine first made his reputation in the chair of "controversial theology" at the Roman College between 1576 and 1588. He eventually became a personal theological advisor to several popes. The "controversial theology" at which Bellarmine excelled was a special genre of Catholic Counter-Reformation thought. It was designed to train polemicists who could answer, in the strongest possible terms, the attacks of the Protestants upon Catholic doctrine and draw the sharpest possible distinctions between the two factions, to the Catholic advantage. Bellarmine believed the Reformation to be primarily an attack on the Church rather than a direct attack on the Nicene Creed's testimony about God himself. Thus he set out to place the Catholic Church as an institution, and especially its truths about the nature of Christian community and divine grace, in sharp relief.[44] Bellarmine's work did much to solidify both the reputation and the self-identification of the Jesuits as the intellectual leaders of the Counter-Reformation.[45] His legacy reveals the paradoxical twins that composed the Jesuit wall against abolitionism, social caution and sectarian militancy.

Bellarmine's first effect in Maryland, therefore, was to confirm the conviction of Jesuits that Protestantism was an enemy with which they were at religious war, and with which they could not compromise theologically, even if that meant rejecting the Protestant principle of abolitionism.

The anti-Protestant attitude permeates an undated sermon by William Hunter, S.J. (1659–1723), who served in Maryland from 1692. Hunter's explicit theme was that what set Catholicism apart from Protestantism was that the Holy Spirit protected the Catholic Church alone in the profession of truth, guarding its doctrine from contamination by error. Why listen to the moral advice of Protestant abolitionists when one had such impeccable guidance oneself?

Preaching for the feast of Pentecost, the commemoration of the descent of the Holy Spirit upon the Apostles, Hunter reminded his hearers to recall their own abiding in the Spirit by virtue of their Catholic baptism. Hunter proclaimed that the most important gift of the Spirit was truth, and that Catholics alone had that gift. He quoted Saint Augustine's observation that only the Spirit of God could speak all truth.

To Hunter, the function of the "spirit of truth" was both positive and negative: sent both to enlighten and to "disabuseth us of our errours." Only such a wise spirit could engage Protestants, who were "subjects so ill-disposed, either for comprehending of truth or for submitting thereto when comprehended, that none but ye God of truth can render them capable thereof." Without the assistance of the spirit, even the greatest of human teachers would not be able to instruct "certain gross minds . . . certain self-conceited obstinate minds."

The opposite of the "spirit of truth" was the "ye spirit of ye world." Hunter catalogued the many pernicious things which this evil spirit nurtured, from a false confidence in material prosperity to a misguided faith that property could ensure permanent happiness. What was most harmful, however, was the fact that the evil spirit also inspired "false conversions . . . false zeal for God." The result was a world "where modest and simple truth" was held captive and in silence." Unless priests like Hunter spoke out, the pernicious spirit would remain unrecognized until it had eclipsed "ye most vivid lights" of both Christian religion and reason.[46]

In his espousal of the Bellarminian tradition of Catholic exceptionalism, Hunter epitomized the fact that Protestants and Catholics in Maryland, as elsewhere, differed radically in their perceptions of *how* and *where* the Holy Spirit spoke its truth. Jesuits indicted Protestants for believing that all revelation was limited to the interplay between scripture and the individual reader's interpretation of those writings.[47] Instead, the Jesuits defended the Catholic proposition that while the Word of God was indeed contained *in* scripture, it was not contained *by* scripture. Decisive to them were the interpretations of scripture handed down by popes, ecumenical councils, and the totality of eighteen and more centuries of Church tradition. Thus arose the Jesuit conviction that such "individualistic" readings of scripture as abolitionism were simply misinterpretations by people who could not have the Spririt because they did not embrace the true Church's whole tradition.

To show a Jesuit scoffing at the idea that insight could come from people other than those appointed to rule over church and society, it is especially helpful to examine a sermon delivered by Richard Molyneux, S.J. (1696–1766), who worked in Maryland from 1730 to 1749. To some, Molyneux "seemed to be the Counter Reformation incarnate," they felt that his death served to dampen considerably Protestant fears of Catholic plotting to overthrow the colonial government.[48] Molyneux's sermon "On Hearing Sermons Diligently" is one of the few surviving sermons of a Jesuit in Maryland to have been given a title by its author. This title was significant. For it was in the content of the sermons delivered before them by ordained priests, Molyneux believed, rather than in personal reading of scripture, that Christians found truth. To Molyneux, ordained clergy were God's specially appointed teachers of the divine will, and no one ungraced by the sacrament of holy orders could replace them.

To Molyneux, listening to proper instruction from duly designated ecclesiastical officials was a crucial duty for the Catholic laity in a colony so dominated by Protestant sects. Molyneux saw the Reformation in England as a cataclysm in which "ye Catholics, God's people, were made a prey to ye adversaries of truth." It was a time of "heresy and schism," when "hell . . . vomited out all its blasphemies, lies and villainies." The office of the apostles, that of bishop, was handed over to "false prophets." The word of "Belsebub" became far more common than the word of God. All this wretchedness was carried out by "Philistines from Luther's and Calvin's camp," and their spiritual descendants among the Protestants of Maryland were to be regarded with prodigious suspicion.

Molyneux's remedy for preventing further victories of the devilish Reformation was for Catholic congregations to listen to their priests alone for moral advice. He stressed that these men, in Maryland almost exclusively Jesuits, were in communion with pope and bishops, and therefore in the company of the only agents of the spirit of truth. What priests had to say in their sermons was trustworthy because it was inspired; people did not need to look elsewhere for enlightenment. Indeed, one could only count on receiving error elsewhere.[49]

When Mobberly, following this tradition, denounced abolitionism as a compound of Presbyterianism, Baptistism, Quakerism and Methodism, it is pertinent that he chose four sects which were all noted for government by congregational participation rather than by centralized authorities. All four denominations posed a direct threat to the social paternalism nurtured by the Jesuits. All four also challenged Roman Catholic clericalism. Mobberly's hostility to them showed that clericalism was a major but unappreciated reason why Jesuits generally resisted abolitionism.

Jesuits trained to make Bellarminian distinctions between Catholicism and other denominations believed that the only good features in Protestantism were those Catholic points which Martin Luther and the other reformers had not bothered to cast aside. Jesuits believed, therefore, that any Protestant tenet which had no parallel in Catholic doctrine should be regarded as gravely erroneous and that any Protestant tenet which corresponded to a Catholic point was not original. Influenced by the Jesuits, the secular Maryland priest Germain Barnabas Bitouzey concurred in this judgment. He wanted to sort out what had been needlessly grafted onto the body of Christ. Bitouzey's conclusion about the Protestants was pithy: "if they are right, we are right with them, and if we are right they are wrong."[50]

Apply this formula to abolitionism, and the implication for Jesuit thought is instantly clear. The people who professed abolitionism were Protestants, but Catholics themselves did not profess it. So abolitionism could not be true.

The Bellarminian heritage led to an extreme sense of the infallibility of the Catholic Church which prevented the Jesuits from dissenting from its official pronouncements on slavery. In another sermon, Bitouzey stated that the existence of the many Protestant sects such as Quakers, Anabaptists, Methodists, Calvinists, Lutherans, Presbyterians and Episcopalians, was the inevitable outcome of their common refusal to acknowledge the infallibility of Catholicism. People who denied the need for some definitive authority over true doctrine inevitably fell to quarreling among themselves, losing themselves in the pursuit of self-interest and personal profit. To Bitouzey, the antidote was for all Christians to "submit our reason and our judgments" to the determinations of Rome. He stressed that infallibility meant that *everything* his Church taught must be true.

This definition went far beyond the official proclamation of infallibility that the Catholic Church as a whole finally would make at Vatican Council I in 1870. On that occasion, the Church limited the exercise of the charism of infallibility to pronouncements in the rarest of cases, in which the pope would speak *ex cathedra* (from his chair as bishop of Rome, out of the assistance granted by the Spirit to the whole Church itself) on very select matters of faith and morals.[51] The tradition of pronouncements on slavery lay outside the restricted definition of 1870, leaving space for modern popes, beginning with Leo XIII in 1889 and culminating with John Paul II in the 1990s, to reverse the Church's approval of slavery after more than nineteen centuries. The broader version of infallibility professed by Bitouzey and his contemporaries in Maryland in the early nineteenth century, however, left the Church's pronouncements on slaveholding within the boundaries of irreformable dogmas during the most crucial years of the abolitionist movement in the United States.

There was another significant difference between the Maryland Jesuit theology of infallibility and the doctrine eventually declared by Vatican I. The Marylanders were much more inclined to see this charism as an exercise of the Church's ecumenical councils than an exercise of the papacy alone. Bitouzey, for example, preached that "when we say the church is infallible, we understand that the decisions upon matters of faith, made by a general Council of the Church, are infallible."[52]

This distinction is important, because a scrutiny of the twenty-one general councils of the Roman Catholic Church reveals that at least four of them produced canons which sanctioned slavery.[53] It can not be stressed enough that Bitouzey and other Catholics of the United States in the early nineteenth century believed that these canons were irreformable because they came from these councils. These were gatherings of all the Church's bishops. Few events could symbolize better the difference between the Catholic sense that doctrinal interpretations must be made by ecclesiastical consensus and the Protestant sense that such decisions could be made by autonomous individuals.

Mobberly wholeheartedly accepted Bitouzey's version of infallibility at the outset of "Slavery or Cham," when he declared his preference for "old systems, old doctrines, and good old morality." His love for the Church, he affirmed, was based on his sense that it always remained the same, a rock supported by the words of eternal truth. If God was unable to deceive Catholics, then the Catholic Church had to be itself incapable of error. It was directly inspired by the creator; therefore, the creatures had no right to reform it. He did not attribute infallibility so much to the papacy as he did to the Church as a whole.[54]

The absurdity of the abolitionist proposition was epitomized for Mobberly by the abolitionists' reliance on St. Paul to justify their cause, even though literal readings of the Pauline epistles revealed Paul's explicit approval of slavery. Mobberly felt that this denial of reality signified the abolitionist mindset that "no matter what St. Paul means, his words must and shall mean what they would have them to mean."[55]

All this Catholic exceptionalism, this Jesuit insistence that the Church of Rome alone was right, set important parameters within which the slavery issue was discussed by Jesuits in Maryland. That was not the limit of Bellarminian influence, however, for Bellarmine also contributed to the Catholic evaluation of slavery with his synthesis of some Catholic philosophies of slaveholding, notably those of Saint Augustine (354–430) and Saint Thomas Aquinas (1225–1274).

Augustine saw slavery as a punishment for sin, while Aquinas attested that it was natural as well as virtuous for the stronger to govern the weaker. Bellarmine was personally more attracted to the Thomistic view which, if taken alone, might have instilled some basis for a greater Jesuit openness to abolitionism. When Thomas stressed that neither masters nor slaves were perfect, since they shared the flawed and perpetually changing human condition, he professed that their status relative to each other was not static. Their relationship of comparative strength and weakness to each other was subject to practical changes which left open both the possibility that the slave would not always require the guidance of the master and the possibility that the master might one day need the care of another.[56] However, Bellarmine's responsibilities as a Cardinal in the Roman curia, responsible by mandate of the Council of Trent for upholding the teachings of the early Church fathers, also forced him to incorporate the Augustinian view of slavery as a punishment for sin into his synthesis.[57] Bellarmine became personally involved in implementing that policy in 1615, during the debate over whether the Church could tolerate the Copernican model of a sun-centered rather than an earth universe. In a letter to Paolo Antonio Foscarini, the head of the Carmelite order, the Cardinal proclaimed his concurrence that "the Council of Trent prohibits interpreting Scripture against the common consensus of the Holy Fathers . . . in case of doubt one must not abandon the Holy Scripture as interpreted by the Holy Fathers."[58]

Bellarmine's correspondence with Foscarini is remembered today for its role in the Church's struggle with the scientist Galileo. However, it also deserves to be remembered for its role in setting Bellarmine's brother Jesuits in Maryland against abolitionism two centuries later, since the Augustine whose positions Bellarmine reiterated as universally normative during the Copernican debate was also the major proponent of slaveholding as a punishment.

The Augustinian assessment of slavery may be found in his fifth century book, *The City of God*. The key passage proclaims that God's original purpose was to give man dominion over irrational nature alone, not over his fellow man. Augustine believed that it was the capacity to think which set man aside from the beasts; he who could think had no need for another governor than himself. However, the normal hierarchy of creatures, of man over beast rather than man over man, was upset by the introduction of original sin into the human condition. Subjection was thereafter deservedly imposed upon certain of the fallen. The wisdom of God, Augustine believed, determined who was deserving of this punishment and who was not. People could follow God's decisions about enslavement with confidence that he is never unjust. Augustine noted that the word "servant" was not used in Scripture until Noah used it in placing a curse upon his son's wrongdoing.[59]

Despite Augustine's punitive portrayal of slavery, there was a positive side to what he said in this passage. At no point did he advance any proposition that slaves were to be held for the financial gain of the master. Augustine, in fact, viewed slavery entirely from the perspective of what it was supposed to do for the slave—correct his moral weaknesses so that he might take his place in the reign of God, when and where all the original equality of master and slave would be restored. In this, Augustine echoed the Pauline view that chastisement was offered out of love, for the refinement of the sinner. For the master, this work was to be a moral duty that took primacy over any needs of his own.

The assessment of slavery by Aquinas, writing about eight centuries after Augustine, was that there simply were practical circumstances in which some people were more wisely governed by people other than themselves. This was a question of utility rather than natural reason; he agreed with Augustine that it was not part of the creator's original plan. It was simply useful for a wise man to rule a less wise man; the first man could help the second.[60]

Once again, this was an emphasis on what slavery should do for the slave rather than what it should do for the master. There was no suggestion in Aquinas' observation that slaves should be held primarily so that the master might profit. Modern scholarship has pointed out that this Thomistic formula theoretically left room for slaves to be manumitted if they reached a point where they could direct their own lives.[61] Bellarmine, searching for common ground between Augustine and Aquinas, was able to find it in their mutual emphasis that slavery existed for the sake of the salvation of those enslaved. That was a perspective that made it harder for Jesuits masters to justify letting go of their slaves merely because Jesuit farms were faring poorly.

Bellarmine developed his own explanation of slavery's existence in the seventh chapter of his treatise *De Laicis*, "On Civil Liberty and Civil Order." Bellarmine based his support of servitude on the premise that "in human society there should be order." Believing that human nature had political and social dimensions from the time of creation, even before the fall, Bellarmine felt that rulers would have been needed even if sin had never emerged as a factor in human relationships. He agreed with Saint John Chrysostom that the divine will in favor of a world divided between rulers and ruled was revealed as early as when the inferior Eve was created from the body of the superior Adam. In this manner, even in the state of innocence, before the sin of Adam and Eve, there was supremacy and subjection, as well as inequalities of height, strength, wisdom and virtue. Bellarmine even proclaimed that there was a hierarchy among the angels, revealing that God's division of the created order between rulers and ruled extended to the purely spiritual realm. He concluded that "right order" demanded that "the inferior be ruled over by the superior." Then Bellarmine listed specific illustrative examples: women must be ruled by men, young people by their elders, the less wise by the more wise, the less moral by the more moral.[62]

This passage of Bellamine's had a direct influence on Mobberly in "Slavery or Cham." When he wished to reject the Protestant principle of individual autonomy, Mobberly penned a passage which closely resembled Bellarmine's. Mobberly used a few different illustrations— the rule of the lion over the animals of the forest, the rule of the eagle over the birds, unnamed kings and masters of the sea who ruled over "the weakest tribes of the finny race"—but the basic construct was the same. If God had a hierarchy in heaven, which was superior to the earth, Mobberly believed that the earth must reflect the same.[63]

Bellarmine's declaration that the need for subjection *preceded* the fall of humanity could have inspired a relatively mild approach to slaveholding among the Maryland Jesuits. If it was not primarily a punishment, but simply a means to carry inferior people through life, there was room for a certain paternal gentleness, even laxity, in their governance. There is testimony that some such influence in fact occurred. Consider some observations made by John Carroll in 1789, responding to charges that Jesuits were draconian masters. He stressed that few priests actually governed slaves, but that those who did treated their slaves mildly, and took particular pains to guard them from hunger and nakedness. Carroll believed that the slaves of priests worked less than the laborers of Europe, and enjoyed much better food, shelter and clothing than those European counterparts. Corporal punishment of priests' adult slaves was almost unknown; their morals were guided and Christian doctrine constantly taught. Therefore, Carroll believed that "a *priest's negro* is almost proverbial for one who is allowed to act without control."[64]

Carroll's declaration was accurate in that it described a situation of chronic disorder on the Jesuit farms. When Peter Kenney inspected the Maryland plantations on his fact-finding mission for the Jesuit curia in Rome in 1820, he reported that he could indeed find no uniform system for governing the slaves.[65] However, it is doubtful that Carroll was entirely correct to attribute this situation only to mercy and benevolence. Disorder grew because, on balance, the Jesuits drew further away from the Bellarminian sense of slavery as a natural institution for the sake of the weak and drew closer to a certain distortion of the Augustinian sense that it was meant for the punishment of the wicked. Deemphasizing Augustine's crucial caveat that any chastisement was intended for the positive purpose of the slave's everlasting salvation, Mobberly, for one, became morbidly preoccupied with the gravity of a special form of original sin which he believed applied only to Africans through a wicked common ancestor, the Biblical Cham, son of Noah.

In Mobberly's exegesis, the curse which Noah pronounced upon Cham and all his offspring brought all Africans not only under an eternal curse of slavery but also under the curse of black skin.[66] This was a very traditional, even conventional, view. It was shared by many Protestant defenders of slavery.[67] However, Mobberly made his own Catholic analysis of the sin which produced two such dire results; it resulted from the insolent attempt of a younger members of Noah's clan to control the elder whom he was meant to defer to. The son violated his place in the paternity, the inferior member failed to keep to his own place in the social hierarchy.

Cham exploited the weakness of Noah, asserting control over him in a triply vulnerable moment by looking upon him when he was drunk, naked and asleep (Genesis 9: 21–27). Cham's behavior was a gross violation of the honor that a son, the person ruled, owed to his father, the person ruling. Furthermore, Cham completed the insult of his father's dignity by informing his brothers of their father's intoxicated and naked condition. Modern exegetes speculate that an unexpunged version of this story would reveal that the son sodomized the father rather than merely looked at him, a monumental insult in a culture which regarded sodomy as an act which sealed the punishment and domination of a defeated enemy.[68]

While Mobberly himself showed no awareness of possible sodomy in the tale of Cham, he did capture the essence of the story, that exploitation of the temporarily weak by the inherently weak was disobedience to God. Mobberly's belief that Cham's sin was to exploit his father's weakness for his own gain may explain the title of his essay. The expression "Slavery or Cham" suggested that Cham had once had a choice as to how to behave with regard to his father. Because Cham had made up his mind, his descendents no longer had control over their fates, but the white people of Maryland still had the freedom to learn from his example. Since Cham seems to have stood in Mobberly's mind for insolent self-initiative and rebellion, the title points to his conviction of what the world would be like without slavery: a place full of individualists out to exploit those whom they should regard as their natural superiors.

Mobberly asserted that the skin colors of people who were not white was the result of sin. In his essay, he discussed the origins of the color of both African and native Americans. Mobberly believed that the sin of Cham, which caused blackness, was particularly offensive to God because it came just after the deluge had purged the world of sin and so reintroduced evil into creation. The Lord found Noah and his family alone worthy of exemption from death in the flood, and even extended to them a new blessing that the earth would flourish in them. Mobberly believed that a sin committed after such a blessing was especially heinous and led to the Lord's decision to color the descendants of Cham black, the darkest possible color, as a perpetual sign of their need to repent of what their ancestor had done to social hiearchy.[69]

Mobberly believed that the native Americans, for their part, descended from

Esau, the son of Isaac and twin brother of Jacob, because Esau was described in the Book of Genesis as having had red complexion. Mobberly acknowledged that Esau was hairier than his purported descendents seemed to be, but he believed that the hair of native Americans was plucked out by the roots during infancy. More importantly, Esau, like Cham, fell under a parental curse. Issac doomed Essau to a nomadic life, to his home far from the richness of earth and the dew of heaven. He would have to live by his sword and serve his brother Jacob (Genesis 27: 39–40). Like the Indians who sold their birthright to the North American land to white folks for a few trinkets and then regretted it, Essau sold his birthright for little but subsequently wanted it back. Mobberly saw in the curse of Isaac and the events of Esau's life the mandate for white people to rule the native Americans just as they did the Africans.[70]

Examination of English attitudes toward the indigenous peoples of North America reveals that English settlers initially attributed the curse of Cham to the Indians, removing that onus from them only after comparing them to the darker skinned first arrivals from Africa. However, they continued to believe that the natives must somehow descend from the nation of Israel, and sought various ways to connect them to the Biblical patriarchs.[71] Mobberly's linkage of them to Esau stood in this tradition of seeking a scriptural antecedent. Many English settlers believed the native Americans to be naturally white, felt that they somehow dyed their skin a tannish hue, and so did not describe them as red skinned until the late seventeenth century. In fact, many Englishmen took the fact that Indians retained their own lightish hue in a hot climate as confirmation that the Africans were black through sin rather than their natural environment.[72] Mobberly's conviction that the native Americans lack of hair was artificially produced echoed somewhat these early beliefs that Indians manipulated their appearance, although he himself appears to have believed that their red skin was natural.

Mobberly's emphasis that both native Americans and Africans were cursed by ancestral sin reflected a hardening of Jesuit racism. He felt that the primordial behaviors of both black and red people justified whatever treatment they subsequently received from whites. This conviction added a racist leaven to Mobberly's already strong sense of clericalism and class distinction. Jesuits were superior not only because they were priests and religious over the laity and learned men over the uneducated, but because they were white over the black and red. Mobberly declared, "The colour, therefore most natural to man, ought to be that which is most becoming man, is naturally white."[73] This was a great change from the idealization of the indigenous expressed by the first recruits for the colonial Maryland mission. When Edward Knott volunteered in 1640, he described them as "redeemed with as great a price as the best in Europe."[74] Mobberly's comparative discussions of Ham and Essau showed that Jesuits had taken the Bellarminian model of a world divided between rulers and ruled and given it a distinctly racist spin. The consequent emphasis on slavery and subjection as everlasting curses was a severe impediment to abolitionism.

Furthermore, this hardened racism was a direct consequence of slaveholding. Jesuits in Maryland had few contacts with native Americans after the mid-seventeenth century. First the political situation in colonial Maryland forced them to stop their work among the native Americans, and soon after the tribes in Maryland virtually died out. What was left to the Jesuits in terms of direct contact with people of color was slaveholding over Africans.

Another factor which hardened Jesuit racism toward their slaves was a distortion of the Catholic doctrine of concupiscence. The manner in which the Jesuits filtered their observations of the world through the prism of this teaching helps to explain why they failed to recognize the full humanity of the slaves who appeared before them.

In Augustine's thought, concupisence "stands, in a general way, for every inclination making man turn from God to find satisfaction in material things which are instrinsically evanescent"; sexual desire is the most powerful of these.[75] It is not the only such desire, however. A contemporary definition broadly describes concupiscence as "The orientation or inclination of lower human faculties toward some *created good* (italics mine) without respect for or subordination to the higher faculties."[76] Catholicism has grown to understand this inclination as "a gravitation away from the good."[77] In everyday language, this means that the senses have difficulty subordinating themselves to reason, giving priority to the observation of the transient material world rather than the invisible but eternal spiritual world. Christians have been traditionally admonished to fight this inclination by relying on their abstract reason to ponder what is good and think about what is right.

Taking advantage of the modern theological tendency to broaden the definition of the doctrine of concupiscence beyond an emphasis upon lust, historians may note that a grave, but little noticed, consequence of belief in this doctrine was that it led Jesuits like Mobberly to mistrust any of their sensate experiences. Whatever they observed, therefore, they fit into preconceived worldviews. Consequently, they used deductive reasoning to apply abstract, racist reasoning to their empirical observations about slaves. Rather than begin their reflections from their experiences of black people, they tried to make experiences fit their preconceived theories of blacks as inherently inferior to whites. They inferred from the general to the specific, rather than formed general principles from particular facts or instances.

A sermon of John Digges, S.J. (1712–1746), which encouraged his congregations to fast frequently, illustrated the beginning of this trend. He stated flatly, "We are indispensably obliged to contradict the inclinations of our nature." People who contradicted reason, gave in to their passions, or preferred pleasure to duty were guilty of behaving like animals; rationality alone made human higher than animal nature. Anything irrational would "tend to the destruction of human society."[78]

John Lewis commented in 1753: "Man's greatest weakness consists in receiving too easily impressions from sensible objects. The cares and solicitudes of this life fill his Heart and its pleasures corrupt it by drawing it from God and ye concerns of a future state. This easiness in our nature of receiving violent impressions from sensible objects, may be looked upon as ye Root of all . . . ye disorder of human life."[79]

Robert Molyneux, S.J. added, "the picture I have been drawing is but the natural representation of man in general. . . . What a warfare hath he to sustain against the Devil, the world, and his own concupiscence. This is the condition of all men, without exception. . . ." The cause of this condition was that mankind had sinned. Concupiscence was God's punishment upon all posterity, allowing the world to be more vivid to the senses than God. This, to Molyneux was true slavery: it left its prisoners mired in sin and doomed to spiritual death, unless they decided to place Jesus Christ above all worldly gain.[80]

In their own battles against the consequences of the human fall, Jesuits often displayed a tendency to mistrust their own sense impressions, manipulating their observations to make them deductively subservient to the theories postulated by reason and the "higher faculties" of the mind. What they observed was placed at the service of what they already believed. In this way, their belief in the doctrine of concupiscence prompted them to see black people as born to be slaves rather than born to be fully human.

There is no better example of this phenomenon than Mobberly's interpretation of the physical characteristics of his slaves. He was unable to stop with the simple observation that their skin was black. Rather, he fit this sensual data into preconceived notions that blackness of skin had extended down the ages since Noah's son uncovered his father's drunkenness. God responded, Mobberly affirmed, with "a mark, which no length of ages, no change of climate, no change of food or treatment, and no alteration of circumstances can ever efface. Nothing but their intercourse with whites can change the colour of their skin. . . . God alone can tell when this mark of reprobation is to cease."[81]

Mobberly likewise believed that the hair texture of his slaves embodied this punishment: "From long, straight, flowing, handsome hair, it became quite short, villous and twisted into odious curls, as if crisped by the application of fire."[82] Mobberly answered the claims of scientists that both the skin and the hair of blacks were simply results of the torrid African climate with the retort that their features had not been altered by the move to the more temperate climate of Maryland. That neither skin nor hair changed, even for several generations born in the United States, Mobberly took as confirmation that those features were manifestations of a perpetual divine curse.

Mobberly's observations of negroes began at their birth, and so did his attempts to fit his observations into his theory. He thought he saw effects of the curse in their infancy: "There is a strange coincidence that takes place in negro children. I once saw an infant of a few days old, almost quite white, tho' its father and mother were even (I think) blacker than a crow. . . . I was informed, that this is pretty commonly the case, + that negro children become black as they grow up."[83] Mobberly noticed a couple of exceptions to this in infants, however: "only that the _____ and _____ (modesty forbids) are black + that they have a black or brown thread or circle on the extremity of the nail. These marks are a certain sign that the infant will be black, and negro fathers who suspect the fidelity of their wives consider the want of them as a sufficient reason for abandoning the offspring."[84]

Mobberly went on to say, "The child is white, or very nearly approaches white at its birth before it is stained with actual guilt. Cham, the *birth* of the African race, was white before the commission of crime. The Infant is white, except where modesty conceals, and Cham committed his crime by looking where modesty forbids. View the contrast, and see how striking a resemblance exists between the circumstances of Cham's crime, and those of Negro Infants at the present day."[85] Mobberly continued to read all kinds of symbolism into what he saw: "The skin is black, denoting the heinousness of sin: The hair is crisped, as if scorched by fire, and yet it is not consumed. Strongly indicating the effects of eternal fire which always burns, but never consumes, and finally they are doomed to be *the servants of servants unto their brethren* (Genesis 9:25)."[86]

Mobberly stood well within an Augustinian theology of concupiscence when he made his observations about African American infants. In the treatise "Contra Julian," written in the fifth century, Augustine emphasized that the mark of original sin lay upon the souls of all infants. All humans were conceived as a result of concupiscence, so from each act of conception by sexual intercourse there "is born a man, a good work of God, but not without the evil which the origin of generation contracts."[87] However, where Augustine looked for the sign of this curse in the behavior of people and the tragic events of life, Mobberly saw it in the physical appearances of black and red people.

Like Augustine, Mobberly believed that original sin manifested itself in the lack of reasonable control that human beings were able to exercise over their passions. Mobberly carried this belief a step further for blacks, however, believing that for them, this meant that the curse of their color would first manifest itself in the genital areas of their bodies. This conviction was an elaborate justification of Mobberly's estimate, shared by many whites, that black people were unusually lustful and in need of governance by more temperate whites.

The most important thing to note from his writings about concupiscence, however, is that Mobberly placed the data before his own senses at the service of his preconceived theories regarding race.

The doctrine of concupiscence greatly emphasized the intimate and the personal; it regarded sin as a force of individual rather than social origin. It thus made it difficult for Jesuits to see that it was the institution of slavery itself that was flawed; they saw its existence as divinely ordained and its faults merely as the consequence of the behavioral failure of individual masters and slaves to take up their preconceived places within a hierarchical world.

Mobberly declared, "Children inherit their parents' dispositions and their parents' vices or virtues." Thus it was possible to trace not only the sign of a slave's original sin in his skin color, but also to predict their typical actual sins throughout life. Due to legends that Cham had been a cannibalistic magician and sorcerer, the forebear of the human-sacrificing Canaanites, Mobberly believed that Africans were inclined to eat their young. He took testimony from "old Africans living in Maryland" who reported "with pleasure" that while dwelling in their native continent they had found a "pickaninny," or roasted infant, to have been "the sweetest morsel they ever tasted."[88]

This conviction made it less likely that Jesuits would support abolitionism, for it showed their fear that Africans unrestrained by civilized masters would revert to such barbaric practices as devouring babies.

One final reason that the Jesuits continued to resist abolitionism was their measured reaction to the Enlightenment. On the one hand, Jesuits like John Carroll recognized that the Enlightenment had inspired the most beneficial result of the American Revolution, that "religious liberty to which we Catholics in the United States are so indebted."[89] However, they were less inclined to attribute this benefit to the personal imagination and initiative of the Founding Fathers than they were to believe that God had used them as instruments of the divine will. The Founders' conscious motive in enacting the Bill of Rights may have been to keep religious controversy from undermining civil order, but Jesuits believed God inspired them to their decision only so that the Catholic Church might enjoy the freedom it needed to evangelize the North American continent.[90] Thus Jesuits accepted the Enlightenment in hopes that it would make America more Catholic rather than with the intent of making themselves more American. They had no intention of embracing every Enlightenment concept in order to become more American.

The influence of the "Principle and Foundation" from the *Spiritual Exercises* of Saint Ignatius of Loyola can be seen in this approach to the Enlightenment. Christians were only supposed to utilize things of the world to the extent that they drew them closer to God. Therefore, the Jesuits embraced the Enlightenment to the extent that it instilled religious liberty in American society, but rejected it to the extent that it undermined social hierarchy and order.

Jesuit toleration of the Enlightenment was ultimately limited by the fact that Catholics were people of the Book, convinced that the teachings of the Bible were the indispensable foundation of Christian doctrine and morality. They felt compelled to resist any suggestion that reason and nature alone might replace or contradict Scriptural revelation in judging right or wrong conduct. Thus John Carroll wrote that "I fear the mischief of the first French Encyclopedie, and other works of the same stamp on Religious subjects, has operated too powerfully, & that the human passions are too much interested in countenancing them. . . . *They have Moses, and the prophets;* if *they hear them not* &c."[91]

What this stance signified was that Jesuits rejected the premise that slavery was immoral because it was unreasonable. Slavery could not be unreasonable, Mobberly replied, because what Scripture said was moral must be *ipso facto* reasonable. Mobberly commented, "Slavery is according to reason. *All men are free; God never made one man to serve another. (Rousseau.)* I should be glad to know whence this text comes. I can find it nowhere but in the mouths of modern sages."[92]

While the Enlightenment often seemed to reject or challenge Christianity, Mobberly believed that it was a natural progression of the Reformation. To him, the many revolutions in Europe and Latin America that broke out after 1789 "moved on the same principle that was formerly hatched in the brain of Martin Luther."[93]

Mobberly's skepticism about the Enlightenment can be seen in what he chose to quote from Thomas Jefferson in his writings. He cited passages which undermined the case for the existence of an absolute right to freedom for slaves. He especially relied on *Notes on the State of Virginia*, in which Jefferson asserted that blacks were inferior to whites in reason and imagination. Mobberly concurred with Jefferson that blacks participated "more of sensation than reflection" and were given "to sleep, when abstracted from their diversions and unemployed in labor."[94]

There is no instance in his surviving writings of Mobberly quoting Jefferson's insistent proclamation in the Declaration of Independence "that all men are created equal."[95] In fact, on the very day of Jefferson's death, July 4, 1826, Mobberly commemorated the fiftieth anniversary of American independence with a diary entry on the nature of true liberty. Mobberly wrote, "Properly speaking, there is no such thing as liberty in the wide sense in which many are willing to take it. No sooner was man created than he was commanded to obey—how then can he look for liberty since his fall?"

To Mobberly, there was only one way to be free: by following the true Church of Catholicism. Like John Carroll, Mobberly's first gratitude as an American was for a government "congenial to the nature of man . . . when every man can regulate his conscience according to the dictates of reason and the rules of the Christian faith."[96] Also like Carroll, however, Mobberly hoped that this religious liberty would result in the conversion of all America to Catholicism rather than the conversion of American Catholics to Americanism.

After Vatican Council II in the 1960s, there arose a historiographical tendency to regard John Carroll as "an Enlightenment bishop." More recent reflection, however, has demonstated that John Carroll and other Jesuits actually had fundamental differences with the Enlightenment. They continued to believe that human reason must be augmented by divine revelation; that God was intimately involved in the lives of his creatures; that human beings were sinners rather than infinitely perfectible through self-initiative; that a divinely revealed religion, Catholicism, was necessary for reaching God.[97] Each of these convictions was used by Jesuits as a justification for anti-abolitionism. Divine revelation and God's will were taken as mandating slavery; the imperfectibility of man argued that some needed the guidance to be provided by masters; there was no divinely revealed mandate against slavery. The impact of Jesuit resistance to the Enlightenment upon their antiabolitionism has been underestimated.

Looking back from the late twentieth century, some scholars saw the story of Maryland Jesuit slaveholding as a warning that the desire missionaries always feel to enter into the culture they are trying to evangelize can lead them to adapt some of that culture's moral blindness. A few argue that the Jesuits of Maryland remained slaveholders because they were too uncritical of the colonial and early federal cultures that valued the practice.[98] However, when the Jesuit hostility to Protestantism and their ambivalence toward the Enlightenment is added to the equation, it becomes clear that there were also aspects of the colonial and early federal cultures of which Maryland Jesuits were too critical. They resisted the truth that the Protestant theologians and Enlightenment writers who sired the abolitionist movements had fresh and valuable perspectives on social morality. In some respects, Jesuits resisted the values of American culture all too carefully.

Joseph Mobberly's "Slavery or Cham," though never published and written by a Jesuit who had fallen out of favor with his superiors, stood squarely in the mainstream of Maryland Jesuit opposition to abolitionism. This manuscript reveals a traditionalism hardened by racism and one that refused to acknowledge any argument that slavery was inherently immoral. The rigidity of this manuscript, however, was actually a defense mechanism against the social flux in which Mobberly and other Maryland Jesuits found themselves in the early nineteenth century. They were struggling to reconcile a somewhat medieval view of social structure and hierarchy, inherited from their Church, with the emerging egalitarianism of the young United States. Jesuits wanted to be faithful Catholics, but they also wanted to fit into the American culture in which they felt called to spread the Catholic interpretation of the Gospel. In such a situation of change, it was inevitable that at least some Jesuits would attempt to cling to old certainties. The attempt to defend slavery in principle while looking for ways to end their personal practice of it must be seen as an attempt to reconcile these tensions. Joseph Mobberly's decision to oppose abolitionism while advocating that Jesuit plantations be freed of slaves was not a reflection of personal eccentricity or merely his own contradiction, but a reflection of a war within the Jesuit soul itself.

NOTES

1. Peter Kenney, S.J., "Statement of Religious Discipline, 1820," Item no. XT1–2, Box 126, Folder 7, Archives of the Maryland Province (MPA), Special Collections Division, Lauinger Library, Georgetown University, Washington, D.C.

2. Joseph Agonito, "St. Inigoe's Manor: A Nineteenth Century Jesuit Plantation," *Maryland Historical Magazine* 72, no. 1 (Spring, 1977), p. 83.

3. Brother Joseph Mobberly, S.J. to Father Giovanni Grassi, S.J., February 5, 1815, Item no. 204K3, Box 58, Folder 6, MPA.

4. Brother Joseph Mobberly, S.J. to Father Giovanni Grassi, S.J., November 5, 1814, Item no. 204 M8, Box 58, Folder 8, MPA.

5. Brother Joseph Mobberly, S.J., "Slavery or Cham," p. 1, Brother Joseph Mobberly, S.J. Papers (BJMSJP), Special Collections Division, Lauinger Library, Georgetown University, Washington, D.C.

6. Agonito, *op. cit.*, p. 98.

7. Mobberly, "Diary, Part IV: Wednesday, October 20, 1824," BJMSJP.

8. Jean B. Lee, *The Price of Nationhood: The American Revolution in Charles County* (New Yorkk: W. W. Norton, 1994), p.75.

9. John W. O'Malley, *The First Jesuits* (Cambridge: Harvard University Press, 1993), pp. 16–18

10. David Fleming, *The Spiritual Exercises of St. Ignatius: A Literal Translation and a Contemporary Reading* (St. Louis: The Institute of Jesuit Sources, 1978), pp. 140–141.

11. "Joseph Mosley and the Eighteenth Century Mission," in Robert Emmett Curran, editor, *American Jesuit Spirituality: The Maryland Tradition, 1634–1900* (Mahwah, N.J.: Paulist Press, 1988), p.106, p. 112

12. John Pulton, S.J. (1697–1749), in Maryland, 1738–1749; Sermon Pu-1, American Catholic Sermon Collection (ACSC), Special Collections Division, Lauinger Library, Georgetown University, Washington, D.C.

13. George Hunter(1713–1779), in Maryland 1746–1756; 1759–1769; 1770–1779; Sermon Hu-2, ACSC.

14. Steven Ozment, *Protestants: The Birth of a Revolution* (New York: Doubleday, Image Books, 1991), pp. 32–41.

15. John Bolton, S.J. (1742–1809), in Maryland 1769–1809; Sermon Bol-2, July 31, 1773, ACSC.

16. Albert J. Raboteau, *A Fire in the Bones: Reflections on African American Religious History* (Boston: Beacon Press, 1995), pp. 117–119.

17. Joseph Mosley (1731–1787), in Maryland 1756–1787; Sermon Mos-2, ACSC.

18. Joseph Mosley, Sermon Mos-6, ACSC.

19. Mobberly, "Slavery or Cham," pp. 1–2, BJMSJP.

20. James Hennesey, S.J., *American Catholics: A History of the Roman Catholic Community in the United States* (New York: Oxford University Press, 1981), p. 145.

21. Robert Emmett Curran, S.J., *The Bicentennial History of Georgetown University , I: From Academy to University, 1789–1889* (Washington, D.C.: Georgetown University Press, 1993), p. 112.

22. Jaroslav Pelikan, *Jesus Through the Centuries: His Place in the History of Culture* (New York: Harper and Row, 1985).

23. Raymond E. Brown, *A Crucified Christ in Holy Week: Essays on the Four Gospel Passion Narratives* (Collegeville, Minn.: The Liturgical Press, 1986), pp. 68–71.

24. James Ashby, S.J. (1714–1767), in Maryland, 1742–1767; Sermon As-11, ACSC.

25. Mobberly, "Slavery or Cham," p. 5, BJMSJP.

26. Mobberly, "Diary, Part VI," BJMSJP.

27. Robert V. Remini, *Henry Clay: Statesman of the Union* (New York.: W. W. Norton, 1991), p. 484.

28. John Carroll, "Funeral Eulogy of George Washington," in Thomas O'Brien Hanley, S.J., *The John Carroll Papers (JCP) II*, (Notre Dame, Ind.: University of Notre Dame Press), p. 295.

29. John Carroll, "Religious Toleration," in Hanley, editor, *JCP*, III, p. 472.

30. Jay P. Dolan, *The American Catholic Experience: A History from Colonial Times to the Present* (Garden City, N.Y.: Doubleday, 1985), pp. 91–93.

31. Marion Normin, "John Gother and the English Way of Spirituality," *Recusant History* 11 (London: The Catholic Record Society, 1972), pp. 306.

32. *Ibid.*, pp. 307–308.

33. *Ibid*, p. 315.

34. Dolan, *op. cit.*, p. 92.

35. Mobberly, "Diary, Part I: Breadth of a Methodist's Conscience," BJMSJP.

36. Normin, *op.cit.* p. 313.

37. Eamon Duffy, "Richard Challoner 1691–1781: A Memoir," in Eamon Duffy, editor, *Challoner and his Church: A Catholic Bishop in Georgian England* (London: Darton, Longman & Todd), pp. 1–26.

38. Dolan, *op. cit.*, p. 92.

39. Richard Challoner, "Caveat Against the Methodists," (Mount Vernon, Ohio: John P. Mardin, 1817; Early American Imprints, American Antiquarian Society, Worcester, Massachusetts), p. 7.

40. Mobberly, "Slavery or Cham," p. 11, BJMSJP.

41. Challoner, *op.cit.*, p. 8.

42. Mobberly, "Slavery or Cham," pp. 1–2.

43. John Bolton, Sermon Bol-1, ACSC.

44. James Broderick, S.J., *Robert Bellarmine: Saint and Scholar* (Westminster, Md.: The Newman Press, 1961), pp. 53–54.

45. Joseph N. Tylenda, S.J., *Jesuit Saints and Martyrs: Short Biographies of the Saints, Blessed, Venerables and Servants of God of the Society of Jesus* (Chicago: Loyola University Press, 1984), p. 338.

46. William Hunter, S.J. (1659–1723), in Maryland 1692–1723; Sermon Hun-1, ACSC.

47. Mobberly, "Slavery or Cham," p. 2, BJMSJP.

48. Lee, *op.cit.*, p. 82.

49. Richard Molyneux, S.J. (1696–1766), in Maryland 1730–1749; Sermon Mo-1, "On Hearing Sermons Diligently," ACSC.

50. Germain BarnabasBitouzey, (died circa. 1815), in Maryland 1794–circa. 1815; Sermon Bi-7, ACSC.

51. Thomas Bokenkotter, *A Concise History of the Catholic Church* (New York: Doubleday Image Books, 1990 edition), pp. 284–293.

52. Germain Barnabas Bitouzey, Sermon Bi-9, ACSC.

53. Luis M. Bermejo, S.J., *Infallibility on Trial: Church, Conciliarity and Communion* (Westminster, Md.: Christian Classics, 1992), pp. 313–314. The councils which condoned slavery in various ways included Lateran III (1179), Lateran IV (1215), Lyons I (1245) and Lyons II (1274).

54. Mobberly, "Slavery or Cham," pp. 7–9, BJMSJP.

55. *Ibid.*, p. 6.

56. Stephen F. Brett, *Slavery and the Catholic Tradition: Rights in the Balance* (New York: Peter Lang, 1994), p. 192.

57. Richard J. Blackwell, *Galileo, Bellarmine and the Bible* (Notre Dame, Ind.: University of Notre Dame Press, 1991), p. 11.

58. Saint Robert Bellarmine to Paolo Antonio Foscarini, April 12, 1615, in Marvin Perry, Joseph R. Peden and Theodore H. Von Laue, editors, *Sources of the Western Tradition, II: From the Renaissance to the Present* (Boston: Houghton Mifflin, 1991), pp. 36–37. For an analysis of why the patristic fathers like Augustine were accorded such importance by the Council of Trent, see. Blackwell, *op.cit.*, p. 11: "This was not merely a general respect for revered ancestors: it was rather a respect for what was understood to be the conduit for a unique body of truth which was to be held in a reverence equal, according to Trent, to that of Scripture itself. . . . The important consequent was that the 'unanimous agreement of the Fathers on matters pertaining to faith and morals was used as a touchstone to determine the content of the Apostolic tradition of revelation from God."

59. Augustine, *The City of God: An Abridged Version from the Translation by Gerald G. Walsh, S.J., Demetrius B. Zema, S.J., Grace Monahan, O.S.U. and Daniel J. Honan, edited by Vernon J. Bourke* (New York: Doubleday, Image Books Edition,1958), p. 461.

60. Saint Thomas Aquinas, *The "Summa Theologica" of Saint Thomas Aquinas*, Second Part of the Second Part, Question 57, Third Article, Reply Objection 2; literally translated by the fathers of the English Dominican Province (London: Burns, Oates and Washburn Ltd., 1929), p. 110.

61. *New Catholic Encyclopedia*, prepared by an editorial staff of the Catholic University of America, Washington, D.C. (New Yorkk: McGraw Hill, 1967), s.v. "Slavery."

62. Saint Robert Bellarmine, *De Laicis, or the Treatise on Civil Government*, Translated by Kathleen E. Murphy (New York: Fordham University Press, 1928), p. 31.

63. Mobberly, "Slavery or Cham," pp. 26–28, BJMSJP.

64. John Carroll, "Response to Patrick Smyth," 1789, in Hanley, editor, *JCP*, I, p. 343.

65. Peter Kenney, S.J., "Statement of Religious Discipline," 1820, Item no. XTI-2, Box 126, Folder 7, MPA.

66. Mobberly, "Slavery or Cham," p. 12, BJMSJP.

67. David Brion Davis, *The Problem of Slavery in Western Culture* (New York, New York: Oxford University Press, 1966), pp. 63–64, pp. 316–317; Winthrop D. Jordan, *White Over Black: American Attitudes Toward the Negro, 1550–1812* (Chapel Hill: University of North Carolina Press, 1968), pp. 17–20.

68. John J. McNeill, S.J. *The Church and the Homosexual* (New York: Next Year Publications, 1985), pp. 58–59.

69. Mobberly, "Slavery or Cham," pp. 42–45, BJMSJP.

70. *Ibid*., pp. 71–78.

71. H.C. Porter, *The Inconstant Savage: England and the North American Indian, 1500–1660* (London: Duckworth, 1979), pp. 92–95.

72. Karen Ordahl Kupperman, *Settling with the Indians: The Meeting of English and Indian Cultures in North America, 1580–1640* (Totowa, N.J.y: Rowman and Littlefield, 1980),pp. 36–37.

73. Mobberly, "Slavery or Cham," p. 102.

74. Christopher Morris to Edward Knott, July 27, 1640, in Curran, editor, *op. cit*., p. 57.

75. J. N. D. Kelly, *Early Christian Doctrines* (London: Adam and Charles Black, 1965), pp. 364–365.

76. "Concupiscence," unsigned article in Joseph A. Komonchak, Mary Collins and Dermot A. Lane, editors, *The New Dictionary of Theology* (Wilmington, Del.: Michael Glazier, Inc., 1987), p. 220.

77. Edward Yarnold, S.J., *The Theology of Original Sin* (Notre Dame, Ind.: Fides, 1971), p. 24.

78. John Digges, S.J. (1712–1746), in Maryland, 1742–1746; Sermon Dig-3, ACSC.

79. John Lewis, S.J (1721–1788), in Maryland 1750–1788; Sermon Le-4, ACSC.

80. Robert Molyneux, S.J. (1738–1808), in Maryland and Pennsylvania, 1769–1808; Sermon Mol-2, 1779, ACSC.

81. Mobberly, "Slavery or Cham," pp. 41–42, p. 44, BJMSJP.

82. *Ibid*, pp. 45–46.

83. *Ibid*., pp. 49–50.

84. *Ibid*. p. 51; Mobberly noted in parentheses that he had obtained this information from the Encyclopedia of Arts and Sciences, vol. 12, p. 795.

85. *Ibid*. p. 51.

86. *Ibid,* p. 52.

87. Augustine, *Against Julian* (New York: Fathers of the Church Incorporated, 1957), p. 147.

88. Mobberly, "Slavery or Cham," pp. 87–88, BJMSJP.

89. John Carroll to Leonardo Antonelli, September 20, 1793, in Hanley, editor, *JCP*, II, p. 102.

90. John Carroll, Undated Sermon "Commemoration of American Independence," in Hanley, editor, *JCP,* III, pp. 460–461.

91. John Carroll to Charles Plowden, February 20, 1782, in Hanley, editor, *JCP*, I, p. 67. Carroll was here paraphrasing the words of Father Abraham in Jesus' parable of the rich man and Lazarus. The rich man, now burning in hell for his lifelong neglect of the beggar Lazarus, wents to send a message to his surviving brothers so that they might avoid the same fate. Abraham replies, "If they will not listen either to Moses or to the prophets, they will not be convinced even if someone should rise from the dead." (Luke 16:31.)

92. Mobberly, "Slavery or Cham," p. 26, BJMSJP.

93. *Ibid.*, pp. 9–10.

94. *Ibid.* See also Thomas Jefferson, *Notes on the State of Virginia*, edited by William Peden (New York: W. W. Norton, published for the Institute of Early American History and Culture at Williamsburg, Viriginia, 1982), pp. 83–85, p. 139.

95. Thomas Jefferson, "The Declaration of Independence," in William Benton, publisher, *The Annals of America, II: Resistance and Revolution, 1775–1783* (Chicago: *Encyclopaedia Britannica, Inc.*, 1968), pp. 447–449.

96. Mobberly, S.J., "Diary, Part V: Fourth of July, 1826," BJMP.

97. Charles Edwards O'Neill, "John Carroll, the 'Catholic Enlightenment' and Rome," pp. 2–3, and Carla Bang, "John Carroll and the Enlightenment," pp. 130–132, in Raymond J. Kupke, editor, *American Catholic Preaching and Piety in the Time of John Carroll* (Lanham, Md.: University Press of America, Melville Studies in Church History II, 1991).

98. Edward F. Beckett, S.J., "Listening to Our History: Inculturation and Jesuit Slaveholding," *Studies in the Spirituality of Jesuits* 28, no. 5 (November, 1996).

CHAPTER SIX

To Serve the Slave or the Immigrant?

IN 1854, THOMAS MULLEDY, S.J., (1794–1860), THE FORMER PROVINCIAL WHO HAD conducted the mass sale of Maryland Jesuit slaves sixteen years earlier, discussed the obligations of masters toward their servants in a lecture delivered at the College of the Holy Cross in Worcester, Massachusetts. The first such obligation which Mulledy proclaimed was that masters must make "a good choice of their domestics. . . . It is not permitted masters, according to the law of the Gospel, to have in their service useless persons, who live in idleness and sloth."[1] This theme, that employers had both the right and duty to choose workers of upright character, had been a factor in Mulledy's resolve years earlier to replace slaveholding with immigrant tenant labor on the Maryland plantations. Many of the characteristics which Mulledy attributed to bad servants in his Holy Cross lecture—that they were violent, swearers, drunkards, insolent in speech, unchaste, immodest, idle and slothful—were traits which Jesuit observers like Joseph Mobberly had ascribed to their slaves during the last years before Mulledy's mass sale. Jesuits also worried that similar qualities were emerging among working class, white Catholic immigrants in the cities of the eastern seaboard whenever they were left too long without the care of priests. In the case of slaves, such conduct became an excuse for Jesuits to get rid of them. In the case of the immigrants, such conduct became a pretext for the Jesuits to draw closer to them through increased urban ministry. Racism was at work in this paradox, for the Jesuits regarded whites as more reformable morally than blacks.

Who was the man whose actions thrust this paradox into the heart of Jesuit life in the United States? The son of an Irish immigrant farmer, Mulledy grew up in Hampshire County in western Virginia. After paying his own way through Georgetown College, he joined the Society of Jesus and was sent to

Rome for his theological studies. There he developed a reputation as an outspoken defender of republican American values against the more authoritarian European clergy who taught there at the time. His position foreshadowed his struggles as provincial, when he would nudge Maryland Jesuits away from their traditional emphasis on rural ministries toward engagement with the city. Mulledy initially wanted to work in ministry to native Americans upon his return home, but superiors assigned him to higher education. By 1829, when he was only 35 years old, Mulledy was president of Georgetown. In January, 1838, he became the second provincial of Maryland. In the aftermath of the controversial sale of the slaves later that year, Mulledy had to resign as provincial and go to Rome to defend his decision to invest income from the sale in construction projects on the Georgetown campus rather than in the training of Jesuit priests. When he did return to the United States in 1843, it was at first to serve in Massachusetts as the founding president of Holy Cross. In 1845, his reputation somehwat rehabilitated, Mulledy returned to the Chesapeake region to head Georgetown for another three years.[2]

Mulledy's proposed transition to white tenant labor on the Jesuit farms did not come to pass without opposition within the order. Between 1814 and 1820, the Jesuits of Maryland first instituted, but then reversed, a policy of gradually selling all their slaves to new masters who would agree to free them after some years of preparation.[3] When the Jesuits finally turned back to the idea of a mass slave sale in 1830s, they shunned their previous resolve to prepare their slaves gradually for freedom and instead sold them to new owners in Louisiana. The long uncertainty about whether and how to proceed with the disposition of their slaves revealed that there remained a strong sentiment within the Society of Jesus to keep them in Catholic hands, no matter how recalcitrant their behavior, out of fidelity to the obligations that Jesuits had traditionally felt to a people they regarded as inferior to themselves.

Still, the basic insight of Mulledy and Joseph Mobberly, that Jesuits now had choice with regard to the people who would work on their land, prevailed in the end. Why? One part of the answer is that these Jesuits correctly foresaw an era of great demographic change for the Roman Catholic Church in the United States, a period which would give the Jesuits many more demands on their ministerial attention than the care of slaves and plantations.

By 1820, some Jesuits anticipated that their church, hitherto largely rural and largely situated in the states of Maryland and Pennsylvania, was poised to become a predominantly urban institution along the eastern seaboard through an increase of European Catholic immigration. This prospect raised the question or whether of not the Jesuit farms had outlived any apostolic utility that they might have once possessed. Related to this was the question of whether the Jesuit order could become numerous enough to operate in both the country and the city, or whether it would it have to choose between ministries in those two areas.

Just two statistics are necessary to demonstrate how correct was the surmise that a demographic revolution would overwhelm Jesuit ministries and their supporting plantations as the nineteenth century proceeded. It is doubtful that the total number of Catholics in what became the United States ever exceeded 35,000 before the establishment of the Constitution in 1789. Between the first federal census in 1790 and 1850, however, over a million Catholic immigrants arrived in the United States from Europe.[4] This was a change of such magnitude that it was inevitable that those Jesuits who foresaw it and sensed its early stages would seek changes in their manner of proceeding in order to meet it. The fate of the Jesuits' slaves hinged in part upon this discernment, with advocates of urban ministry, like Mulledy, tending to view the old plantation system as an obstacle to be discarded and defenders of rural ministry, like Peter Dzierozynski (1779–1850), arguing that the order simply could not walk away from the moral obligations it had long incurred in the countryside—especially duties toward the slaves.

Efforts have been made to trace the motivations of those Jesuits who took particular sides in this discernment. The history of the Georgetown faculty reveals that there was a basic cultural dichotomy between two groups, who may be designated as "native" and "continental" Jesuits.[5] This cleavage was not unique to the Jesuits, but a general characteristic of the American Catholic Church during the early decades of the nineteenth century.[1]

The "native" Jesuits may be generally defined as those who were raised in the United States or in the British Isles. Heavily influenced by Anglo-American and/or Irish culture, they placed great stress on individual liberty, self-initiative, and the provisions of the Constitution, particularly the Bill of Rights. Indeed, they hoped that the Catholic Church would apply some of the republican ideals of the Constitution to its own internal governance.

The "continentalists," by contrast, may be generally defined as those Jesuits who came from the European mainland. They immigrated to the United States because of the harassment they were subjected to during the suppression of the Society and also because of the anti-clericalism fostered by the French Revolution. Basically, these Jesuits were representative of Europe's *ancien regime*. The continentalists tended to be skeptical of American culture, wanted to see Catholics maintain a critical distance from republican ideals, and felt that the Church should continue the authoritarian structure of government that it had developed during the Counter-Reformation.[7]

Place of origin, however, was not always indicative of the positions which specific Jesuits took on the slavery question. The Italian Giovanni Grassi (1775–1849) was a continentalist by birth, but he was supportive enough of the Constitution to perceive that slavery contradicted it. He predicted that it would be allowed to die out gradually. A more adamant continentalist advocate of disposing of the slaves was the Alsatian Anthony Kohlmann (1771–1836), whose vision of more schools in the eastern seaports was an impetus to those who wanted to abandon the rural ministry epitomized by the plantations.[8] There were both natives and continentalists who favored keeping the slaves, and both natives and continentalists who favored disposing of them.

It is better, therefore, to analyze the division over slavery not according to where various Jesuits came from, nor in terms of how they felt about secular and ecclesiastical government, but in terms of where they believed the future needs of Jesuit ministry lay. If a specific Jesuit was convinced of the coming urgency of ministry to the urban immigrant, he often advocated discarding the plantations and/or selling the slaves.

The immigrants, by the weight of their numbers and the strength of their cultural background, came to offer some hope that the United States might one day become a majority Catholic country. In 1820 the 124 Catholic church buildings in the United States represented a lower sum than those of any other denomination, and the 195,000 Catholics in the nation represented fewer adherents than either Methodists or Baptists. By 1850, just thirty years later, immigration had pushed the total number of Catholics to 1,606,00, making Roman Catholicism the largest single denomination in the nation. The second largest group in 1850, the Methodists, had more than a quarter million fewer adherents than the Catholics.[9] One reason that the hope that enough immigrants might come to America to make it a more Catholic country moved Jesuits was that it seemed to offer a chance to foster more vocations to religious life or priesthood. In the racial climate of the early nineteenth century, it was not possible for African Americans to become clergy, but it was possible for Americans of European origin to. The Jesuits were drawn to immigrant ministry as a means of perpetuating the existence of their own order. When Mulledy arrived at Holy Cross in 1843, for example, he followed the wishes of Bishop Benedict Fenwick of Boston, a fellow Maryland Jesuit, and wrote to the Jesuit general that the new college would admit Catholic boys only. The "dangerous communications with the Protestant boys" which Mulledy believed marked Georgetown, the centerpiece of the old rural ministry in Maryland, thus would be avoided in Massachusetts. Mulledy anticipated that "in all probability" that there would be more vocations at Holy Cross alone, than there would be in all the Catholic colleges that admitted Protestants put together.[10] Contrast this conviction with the "Proposals for Establishing an Academy at George-Town" in 1789, which stated "Agreeably to the liberal Principle of our Constitution, the SEMINARY will be open to Students of EVERY RELIGIOUS PROFESSION."[11]

The ultimate decision to hold a mass sale in 1838 may be regarded as a compromise between the ruralists and the urbanists. The Jesuit farms were retained—a concession to the ruralists—but the slaves were sold—a concession to the urbanists. The hope was that efficient farms, run by free labor, would play a role in supporting the new Jesuit ministries in the cities. This hope was realized, for the farms began to prosper for the first time during the generation after the mass sale. By the beginning of the Civil War, events had vindicated Mobberly's anticipation that Jesuit farms would do quite well without slaves.[12]

One reason this solution was so long delayed, however, was a tactical error of the urbanists. Such pioneering urbanists as Kohlmann tried to promote their vision by stressing the financial benefits that would eventually accrue to the Society as a result of concentrating ministries in the cities. This emphasis ran up against a cultural bias, the longstanding Jesuit hostility to profits. This hostility had long impeded the progress of the plantations; now it became an impediment to effective urban ministry, too.

Kohlmann showed his basic continentalism through the authoritarian methods he adapted as President of Georgetown from 1817–1820. However, he also worked in Manhattan between 1808 and 1813, there founding the New York Literary Institution, a short-lived secondary school. This experience convinced Kohlmann that Catholic immigrants in great cities like Boston, New York and Philadelphia already needed more priests, and also that there was going to be much more immigration. What Kohlmann seems to have feared was that the new arrivals would drift too far toward American republicanism and individualism unless their adjustment to their new country was mediated by the Church. Confirmation that this was his anxiety may be found in Archbishop Carroll's assessment that one reason Kohlmann's school failed was his refusal to hire lay teachers who had not been trained in the Jesuit method of education. Carroll felt that Kohlmann was overly anxious to leave all the instruction in Jesuit hands, an unnecessary move in such a populous city with many well-qualified foreign-born schoolmasters.[13] Kohlmann's scrupulosity may have doomed the New York Literary Insitute, but it also apparently became a means by which this Jesuit of continental European origin reconciled the tension between the traditional committment to the plantations and the growing needs in the cities. Jesuits, he felt, were simply more needed in the cities than the countryside because there now was a greater need to strengthen Catholic identity in the motley cultural atmosphere of places like New York.

Kuhlmann's ill-advised emphasis on the potential profitability of urban ministry arose through his reaction to the news that his Manhattan school must close because there were not enough Jesuits to station both there and at Georgetown College and the other apostolates in Maryland. Kuhlmann's perspective was similar to the characteristic attitude of members of the American Colonization Society when they sought money for their scheme of relocating slaves to Africa. Commercial and trading centers like New York offered more opportunities for voluntary charitable activities than landed towns like Washington.[14] That was not a small consideration for a school administrator like Kohlmann in an era when Jesuit schools were forbidden to charge tuition. He was convinced his school in New York had great potential to become self-supporting because it was located in a more dynamic economic setting than the Maryland plantations.

The ban on Jesuits charging tuitions lasted until 1832–1833, when Maryland Jesuits, as part of the reorganization process that made their mission an independent province of the Society of Jesus, successfully petitioned the Jesuit general in Rome for permission "to receive pensions from day scholars" in places where the schools lacked foundations and other adequate means of support.[15] The traditional policy of free marticulation was based upon an ideal of Saint Ignatius of Loyola that Jesuit ministries should be offered gratuitously whenever possible. The Constitutions of the Society of Jesus stated that alms could be accepted but not begged, "for the greater edification of the people."[16] This norm was a reaction to the late medieval clergy's fattening upon fees for their ministries, an abuse which Jesuits viewed as a major cause of the Reformation.[17] Thus there was a great demand on the plantations to provide compensating support for schools like Georgetown, but plantations as poorly run as the Jesuit ones had trouble carrying one school, let alone several. Kohlman warned that the Jesuits would "starve and go ragged" in Maryland but could have $60,000 invested in New York banks within ten years if they cultivated well-disposed donors in the business community. That would be a financial foundation which the plantations could never come close to providing.[18]

Schools founded in the Protestant tradition did not have to contend with the Jesuit antipathy to tuition. The records of Harvard College make it clear that tuition was charged there from the earliest days. In the seventeenth century, when there was a shortage of hard money, students often paid Harvard with wheat, malt, cattle or poultry. When tuition was raised, the cost of living and the expenses of paying tutors and supporting more students were the reasons. Sometimes students were assessed extra money if they took a course with a professor to whom the college could not give an adequate salary otherwise. Always, however, there was the expectation that students would bear some of the cost of their own education.[19] This was so even though most colleges founded during the colonial period also received measures of governmental support, beginning with the 400 pounds that Massachusetts Bay contributed to the founding of Harvard in 1636. Later, the college received grants of land and further tax levies from Massachusetts. In Virginia, tobacco was taxed to support William and Mary, and land control fees also went to the school—including George Washington's surveying license.[20] A system of state support for education emerged in New England, especially, because the Puritans there believed that learning was necessary in order to distinguish between true and false religion.[21] However, since most Protestant Americans of the early nineteenth century still believed that Catholicism was one of the false religions, there was no tradition of state support for a schools like Georgetown or the New York Literary Institute.

At the same time that he was trying to promote his hardheaded financial view of the Society's affairs, even Kohlmann fostered sentimentality about slaveholding among Jesuits in a sermon which included a tale of how a Brazilian slave woman had edified her master. She had consecrated her life to God and wore a crucifix around her neck as a sign of her perpetual virginity. When the master approached her sexually, she begged him to look upon her crucifix and contemplate the high price Jesus had paid to redeem each of them. Would he take an action which would destroy two such dearly bought souls? Moved, the master abandoned his harassment of "her who was indeed a slave by her condition but a heroine by her faith."[22]

Kohlmann's sermon echoed a widespread Jesuit conviction that there was much grace for a master himself to gain through slaveholding, so long as he conducted it with humility and a realization that the slaves were children of God. Opportunities to draw souls to Christ would be lost if slaves were let go. The "Principle and Foundation," from the *Exercises*, as applied here, still saw slaveowning as one of the means by which a Jesuit could attain his own salvation through caring properly for the slaves entrusted to his charge.

Those who wished to retain the slaves typically feared what would happen to them if they passed out of Jesuit supervision. Would lecherous new masters await them, along with other dangers to their moral and religious development? Typical of these doubters was Francis Dzierozynski, a Polish emigre who was appointed as the Jesuit General's unofficial permanent representative in the United States in 1821 after expulsion from his homeland by occupying Russians.[23]

Dzierozynski believed two things. First, the plantations should be cherished as a "perpetual good," no matter what their economic record. Second, the slaves who dwelt on them should not be regarded as an economic investment, but as spiritually needy "children" whose needs had been entrusted to the Society of Jesus by divine will.[24] Even if the Society were to respond to the needs of Catholics in the cities, Jesuits would still have a moral obligation to care for the slaves.

In pondering the plantations, Dziezorynski took a classicist view of moral problems. This perspective is dominated by a sense that the world is complete, fixed for all eternity, and marked by the harmony of an objective order. It describes the world in terms of sharply defined essences using absract, universal concepts. Its conclusions remain the same, and it emphasizes the mandate to sustain the established order.[25] When Dzierozynski said that the plantations were a perpetual good that must be cherished no matter what their economic condition, he epitomized this cultural paradigm.

Set against this classicist view was an ideal in the Jesuit Constitutions that Jesuits should go where the greater apostolic need lay. Ignatius gave two justifications for this principle, the shortage of available workers and "the wretchedness and infirmity of the people there and their danger of eternal condemnation." Ignatius also stressed that an estimate should be made as to where the greater fruit was likely to be reaped through the usual means of the Society of Jesus: "where one sees the door more widely open and a better disposition and readiness among the people to be profited."[26] Ignatius believed that in some cases, these norms would involve travel to new sites for ministries, while in others they would involve "residing steadily and continually in certain places."[27] The criterion, however, was heavily related to the need and receptivity of the people who were to be ministered to.

The question of who might be more receptive to Jesuit ministries was an issue that could be manipulated to favor the immigrants against the slaves. Indeed, the 1820s began a strong transition in Jesuit rhetoric toward concentration on the unworthiness of the slaves to receive Jesuit ministrations.[28] This change can be noted in the comments of Mulledy regarding the obligation to select good servants, and in the comments of Peter Kenney regarding the peace that would fall upon the Maryland mission once it was freed of the burden of slaveholding.

For a time, the parameters of the discussion assumed that the Jesuits faced an either/or choice between rural and urban ministry. Either everything in the countryside must go or not. Mobberly, however, envisioned a possible compromise in which the Jesuits would keep some presence in rural areas through farms operated with white tenant labor. This was an important insight, for it allowed the future of slaveholding and the future of the plantations themselves to be considered separately.

Mobberly began to ruminate on the unprofitability of slaveholding as early as 1812, when he completed a census of the longevity of the slaves at St. Inigoe's. While records were poorly kept, he believed that many lived to be nonagenarians and even centenarians. It was a fact that only nine of fifty-five slaves at St. Inigoes had died during Mobberly's first six years of management there, beginning in 1806.[29] These statistics apparently convinced Mobberly that the Jesuits were fulfilling their paternal obligations to the slaves quite well, but at great practical expense.

Mobberly's testimony contradicts the conclusion that the vortex of poor living conditions, greater exposure to contagion, heavier tasks, and deficient medical attention gave slaves shorter life expectancies and higher mortality rates than whites throughout the South. There has been some skepticism concerning a tradition that many aged slaves spent a long decline living off the largess of their masters.[30] Had Mobberly possessed more reliable information on the ages of his slaves, it is possible that his data might not have been so far out of alignment with this tradition after all. However, the crucial effect of this episode was that Mobberly believed in the longevity of his slaves and spoke from that perception.

On February 5, 1815, Mobberly sent his first detailed proposal for free labor plantations to Grassi, now the mission superior. Mobberly gave three motives for his proposal.

The first was that the Jesuits should no longer risk their own salvation by taking upon themselves the responsibility of governing the morally obtuse slaves. As their "parents" in the Lord, the Jesuits would be blamed at the last judgment for the slaves' failure to learn and practices the basics of Christian living, so it was best to abandon them as hopelessly incapable of enculcating the same. This was Mobberly's own interpretation of the "Principle and Foundation. Since Christians should only make use of created things so long as they helped them achieve everlasting life, the Jesuits should now concede that their slaveholding no longer served their own best end.[31] Contrast Mobberly's thought here with Mulledy's comments on the damnation that would await Jesuits who abandoned immigrant orphans: "If these children be this day deserted by you . . . the blood of the murdered Abel calls aloud for vengeance upon you."[32]

Mobberly's second motive was that the slaves had become much harder to govern than even a generation earlier.[33] He chose to attribute this moral decay to a decline in the character of the slaves rather than to any problems of the plantation system itself. This was a telling lack of connection, for Mobberly was aware of the decline of the system. To him, however, the slaves' unruliness were a cause rather than a symptom of the plantations' difficulties.

Mobberly did not linger over his first two reasons, however, for he believed that they were already well-known to Grassi. Instead, Mobberly devoted most of the letter to developing his point that "we shall make more and more to our satisfaction" without slaves.[34]

One of his first points was that slave labor involved difficulties with white hired labor as well as with the slaves themselves. Mobberly's experiences in plantation management exposed him to many problems with overseers. He deplored the necessity that "The planter must overlook his overlooker," for such a situation was inevitably the source of time-consuming and expensive quarrels between them. Mobberly grasped the point that laborers worked better when they could work for themselves. This led him to the conclusion that a tenant farmer, working the land with some potential of keeping some profits for himself, was much more likely to produce for the Jesuits than either an overseer or a slave.

Overseers were enormously demanding of compensation. Typically, Mobberly found that they wanted, annually, 300 pounds of pork, three barrels of corn, a furnished house, a personal garden, firewood to be cut and hauled to their door, the right to graze their own poultry and from $150 to $200 in cash.[35] When George Williams was hired as overseer at St. Inigoe's without informing the Jesuits of his poor health, they soon found themselves bearing the expenses of his mortal illness from tuberculosis and "slow fever."[36]

Even more problematic than an ill overseer was an ill-behaved one. Samuel Leach, the overseer at St. Inigoe's in 1818, was uncooperative in so many ways that Mobberly began to keep a day-to-day record of his offenses. At first, Leach tended to stay at his own house, either lounging or working in his own garden. He consistently neglected Mobberly's commands to thin corn, cut weeds, or help in the harvest field. Later, Leach began traveling away from the plantation on his own business, often attending feasts at neighboring farms and harvesting oyster for himself in Chesapeake Bay. Despite ample documentation of these transgressions, Mobberly could not fire Leach outright. Under the direction of two arbitrators, he was merely able to deduct $35.26 from the overseer's annual salary of $100 before Leach would resign.[37] Mobberly rued the waste.

One reason the employment of overseers in the antebellum South was precarious was their difficult task of balancing leniency and strictness. Overseers had to be benevolent enough to inspire the slaves to work, but strict enough to remind them of their servile status. Masters and overseers alike frequently were dismayed by the ambivalent results, so turnover was high. There is broad consensus concerning this analysis.[38]

Mobberly's own case against overseers seems to have been more complicated. The overseer's absenteeism and passivity no doubt were no inspiration to the slaves to work themselves, but Mobberly was more interested in the contrast between the apathy Leach displayed when working for the Jesuits and the zeal with which he pursued his own money-making pursuits, like gardening and oystering. Unlike many of his Jesuit contemporaries, Mobberly had an appreciation for market capitalism. He was convinced that it was entirely moral for the Jesuits to look out for their own interests in accordance with that system. Was there a way to make a zealous white laborer like Samuel Leach work for the Society of Jesus as well as for himself? Tenant farming seemed to offer the best chance of that.

Many Jesuits resisted Mobberly's zeal for economic reform, however. This fact came home to Mobberly when he noted that for all his painstakingly drafted reports of expenses, losses, and demands for change, his superiors tended to ignore him. Briefly, he wondered whether this was because his rank as a brother made it impertinent for him to speak up to priests on these matters.[39] Soon enough, however, he reflected that the problem was not his rank but his topic. Jesuits were still uncomfortable with all this talk of making money. Perhaps it would be best to change his emphasis to the topic so often proposed at the meetings of the clergy corporation, that any sale be motivated by the hope of improving the moral character of the slaves.

This topic became clearly articulated in his diary around 1817, when Mobberly recorded the decision of Father John Henry, the manager of Bohemia, to sell some slaves from that plantation. Henry did this, Mobberly asserted, because he "found the blacks so ungovernable and so corrupt in their morals" that he deemed it better to send them away. Mobberly's text, which implied that he had not personally discussed these motives with Henry, speculated that the manager had "probably supposed" that a change in climate and locality would inspire the slaves to reform their morals. In any case, five of the slaves were sold, prophetically, to a neighbor who was acting as an agent for planters in Louisiana.[40]

It is significant that all five of these slaves were young males, of a most desirable gender and age for labor. In any case, Mobberly's record of this episode marks the earliest appearance in the Maryland Jesuit literature of the proposal to relocate Jesuit slaves to the Deep South.

Church policy regarding the family life of slaves was a further spur to the idea of replacing them with tenants. If the child of a tenant laborer, or the laborer himself, needed to go elsewhere to find adequate work, he could do so. Canon law, however, decreed that heroic efforts must be made to keep slave families together on the same plantation, even when individual members of the family were not really needed for the work. Married couples could not be separated at all, and every effort was to be made to keep their children with them, too.[41] Slaves throughout the South actually had their own high degree of success in sustaining long marriages and close family ties, learning from their experience of servitude to establish their own standards and rules of conduct for family preservation.[42] The behavior of the Jesuits, however, simply failed to recognize any self-responsibility of the slaves in this regard. The Jesuits took it for granted that they, not the slaves, had to safeguard the slaves' marriages.

There was good reason for this skepticism. Circumstances in Maryland and the Upper South were much less favorable for keeping slave families together than was the case in the Deeper South. Throughout the period between 1800 and 1860, possession of slaves in the state declined to the point where the typical holding was just one slave. Ninety-percent of Maryland slaveholders in 1860 owned eight slaves or less.[43] When these figures are compared with the fact that the Maryland Jesuits collectively owned 272 slaves as late as 1838, it becomes obvious why they were hard pressed to find local buyers. Since keeping families together was a higher priority for the Jesuits than avoiding the transportation of slaves into harsher working conditions, the Jesuits had few compunctions about sending the slaves to Louisiana, where it seemed that there were still Catholic masters who capable of taking on large slave families.

Slaves could often exploit their own broader cultural definition of family to exert more control over how owners might dispose of them. They preferred an "exogamous" model of marriage, in which bonds outside their own clans and plantations were frequent. The slaves championed the inclusion of the extended family—including aunts, uncles, cousins and grandparents—in their model of the unit that must be kept intact.[44] This philosophy, however, while it may have been used to stop sale within Maryland, was also a dangerous advocacy for the slaves to make, for it provided a further incentive to transport such masses of slaves to the Deep South.

Meanwhile, Jesuits were emphasizing an unfavorable impression of the incorrigibility of slaves, which contrasted with their expectations that immigrants would develop good character. Mobberly's diary reveals that by the

1820s, bitter experience in plantation management had hardened his racism. Gone were the affectionate nicknames for the elderly slaves he had counted in the St. Inigoe's census of 1812. Mobberly now believed that African Americans were intrinsically dishonest. He kept a list of the items they had supposedly stolen from their Jesuit masters: pigs, sheep, geese, turkeys, tobacco, corn and wheat. They would even stealthily run their master's horses on exhausting night rides so that the animals would not work productively the next day. Meanwhile, plantation tools were abused through neglect and breakage. Always in the background was the specter of a slave uprising. To Mobberly, all these misdeeds, actual and potential, constituted a sign that the African American character was perverted rather than a rebellion against injustice.

While Mobberly was prophetic in some respects, particularly when writing about business and financial matters, he reflected conventional Roman Catholic morality of his era in analyzing slave misbehavior. He took it as a product of the individual characters of unruly slaves and slothful masters rather than the rejection of corrupt social structures. Not until Pope Leo XIII's encyclical letter of 1890, *Rerum Novarum*, which discussed the situation of the European laboring class, did the Church begin to draw more explicit connections between living and working conditions and individual moral conduct. This connection reached maturity only in the twentieth century, when the "theology of liberation" was developed by Catholic theologians in Latin America to emphasize that social structures could themselves be sinful.[45] None of these insights occurred to Mobberly.

Mobberly believed that slaves born in the United States were harder to govern than their imported counterparts. This phenomenon he attributed more to the breakdown of discipline on the masters' part, which had allowed a latent African unruliness to flourish. Mobberly condemned his peers for "losing sight of the old observation that the better a negro is treated, the worse he becomes." Mobberly resorted to poetry to describe the way for a master to proceed:

> Tender handed brush a nettle
> And it stings you for your pains
> Grasp it like a man of mettle
> And as silk it soft remains
> It is the case with common natures
> Treat them kindly, they rebel
> But be rough as nutmeg graters
> And the rogues obey you well.[46]

The poor behavior of the slaves may have had another cause, however. Slaveholding attempted to rob slaves of their own African cultural identity.[47] The deteriorating deeds of the Jesuits slaves may have been a reaction to this deprivation. As they became generations more and more removed from the African way of life from which their ancestors had been torn, the slaves felt increasingly rudderless and rebellious.

Another difficulty for Mobberly's scheme for harsher discipline was that he believed that many whites in Maryland now frowned upon the corporal punishment of slaves. A master who complained too openly about his slaves' misdeeds, Mobberly claimed, would be suspected of harshness by the vocal and growing numbers of abolitionists. His reputation would grow even worse if the abolitionists saw him resort to whipping. Mobberly was particularly wary of Methodists, whom he described as especially vigorous opponents of Jesuit slave labor. He recorded that on one occasion, Methodist abolitionists brought up kidnapping charges against the Jesuits for trying to transport slaves out of state to Louisiana.[48]

Mobberly's combined pursuit of the goals of agricultural profit and punishment of slave misconduct had some effect on the thinking of his confreres by 1822. In that year, the trustees of the Roman Catholic clergy corporation authorized the sale of slaves whose conduct had been "refractory." However, just three months later the same trustees authorized their corporate agent to sell up to thirty slaves from the Whitemarsh plantation, but only "provided the loss of so many does not materially injure the the cultivation of the farm."[49] The corporation was now capable of embracing both punitive and financial motives for sales.

Mobberly, in his racism, focused so deeply on slave perversion that he overlooked an opportunity to demonstrate how profits could help slaves. This omission came when, continuing his focus on the "Principle and Foundation," he made a list of ten forms of slave mistreatment through which masters had alienated themselves from God. Several of these abuses involved material neglect, deprivations of food, clothing and shelter that arguably occurred because the plantations were not making enough money. Mobberly could have made a good case that increased profits would have avoided these sins of omission, allowing the Jesuits to both support their ministries and their slaves. Instead, by choosing to argue that profitability was possible only without slaves, Mobberly left that line of argument untouched.

For example, the first mistreatment that Mobberly listed was that the health of the slaves was afflicted when masters did not provide adequate huts and beds for them. More profits could have led to improvements in shelter. He also noted that masters did not provide the slaves with proper nourishment and winter clothing, which he felt would have been the nearest thing to just wages that the slaves could have received in their servile status. More profits would have purchased that food and clothing. Mobberly did acknowledge that the deprivation of so many things to slaves constituted "a sin which cries to Heaven for vengeance." In general, too, Mobberly believed that masters neglected slaves once they became too old or fell too ill to work. He specifically said that the only way the Jesuits could avoid further multipication of these sins would be to relinquish the slaves to better providers.

The remaining six failures of masters to serve their slaves were moral and spiritual rather than material, reflecting that even the pragmatic Mobberly shared the Jesuit tendency to worry more about the moral than the material lives of their slaves. Mobberly condemned the practice of having slave children sleep in the same bed, regardless of their sex or age. This practice was an invitation to carnal corruption. Temptation was compounded when masters forbad their slaves to marry young, thus increasing the possibility that they would commit fornication.

Accompanying this was a failure to instruct slaves in Christian doctrine or to prepare them properly to receive the Sacraments. They were not "compelled by proper means" to carry out Christian duties. Little restraint was applied when slaves acted wickedly; there was almost no chastisement for such behavior. When they finally were corrected, cruel means were often used. Finally, they were often sold under "grievous circumstances" which separated husband from wife, directely violating canon law. Pondering this long list of problems, Mobberly did not consider the possibility that masters simply had been exhausted by the strain of trying to administer an impossible system. Instead, he concluded that God would blame them for a failure of vocation:

> How many masters will be infallibly lost for the commission of the above crimes? In this life, they are impoverished by keeping slaves; their lives are filled with cares and vexations; their prospects of happiness are marred and when they die, they lose all for ever! Who, then, would possess a slave?[50]

The pessimism of this peroration is remarkable and manifests a striking contrast between Jesuits and other southern slaveholding intellectuals of the era. Such commentators as William Gillmore Simms, James Henry Hammond, Edmund Ruffin, Nathaniel Beverley Tucker and George Frederick Holmes consciously promoted and sought to strenghten slavery as part of their program for the moral reform of the South.[51] Mobberly did not share their convictions that slavery could be made to operate better or that it would make masters themselves more virtuous. When he did write in its defense, as he did in "Slavery or Cham," Mobberly basically used slavery as a rhetorical weapon in disputations with Protestantism. But when he measured the actual conduct of Jesuit slaveholding against the moral standards of the Roman Catholic Church, Mobberly found it sorely wanting.

The antebellum period has been seen as a time when the Southern planter class evolved from accepting slavery as a necessary evil to proclaiming that it was a positive good in comparison with the Northern wage earning system.[52] Mobberly was one Southern planter who did not reach that conclusion. Not only did he continue to view slavery as a necessary if divinely willed evil, he also preferred the wage labor system. This record suggests that Mobberly fell outside the mainstream of Southern thought on slaveholding.

When Mobberly's stance is compared with that of the Reverend Thornton Stringfellow, a proslavery Baptist evangelical minister, the Jesuit's lack of enthusiasm for slavery becomes even more manifest. Stringfellow felt that he had a moral duty to foster respect for slavery. So convinced was he of slavery's righteousness that he did not take its abolition in 1865 as an indication of its failure. Rather, Stringfellow saw abolition as a mysterious test of faith to which God was subjecting the South before vindicating its way of life.[53] Such mysticism was far removed from Mobberly's practical conclusion that Jesuits could easily survive and even prosper without slavery.

Mobberly's pessimism about the possibility of developing the character of slaves also turned sharply away from the usual Roman Catholic view of human sinfulness. This ordinarily might be defined, in one theologian's phrase, as "sober hope." It involved a realistic appraisal that evil was a factor in all human situations, but was accompanied by a deep conviction that the redemption wrought by Christ had provided the means to check this evil. Mobberly, by contrast, had gone so far as to despair that the slaves were capable of responding to the Gospel.

Ironically, as this despair spread and hardened among his fellow Jesuits, there was a dissipation of belief in Mobberly's racist conviction that blackness of skin resulted from a Biblical curse. Mulledy, for example, endorsed a revised exegesis of the Noah and Cham encounter in a lecture that he delivered at Nice, France in 1840. Mulledy was in Europe to explain his conduct of the recently concluded slave sale to the Jesuit curia in Rome. Superiors advised him to remain abroad until feelings cooled at home, so Mulledy spent some time as a teacher to the American expatriates at Nice.

In his discourse, Mulledy denied that any such curse had carried down through the ages to any African peoples. Rather, he saw Noah's pronouncement as having applied only to certain nations of literal descent from Noah, nations which had existed in the ancient Middle East during Biblical times but which were long extinct by the nineteenth century.[54] Mulledy took the Bible literally in the sense that he still believed that Noah's curse was historical, but he also believed that no one subject to it was anymore alive anywhere in the world.

Mulledy's abandonment of curse theology did not represent a conversion from racism, as is shown by the imagery he used in denouncing the old theory as a silly pious fable:

> If looking glasses were, in those days, in use, only think what a fracas and turmoil those good ladies (of Cham's family) must have excited, on beholding themselves suddenly changed. . . . This is nothing but a fable, calculated to frighten children, by telling them, that if they are disobedient and naughty, they will turn black and ugly, which if it were true, I am apprehensive that the number of negroes would be woefully multiplied.[55]

In this mockery, Mulledy made an ugly suggestion. There was no need to attribute guilt to African Americans for a misdeed of thousands of years ago because there were plenty of misdeeds to blame them for in Mulledy's own time. The idea that white children might be genuinely frightened by the thought of turning black when they misbehaved suggests that Mulledy still accepted the bleak analysis of the African American character outlined by Jesuits like Mobberly.

Mulledy's goal here was not really to disavow a curse on the slaves, but to deny any curse on the masters. If it was true that there was no divine mandate to enslave people of black skin color, then there was no mandate for Jesuits to hold them as slaves. This idea had obvious appeal for Mulledy at a time when his sale of the Jesuit slaves had endangered his credibility and his career.

Corresponding to this zeal to rid the Jesuits of the burden of the slaves was their eagerness to embrace ministry to the immigrant. Even Mobberly, who wanted to sell the slaves so that the plantations would be more likely to remain in Jesuit hands, himself believed that the European Catholic immigrant would be a good influence in the United States. This attitude becomes clear through some reflections on liberty that Mobberly entered in his diary at Georgetown on the fiftieth anniversary of American independence in 1826. A classics student before his days in plantation management, Mobberly remained well read in American literature throughout his life. References to both books and newspapers marked his diary. He liked to respond to what he had read, particularly if it seemed to challenge Catholicism in any way. Seeing Jefferson's *Notes on the State of Virginia* as potentially useful in warning the American Republic against "Luther's principle . . . of irregular and unbounded notion of liberty," Mobberly offered a nuanced response to some anti-immigration sentiment that Jefferson expressed in his book.

In the passage to which Mobberly responded, Jefferson wondered if there were any disadvantages to be weighed against the advantages some expected from increased immigration. He believed that those who must join together in a society must have some consensus about their common business if they were to be happy. Societies were formed to support civil government, so its administration must be conducted by common consent. The principles that formed the consenus underlying American government, Jefferson added, were unique in the world, the offspring of the English constitution and the best principles of natural right and reason. The principles of absolute monarchies were directly opposed to these, yet from such states the greatest number of immigrants were likely to come. Either they would prefer their original country's principles, or throw them off in favor of unrestrained licentiousness. The American ideal of ordered liberty would be too foreign for them. They would propose legislation against ordered liberty, and render it incoherent and confused. [56]

Mobberly saw value in this Jeffersonian analysis, but only to a point. Basically, Mobberly felt that Jefferson was correct to the extent that he described potential immigrants of *Protestant* origin and influence. The damage which such people could do to social order was indeed to be feared. However, Mobberly believed that anyone who been cultivated in the *Catholic* tradition of obedience to legitimate authority would know how to distinguish among tyranny, licentiousness and ordered liberty. Such a man would know how to "regulate his conscience according to the dictates of reason and the rules of the Christian faith."[57]

Therefore, Mobberly retorted that the presence of more European Catholics in the United States would strengthen the moral life of the country, but only if these people were provided with enough priests, churches and schools to sustain their Catholic faith. He hoped that reformed plantation management would make such expansion of ministries financially possible.

Like Kohlmann, Mobberly was convinced that the Church would have to remain in constant contact with Catholic immigrants if there was to be any chance of saving their faith from Protestant and exaggeratedly republican influences. Unlike Kohlmann, Mobberly did not believe that the plantations had to be totally abandoned in that effort.

Mobberly's convictions became clearer in another diary entry of 1826. In this further reflection, Mobberly felt that Jefferson's bleak assessment of the prevalence of absolute monarchy in continental Europe was too pessimistic an analysis of what these governments were like:

> I do not aim at royalty—I respect majesty; and tho there may be at present some petty instances of domineering rule in certain corners of Europe . . . yet Europe at the present day is blessed generally with good and gracious Sovereigns, who labour to render their subjects happy, by guaranteeing to them the rights and privileges of free citizens.[58]

This comment added to Mobberly's dissent from the Jeffersonian proposition that people from continental Europe had so little experience of "temperate liberty" that they would be unable to adjust to life in the United States. Such maladjustment would only be true of arrivals who were fallen under the sway of Luther. Where Jefferson attributed ordered liberty to the influence of the English constitution, Mobberly attributed it to the influence of Catholicism. The great events of seventeenth century English Constitutional history—the attainment of Parliamentary supremacy over the monarchy through the efforts of the Puritans—had been disastrous for Catholicism. Jesuits like Mobberly preferred to see the origins of ordered liberty much earlier, in the undivided medieval Church.

On this point, Mobberly agreed with some conservative Protestant proslavery commentators of the Deep South. While these writers rued what they believed to have been the scandal, corruption and idolatry of the medieval clergy, they acknowledged that the Roman Catholic Church of the Middle Ages had fostered social stability. There was an organic social structure to the Middle Ages, a society of mutual obligations and mutually recognized rights, which some Protestant slaveholding intellectuals felt contrasted well with the rampant individualism of modern capitalism.[59]

To a Jesuit trained in the Counter-Reformation ethos, such tributes to Catholicism came as a vindication. The English Constitution was an unsatisfactory source of order for Mobberly because it was corrupted by the Reformation. It was better to trace liberty back to medieval Christendom. Since he was Catholic, Mobberly did not have to look upon this source as sheepishly as the Protestant intellectuals of the day did.

Mobberly shared the views of many European Jesuits who had fled to the United States during the French Revolution that exaggerated Lutheran notions of liberty had recently ruined the nominally Catholic country of France. The French Revolution had expanded the concept of liberty to include the insupportable notion of equality. The events of 1789 provided this combination with a fair trial, but its futility was illustrated when that Revolution descended into what Mobberly believed was a new and worse form of despotism than that which it had sought to replace. The paradoxical result was more inequality than France had ever experienced before, with the new despotism of Bonaparte replacing that of the Bourbons.[60]

Like Kohlmann, Mobberly believed that the United States could avoid a similar fate only if it cultivated the growth of a citizenry with some regard for hierarchy, people who would know that social equality was an absurb proposition. Mobberly saw much potential for the devout Catholic immigrant to temper egalitarian sentiment in the United States—this would be the perfect means to fight the "unbridled licentiousness" that had so frightened Jefferson.

Mobberly noted that life in the military, and the "galling yoke" of life as a slave, were often cited as proof that manifestations of tyranny survived in the United States. However, Mobberly begged people who held these opinions to look beneath appearances. Both the military and slavery were guardians against anarchy and self-destruction. He felt that human nature, reason, and the will of the American nation called upon the government to safeguard the political system through the cultivation of discipline. No laws, no liberty; no rulers would mean unrestrained behavior.[61]

The fear of "unbridled licentiousness" was important for the Jesuit discernment about how to discard their slaves. Since Mobberly felt that the excessive pursuit of equality actually led to inequality during the French Revolution, he refused to recommend a step like slave emancipation for the United States, which he believed would only inspire futile attempts to treat free blacks as equal in ability to free whites. To give freedom to the slaves would be a step toward complete despotism, for order would collapse if those who needed the moral governance of people of greater natural ability and superior color were to be set loose in American society. Had he lived to see it, Mobberly would likely have supported proposals in 1834 that Jesuits join in the colonization movement to send manumitted slaves back to Africa.[62]

Jesuits like Mobberly and Mulledy were racist elitists. They felt that slaves needed guidance from white religious leaders. However, in another sense they were also nonracist elitists, for they felt that working class white immigrants needed ruling, too, and they gradually gave this second need precedence over the first.

Mobberly was concerned that the distorted ideals of the French Revolution remained in circulation in the United States, and this conviction determined his strategy for ending Jesuit slaveholding. What America needed was honest laborers who would know how to use their liberties with measure, in the Jeffersonian tradition. Former slaves could not fit that definition, but pious Catholic immigrants might, with proper direction.

To Mobberly, the slaves would not fit that description because he wholly agreed with Jefferson's analysis of the African character. He quoted approvingly Jefferson's declaration that black people were more sensate than reflective, living more out of passion than reason. Mobberly also asserted that his experiences as a plantation manager supported Jefferson's observation that Africans were likely to sleep when deprived of work or amusements.[63]

These racist observations of Jefferson's were used by Mobberly to support two of his own convictions. The Jesuit farms would be better off with enterprising immigrant tenant laborers than with apathetic slaves, and the lethargy of the slaves clearly made them morally incapable of governing themselves.

Mobberly's nuanced respect for the thought of Jefferson—the fact that he tempered the observations on immigration but wholeheartedly endorsed the racist comments—demands an augmentation to traditional analysis of the political beliefs of American Jesuits during the early republican and antebellum periods. Early on, Jesuits like John Carroll were essentially Federalists.[64] They honored that party not only for its advocacy of a Revolution and a Constitution that had secured religious liberty, but also for its sense of social patriarchy. Later, Jesuits like Mulledy displayed Whiggish economic convictions, advocating that the Society invest its wealth in banks rather than land as a means of better supporting its educational endeavors.[65] However, Mobberly showed that some Jesuits also shared the basic Jeffersonian belief that life in the countryside was more virtuous and more likely to promote social and political order than the urban, industrial order championed by the Hamiltonian Federalists. The difference between Jefferson and Mobberly was that the latter saw room to to include Catholics in this yeoman agrarian order.

Mobberly feared that either emancipation or the concentration of unemployed immigrants in the cities would lead to pauperism and anarchy. Citing an article which had appeared in *The Washington Republican* in June, 1823, Mobberly described the huge number of unemployed and beggars in European nations, even though formal slavery did not exist there. His observation is worth quoting extensively, for it summarizes his conviction that there were people whose nature required that they live in subjection, for their own good:

> All the above paupers are lost to society in a two-fold light. Society is not only deprived of their services, but it must also spend its treasures to support them. If those unhappy people had good masters, they would then be in a comfortable situation. They would be saved from a habit of indolence, which paralizes their every nerve, + entails upon them a crowd of various and afflicting diseases. In their infirmities, the medical balm of comfort would be administered, and the soothing care of a kind master would drown their multiplied sorrows. Society would be relieved from a troublesome burden, and States and Provinces would be freed from an enormous tax. When slavery exists, beggars are rarely found. We must therefore conclude, that slavery is not only lawful, reasonable, and good, but that it is also necessary.[66]

Mobberly's definition of slavery was an expansive one. He clearly believed that there were more forms of servitude than the variety applicable to African Americans. Mobberly did not suggest that European paupers be made slaves in the same legal sense that African Americans were. Rather, he suggested that poor people were better off when people of means and superior ability answered a vocation to govern the poor responsibly. This was the obligation of the elite to which the Jesuits belonged, to provide the poor with moral and religious direction as well as appropriate supervision of their work. Mobberly felt that if American society resisted egalitarianism and kept in mind the natural distinction between rulers and ruled, those gifted for ruling would absorb the immigrants and guide them to a condition best conducive to social order. This scenario would give the religious orders of the Church, most especially the Jesuits, with their Catholic wisdom and extensive educations, a crucial role in the American future as Mobberly envisioned it.

A strain of Southern thought regarded slavery as a broad principle of life that transcended any of its institutional embodiments. There was a conviction that "the normal and necessary condition of labor was some form of personal servitude within the extended biblical model epitomized by Abraham."[67] This condition was neither exhausted nor necessarily epitomized by the chattel version of slavery found in the American South. Mobberly shared this conviction, and he sensed that the number of servants whom the Jesuits were broadly responsible for was about to expand dramatically.

This new obligation demanded some form of adjustment for the older sense of obligation to African American slaves. Of the alternatives, manumission within the United States looked unlikely to succeed. If the slaves were to be cast off on their own along the eastern seaboard, an area then straining to absorb massive immigration, the employment crisis in those states would only grow worse. The realization that freed slaves and immigrants would compete for jobs at the pit of the economy has been cited as a major reason why Catholics of the mid-nineteenth century were skeptical about the abolitionist movement.[68] Manumission accompanied by transportation to Africa was another possibility. The Jesuits considered that course and did not pursue it, apparently out of the fear that the colonization groups had too many ties to anti-Catholic nativists[69] A third option was to sell the slaves to a state of the Deep South where they could remain under Catholic ownership without impeding the need for the Church to minister to immigrants along the Eastern Seaboard. Louisiana not only still had a massive slave labor economy, but an extensive Catholic heritage which seemed to promise that the slaves would be governed in a traditional manner there.

Jesuits of the 1820s and 1830s did not abandon their longstanding conviction of a vocation to the role of master. Rather, led by Mobberly and Mulledy, they broadened their definitions of just whom masters were responsible for among the world's servants. Jesuits discerned that they were masters by vocation—masters who were about to receive more subjects and greater responsibilties. The modern mind is so accustomed to distinguishing between the chattel slave and the immigrant that it has overlooked the extent to which the elitist Jesuits of the middle nineteenth century linked these two groups together in their thought as people in need of the care and governance of wise priests. The Jesuits looked upon any people of the working class, whether white or black, as servants by nature.

Jesuit antiabolitionism erected a tremendously high wall against the suggestion that they should free their African American slaves. However, there were three serious cracks in this wall that left an opening for selling off the slaves instead: the Jesuit sense of their obligation to the coming working class immigrants from Europe, the increasingly intractable financial situation on the farms, and the growing conviction that African Americans were incapable of moral conversion. Each of these factors left room for the argument that the problems facing the Maryland Jesuits could be resolved by selling off their chattel. As the 1830s approached, the Jesuit slaves fell into this vortex, assuring that some of the wall erected by Jesuit antiabolitionism would tumble down after all in the decade to come.

NOTES

1. Thomas Mulledy, S.J, "87th Instruction in Moral Theology," 1854, The Thomas Mulledy, S.J. Papers (TMSJP), Special Collections Division, Lauinger Library, Georgetown University, Washington, D.C.

2. Robert Emmett Curran, S.J., *The Bicentennial History of Georgetown University, I: From Academy to University, 1789–1889* (Washington, D.C.: Georgetown University Press, 1993), pp. 107–108, p. 120, p.129.

3. Proceedings of the Roman Catholic Clergy Corporation of Maryland (RCCC), 1814 and 1820, Item no. 2N 7–10, Box 2, Folder 6, Archives of the Maryland Province (MPA), Special Collections Division, Lauinger Library,

Georgetown University, Washington, D.C.

4. John Tracy Ellis, *American Catholicism* (Chicago: The University of Chicago Press, Chicago History of American Civilization Series, Second Edition, Revised, 1969), p. 43, p. 50.

5. Curran, *op. cit.*, pp. 80–81.

6. Jay Dolan, *The American Catholic Experience* (Garden City, N.Y.: Doubleday, 1985), p. 124.

7. Curran, *op. cit.*, p. 80

8. *Ibid.*, p. 112.

9. Dolan, *op. cit.*, p. 160–161.

10. Thomas Mulledy, S.J., to the Jesuit General, 1843, Box 3, Dzierozynski Folder, Catholic Historical Manuscripts Collection (CHMC), Special Collections Division, Lauinger Library, Georgetown University, Washington, D.C.

11. "Proposals for Establishing an Academy at George-town, Patowmack River, Maryland," 1789, in Curran, *op. cit.*, p.26.

12. Brother Joseph Mobberly, S.J., to Rev. Giovanni Grassi, S.J., February 5, 1815, Item no. 204 K3, Box 58, Folder 6, MPA.

13. John Carroll to Rev. Giovanni Grassi S.J., September 24, 1813, in Thomas O'Brien Hanley, editor, *The John Carroll Papers (JCP)*, III (Notre Dame, Ind.: University of Notre Dame Press, 1976) p. 231.

14. P.J. Staudenraus, *The African Colonization Movement, 1816–1865* (New York: Columbia University Press, 1961), p. 23.

15. "Minutes of the Extraordinary Consulation at Georgetown College, August 2, 1832," Box 126, Folder 2, MPA.

16. John W. Padberg, S.J., *The Constitutions of the Society of Jesus and their Complementary Norms* (St. Louis: The Institute of Jesuit Sources, 1996), no. 331, p. 138.

17. John W. O'Malley, S.J., *The First Jesuits* (Cambridge: Harvard University Press, 1993), pp. 305–306.

18. Curran, *op. cit.*, p. 59, pp. 60–61, pp. 70–71.

19. Seymour E. Harris, *Economics of Harvard* (New York: McGraw-Hill, 1970), pp. 53–55.

20. Roger E. Meiners, "The Evolution of American Higher Education," in John W. Sommer, editor, *The Academy in Crisis: The Political Economy of Higher Education* (New Brunswick, N.J.: Transaction Publishers, 1995), pp. 22–23.

21. Warren A. Nord, *Religion & American Education: Rethinking a National Dilemma* (Chapel Hill: University of North Carolina Press, 1995), pp.64–65.

22. Anthony Kohlmann, S.J., "Sermon Notes, 1813–1819," Item no. 9 Kohlmann, Box 6, Folder 2, MPA.

23. Curran, *op. cit.*, pp. 90–91.

24. *Ibid.*, p. 112.

25. Richard M. Gula, S.S., *Reason Informed by Faith: Foundations of Catholic Morality* (Mahwah, N.J.: Paulist Press, 1989), pp. 32–33.

26. Padberg, *op. cit.*, no. 622, p. 284.

27. *Ibid.*, no. 603, p. 276.

28. Edward F. Beckett, S.J., "Listening to Our History: Inculturation and Jesuit Slaveholding," *Studies in the Spirituality of Jesuits* 28, no. 5 (November, 1996), p. 34.

29. Brother Joseph Mobberly, S.J., to Father Giovanni Grassi, S.J., Summer 1812, Item no. 203–C12, MPA, Box 57.5, Folder 3.

30. Kenneth M. Stampp, *The Peculiar Institution: Slavery in the Antebellum South* (New York: Random House, Vintage Books Edition, 1989), p. 318.

31. Brother Joseph Mobberly, S.J. to Rev. Giovanni Grassi, S.J., February 5, 1815, Item no. 204K3, Box 58, Folder 6, MPA.

32. Thomas Mulledy, S.J., Miscellaneous Undated Notes, Box 8, Folder 5, TMSJP.

33. Brother Joseph Mobberly, S.J. to Rev. Giovanni Grassi, S.J., February 5, 1815, Item no. 204K3, Box 58, Folder 6, MPA.

34. *Ibid.*

35. Brother Joseph Mobberly, S.J., "Diary, Part I: Systems," pp. 72–75, The Brother Joseph Mobberly, S.J. Papers (BJMSJP), Special Collections Division, Lauinger Library, Georgetown University, Washington, D.C.

36. Brother Joseph Mobberly, S.J. to Rev. Giovanni Grassi, S.J., Summer, 1812, Item no. 203 C12, Box 57.5, Folder 3, MPA.

37. Brother Joseph Mobberly, S.J., Entry for the year 1818 in the St. Inigoes' Account Book, Item no. 170–G, MPA, Box 44, Folder 1.

38. Eugene D. Genovese, *Roll, Jordan, Roll: The World the Slaves Made* (New York: Random House, Vintage Books Edition, 1976), p. 14; Peter Kolchin, *American Slavery, 1619–1877* (New York: Hill and Wang, 1993), p. 36.

39. Brother Joseph Mobberly, S.J. to Rev. Giovanni Grassi, S.J., November 5, 1814, Item no. 204 M8, Box 58, Folder 8, MPA.

40. Brother Joseph Mobberly, S.J., "Diary, Part I: Negroes Taken out of Prison," p. 111, BJMSJP.

41. Curran, *op. cit.*, p. 119.

42. Herbert G. Gutman, *The Black Family in Slavery and Freedom, 1750–1925* (New York: Random House, Vintage Books, 1976), pp. xxii-xxiii.

43. Barbara Jeanne Fields, *Slavery and Freedom on the Middle Ground: Maryland during the Nineteenth Century* (New Haven: Yale University Press, 1985), p. 24.

44. *Ibid.*, p. 25.

45. James Bretzke, S.J., "A Taxonomy of Contemporary Chrisitan Ethics and Moral Theology," unpublished lecture notes, Jesuit School of Theology at Berkeley, Berkeley, California, 1995.

46. Mobberly, Diary, Part I, Systems, p. 77, pp. 141–142, BJMSJP.

47. Robert William Fogel, *Without Consent or Contract: The Rise and Fall of American Slavery* (New York: W. W. Norton, 1989), p.398.

48. Mobberly, "Diary, Part I: Negroes Taken out of Prison," pp. 11--115, BJM-SJP.

49. Proceedings of the Roman Catholic Clergy Corporation of Maryland (RCC), November 30 and August 22, 1822, Item no. 91.2, MPA, Box 24, Folder 2.

50. Mobberly, "Diary, Part I: Systems," pp. 142–143, BJMSJP.

51. Drew Gilpin Faust, *A Sacred Circle: The Dilemma of the Intellectual in the Old South, 1840–1860* (Baltimore: The Johns Hopkins University Press, 1977), p xi.

52. Lawrence B. Goodheart and Hugh Hawkins, editors, *The Abolitionisits: Means, Ends and Motivations* (Lexington, Mass.: D.C. Heath, Third Edition 1995), p. xx.

53. Drew Gilpin Faust, "Evangelicalism and the Proslavery Argument," in her book *Southern Stories: Slaveholders in Peace and War* (Columbia: University of Missouri Press, 1992), pp. 15–28.

54. Thomas Mulledy, S.J., "46th and 47th Lectures on Genesis, delivered at Nice, France, on March 26 and April 4, 1841," Box 8, Folder 2, TMSJP.

55. *Ibid.*

56. See Mobberly, "Slavery or Cham," pp. 23–25, BJMSJP; also, William Peden, editor, Thomas Jefferson, *Notes on the State of Virginia* (New York: W. W. Norton, published for the Institute of Early American History and Culture at Williamsburg, Virginia, 1982), pp. 84–85.

57. Mobberly, "Diary, Part V: July 4, 1826," BJMSJP.

58. *Ibid.*

59. Eugene D. Genovese, *The Slaveholders' Dilemma: Freedom and Progress in Southern Conservative Thought, 1820–1860* (Columbia: University of South Carolina Press, 1992), pp. 5–6.

60. Mobberly, "Slavery or Cham," pp. 30–3, BJMSJP.

61. Mobberly, "Diary, Part V: July 4, 1826," BJMSJP.

62. Will Erkead to Reverend William McSherry, S.J., October 17, 1834, Box 13, Folder 4, MPA.

63. Mobberly, "Slavery or Cham," p. 60.

64. Charles Edward O'Neill, "John Carroll, the Catholic Enlightenment and Rome," in Raymond J. Kupke, editor, *American Catholic Preaching and Piety in the Time of John Carroll* (Lanham, Md.: University Press of America, 1991), p. 7.

65. Curran, *op.cit.* p. 112.

66. Mobberly, "Slavery or Cham," pp. 35–36, BJMSJP.

67. Genovese, *The Slaveholder's Dilemma*, pp. 62–63.

68. James Hennesey, S.J. *American Catholics: A History of the Roman Catholic Community in the United States* (New York: Oxford University Press, 1981), p. 43.

69. Will Erkead to Rev. William McSherry, S.J., October 17, 1834, Box 13, Folder 4, MPA.

CHAPTER SEVEN

The End of Maryland Jesuit Slaveholding, 1838

BETWEEN 1830 AND 1832, FATHER PETER KENNEY CONDUCTED HIS SECOND visitation to the Jesuits of the United States on behalf of the Jesuit General in Rome, Jan Roothan. An immediate concrete result of this inspection occurred on February 2, 1833, when Roothan accepted Kenney's recommendation to raise the Maryland mission to the adminstrative status of a province of the Society of Jesus. This move was an ecclesiastical parallel to the American constitutional process of elevating a territory to statehood. It was a recognition that the Jesuits of Maryland had formed a mature branch of the Society of Jesus that was capable of taking an equal place with its elder branches. Roothan's announcement of this promotion was signed on the Feast of the Purification, the celebration of the announcement of the prophet Simeon to Mary that her son, Jesus, was the fulfillment of God's promises to Israel. A similar feeling, that the moment had arrived for the fulfillment of God's pledges to the American Church and its Jesuits, permeated Roothan's proclamation of the Maryland Province.[1]

The establishment of the new province instigated a reorganization of its institutions that lasted five years, culminating in the sale of all the Jesuit slaves and the reform of plantation administration. Kenney's first inspection, in 1820, had recommended that American Jesuits look for an opportunity to dispose gradually of their slaveholdings.[2] During the years that intervened before his second inspection, five important influences finally came together to make that step more likely. These included alarm concerning the moral behavior of Jesuit slaves, optimism about the growth of Catholicism in the United States, the pressures imposed upon all slaveowners by the abolitiont movement, the enmity posed to American Catholicism by the nativist movement, and the practical need for Jesuits to deal with American economic realities of the 1830s. All these factors influenced Kenney's conduct of his second visitation, and they helped to destroy the exceptional institution that was the Jesuit variation of slaveholding.

Kenney was convinced that the immorality of the slaves was undermining the work of the plantations. In June, 1831, he visited the small mission of Bohemia. There Kenney found seven slaves—five males and two females, and their stymied overseer, Brother Heard. Three of the slaves, two males and a female, were under the age of eighteen. The three adult males were married to wives who did not belong to the Jesuits. That last statistic alone left Heard vulnerable to church tradition that slave spouses must not be broken up. As St. Thomas Aquinas had written in the thirteenth century, "a slave can by marrying give another person power over his body without his master's consent. . . . If the master command his slave not to marry, the slave is not bound to obey his master."[3]

Kenney was disturbed by the behavior of all the Bohemia slaves—heavy drinking, illicit sexual relationships and theft. Seeing a chance both to punish them and to experiment with tenant labor, Kenney ordered Heard to sell the slaves. When Kenney returned in July of 1832, he recorded happily that "Brother Heard looks much better than he did last year. He attributes much of his renewed health to the peace, which the absence of the wicked slaves allows him to enjoy."[4] This apparent success on the smallest plantation supported the idea of doing the same on all the others. Jesuits had complained about slave decadence for many years without acting against it, but now they had a new sense that such obstinancy was hindering an otherwise thriving church. The development of Catholicism within the young republic was encouraging by 1830. In 1790, there was only one American diocese, Baltimore. In 1808, this number expanded to five with the addition of dioceses in Boston, New York, Philadelphia and Bardstown, Kentucky. By 1830, there were ten dioceses.[5]

The new Maryland Province reflected this growth. In 1805, the Society of Jesus was reestablished in the Maryland area by five members, all elderly men who had been Jesuits before the suppression of 1773. As early as October, 1806, however, eleven younger men entered the novitiate.[6] 1833, the first year of the full Province, saw a total membership of seventy-eight Jesuits. Thirty-four were priests, seventeen were preparing for ordination, and twenty-seven were brothers. The Province's geographical range included the entire state of Maryland, three counties in Pennsylvania (including a parish in Philadelphia), and the city of Alexandria, Virginia. There were the eight Jesuit plantations, twenty two missions, a university at Georgetown, a college at Frederick and one secondary school. It included a novitiate and a scholasticate (a specialized school where Jesuits studied for ordination).[7] A fact that underscored the size of Jesuit Maryland was Roothan's concurrent decision that the Missouri Mission of the Jesuits not be incorporated within the new province but left as an independent region which would develop into its own province.[8]

This Jesuit revitalization, however, coincided with a similar increase of confidence and boldness within the abolitionist movement. At a time when the Jesuits believed that their choice regarding the future of their slaves lay between a mass sale and a gradual manumission, the New England activist William Lloyd Garrison (1805–1879) announced his conversion to the concept of immediate emancipation. Founding the important abolitionist newspaper *The Liberator* on January 1, 1831 in Boston, just a few months after Kenney's second arrival from Europe, Garrison declared that his earlier support of gradual manumission had been made "unreflectingly," and asked pardon for that sinful advocacy.[9]

On December 4, 1833, ten months and two days after the establishment of the Maryland Province, the newly formed American Anti-Slavery Society announced that it would "aim at a purification of the churches from all participation in the guilt of slavery."[10] On June 17, 1837, one year and two days before Father Thomas Mulledy signed a final contract for the sale of the Jesuit slaves, the feminist abolitionist Angelina Grimke (1805–1879) declared that Christians had a moral obligation to disobey unjust laws forbidding manumission. Denying that there could be such a thing as a practical obstacle to setting slaves free, Grimke affirmed of the slaveholder that "*he is able* to let the oppressed go free, and that such heaven-daring atrocities ought to *cease now*, henceforth and forever."[11] This attitude left no room for the Jesuits' agonizing over whether to keep or sell their servants.

Kenney recognized that Jesuit Maryland was vulnerable to this abolitionist surge. In August, 1832, he advised Father General Roothan to allow "the adoption of some arrangement that will gradually liberate the mission from such servants and substitute free laborers in their place." Such a step was desirable due to "the state of public feeling on the subject of slavery." While Kenney acknowledged that there were other problems with slaveholding, the abolitionist agitation was the only problem that he specified in this memorandum.[12] Note that Kenney's call for gradual manumission came ninteen months after Garrison's newspaper demanded immediate emancipation.

These years also coincided with an increase in nativism, a movement of resistance to foreign and Catholic influence in the United States. Many Protestants feared that Catholicism was inimical to the American manner of proceeding, and some saw Jesuits, in particular, as master organizers of a Catholic conspiracy against the United States. Arguing that their ignorance made Catholic immigrants vulnerable to Jesuit manipulations, an alarmed Samuel F. B. Morse (1791–1872) asked whether "their darkened intellects can suddenly be illuminated to discern the nice boundary where their ecclesiastical obedience to their priests ends, and the civil independence of them begins?"[13]

With their reputation for intrigue and close dealings with the papacy and the Catholic monarchs of Europe, Jesuits were frequent targets of such nativist rhetoric. From its founding in 1816, the American Bible Society warned that Jesuits wished to prevent the scriptures from being distributed to the general population. When a journalist named William S. Stone documented that allegations of sexual debauchery in Catholic convents were false, he was accused of accepting payment from Jesuits to discredit the accusers. One nativist newspaper, the *American Protestant Vindicator*, even claimed that the pregnancy of one such accuser, Maria Monk, had been arranged by Jesuits determined to discredit her exposures. There was even talk that Jesuits were trying to infiltrate the American West before Protestants could.[14]

Kenney's papers reveal that he and the individual Jesuits whom he consulted were aware that nativism posed a problem for the Society. Kenney begged Roothan to understand the legal and political situation that affected American Jesuits. In particular, he wished the General to comprehend that in the United States, the permission of the Pope was not required for the disposal of ecclesiastical property. Jesuits believed that they could sell land on their own local initiative, so long as it was done for the church's good. The alternative, that they would have to wait for months at a time for officials in Rome to approve any sales, would "tend to raise against us, however unjustly, the charge of supporting the Pope's domain in temporals, a doctrine greatly odious in all its brands in Catholic countries."[15]

In a second manuscript from 1832, Kenney again showed his sensitivity to nativist criticism. Instructing the Jesuits of the Missouri Mission concerning their college at Saint Louis, he placed sharp conditions on their permission to publish in Missouri. Kenney believed that the time had come for Catholic dogma to be proclaimed more vigorously, but he wanted it done anonymously. He stipulated that the articles must be published under pseudonyms, and that the order should not assume public responsibility for what an individual Jesuit might say. Exceptions to this discretion could only be made by the mission superior after meeting with his consultors, an advisory board within the Society.[16]

Maryland Jesuit archives for the 1830s show that the Society was under assault from widely scattered parts of the nation, both north and south. Writing from his post as bishop of Boston in 1830, Benedict Fenwick described how the anti-Masonic party in New England had linked the Jesuits to an alleged conspiracy against the Constitution. Fenwick also had to deny charges in the Boston press that the Jesuits had committed massacres in France, Italy, Spain, and Ireland.[17] In a letter of May 6, 1838, James Ward, S.J. described the experiences of a Georgetown alumnus named Mr. Aiken, who had converted to Catholicism as a student. Aiken returned to his native Tennessee on vacation, only to be told by a Presbyterian that Catholicism was the one denomination beyond toleration in the United States. Aiken himself "fought with tongue and pen in the cause of truth," and found in his response to the bigot's words a call to enter the Jesuits. Ward worried, however, about the large number of Catholics who folded under such fire and apostasized, particularly when far from the ministrations of a priest. Ward felt that the fact that Aiken was the only new novice that year was a sign that the nativist rhetoric had taken its toll in the territory covered by the Maryland province.[18]

Under these circumstances, there were many Jesuits and other Catholics who felt that priests and religious must distance themselves as much as possible from the growing controversy over slavery, presenting themselves instead as representatives of a cautious Church whose "conservative, law-abiding, unifying influence . . . would leave the settlement of the slavery question to the legally constituted authorities of the country."[19]

The final factor in the transition from Jesuit slaveholding was that the new Province set about organizing its business affairs in the midst of an economic revolution that swept across the United States during the decades between the War of 1812 and the Civil War. The process of this change may be described succinctly: "History's most revolutionary force, the capitalist market, was wresting the American future from history's most conservative force, the land."[20] The overriding characteristic of American life during these years was social and economic transformation. There were dramatic shifts in population as more immigrants arrived from Europe and many people moved west. The advent of steamboats, canals and railroads made both transportation and communication easier, uniting the domestic economy into an interdependent whole of regional specialization, urbanization, and a factory system based on cheap labor. While much about these changes was exciting, much about them was disconcerting, too.[21]

The state of Maryland was both caught up in and resistant to this transition. Northern Maryland had a largely industrialized economy based on free labor by 1850, while southern Maryland remained more wedded to the land and slave labor.[22] The momentum lay in the direction that northern Maryland was taking, but not everyone felt comfortable with the transition. It was during this era of choice and transition that the Jesuits decided to sell their slaves.

The market revolution encouraged many Americans to turn inward to private religious concerns and certainties. For Protestantism, this trend was represented by the theological ferment of the Second Great Awakening in the 1820s and 1830s. Devout Protestant Americans met the disruption of the market with creative thought about domesticity and Christian benevolence. The anxieties of such people revealed that they did not necessarily share in the mythology of capitalist change as a constant engine of human fulfillment.[23] They felt that Christian principles were necessary to check the market's encouragement of human greed.

How did Catholicism respond to the market revolution? The emphasis on reorganization and consolidation among the Maryland Jesuits during the 1830s suggests that Jesuits, for one, shared the general introspection characteristic of Protestant denominations during these years. Even the Jesuits found themselves in theological ferment, not in terms of changing any dogmas, but in considering the practical implementation of their moral worldview. Quite simply, they took another look at such issues as profit and earning money at interest.

In these matters, American Jesuits experienced tensions with their superiors in Rome. One feature of the changing economy, for instance, involved banking. The concepts of fluid capital and interest were difficult for Catholic authorities, who faced their Church's long heritage of regarding usury as immoral.[24] Kenney had to reassure Father General Roothan that Maryland Jesuits had no present desire or intention to exchange their land for stock in banks. However, they also wished Kenney to remind Rome that any future change in this policy was theirs alone to make.[25] The thought that they might receive much bankable money from a slave sale was already attractive to those Jesuits who sought means to build many more schools and parishes along the eastern seaboard.[26] In short, the market revolution had weakened one of the most exceptional features of Jesuit slaveholding, the reluctance to view slaves as means of profits.

The challenge of reorganizing Jesuit life in the ferment of the 1830s first fell to the young Father William McSherry (1799–1839), who was appointed the first Provincial of Maryland in 1833. McSherry was the son of an Irish emigre who had become wealthy, first as a merchant in Jamaica and then as a slaveholding planter in the western part of Virginia.[27] The son's family awareness of Ireland was reinforced when he became a Jesuit and worked in Rome under the patronage of the Irish-born Kenney.

This was a fateful connection for the future of the Jesuit slaves, for Kenney handed on to McSherry a belief that slaves in America were not so badly off as the peasantry of Ireland. Kenney wrote to an American Jesuit correspondent in 1822, "You hear dreadful things of the South of Ireland. . . . Your slaves, even in the South, are better provided for in many respects than a great portion of our peasantry."[28] To Kenney, the triple evils of a tithe system, oppressive rents, and absentee landlords were much worse than anything to be found on American plantations.[29] In this analysis, Kenney was quite close to the feelings of the "Young Irelanders," members of a nationalist movement in his homeland who believed that the liberation of Ireland was a more urgent need than the emancipation of slaves elsewhere in the world.

Even Daniel O'Connell, the most influential Irish nationalist leader of the first half of the nineteenth century and an advocate of immediate and universal slave emancipation, felt that most slaves were better off than Irish peasants. O'Connell attributed this difference to the need for masters to keep slaves healthy enough to be productive.[30] He did proceed to say that he did not see this difference in conditions as any reason to spurn abolitionism.[31] Jesuits like Kenney and McSherry drew precisely the opposite conclusion, however, refusing to universalize the movement for liberty as O'Connell had.

Nativist rhetoric close to home may have influenced the Maryland Jesuits in thus distancing themselves from O'Connell. The last thing they felt they needed was association with European revolutionaries. A declaration of the Protestant Association of Baltimore in 1835, for example, asserted that European despots were trying to eliminate the model of liberty that was the United States by sending subversive money to American Jesuits. This plot, the Association said, was similar to the manner in which O'Connell and his "Romist auxiliaries" were undermining the liberties of the United Kingdom.[32] Kenney and McSherry also believed that while liberated white peasants might thrive in a reformed Ireland, inferior and debauched black slaves would not fare as well if manumitted in the United States. One of McSherry's early acts as provincial, therefore, was to consider transporting the slaves to Africa. In 1834, he entered into secret negotiations with the Maryland branch of the American Colonization Society about sending them to Liberia.

The colonization movement was inspired by the feeling that whites and blacks would never be able to live together harmoniously in the United States. Therefore, it envisioned the mass migration of the slaves to their ancestral continent as the only humane alternative. An early exponent of this project was Thomas Jefferson.[33] The foundation of the American Colonization Society in December, 1816 was an attempt to make the idea concrete.[34] This organization immediately drew the loathing of free blacks, who saw it as an attempt to deny them citizenship in a nation their ancestors had involuntarily but extensively labored to build.[35]

White Maryland, however, welcomed the movement. The early 1830s saw much official encouragement for the state's slaveholders to consider transportation. In 1832, the legislature responded to Nat Turner's insurrection in neighboring Virginia by providing the Maryland auxiliary of the American Colonization Society with a $20,000 annuity for ten years. Laws were also passed providing that freed slaves who refused transportation face either ejection from the state or a reversion to bondage.[36] In this vortex, it is not surprising that the Maryland Jesuits considered transportation as part of their discernment concerning their new Province.

Fear of nativism prompted the Jesuits to conduct their dialogue with the Colonization Society anonymously. They appointed an intermediary, a layman named Will Erkead, to represent them in the discussions. All Erkead was authorized to reveal was that he spoke for a certain "large Catholic proprietor of slaves." On their behalf, he demanded that that these slaves be guaranteed the free exercise of the Catholic faith in Liberia. The board members were reassuring in response, even claiming that Catholic blacks were "emphatically the best part of the coloured population and would make the best settlers."[37] This was probably a sincere comment, since the Maryland branch of the society included in its membership such prominent Catholic laymen as Charles Carroll, the last surviving signer of the Declaration of Independence, and Roger Brooke Taney, a future Chief Justice of the United States.[38]

Erkead himself hoped that the example set by the Jesuits in transporting their slaves might "prove a good lead to many Catholic slaveholders who viewed the evils of a slave population precisely as ourselves, but could not consistently send them away from their churches."[39] Because Catholic masters felt such a paternalistic sense of responsibility for the devotional lives of their slaves, it was difficult for them to contemplate sending them away without supervision. Erkead recognized that this attachment had been a hindrance to the prophecies of such colonizationists as Ferdinando Fairfax, who had once predicted that masters would rush to free their slaves if only assured that they would not remain nearby once freed.[40]

Unfortunately for Erkead's assignment, McSherry's inquiries coincided with a period of considerable turmoil within the colonization movement itself. The Maryland chapter of the national Colonization Society declared its independence in 1834, and declared an intention to establish its own colony in Liberia. Meanwhile its spread stories of disorder in the settlement already existent in Liberia under the direction of the national organization. At one point, the dissidents even discouraged further emigration as long as the Liberian situation went uncorrected.[41] McSherry determined that it would not be advantageous to get involved in such quarrels.

There was a deeper reason for the Jesuits' rejection of colonization, however. The premise that the white and black races could not ever mix together was not supportive of the Catholic universalism that the Jesuits espoused. They were strong believers that all human beings, including African American slaves, were united in one Lord—"members of Jesus Christ, redeemed by his Precious blood," and so to be treated with charity, if paternalistic charity.[42] The idea of setting white and black people an ocean apart was just too foreign to their inclusive ecclesiology.

An opportunity was possibly missed here. For some Americans, participation in the colonization movement served as a transition between support for gradual manumission and advocacy of immediate emancipation. William Lloyd Garrison was an exemplar of this phenomenon. His participation in the colonization movement accelerated not only Garrison's abhorrence of slavery, but also his awareness of the racist impediments that free American blacks had to endure.[43] He eventually concluded that they had a right to live in the United States as freemen. The same thing might have happened to the Jesuits had McSherry associated with the colonizationists longer. However, he turned away from negotiations with the Colonization Society to survey his slaveholdings and attempt to calculate how much would be obtained from their sale. This task took several years.

McSherry found that forty-five slaves lived at St. Thomas' Manor in 1833. Nine men and boys and seven women were capable of work; the twenty-nine remaining were elderly and children. The burden of caring for these slaves was so great that the plantation usually had to borrow money from the General Fund of the Maryland Province rather than live off its own income. St.

Thomas' had contributed to the pension fund for Maryland Jesuits only occasionally, once with money obtained by exchanging produce with local merchants.

McSherry planned to spend $700 per year on tenant labor at St. Thomas'. McSherry calculated that a sale of the slaves there should bring in at least $16,000, with $1000 in interest.[44]

At Newtown in 1837, McSherry found thirty-six slaves—thirteen capable men, four capable women, the remaining nineteen elderly or children. Their burden had led to Newtown's contributing only twice to the General Fund recently: $600 for the year 1833, and $780 for all the years since then.

McSherry envisioned spending $1100 on tenant labor at Newtown. McSherry thought the sale of the slaves would bring at least $25,000. The interest would likely be 5 per cent, or $1100, but he felt 6 per cent or more might actually be obtained—if so, the sale would bring in an extra $1500.[45]

Also in 1837, McSherry surveyed the slaves at St. Inigoe's. There were ninety slaves there. Less than half of the slaves, forty-three—twenty-four men and nineteen women—were able to work. There were tenant farms, but most went unrented, so that the Jesuits had to raise at least $600 on the home farm to have any chance of meeting the annual province tax of $1000 to the General Fund. However, so much grain was absorbed in feeding the slaves that even the grain produced by the tenants was never sold off the plantation.[46]

By the 1830s, the weight of these financial problems had cost the Jesuits some human perspective on the lives of their slaves. Consider a petititon for manumission sent to McSherry on October 21, 1833 by Thomas Brown, who had been hired out to the Jesuits at St. Louis University on the Missouri mission. Brown had been owned by Jesuits since 1795, and his wife, Molly, had been a Jesuit slave from birth. The Browns' complaint was that they had been cast off into poor housing in their old age, a "rotten log house" owned by a campus neighbor. When Thomas asked the university president, Father Verheagen, if they could return to Jesuit quarters, he was offered an outlying house with no fireplace. Believing that he and Molly would freeze to death during the winter, Brown asked McSherry if he could buy his freedom for $100, $50 in immediate down payment and the rest as soon as possible. If this request were to be granted, Brown promised to pray for McSherry in perpetuity.[47]

Brown's petition is one of the few manuscripts in the voice of a Maryland Jesuit slave. Whether he actually wrote it, or whether he dictated it to someone who polished the presentation for him, is unclear. However, it deserves to be evaluated as a rare indication of how a Jesuit slave himself felt about his own treatment. Thomas knew enough about Jesuit structures to realize that McSherry, as a Provincial, outranked and could overrule Verheagan, a university administrator. He also understood that the treatment accorded to him and Molly signified that the Jesuits had changed their exceptional way of looking at slaves as humans first and vehicles for profit only incidentally.

Contrast Brown's testimony of 1833 with the voice of Granny Sucky, recorded in 1806. As a youth, she was punished for her spiritual audacity, forgetting her call to obey her Jesuit master long enough to advise him not to use the prayer of self-mortification. After her whipping, she kept a resolve never to challenge a Jesuit about his prayer again.[48] Brown was more self-confident in the insistence of his demand for freedom.

As Provincial, McSherry's power to determine the future of slaveholding was not absolute. He faced two checks on his discernment: the counsel of his men in Maryland gathered in a Province congregation, and the review and final decision of Father General Roothan.

In 1835, ten Jesuits attended the first Congregation of the Maryland Province. Their deliberations ended with the dispatch of a number of "postulata," or policy recommendations, to Rome. Two addressed the interrelated questions of plantations and slavery.

There was sentiment to sell all the farms as well as all the slaves. However, there were not enough votes for such a radical alternative. A compromise, passed by the narrow vote of six to four, retained the proposal for the slave sale but suggested that some plantations be kept and operated with free labor.[49] The hope behind this compromise was that the Jesuits could thereby find a way to incorporate both rural and urban ministry in their apostolic activities.

When Roothaan first replied to this postulatum, he demonstrated the traditional priority that Jesuits had accorded to the care of slaves by ignoring the suggestion about the lands altogether, merely commenting that the proposal regarding the slaves was a grave matter that required more study before he could give an answer.[50]

The second postulatum on the plantations underscored how much the anticipation of massive European immigration influenced the deliberations of American Jesuits by 1835. It requested that the number of rural missions and parishes be sharply if gradually cut, so that Jesuits might found colleges in Richmond, Philadelphia and New York to augment the ones already established at Georgetown and Frederick, Maryland. It also made a recommendation that profits from any farms which might be sold be used to buy urban land that would be suitable for college construction. Finally, it requested that priests who had hitherto ridden around the countryside from plantation bases rural should now travel from town to town to preach and offer retreats based on the *Spiritual Exercises* to city dwellers.

This postulatum had a clear preference for urban parishes and schools over rural missions. It argued that opening new schools would be almost impossible if too many of the old missions were maintained. Interestingly, it also argued that in the likely event of a division of the northern and southern states into separate countries, it would be desirable for the Jesuits to have houses of refuge for themselves in all parts of the land.[51] This comment was a concrete sign of Jesuit pessimism regarding the future of the Union.

Roothaan was slow to respond to the Congregation's advice. Meanwhile, two participants in the deliberations took some time to record the arguments that had been made during the meeting. One was the Province "procurator" or business agent, Father Vespre. Himself an advocate of selling the slaves, Vespre nevertheless wrote a memoir of the proceedings which preserved some of the objections made to the sale. The other record was left by Father Stephen Dubuisson, a former President of Georgetown, a staunch opponent of the sale. Vespre recorded the opponents' belief that to dispose of the slaves would guarantee the damnation of both the slaves and the Jesuits. Even if the first buyers were Catholics, the Jesuits would have no control over whether they would actually keep the slaves or sell them again, this time to Protestants for a profit. More pragmatic opponents of the sale argued that the slaves should be retained in case there were ever to be compensation from the government following upon a general emancipation—a point which showed that even the more traditionally minded Jesuits were moved by a new appreciation for profit. Also, Vespre recorded the fear of some that all white Americans, Catholics and Protestants, would be scandalized if there were a sale of slaves by the same priests who had spent so many decades proclaiming the vocation of the master to parent the slave.[52]

Dubuissson recorded the cases for and against the sale in much greater detail than Vespre did. Dubuisson wrote in the style of Thomas Aquinas in the *Summa Theologica*: he would state the issue, summarize the positions of his opponents, give an answer to their specific objections, and finally give his own opinion.[53] The advantage of this technique for historians is that it gives a full summary of the discussion at hand.

Dubuisson's opponents argued that the possession of slaves was damaging to the Jesuits in two ways. First, the burden of governing them distracted Jesuits from prayer. Second, the preoccupations of slave ownership made the Jesuits adopt the same worldly values as other masters in Maryland.

Dubuisson answered that Jesuits could just as easily lose their perspectives and souls in city parishes. Wherever a Jesuit might live, he would destroy his spirituality if he did not make the time for prayer. Any distractions from prayer on the plantations could easily cease if only the administration was reformed to allow for less day to day involvement by Jesuits themselves. Dubuisson felt that the portrayal of plantation life as morally dangerous for priests had been contrived by advocates of urban ministry.

Dubuisson then offered his own four reasons why Jesuits of the 1830s encountered spiritual difficulties in the United States. Infected with the overly individualistic American spirit, many neglected the communal dimension of religious life. The economy of the young republic promoted commerce and industry rather than agriculture, so that fewer Jesuits experienced the contemplative value of rural culture. Too many Jesuits also appeased nativism, discarding Catholic devotional practices that drew Protestant criticism. Finally,

Dubuisson argued that many young Jesuits, particularly those of Anglo and Irish background, interpreted rules in their own interest rather than for the good of the Society and lacked proper piety.

Dubuisson's opponents presented as their second argument the case that the Bohemia plantation had become prosperous since Kenney's sale of its slaves four years earlier. Dubuisson responded that this phenomenon was not due to the absence of the slaves, but to the financial competence of the Jesuit now managing that farm. Dubuisson therefore proposed that those Jesuits who did remain in farm administration should simply be trained better.

The third argument of Dubuisson's opponents was that their religious vows and priestly consecration would impede Jesuits from fighting against any slave insurrection. Such revolts seemed more likely in the controversial atmosphere stirred up by the abolitionists. However, Dubuisson continued to insist that the greater danger would be to set the slaves free, for the climate of violence would still encourage them to believe that they could do things for themselves of which they were not capable. Dubuisson pointed out, as Kenney had also argued in 1820, that it would always be possible to find laymen who could carry out any needed suppression. Dubuisson's own position was that to set the slaves free in such a dangerous climate would actually make it more likely that Jesuits would be caught in violent clashes between remaining slaveholders and abolitionists.

Dubuisson's opponents believed that the finances of the Province would be assisted by a sale. Revenue from harvests alone, it was said, had not met such recent expenses as a construction debt incurred at Georgetown, the failure of the government to fulfill a promised $25,000 donation to that university and, the needs of the novitiate at Frederick. Dubuisson, however, stubbornly maintained that these problems could be met by administrative reform of the farms, not by elimination of the slaves.

Having answered Thomistically all these objections, Dubuisson now offered his own reasons to keep the slaves. He had a conviction that plantations operated with slave labor could become places of refuge for unhealthy and ill-tempered Jesuits unable to function in schools or parishes. Dubuisson believed that elderly Jesuits could comfortably retire to the plantations, as could immigrant Jesuits unable to master English. Where else could such people go?

Dubuisson also objected to the proposed transfer of slaves to the Deep South. He wished to respect the slaves' repugnance to that part of the country. He also thought that it was unfair to ask masters and slaves to separate, both physically and emotionally, when they had liked each other. Moreover, the interests of the aged and the married couples required that at least some such slaves remain in Maryland.

Dubuisson offered two final points. One, he feared that some Protestants would try to embarrass the Jesuits by freeing their own slaves just as the Jesuits were selling theirs. They would then mock the Catholic Church for its failure to embrace manumission. Dubuisson wished to avoid the scandal such an event would cause for the Church.

Dubuisson, finally, mistrusted the good faith of banks in accrediting the money that would be involved in such a massive transaction. He preferred that the society rely on land rather than money to secure its future.[54]

Dubuissson's objections did not sway Rome in the end. Roothan's permission to sell the slaves finally came in October, 1836, although it was accompanied by six conditions.[55] Basically, each of these conditions showed Father General's desire to preserve the traditional Catholic moral theology of slaveholding, which stipulated that the interests of the slaves be placed ahead of the needs and desires of their masters. The fact that he took such trouble to state these conditions suggests that Roothan had developed a mistrust of Maryland Jesuit fidelity to the traditional theology.

Roothan's first condition was that negotiations could only be conducted with potential masters who would both recognize and assist the slaves' right to freely practice their Catholicism. His third condition made this first stipulation more concrete, requiring that such provisions be made a condition of the actual bill of sale. Above all else, the slaves must be provided with priests.

Roothaan's second condition was that the slaves must be sold directly to their new masters rather than to intermediary agents. This decree was designed to prevent the danger that avaricious agents might break up married couples and families and sell them to Protestant buyers.

The fourth and fifth conditions were likewise concerned with marriage bonds and family ties. The fourth decreed that husbands and wives were never to be separated from each other, and that children were preferably not to be separated from their parents. The fifth condition was that any Jesuit slave married to a slave from another plantation must be brought together with their spouse rather than sold to a distant place. The sixth and final condition was that slaves whose age or health prevented their sale or transport must be provided for "as justice and charity demands," even if that meant their retention by the Jesuits.[56]

Not once, in all these conditions, was there any directive that the fiscal and financial condition of prospective buyers be investigated. The underlying concern was that, to the end, the Jesuits fulfill their paternal religious obligations toward their slaves. No thought was given to the possibility that new owners might neglect these tasks due to their own business reverses.

Roothaan's only instructions about finance concerned how to spend the money received from the sale. It could not be used to purchase supplies for the farms, or for the retirement of debt. Roothan suggested investment in ground rents in the cities of Pennsylvania and New York State.[57] This rent money could then be used for the education of young Jesuits. None of it should be used on construction of Jesuit schools for lay people, as Roothan wished to prioritize the training of greatly needed priests.[58]

Richard McSherry did not have the opportunity to implement these conditions. In 1837, he fell ill with stomach cancer and resigned as Provincial, only to die in 1839. His successor was another Irish American, the man who would actually conclude the slave sale, Thomas Mulledy.

The year 1837 offered the faces of Janus to Irish Americans. They stood at the hinge between two cultures. Both Ireland and the United States embodied strong heritages, both of which vied for Jesuit attention. Irish tradition included a legacy of anti-slavery thought, while American culture called on immigrants to assimilate to their new country through loyalty to a constitutional order which protected slavery.

If McSherry and Mulledy had followed the more Irish side of their heritage, they might have become outright abolitionists. Daniel O'Connell, the most prestigious and influential Irishman of the first half of the nineteenth century, had already linked the struggle of Ireland's Catholics for political and religious liberty with the struggle of African Americans for emancipation from bondage. As early as 1829, and frequently throughout the 1830s, O'Connell denounced the hypocrisy of Americans who supported Irish liberty while continuing to countenance slavery in their own country.[59] In colorful oratory, O'Connell portrayed slavery as a "stain on the star spangled banner."[60] As the Jesuits prepared for their sale, abolitionists operating within the British Empire began to focus more attention on the United States, for their goals of ending both colonial slavery and apprenticeship in the Empire had now been met.[61]

O'Connell's idealism was not an aberration, for he continued an ancient Irish tradition of firm opposition to slavery. Some scholars trace this position as far back as Saint Patrick in the fifth century. Himself an escaped slave who later returned to convert his former masters, Patrick publicly condemned Christian chieftains from Roman Britain for selling their fellow Christians among the Irish into slavery under pagan tribes like the Scots and Picts.[62] Patrick condemned the idea of basing freedom on ethnic and secular claims like Roman citizenship, arguing that Christian profession entitled all the baptized to live in freedom. The Irish Church affirmed this insight at the Council of Armagh in 1177, when it prohibited the Irish, in their turn, from trading in British Christian slaves.[63]

O'Connell's attempts to link Irish liberty and American abolitionism provoked two forms of opposition, however. In Ireland, there were many political leaders who wanted an exclusive focus on the overriding problems of their own country, particularly the need to repeal the 1801 act of Union with Great Britain. They feared, prophetically, that O'Connell's abolitionism would cost the repeal movement important financial support from proslavery Irish Americans.[64] This was a cultural clash between O'Connell, a man of the eighteenth century Enlightenment who saw liberty as a universal issue, and such groups of romantic nationalists as the "Young Irelander" movement, which focused on Ireland alone.[65]

Another factor was that many Irish Americans wanted nothing to do with an antislavery position. Highly anxious to demonstrate what they had in common with the American majority, they emphasized the white skin which separated them from African Americans but united them to the Protestant majority.[66] Such Catholic bishops as John Hughes of New York City and John England of Charleston, South Carolina, hypersensitive to the nativist charge that Roman Catholicism was set on foreign interference in the domestic affairs of the United States, denounced O'Connell as a meddler.[67] England went so far as to question O'Connell's interpretation of Saint Patrick's teachings, asserting that the latter was against slave trading but not slavery itself.[68]

O'Connell's most dramatic appeals to Irish Americans to embrace abolitionism came in the early 1840s, several years after the Jesuit slave sale, when he became the first of 70,000 signers of "An Address of the People of Ireland to their Countrymen and Countrywomen in America." This statement was widely circulated in immigrant communities by William Lloyd Garrison and his followers, but did not win much support from Irish Americans.[69] Many Irish Americans, in fact, even stopped contributing to the repeal movement completely in response to O'Connell's linking it to emancipation.[70]

There is evidence that Garrison, anxious to see cooperation between the Irish freedom and American abolitionist movements, and eager to win the votes of Irish Americans for emancipation, tried to reassure O'Connell that American Protestant abolitionists were not as anti-Catholic as their reputation suggested. Garrison, therefore, may have deliberately muted criticism of Catholic slaveholders during the years after he met O'Connell in London in 1833. This desire might explain Garrison's failure to mention Jesuit slaveholding in his papers. Writing to O'Connell in 1843, Garrison declared that his followers issued a thousand attacks against Protestant slaveholders for every one they made on Catholic slaveholders. The reason for this, Garrision asserted, was that the Protestant clergy and churches had been biased against the abolitionist movement from its outset.[71]

There is little likelihood, however, that any appeals from either Garrison or O'Connell would have dissuaded the Jesuits from their course of putting their American identity ahead of immediate emancipation. Both McSherry and Mulledy wanted to win recognition of Catholics as true Americans, and especially wanted to see Georgetown College in the capital city achieve status as a national university. At Georgetown, Mulledy cultivated the message that Catholics were true Americans. He had his students march to the Capitol in their school uniforms for the second inauguration of President Andrew Jackson in 1833, and he encouraged both Presidents Jackson and Martin Van Buren to enroll relatives in the college. Members of Congress were frequently feted on campus, and great patriotic celebrations were staged each year for Washington's Birthday and the Fourth of July.[72]

Mulledy wrote a sermon on liberty, which he is known to have delivered at

Frederick, Maryland on the Fourth of July, 1852. Although delivered long after the slave sale, it contains clues to that cautious approach to the exercise of American citizenship that influenced him to prefer sale to manumission. Mulledy stated that while government has an obligation to protect political liberty as the foundation of a successful secular government, the individual must view his personal liberty only as a means to freely choose the law of God and attain eternal life. Mulledy felt that God had offered the Americans their great individual freedoms only as a test, to see if they would remain faithful to the right things in life.

Therefore, Mulledy argued, liberty must not be exploited. He compared God to a master who measured the character of his servants by leaving alluring articles around the house to see if they would steal them. In a statement that explains much of his toleration of slaveholding, Mulledy declared that the only true form of slavery was that to sin and wrongdoing.[73] What was needed, then, was a cautious approach to life in the United States. Catholics must be obedient Americans. Challenging the constitutional order regarding slavery because Daniel O'Connell called for abolitionism would have disrupted this goal.

In 1857, Mulledy also wrote a homily on the "Duty of Citizens to their Rulers." He took as his text Romans 13:1, "Let every soul be subject to higher powers," and argued that the fourth commandment, the order to honor one's parents, "extended to rulers and governors of the earth," including heads of republics, who were to be regarded as parents of their people. To Mulledy, it was "prohibited to speak of them with contempt, to murmur against their government, to defame them and to inspire others with a spirit of discontent, revolt, and mutiny." His role model in this regard was the Christian community of ancient Rome, who obeyed the just temporal authority of the Roman Emperors even though they persecuted the faith. The alternative would have been secular anarchy, which would have impeded the liberty of the church just as much as any persecution.

The only restriction that Mulledy placed on obedience to secular authority was that citizens must spurn commands to contradict the will of God. Even here, however, he tempered this qualification with a call to give authorities as much benefit of the doubt as possible. When the government imposed new taxes, for example, it was necessary to suppose that the interest of the state compelled the new levies, and "not trouble the peace of society by complaints and murmurs."[74]

These thoughts demonstate that Mulledy clearly fit into a certain Irish American manner of responding to the nativist movement. To divert criticism of themselves, they resorted to vigorous expressions of American patriotism and veneration for the Constitution just as the Garrisonians were attacking both national unity and the morality of the Constitution.[75] Not for Mulledy was the universal call for liberty issued by the O'Connellites and the Garrisonians; he worried only about his own liberty and the liberty of the religious order he belonged to.

As Provincial, therefore, Mulledy quickly revived the project of finding suitable buyers, which had been delayed by McSherry's ill-health and the financial Panic of 1837. In June of 1838, after a few days on the farms of southern Maryland, he wrote to Father Francis Dzierozynski at Georgetown that the task was vexed. Concerning one prospective buyer, Mulledy wrote that he had tried to convince the man that a fair price would have to be at least $400 per head, not the $345 the man was willing to offer. While Mulledy continued to hope for $450 per head, he had come to realize that it was difficult to dispose of the slaves to persons in a Catholic neighborhood.[76]

While he could play the role of the hard-headed businessman, the conviction that the slaves were human and Catholic continued to unsettle Mulledy's conscience. On June 30, eleven days after concluding their sale, he recorded in his diary that he had celebrated Mass for the intention of the "poor negroes."[77]

Two buyers were finally found in Louisiana, a state whose French heritage gave it a prominent Catholic culture and whose sugar economy, unlike Maryland's seemed capable of supporting the massive plantations that alone could prevent slave families from being broken up. On June 19, 1838, therefore, a contract was signed with former Governor Henry Johnson (1779–1867) and his associate, Dr. Jesse Battey. The price was $115,000 for 272 slaves; the down payment was $25,000 on a mortgage of ten years.[78] The slaves were mostly transported during the autumn of that year.

Johnson's political record as Governor and United States Senator from Louisiana suggests that more than his Catholicism attracted Mulledy's approbation. A leading Southern Whig, Johnson promoted banking. He signed legislation creating a Bank of Louisiana, in which the state government held half the stock of four million in capital. He also implemented a Planters' Banking Association, which had a fund of two million.[79]

Mulledy appreciated this record because he valued banking himself and wanted Jesuits to invest more money in them. He may have sensed an even deeper philosophical affinity between Jesuits and southern Whigs. Southern Whigs faced a dilemma, for they were torn between the national party's attraction to a modern economy of specialization and bourgeois values and the lingering premodern values of agrarian Southern society.[80] This is also a fair description of the conflict that wracked the Maryland Jesuits as they contemplated the sale of their slaves, as symbolized by Mulledy's own vexed combination of public sale negotiations and private Masses for the slaves.

The conflicted attitude of the Jesuits, in fact, guaranteed that the sale was executed only with difficulty in almost every respect. Neither the transportation of the slaves, the disposition of the money received, the capacity of the buyers to pay off their mortgage, nor the subsequent religious lives of the slaves worked out well. Only the condition of the farms in Maryland changed for the better through this transaction.

Mulledy was afraid that diehard Jesuit opponents of the sale might assist slaves to escape before transportation, so he arrived on the plantations, unannounced, accompanied by Johnson and a sheriff, to confiscate as many slaves as possible by force. Not all the slaves could fit in one ship, however, so there had to be a second transportation a few weeks later. During the interval, several Jesuits indeed encouraged their slaves to hide in the woods. At least a dozen slaves avoided transportation altogether by so doing. In the confusion, however, it seems quite likely that several slave families were separated.[81]

Mulledy's manner of dividing up the money from the sale caused him great trouble. Against the specific order of Roothaan to reserve it for the training of Jesuits, he applied $17,000 of the proceeds toward a $30,000 construction debt at Georgetown—a debt incurred through building projects Mulledy himself had undertaken as President of that institution.[82] Mulledy was soon forced to resign as Provincial and come to Rome to justify this application.

The third problem in the execution of the sale was that Johnson and Battey had financial difficulties that prevented them from either meeting all their payments or keeping their promises about providing religious devotion for the slaves. There survives a correspondence between Mulledy and Edmund Forstall, an attorney for the Jesuits who maintained contact with Johnson, in 1844. Unsuccessful in collecting some debts which were owed to him, forced to spend some of the proceeds from that year's crop on the construction of a sugar house and the establishment of a mill, Johnson feared he would be unable to meet his own mortgage payments that would fall due the following March. His only chance was to re-mortgage his main plantation or sell his interest in a nearby sugar plantation. Johnson hoped that he could relocate all the former Jesuit slaves on his home plantation so that they might be remortgaged. Johnson declared that he was still "intending . . . to discharge the notes . . . held against me."[83]

In 1851, Dr. Batey requested release from his mortgage on sixty-four of the slaves.[84] The subsequent financial travails of Johnson was reported to Mulledy by Father C.C. Lancaster in a letter of March 1, 1859. The Senator had eventually sold to a certain John Thompson, a graduate of the Jesuit university at St. Louis, the obligation of paying off the slave mortgage. Thompson himself applied for an extension of the mortgage to March 31, 1860, after which Johnson made a vain attempt to reassume responsibility for the debt.[85]

These events were partially the consequence of the exclusive focus that the Jesuits had placed upon finding buyers who would provide for the spiritual lives of the slaves. In neglecting to investigate potential buyers' financial credentials, the Jesuits unintentionally set up a situation in which the actual buyers proved unable to care for either the material or the spiritual needs of the slaves. The Jesuits had embraced the culture of the American marketplace to a certain extent, but not entirely.

The fate of the slaves under their new dispensation was a troubled one. In

1848, James VandeVelde, S.J. toured Louisiana and visited Thompson, one of his former pupils. VandeVelde traveled there in hopes of determing what had happened to the slaves in the decade since their transportation. He wrote to Mulledy in detail about the spiritual problems he found on the neighboring plantations of Johnson and Thompson.

About one-third of the slaves already lived on the Thompson plantation. The nearest Catholic church was at Donaldsonville, about ten miles across the bayou of Lafourche. Walking to mass was troublesome for the infirm and taxing for those who worked all week. Only one small cart was available, enough to hold only a few of the women and children. Many mothers stayed home on Sundays in order to care for their children and attend to domestic duties in the master's house. For those who did reach church, the sermon was in incomprehensible French.

VandeVelde approached a priest at Donaldsonville about calling at the plantations one Sunday a month for Mass and catechism lessons. However, the priest felt that he would only be able to do that on a weekday, when many slaves would be working in the fields.

The remaining slaves were in similar difficulties. They lived on two plantations, Bayou Tabou and Bayou Mongo, which were far from any church or priest. Furthermore, Johnson had sold them to Protestant masters who had no basic interest in their religious devotions, meanwhile claiming that his financial problems made it impossible for him to build the promised chapel.

VandeVelde found several other Catholic plantation owners nearby who were willing to contribute toward the construction of a church, on two conditions. They wanted the church to be open to their own slaves, and they wanted the Maryland Jesuits to head the subscription list with a $1000 contribution. VandeVelde counseled Mulledy:

> To tell you the truth, I am of opinion that the Province of Maryland is in conscience bound to contribute to it, and thus to provide for the salvation of those poor people, who are now utterly neglected, and whose children grow up without any notion of religion. Justice as well as charity require that their former masters should step in to aid other well-disposed persons to procure them the means of salvation. . . . Mr. Johnson will probably be still in Washington when this will reach you, and might be consulted as regards the manner of providing for the spiritual welfare of the coloured people. [86]

Thus Vandevelde documented how the faith lives of the slaves had been neglected over the decade following their departure from Maryland. Any response Mulledy may have made to this letter has not survived.

The one conspicuous success of the slave sale was that the Jesuit farms now began to prosper. Two sets of reports, those of Peter Havermans, S.J. in 1841 and those of John McElroy, S.J. in 1842, demonstrate that this change occurred because the departure of the slaves encouraged Jesuits finally to address their problems systematically.

Havermanns hoped to diversify Bohemia by selling its marl as fertilizer. Two tenants were already using a two-field system to revitalize the land. There were plans to establish one more tenant farm and a mill to exploit the nearby timber and water power.[87]

Havermans wanted to drain the swamp at St. Joseph's for meadlowland. A young Jesuit, Charles Lancaster, was manager there, and was employing both white and black farmhands—the first recorded indication of Jesuit willingness to hire manumitted slaves after the mass sale. Lancaster had already constructed several houses for tenants. He had also developed a corn house, facilities for graining, a stable and carriage house. The land already was producing twice as much as under slaveholding.[88]

At Jesuit direction, two tenants at Newtown Plantation had already completed a new meat house and corn house; a kitchen was nearly finished. Havermans found abundant livestock on all the Jesuit farms he inspected; more clover was needed to feed them. Thus he determined to adopt a four-field system.[89]

In 1842, John McElroy found St. Inigoe's occupied by six honest but unlucky tenants. Wheat, corn and tobacco had all failed, forcing the payment of rents by cash. McElroy devised two projects to address these losses, however. The first was to sell pine from the heavily wooded St. George's Island. While this wood only brought in $10 an acre, it replaced itself quickly. He also introduced sturdier construction material in order to cut repair costs on farm buildings.

McElroy had spent much time working at Frederick in northern Maryland; he knew that farmers there were more prosperous than the slaveholding neighbors of the Jesuits at St. Inigoe's. He realized that it would take awhile for the Jesuits to catch up with the farmers of Frederick. "That we shall succeed any better in *future* than we *have done* in this estate, is very doubtful. It is worthy of consideration now to see if something can not be devised to secure our property, and make it competent to the object it has in view." It was clear to him, however, that the end of slaveholding had been a necessary first step: "For the last forty years, I question whether this manor, with its 2000 acres, has yielded to the Society one hundred dollars a year, or four thousand dollars clear of all expenses."[90]

At Newtown, collection of rents was a big problem. McElroy noted that "this difficulty occurs frequently when renting to poor men, as crop failures, family accidents, prevent them from meeting engagements on small farms." The grain crop at Newtown had also failed, although not to the same extent as St. Inigoes. McElroy responded to these difficulties by investing less in repairs at Newtown than at other plantations.[91] It was now made clear to the tenants that they must produce if improvements were to occur.

Turning to St. Thomas', McElroy reported that there were two tenants. Both paid one-third of their crops for rent, but McElroy wanted them to pay cash for 1843 and 1844. He decided to charge $400 for one tenement and $500 for the other, the difference being attributed to the greater amount spent on improvements for the second farm. McElroy had already persuaded the tenants to sow clover on the land each year in hopes of improving the soil. McElroy could also report a substantial savings on the construction of a barn. Since a Jesuit brother had been able to build the barn himself without employing an outside carpenter, expenses were much reduced. Only a kitchen was now needed to make this building complete. Unfortunately, the wheat crop at St. Thomas' had been very deficient that year.[92]

Regularization of bookeeping was the challenge at Cedar Point, whose manager, Mr. Higdon, had died shortly before McElroy's inspection of the place. No one had audited Higdon's accounts in years. McElroy quickly found that the man had not known how to do proper bookkeeping—-"he had strict integrity and excellent moral character but kept *no cash account*—-no account against the procurator and a want of dates in all his credits." McElroy found that there was not even a separate account kept for each tenement.

Nevertheless, McElroy believed that "with careful supervision and economy" the farms at Cedar Point would become profitable over a reasonable number of years. He hoped to award leases of eight to ten years on the principal tenements, and to require the raising of certain crops. He also wanted to require that tenants themselves keep the buildings in repair and leave the houses in the same state as found. "This would enlist the tenants in *our* interest, whilst seeking their own, and would give somewhat of character to our property."[93]

The final estate which McElroy surveyed in this report was White Marsh. Four tenants there paid $875 each year in rents. There was hope to raise that amount to $1000, but the case of one tenant who was fighting eviction had delayed the new arrangement by a year. 450 acres of this farm were in Anne Arundel County, and a Mr. Hopkins wanted to buy that portion for $9.25 per acre. McElroy noted that this was the price that a Barton Dural had recently paid to the Jesuits for land of similar quality and quantity.[94] There was an effort to standardize prices.

While Johnson and Battey foundered in Louisiana, the Jesuit plantations in Maryland thus began to prosper. Ironically, "the Society abandoned its slave labor at the very time that the estates were beginning to produce." The turnaround was attributed to the introduction of tenant farming and sharecropping, plus the emergence, at long last, of some Jesuits who showed skill at financial management.[95] One of these was Lancaster, who recorded that the income of the farms rose from $6000 in 1847 to $10,000 in 1849 to $16,000 in 1861.[96] These statistics are an exception to the general portrayal of southern Maryland in the mid-nineteenth century as a place where a stagnant slave economy had not yet been challenged by the emergence of a vital alternative.[97]

The facts show that the Jesuits were challenging the old order in a remarkably successful way.

The Jesuits had thus largely solved their plantation problem. In two other areas, however, the slave sale brought no relief to the Society. These were the pressures that nativism and abolitionism continued to exert on Jesuit life.

In September, 1838 Benedict Fenwick, a Jesuit serving as Bishop of Boston, predicted to his brother that the slave sale would relieve abolitionist and nativist attacks on the Society.[98] Still ahead, however, were the events of the 1840s and 1850s, and the massive Irish Catholic immigration to be provoked by the potato blight of 1845. The reaction to the ensuing influx of Catholics led to the formation of the American, or "Know-Nothing" Party.[99] When this party entered former President Millard Fillmore in the presidential election of 1856, Maryland was the only state whose electoral votes Fillmore captured.[100] These events, taking place well beyond the influence of the Jesuit plantations, negated any benefit from the sale.

Charles Stonistrust, S.J. of Georgetown spent much time refuting nativist charges against Jesuits during these years. In 1855, he responded to a query from the War Department by denying that Jesuits took an oath to subvert the Constitution.[101] During the presidential election campaign of 1856, a Georgetown alumnus living in Alabama, H. P. Thompson, sought Stonistrust's help in denying a Know-Nothing rumor that Catholicism was an abolitionist religion. Thompson contrasted Georgetown alumni, who were loyal to the Constitution, with graduates of Princeton, Dartmouth and Yale, who were disdainful of the Constitution and hostile to the South. Thompson felt that Georgetown had taught Catholics to vote for national rather than sectional candidates like the Republican nominee that year, John C. Fremont.[102]

Defying Fenwick's expectations, Jesuits after the slave sale still had to search for ways to demonstrate their Americanism. One tactic was to promote a holiday called "Maryland Pilgrim's Day," a recollection of the first Catholic settlers and their role in securing religious freedom and toleration in the colony and, eventually, the nation. In an unusual gesture for the usually politically reticent Jesuits, Reverend John McCaffrey, S.J. himself delivered a public oration on this holiday in 1842. He subseqently published his address as a pamphlet.[103] McCaffrey tried to stem the accusation that Catholics opposed religious liberty for Protestants by arguing that the Jesuits stood for the principle that Jesus had died in love for all humanity, and that all must be left to accept or reject him freely. These remarks were necessary because the slave sale had not removed skepticism about the Jesuits' motives for participating in American culture.

However great the doubt that the Jesuits were true adherents to American values, it was the Society's full absorption in the dynamics of antebellum America that destroyed the exceptional institution of Maryland Jesuit slaveholding. During colonial times, the Jesuits envisioned slaveholding as something conducted for the slave's benefit, with Christian masters turning aside aspirations for profit to provide for servants unable to govern their own lives. In the nineteenth century, however, the Jesuits tired of trying to discipline slaves who persistently showed their resentment of their servile condition by rebelling against Catholic morality. It seemed futile to remained mired in such an impasse when the Catholic Church was otherwise beginning to grow in the United States. Meanwhile, such movements as abolitionism and nativism enmeshed the slaveholding Jesuits in controversies they sought to escape. In particular, their desire to be seen as loyal Americans and men faithful to the Constitution led them to reject the abolitionist impulses coming from Daniel O'Connell in Catholic Ireland, and to resist appeals that they join hands with American abolitionists like William Lloyd Garrison. The pressure of a market shifting from land to money based wealth was sufficient to instigate the Jesuits to defy Roman suscipions of new ways of making wealth.

All these forces came together in the mass Jesuit slave sale of 1838, an event which made the farms prosperous at long last, but which did little to ease the Jesuits' other problems. Despite painstaking effort by the Jesuits, their former slaves were quickly denied the practice of Catholicism through the negligence of their new owners. Meanwhile, abolitionists and nativists remained wary of Catholicism, and even became more hostile as immigration grew greater in the years after the sale. There was little about any of these events which made the Jesuits' lives easier, but one thing was certain—their own conduct of slaveholding in Maryland had come to an end.

NOTES

1. Roman Archives of the Society of Jesus (RASJ), IX, "General and Miscellaneous Letters, 1833–1837," Archives of the Maryland Province (MPA), Special Collections Division, Lauinger Library, Georgetown University, Washington, D.C.

2. Father Peter Kenney, S.J., "Statement of Religious Discipline, 1820," Item no. XT1–2, Box 126, Folder 7, MPA.

3. "From the *Summa Theologica* of St. Thomas Aquinas, c. 1265–1272," in Kenneth J. Zanca, editor, *American Catholics and Slavery, 1789–1866: An Anthology of Primary Documents* (Lanham, Md.: University Press of America, 1994), p. 17.

4. Father Peter Kenney, S.J., "Observations made by Reverend Father Visitor at the Residence of St. Francis Xavier, Bohemia, Cecil County, Maryland, June, 1831," Item no. XP5, MPA, Box 126, Folder 4; Peter Kenney, S.J. to Thomas Mulledy, S.J., July 16, 1832, The Thomas Mulledy, S.J. Papers (TMSJP), Box 1, Folder 4, Special Collections Division, Lauinger Library, Georgetown University, Washington, D.C.

5. John Tracy Ellis, *American Catholicism* (Chicagos: University of Chicago Press, 1969), p. 48.

6. Robert Emmett Curran, S.J. *The Bicentennial History of Georgetown University, I: From Academy to University, 1789–1889* (Washington, D.C.: Georgetown University Press, 1993), p. 58.

7. Robert K. Judge, "Foundation and First Administration of the Maryland Province," *Woodstock Letters* 88 (November, 1959), p. 378.

8. Gilbert J. Garraghan, S.J., *The Jesuits of the Middle United States, I* (New York, New York: America Press, 1938; impression reprinted in Chicago: Loyola University of Chicago Press, 1983), p. 328.

9. William Lloyd Garrison, "To the Public," 1831, in Lawrence B. Goodheart and Hugh Hawkins, editors, *The Abolitionists: Means, Ends, and Motivations* (Lexington, Mass.: D.C. Heath, Problems in American Civilization Series, 1995), pp. 42–43.

10. American Anti-Slavery Society, "Declaration of Sentiments, " 1833, *Ibid.*, p. 46.

11. Angelina Grimke to Catherine E. Beecher, June 17, 1837, *Ibid.*, pp. 50–52.

12. Fr. Peter Kenney, S.J., "Minutes of Extraordinary Consultation at Georgetown College, Washington, D.C.," MPA, Box 126, Folder 2.

13. "From Samuel F. B. Morse's *Imminent Dangers to the Free Institutions of the United States, Through Foreign Immigration*," in Zanca, *op. cit.*, p. 98.

14. Ray Allen Billington, *The Protestant Crusade, 1800–1860: A Study of the Origins of American Nativism* (New York: Macmillan, 1938), pp. 42–42; pp. 105–106; p. 108; pp. 120–135.

15. Father Peter Kenney, S.J., "Minutes of Extraordinary Consultation at Georgetown, August 2, 1832," MPA, Box 126, Folder 2.

16. Fr. Peter Kenney, S.J., "Memorial to the Missouri Mission," 1832, Item no. XSI, MPA, Box 126, Folder 6.

17. Benedict Fenwick to George Fenwick, January 21, 1830, Item no. 209 NI-15, MPA, Box 62, Folder 19.

18. James Ward, S.J. to Samuel Barber, May 6, 1838, Item no. 212 Pl 13, MPA, Box 66, Folder 5.

19. Madeline Hooke Rice, *American Catholic Opinion in the Slavery Controversy* (New York: Columbia University Studies in History, Economics and Public Law #508, 1944), pp. 93–94.

20. Charles Sellers, *The Market Revolution: Jacksonian America, 1815–1846* (New York: Oxford University Press, 1991), p. 4.

21. Ira M. Leonard and Robert D. Parmet, *American Nativism, 1830–1860* (New York: Van Nostrand Reinhold, 1971), p. 34.

22. Barbara Jeanne Fields, *Slavery and Freedom on the Middle Ground: Maryland during the Nineteenth Century* (New Haven: Yale University Press, 1985), pp. 1–22.

23. Sellers, *op. cit.*, p.202.

24. John F. Sleeman, "Usury and Interest," in James F. Childress and John MacQarrie, editors, *The Westminster Dictionary of Christian Ethics* (Philadelphia:

The Westminster Press, 1986), pp. 639–640.

25. Kenney, Minutes of Extraordinary Consultation at Georgetown, 2 August 1832, MPA, Box 126, Folder 2.

26. Curran, *op. cit.*, p. 112.

27. Curran, *op. cit.*, p. 108.

28. Peter Kenney, S.J. to John McElroy, S.J., March 30, 1822, Item no. 205 Z10a, MPA, Box 60, Folder 17.

29. *Ibid.*

30. Douglas C. Riach, "Daniel O'Connell and American Anti-Slavery," *Irish Historical Studies* XX, no. 77 (March, 1976), pp. 3–25.

31. Douglas C. Riach, "O'Connell and Slavery," in Donal McCarthy, editor, *The World of Daniel O'Connell* (Dublin, Ireland: Mercer Press, 1980), p. 176.

32. Mary McConville, *Political Nativism in the State of Maryland, 1820–1860*, (Washington, D.C.: Catholic University of America Press, 1928), pp. 92–93.

33. Thomas Jefferson, *Notes on the State of Virginia* (New York: W. W. Norton edition, edited by William Peden, 1954), p. 143.

34. P.J. Staudenraus, *The African Colonization Movement, 1816–1865* (New York: Columbia University Press, 1961), pp. 29–30.

35. "Philadelphia Blacks Protest Against Colonization, 1817," in Goodheart and Hawkins, editors, *op. cit.* pp. 37–38.

36. Staudenraus, *op. cit.*, p. 142.

37. Will Erkead to William McSherry, S.J., October 17, 1834, MPA, Box 13, Folder 4.

38. Staudenraus, *op. cit.*, p. 110.

39. Erkead to McSherry, S.J., October 17, 1834, MPA.

40. Staudenraus, *op. cit.*, p. 3.

41. Staudenraus, *op. cit.*, pp. 232–234.

42. Father George Hunter, S.J., "Notes in his Spiritual Retreat at Port Tobacco, December 20, 1749," Item no. 202A7, MPA.

43. James Brewer Stewart, *William Lloyd Garrison and the Challenge of Emancipation* (Arlington Heights, Ill.: Harlan Davidson, 1992), p. 41.

44. William McSherry, S.J., "Report of Incomes of St. Thomas' Manor, 1833," Item no. 99L-4, MPA, Box 26, Folder 3.

45. William McSherry, S.J., "Report on Newtown, 1833–1837," Item no. 99 L 1–4, MPA, Box 26, Folder 3.

46. William McSherry, S.J., "Report on St. Inigoe's, 1833–1837," Item no. 99.LI-4, MPA, Box 26, Folder 3.

47. "Petition of the slave Thomas Brown to Father Richard McSherry, Provincial," October 21, 1833; MPA, Box 40, Folder 5.

48. Brother Joseph Mobberly, S.J., "Diary, Part VI," p. 21; the Brother Joseph Mobberly, S.J. Papers (BJMSJP), Special Collections Division, Lauinger Library, Georgetown University, Washington, D.C.

49. "Proceedings of the First Maryland Province Congregation, 1835," in *Acts of*

the Province Congregations, 1832–1896, MPA.

50. *Ibid.*

51. *Ibid.*

52. Father Francis Vespre, S.J, "Memoir of the First Province Congregation, 1835," RASJ, IX, MPA.

53. For a comparison of the writing styles of Aquinas and Duboisson, see Anton C. Pegis, editor, *Introduction to St. Thomas Aquinas: The Summa Theologica and the Summa Contra Gentiles* (New York: Modern Library, 1948), pp. 3–5 and Judge, *op. cit.*, pp. 395–397.

54. Father Stephen Dubuisson, S.J., "Memorial Regarding the Proposed Sale of the Slaves," 1836, IX, "General and Miscellaneous Letters, 1833–1837, RASJ, IX, MPA.

55. Note that applying to the Jesuit general for this permission was a very different matter to the Maryland Jesuits than applying to the Holy See itself would have been. An application to the General kept the question of their property within the Jesuit order, and thus did not violate the Maryland Jesuits' belief that they owned land autonomously, without the intervention of the greater Church.

56. Edwin Beitzell, *The Jesuit Missions of St. Mary's County, Maryland* (Abel, Md.: Privately Printed by the Author, 1960), p. 139.

57. Judge, *op. cit.*, p. 398.

58. Robert Emmett Curran, "'Splendid Poverty': Jesuit Slaveholding in Maryland, 1805–1838," in Randall M. Miller and Jon L. Wakelyn, editors, *Catholics in the Old South: Essays on Church and Culture* (Macon, Ga.: Macon University Press, 1983), p. 142.

59. Riach, "Daniel O'Connell and American Anti-Slavery," p.5.

60. Gilbert Osofsky, "Abolitionists, Irish Immigrants, and the Dilemmas of Romantic Nationalism," *The American Historical Review* 80, no. 4 (October, 1975), p. 890.

61. Riach, "Daniel O'Connell and American Anti-Slavery," p. 4.

62. Thomas Cahill, *How the Irish Saved Civilization: The Untold Story of Ireland's Heroic Role from the Fall of Rome to the Rise of Medieval Europe* (New York: Doubleday Anchor Books, 1995), p. 114; see also Patrick, "Letter to the Soldiers of Coroticus," in Martin P. Harney, S.J., editor, *The Legacy of Saint Patrick: As Found in his Own Writings* (Boston: Daughters of Saint Paul, 1979), pp. 121–129.

63. Noel Ignatiev, *How the Irish Became White* (New York: Routledge, 1995), p. 7.

64. Riach, "Daniel O'Connell and American Anti-Slavery," p. 22.

65. Maurice R. O'Connell, *Daniel O'Connell: The Man and His Politics* (Dublin, Ireland: Irish Academic Press, 1990), p. 122, p. 130.

66. Ignatiev, *op. cit.*, pp. 6–31.

67. O'Connell, *op. cit.*, pp. 122–123.

68. Riach, "Daniel O'Connell and American Anti-Slavery," p. 21.

69. Osofsky, *op. cit.*, p. 897.

70. *Ibid.*, p. 902.

71. William Lloyd Garrison to Daniel O'Connell, December 8, 1843, in Walter M. Merrill, editor, *The Letters of William Lloyd Garrison, III: No Union with Slaveholders, 1841–1849* (Cambridge: The Belknap Press of Harvard University Press, 1973), p. 230.

72. Curran, *Bicentennial History*, p. 110–111.

73. Thomas Mulledy, S.J., "Homily on Liberty," July 4, 1852.

74. Thomas Mulledy, S.J., "Duty of Citizens to their Rulers," January 11, 1857; TMSJP, Box 7, Folder 5.

75. Osofsky, *op. cit.*, p. 900.

76. Rev. Thomas Mulledy, S.J. to Rev. Francis Dzierozynski, S.J., June 12, 1838, Item no. 212 Pl-13, MPA, Box 66, Folder 5.

77. Rev. Thomas Mulledy, S.J., "Index of Mass Intentions and Diary," 1824–1851, TMSJP, Box 8, Folder 4.

78. Curran, "'Splendid Poverty'," p. 142.

79. "Biographical Sketches of Louisiana's Governors, from D'Iberville to Foster, by a Louisianaise, as a Contribution to the Exhibit of Woman's Work, in the Louisiana State Department, at the World's Industrial and Cotton Centennial Exposition, New Orleans, La, 1884–1885," (Baton Rouge, La.: The Advocate, Book and Job Office, 1893), pp. 28–29.

80. Daniel Walker Howe, *The Political Culture of the American Whigs* (Chicago: University of Chicago Press, 1979), p. 239.

81. Curran, " 'Splendid Poverty'," p. 143.

82. *Ibid.*, p. 142.

83. Henry Johnson to Edmund Forstall, circa. 1845, Item no. 112 R1–R4, MPA, Box 40, Folder 6.

84. Doctor Jesse Batey, Request for Mortgage Release on his Slaves, 1851, Item no. 112 B1–P6, MPA, Box 40, Folder 5.

85. Father C.C. Lancaster, S.J. to Father Thomas Mulledy, S.J., March 1, 1859, Item no. 112 B1–P6, MPA, Box 40, Folder 5.

86. James VandeVelde to Thomas Mulledy, S.J., March 28, 1848, Item no. 216 711, MPA, Box 70, Folder 5.

87. Peteer Havermans, S.J., "Report of Bohemia, June 7, 1841," Item no. 99LI-4, MPA.

88. Peter Havermans, S.J., "Report of St. Joseph's, Eastern Shore," June 7, 1841, Item no. 99 Li-4, MPA, Box 26, Folder 3.

89. Peter Havermans, S.J., "Report on Newtown," 1841, MPA, Box 26, Folder 3.

90. John McElroy, S.J., "Notes on the Present State of our Farms by the Agent in his late Visit," December 17, 1842, Item no. 99.LI-4, MPA, Box 26, Folder 3.

91. *Ibid.*

92. *Ibid.*

93. *Ibid.*
94. *Ibid.*
95. Curran, "'Splendid Poverty'," p. 146.
96. Peter C. Finn, "The Slaves of the Jesuits in Maryland," (masters dissertation, Georgetown University, 1974), pp. 132–133.
97. Fields, *op. cit.*, pp. 6–7.
98. Benedict Fenwick, S.J. to George Fenwick, S.J., September, 1838, Item no. 212 N2, MPA.
99. Ellis, *op. cit.*, pp. 61–69; pp. 84–86.
100. David C. Whitney and Robin Vaughn Whitney, *The American Presidents* (Garden City, N.Y.: Guild America Books, Eighth Edition, 1993), p. 110.
101. Correspondence of Jefferson Davis, Secretary of War, and Charles Stonistrust, S.J., July 6 and 16, 1855, Item no. 213Z2 and no. 223Z2, MPA, Box 75, Folder 22.
102. H. P. Thompson to Charles Stonistrust, S.J., August 24, 1856; MPA, Box 76, Folder 1.
103. Rev. John McCaffrey, S.J., President of Mt. St. Mary's College, "Oration Delivered at the Commemoration of the Landing of the Pilgrims in Maryland, Emittsburg, Maryland, May 16, 1842," MPA.

EPILOGUE

A Slaveholding both Anglo-American and Catholic

In broad particulars, the story of Jesuit slaveholding parallels the general story of slaveholding in Maryland. The Jesuits began to hold slaves around the same time that other colonial Marylanders did, and ceased to hold slaves around the same time that the "peculiar institution" was in general decline within the state of Maryland. These facts can tempt one to the conclusion that there was nothing exceptional about Jesuit slaveholding. These same facts, however, can also blind posterity to some exceptional features of Jesuit practice.

Slaveholding arose among Marylanders for reasons of economic expediency that were leavened by assumptions of race and class. In a culture which took the superiority of the white race and the English emphasis on rule by a landed upper class for granted, slavery seemed like the most efficient form of labor with which to harvest the tobacco crop. Practical experience showed Marylanders, pragmatic Anglo-Americans that they were, that such forced labor could accomplish the task once the market for indentured servants had eroded. The Maryland Jesuits were not just Anglo-Americans, however. They were also Catholic. This meant that there was an overlay of abstract principles concerning slaveholding, derived from the Catholic intellectual tradition, which they applied to the personal governance of their own slaves. Thus these Jesuits early manifested a tension between their Anglo-American and Catholic identities that would dominate their entire history as slaveholders.

As English settlers, the Jesuits shared in the development of slavery in Maryland. In administering their slaveholding, however, they attempted to apply the abstract ideals of Catholic philosophy and theology. Derived from deductive reasoning, mostly from such thinkers of ancient, medieval and Renaissance Europe as Augustine, Aquinas, and Bellarmine, these principles often had little to do with the actuality of slaveholding in eighteenth and nineteenth century Maryland. They had been developed before the emergence of a modern plantation system of slavery in the southern colonies of British North America. The result was that the Jesuits struggled to apply ideals of humane treatment and personable relationships between masters and slaves to a situation which could not accommodate those ideals. A tension between a typically American and a typically Catholic form of slaveholding arose. The failure of the Jesuits to balance this tension was the probable reason why their plantations never really became prosperous during the slaveholding era. While their Anglo-American sense of expediency prompted them toward economic efficiency, the ideals of the Church inhibited the Jesuits from feeling comfortable with the acquisition of wealth.

This contradiction is why the Jesuits treated their slaves harshly despite their own rhetoric that they would treat them kindly as an example to other masters. Trapped between two tenacious identities that were difficult to reconcile, the Jesuits formed a reservoir of frustration and rage which they had to express somehow. The slaves became convenient targets. Jesuit mistreatment of the slaves was not designed to motivate the slaves to work harder, but rather simply to punish them for misbehavior that made the Jesuits' desire to reconcile temporal and religious values more difficult to realize.

The ideological evolution of American proslavery thought proceeded from an early stage of regarding slaveholding as a necessary evil to the assertation that slavery was a positive good. Their Catholic tradition prevented the Jesuits from fully making this shift themselves. They held to the theory that slaveholding was one of the sad results of the fall of humanity, one of those unfortunate consequences of original sin that would be wiped out when the Second Coming restored creation to its original order. Meanwhile it would be necessary for some people to remain enslaved as a consequence of their fall from grace. Because the Jesuits regarded slavery as a necessary evil, it was difficult for them to complete the transition to regarding it as a positive exercise for the pursuit of profit.

This anachronism persisted among Catholics because their theology regarded human work more as an expression of humility and submission to God than as a means of self-fulfillment.[1] The Jesuits were also influenced, however, by a major impetus to regard slavery as a punishment for the sin of racism. They considered people of dark color as morally inferior to people of white skin color, reinforcing the idea that Africans were under a perpetual curse of slavery due to some primeval flaw of their character. For the Jesuit missionaries to Maryland, there were two antecedents for this prejudice, their English heritage and certain attitudes which had early sprung up within the Jesuit order itself. The first antecedent they shared with their English Protestant neighbors; the second was their own.

The English of the colonial era characteristically approached all foreigners with insularity. They believed that England had a superior way of life which others would have to recognize and join in order to prove themselves fully worthy of being called civilized. Since the English even approached Europeans with this attitude, they certainly could not have regarded peoples of other continents as their equals either.[2] Some Englishmen came to regard black skin as a quality which truly set an individual radically apart from themselves.[3] Thus the English Jesuit missionary Joseph Mosley could write home in 1773 from Tuckahoe, Maryland that "I've lived alone for these nine years past, not one white person with me."[4] Whatever Mosley might have thought regarding the spiritual rights of slaves to Christian baptism, socially he regarded them as less than human.

While Jesuits were unusual compared to other European missionaries in having an ability to respect and sometimes even enter into the non-European civilzations they encountered, this dexterity at adapting to other cultures for the sake of spreading the Gospel within them did not extend to dealings with people of black skin and African origin. The French Jesuits in New France eventually absorbed themselves in the native culture they encountered there.[5] Southern European Jesuits initially displayed remarkable adaptation in East Asia, where missionaries like the Italian Matteo Ricci envisioned and sought a great synthesis of Confucian culture and Christianity. It was also in Asia, however, that Jesuit dislike for the dark-skinned first manifested itself in contempt for the peoples of India and Southeast Asia, whose supposed backwardness some missionaries contrasted with the brilliance of the "white" peoples of China and Japan.[6] In colonial Maryland, a similar Jesuit bias manifested itself in English Jesuit appreciation of Indians and a dislike of slaves. Christopher Morris described the native Americans as "as deare unto Christ our Lord and redeemed with as great a price as the best in Europe."[7] Joseph Mosley, however, wrote disparagingly of "negroes, a stubborn, dull set of mortals, that do nothing but by driving."[8] A root of these contrasting feelings was the fact that Jesuits, themselves men of initiative and hard work through their spirituality of laboring for the Lord and the spread of the Gospel, respected industrious people and had trouble honoring people who seemed to take a more resistant approach to work. The hard work of the Indians to master the North American wilderness impressed them; the resistance of Africans to working the plantations did not.

Thus the English Jesuits who founded the Maryland mission derived racism from both their English and their Jesuit heritage, and found it natural to enslave Africans. Even when some Jesuits began to question the utility of their slaveholding, as many did from the time of the American Revolution and the papal suppression of the Jesuit order, they did so for largely racist reasons. They correctly saw the lethargy of the slaves as a major reason why the plantations were unprofitable. Their racist assessment of the African character prevented them from realizing that this lack of industry was the slaves' way of protesting their involuntary servitude, so the Jesuits took the lack of hard work as confirmation of the dogma that people of dark skin color were inherently lazy and licentious. The Jesuits supported the American Revolution because of its promise of religious liberty for Catholics, not to achieve fundamental equality between slaves and white folks. Instead, they saw the idea of selling off all their slaves as a possible means of breaking the financial dependence of the plantations upon the deficient African-American character.

The racism of the Jesuits was a major cause of their ambivalent attitude toward the Enlightenment, the Western intellectual movement whose emphasis on the rights of man played such a pivotal role in the founding of the United States and in the rise of the abolitionist movement. To be sure, racism was not the only reason Jesuits were wary of this movement. They believed that the Enlightenment was a derivative of the heretical Protestant Reformation. They also disliked the Enlightenment's preference for rationality instead of religious doctrine and its emphasis on the individual rather than the community. Also essential to both the Enlightenment and romantic Protestantism, moreover, was a confidence in the perfectability of humanity that was difficult to square not only with the traditional Catholic emphasis upon sin and the flawed quality of human nature, but also with the idea that some people were racially inferior. Since Jesuits baptized their slaves, they clearly regarded them as human. However, they could not accept the idea that their slaves could be as morally perfectable as any other human beings. They baptized them so that they might receive God's mercy for their flaws, not that they might be set on a path to wordly accomplishment.

Even after slaveholding ended, Jesuits in Maryland continued to regard even partial African ancestry as a sign of inferiority. This fact was manifested by their postbellum treatment of a group in southern Maryland known as the "Wee-Sorts." These were people of a disputed mixture of racial backgrounds. Their nickname was apparently a mockery of the Wee-Sorts' own strong sense of distinction and exclusivity from full-blooded black people. They were reputed to say "We sort of people consider ourselves different from you sort," when black people treated them with undue familiarity. It is significant that during all the years that the Wee-Sorts expressed this sort of prejudice, Jesuits served as their pastors.

However, this did not mean that the Wee-Sorts themselves received fully sympathetic treatment from the Jesuits of Maryland. While the Wee-Sorts proclaimed themselves to be of native American origin, Jesuits believed that there were European and African strains in the Wee-Sort ancestry as well. Some scholars speculated that they descended from shipwrecked Spanish sailors of the sixteenth century who became involved with native American women; others speculated that French traders from Canada sired the group. In any case, the Wee Sorts were proud of their European and native American ancestry, but they resented any talk of African strains in their ancestry and shunned social contact with blacks.

White Marylanders felt otherwise, and the Wee Sorts were counted as "negroes" in United States census reports as late as 1950. They were subjected to ostracism and prejudice, particularly under the laws against interracial marriage that applied in the state for much of the twentieth century. This treatment showed the continuing heritage of the resistance to racial amalgamation that began in the colonial Chesapeake. The English could not stop all sexual relationships between white and black people, but they could and did refuse to grant status in white society to the mixed race offspring of such unions. In British North America, there was no recognized "mulatto" status creating a social status midway between white and black. Rather, the smallest amount of African ancestry designated an individual as wholly black.[9] However, the Jesuits made a small spiritual exception to that general secular practice by making a special place for Wee-Sorts in their church of Saint Ignatius at Bel Alton, Maryland—in the pews at the rear of the main floor. The whites were seated down front and the full-blooded blacks in their customary place in the balcony at the very rear, with the Wee-Sorts effectively in between. This segregation of seating arrangements ratified a Jesuit sense of social hierarchy among the races that persisted until the civil rights movement of the 1960s.

In 1965 the pastor of Saint Ignatius, Father Robert Thoman, celebrated the fact that the Wee-Sorts were tri-racial. He felt that they were the only group of people who embodied the complete image of the Catholic Church in the United States itself.[10] This remark was an attempt to affirm the Wee-Sorts at a time when legal segregation was near elimination in the United States and Jesuit attitudes themselves were finally changing. Thoman overlooked the roles of Hispanic and Asian communicants in the American Catholic population, but it was certainly one of the first times that the ideal of racial mixing received enthusiastic endorsement from a Jesuit in Maryland.

It is clear, therefore, that the decision of the Jesuits to end their slaveholding in 1838 must be linked to some other cause than racial liberalism. The key to understanding the sale lies in the simple fact that the slaveholding of the Jesuits, unlike that of their Protestant neighbors, was perpetually linked to the Catholic struggle to win acceptance and assimilation in British North America and the United States. Within this context, there was no deep inconsistency between the Jesuits' decision to acquire slaves in the seventeenth century and their reverse decision to dispose of them in the nineteenth. Each choice was motivated by the desire to fit in—a dilemma that Anglo American *Protestant* slaveholders did not face.

In colonial Maryland, the Jesuits realized from the outset that Catholics must achieve recognition of their status as propertyholders if they were to overcome the stigma of religious minority in a Protestant culture. Thus their possession of slaves initially served Catholic civil and religious liberties. By the antebellum era in Maryland, Jesuits felt instead that they must avoid vulnerability to the abolitionist controversy in order to innoculate themselves against nativist attempts to roll back their now secured religious liberties. They made no move to show agreement with the abolitionists, but they did try to inoculate themselves against them by selling off any slaves whose treatment the abolitionists could have fussed about. In the first case, slaveholding happened to serve the cause of Catholic liberty. In the latter case it happened that slaveholding did not. In each case, therefore, the decision that was made served the broader cause of Catholics' civil liberty in Maryland.

The slavery conundrum was finally solved, in the words of Abraham Lincoln in the Gettysburg Address, by " a great civil war, testing whether that nation, or any nation so conceived and so dedicated, can long endure."[11] Lincoln decided to end slavery for the same reason that Jefferson had once consented to preserve it. Each leader did what, on his watch, seemed most likely to preserve the unity of the nation. Similarly, the Jesuits made a utilitarian use of slaveholding, embracing it when it served their own liberty and discarding it when it did not. The Jesuits even found a spiritual justification for this expediency in the writings of their founder, Ignatius of Loyola, who wrote that the goods of the world were created for men to use or discard according to their judgment of whether those goods served the cause of their eternal salvation.

At the time that they sold their slaves, Jesuits were beginning to respond to and anticipate massive Catholic immigration to the United States from Europe. If the Catholic population of the nation was about to become much larger, it seemed expedient to avoid any impression that the Jesuits might be combining large concentrations of lower-class immigrants and slaves near the eastern coast of the United States. Jesuits had a conspiratorial reputation in Anglo-American culture, and the idea that they were plotting to overthrow the Constitution as they and Guy Fawkes were once supposed to have plotted the bombing of the English Houses of Parliament was never far from the imaginations of nativists. For the Jesuits to rid themselves of the slaves in 1838 gave the nativists one less excuse to warn of Jesuit insurgency.

Here also the Jesuits' racism played a subtle role. The Jesuits were better disposed toward the white laborer from Europe than the black African. With the Catholic population about to swell even while no corresponding increase of Jesuit vocations seemed likely, it seemed wasteful to concentrate scarce manpower on rural backwater plantations when Jesuits would be more needed in the cities to care for the masses of immigrants. Jesuits like Thomas Mulledy, the architect of the slave sale, stressed the choice of servants that was now possible for Catholics of means and argued that the morally superior laborers should be chosen. That was a code for the choice not only to employ whites socially, but also for the choice of Jesuits to work *with* whites spiritually. Jesuits could respond to the nativist threat with the disposition of their slaves because they had confidence that they could soon meet all their labor needs from a new and supposedly superior source and also minister to that same, potentially more fruitful source.

Joseph Mosley's expression "Negroes of Ours" points to this Jesuit tendency to condescend socially to the people they ministered to spiritually. Mosley entered this expression whenever he recorded the baptism of a Jesuit-owned slave in his parish register in Tuckahoe, Maryland. By saying that such an individual was "ours," meaning the communal property of the Society of Jesus, Mosley condescended socially to that person. Yet, by granting the same person initation as a Christian, Mosley accorded that individual great spiritual respect. Jesuit attitudes toward the immigrants from Europe began in much the same fashion. This combination of social condescension and spiritual egalitarianism descended from attitudes which Jesuits had long since developed in countries like France: a concentration on ministry to the elite while hoping the cultivation of such a devout upper class could help to keep the lower classes suitably Catholic and moral.[12]

Yet, when it came to white European Catholics who immigrated to the United States, this contradictory treatment did not last. In fact, the most enduring reputation of the American Jesuits became their assistance of such immigrants into the middle class of their new country. The social condescension quickly disappeared when its recipients were Irish, Italian, German or eastern European. The large network of secondary schools and institutes of higher education which the Society of Jesus developed throughout the United States during the nineteenth and twentieth centuries allowed many Catholics to advance professionally and socially. This mobility was exactly the opposite of what happened to African Americans both during all the years that the Jesuits owned slaves and the long decades afterward. The contrast raises the disturbing likelihood that the racism of the Jesuits prevented them from doing for African-Americans and Wee-Sorts what they were able to do for the white European immigrants.

Are there contributions that the lamentable saga of the Jesuit slaves may make to the historiography of the Catholic Church in the United States? Yes, there are. The tale adds weight to the testimony that American Catholicism was fully caught up in a national tendency toward racism. The tale also lends insight to a debate as to whether American Catholics have been typically more intent on resisting or assimilating to broader American culture.

This debate continues today. On one side is a resistance thesis, arguing that the Roman Catholic Church, both clergy and laity, might historically be characterized as in and for America, but never precisely of it.[13] Alternatively, there is a thesis that a tension between resistance and assimilation has been the major theme of American Catholic history, with the assimiltationists prevailing most of the time through the manner in which the necessary immersion of the laity in everyday secular culture has offset the structural aloofness of the clergy.[14] The Maryland slavery controversy shows that the Jesuits, at least, took a clerical lead in a dubious form of assimilation: using slaves as pawns in a larger struggle to fit into American culture. Whatever the general balance of the tension between resistance and assimilation, in the specific instance of the Jesuit slaves, there was little clerical resistance to the idea of Catholics becoming more American.

By making their slaves pawns in the struggle to assimilate as Americans, Jesuits contradicted the doctrine they professed as the Incarnation. This is the basic Catholic teaching that God becomes human, and it is imagined for Jesuits as an especially effective way through the *Spiritual Exercises* of Ignatius of Loyola. The decisive passage is from the first day of the second week of the *Exercises*—the time in his month-long retreat when the Jesuit ponders unity with Christ on mission to the world and the Church. It reads as follows:

> Here, it is how the Three Divine Persons looked at all the plain or circuit of all the world, full of men, and how, seeing that all were going down to Hell, it is determined in their Eternity, that the Second Person shall become man to save the human race. . . . how They look on all the surface and circuit of the earth, and all the people in such blindness, and how they are dying and going down to Hell.[15]

In order for this belief to be expressed in the daily conduct of any individual Catholic, it means that he/she must treat others with a fullness of both spiritual and bodily dignity, giving them the respect that their identity as redeemed creatures demands. According to the doctrine of the Incarnation, each and every person born into the world has an indwelling of Jesus Christ and deserves their full human rights.

The point here is not whether this norm signified that there was a universally applicable theology or standard of morality, but that the Jesuits in Maryland claimed to believe that there were such things. It is reasonable to measure their actual conduct against what they professed to be real and true. Consider, then, how the Jesuits contradicted their own teaching about human dignity through their possession of slaves. The Jesuits acknowledged in their rhetoric that their slaves had full spiritual equality with all other Catholics, but they also claimed that these same individuals had to be enslaved bodily and so could not enjoy full rights of secular citizenship. To make this contradiction possible, Jesuits had to also profess that the slaves needed owners to guide their religious observance. It was a perfect reinforcement for racism.

As long as the fullness of this legacy remains unconfronted by the Jesuits of today, the slaves will remain theirs, despite their sale so many years ago.

NOTES

1. Eugene D. Genovese, *Roll, Jordan Roll: The World that the Slaves Made* (New York: Random House, Vintage Books Edition, 1976), p. 287.
2. James Axtell, *The Invasion Within: The Contest of Cultures in Colonial*

North America (New York: Oxford University Press, 1985), p. 131.

3. Winthrop D. Jordan, *White over Black: American Attitudes toward the Negro, 1550–1812* (Chapel Hill: The University of North Carolina Press, 1968), p. 20.

4. Joseph Mosley to Helen Dunn, July 5, 1773, in Robert Emmett Curran, S.J., editor, *American Jesuit Spirituality: The Maryland Tradition, 1634–1900* (Mahwah, N.J.: Paulist Press, 1988), p. 109.

5. Axtell, *op.cit.*, especially Chapters 2–6, pp. 23–127.

6. See Andrew C. Ross, *A Vision Betrayed: the Jesuits in Japan and China, 1542–1742* (Maryknoll, N.Y.: Orbis, 1994), especially p. 42 and pp. 204–205.

7. Christopher Morris, S.J. to Edward Knott, S.J., July 27, 1640, in Curran, *op.cit.*, p. 57.

8. Joseph Mosley, S.J. to Helen Dunn, June 5, 1772, reproduced in *Woodstock Letters* XXXV (1906), p.50.

9. Gary B. Nash, *Red, White and Black: The Peoples of Early North America* (Englewood Cliffs, N.J.: Prentice Hall, 1992 Edition), pp. 289–290.

10. Benjamin Herman, "Unexplained WeeSorts Still Insist They're Different," *Washington Post*, May 16, 1954; Roger Treat, "Wee Sorts of Chapel Hill: Their Tribal Pride has let them Survive," *Baltimore News American*, June 1965; MPC, Box 9, Folder 5.

11. Abraham Lincoln, "The Gettysburg Address," in Richard N. Current, editor, *The Political Thought of Abraham Lincoln* (New York: Macmillan, the American Heritage Series, 1967), p. 284.

12. A. Lynn Martin, *The Jesuit Mind: The Mentality of an Elite in Early Modern France* (Ithaca, N.Y.: Cornell University Press, 1988), Chapter 12, "The Social Order," pp. 201–216.

13. See "Preface," pp. vii-xi, in Charles R. Morris, *American Catholic: The Saints and Sinners Who Built America's Most Powerful Church* (New York: Times Books, 1997).

14. See Jay Dolan, *The American Catholic Experience: A History from Colonial Times to the Present* (Notre Dame, Ind.: University of Notre Dame Press, 1992 edition).

15. David L. Fleming, S.J., *The Spiritual Exercises of St. Ignatius: A Literal Translation and a Contemporary Reading* (St. Louis: The Institute of Jesuit Sources, 1978), pp. 70–72.

Bibliography

MANUSCRIPT SOURCES

I. Unpublished Manuscripts

The American Catholic Sermon Collection. Special Collections Division, Lauinger Library, Georgetown University, Washington, D.C.

Archives of the Maryland Province of the Society of Jesus. Special Collections Division, Lauinger Library, Georgetown University, Washington, D.C.

Catholic Historical Manuscripts Collection. Special Collections Division, Lauinger Library, Georgetown University, Washington, D.C.

Lafarge, John, S.J. The John Lafarge, S.J. Papers. Special Collections Division, Lauinger Library, Georgetown University, Washington, D.C.

Maryland Province Collection. Special Collections Division, Lauinger Library, Georgetown University, Washington, D.C.

Mobberly, Brother Joseph, S.J. The Brother Joseph Mobberly, S.J. Papers. Special Collections Division, Lauinger Library, Georgetown University, Washington, D.C.

Mulledy, Thomas, S.J. The Thomas Mulledy, S.J. Papers. Special Collections Division, Lauinger Library, Georgetown University, Washington, D.C.

Proceedings of the Roman Catholic Clergy Corporation of Maryland. Special Collections Division, Lauinger Library, Georgetown University, Washington, D.C.

II. Published Manuscripts

Abbott, Walter M., S.J., editor. *The Documents of Vatican II*. New York: America Press, 1966.

Attwood, Peter, S.J. "Liberty and Property: or, the Beauty of Maryland

Displayed (1718). *United States Catholic Historical Magazine* III. New York: Press of the Society, 1890.

Augustine. *Against Julian*. New York: Fathers of the Church Incorporated, 1957.

———. *The City of God: An Abridged Version from the Translation by Gerald Walsh, S.J., Demetrius B. Zema, S.J., Grace Monahan, O.S.U. and Daniel J. Honan, edited by Vernon L. Bourke*. New York: Doubleday Image Books, 1958.

Bellarmine, Robert. *De Laicis, or the Treatise on Civil Government*. Translated by Kathleen E. Murphy. New York: Fordham University Press, 1928.

Bowden, Henry Sebastian, editor. *Mementoes of the Martyrs and Confessors of England and Wales*. Wheathampstead, England: Burns and Oates, 1962.

Catechism of the Catholic Church. New York: Doubleday, Image Books Edition, 1995.

Challoner, Richard. "Caveat Against the Methodists." Mount Vernon, Ohio: John P. Mardin, 1817. Early American Imprints, American Antiquarian Society, Worcester, Mass.

Current, Richard N., editor. *The Political Thought of Abraham Lincoln*. New York: Macmillan, The American Heritage Series, 1967

Curran, Robert Emmett, S.J., editor. *American Jesuit Spirituality: The Maryland Tradition, 1634–1900*. Mahwah, N.J.: Paulist Press, 1988.

Davitt, Edward, S.J., editor. "Letters of Father Joseph Mosley, S.J., 1757–1806." *Woodstock Letters*, XXXV, 1906.

"The Declaration of Independence," in *The Annals of America,II: Resistance and Revolution, 1775–1783*. Chicago: Encyclopedia Britannica Inc, 1968.

Ellis, John Tracy, editor. *Documents of American Catholic History*. Two Volumes. Wilmington, Del.: Michael Glazier, Inc., 1986.

Elton, G. R., editor. *The Tudor Constitution: Documents and Commentary*. Cambridge: Cambridge University Press, 1975 Reprint.

Faust, Drew Gilpin, editor. *The Ideology of Slavery: Proslavery Thought in the Antebellum South, 1830–1860*. Baton Rouge: Louisiana State University Press, 1981.

Fleming, David L., S.J. *The Spiritual Exercises of Saint Ignatius Loyola: A Literal Translation and a Contemporary Reading*. St. Louis: The Institute of Jesuit Sources, Revised Edition, 1986.

Goodheart, Lawrence B., and Hawkins, Hugh, editors. *The Abolitionists: Means, Ends and Motivations*. Lexington, Mass.: D. C. Heath, Third Edition 1995.

Hall, Clayton Colman, editor. *Narratives of Early Maryland, 1633–1684*. New York: Scribners, 1910.

Hanley, Thomas O'Brien, S.J., editor. *The John Carroll Papers*. Three Volumes. Notre Dame, Ind.: University of Notre Dame Press, 1976.

Harney, Martin P., S.J., editor. *The Legacy of Saint Patrick: As Found in His*

Own Writings. Boston: Daughters of Saint Paul, 1979.

Hughes, Thomas, S.J. *History of the Society of Jesus in North America, Colonial and Federal*. Four Volumes. London: Longmans, Green and Co.: 1917.

Hunter, George, S.J. "A Short Account of the State and Condition of the Roman Catholics in the Province of Maryland, Collected from the Authentic Copies of the Provincial Records and Other Undoubted Testimonies." *Woodstock Letters* X, #1 (1881).

Jefferson, Thomas. *Notes on the State of Virginia*. Edited by William Peden. New York: W. W. Norton, 1954.

Miller, Walter M., editor. *The Letters of William Lloyd Garrison, III: No Union with Slaveholders, 1841–1849*. Cambridge: The Belknap Press of Harvard University Press, 1973.

More, Thomas. *Utopia*. Harmondsworth, Eng.: Penguin Classics Edition, 1965.

Moulton, Phillips P., editor. *The Journal and Major Essays of John Woolman*. New York: Oxford University Press, 1971.

Nolan, Hugh J., editor. *Pastoral Letters of the American Hierarchy, 1792–1870*. Huntington, Ind.a: Our Sunday Visitor, Inc., 1971.

O'Brien, David J., and Shannon, Thomas A., editors. *Catholic Social Thought: The Documentary Heritage*. Maryknoll, N.Y.: Orbis, Second Edition, 1995.

Padberg, John, S.J., editor. *The Constitutions of the Society of Jesus and their Complementary Norms*. St. Louis: Institute of Jesuit Sources, 1996.

Perry, Marvin, Peden, Joseph R. and Von Laue, Theodore H., editors. *Sources of the Western Tradition, II: From the Renaissance to the Present*. Boston: Houghton Mifflin, 1991.

Persons, Robert, S.J. "An Answere to the Fifth Part of Reportes, 1606," in Rogers, D. M., editor. *English Recusant Liteature, 1558–1640*, no. 245. London: Scolar Press, 1975.

Pleasants, J. Hall, editor. *Archives of Maryland, L: Proceedings and Acts of the General Assembly of Maryland, 1752–1754*. Baltimore: 1933.

Rogers, D. M., editor. *English Recusant Literature, 1558–1640*, #245. London: Scolar Press, 1975.

Southwell, Robert, S.J. *An Humble Supplication to Her Maiestie*. Bald, R. C., editor. Cambridge, Eng.: At the University Press, 1953.

Thomas Aquinas. *The "Summa Theologica" of Saint Thomas Aquinas*. Translated by the Fathers of the English Dominican Province. London: Burns, Oates, and Washburn Ltd., 1929.

Zanca, Kenneth J., editor. *American Catholics and Slavery, 1789–1866: An Anthology of Primary Documents*. Lanham, Md.: University Press of America, 1994.

II. Published Secondary Sources

Agonito, Joseph. "St. Inigoe's Manor: A Nineteenth Century Jesuit Plantation." *Maryland Historical Magazine* 72, no. 1 (Spring, 1977).

Al-Anon Family Groups. "*. . . In All Our Affairs: Making Family Crises Work for You*. New York: Al-Anon Family Group Headquarters, 1990.

Axtell, James. *The Invasion Within: The Contest of Cultures in Colonial North America*. New York: Oxford University Press, 1985.

Bang, Carla. "John Carroll and the Enlightenment," in Kupke, Raymond J., editor, *American Catholic Preaching and Piety in the Time of John Carroll*. Lanham, Md: University Press of America, 1991.

Bangert, William V., S.J. *A History of the Society of Jesus*. St. Louis: The Institute of Jesuit Sources, 1986.

Beckett, Edward F., S.J. "Listening to Our History: Inculturation and Jesuit Slaveholding." *Studies in the Spirituality of Jesuits* 28, no. 5 (November, 1996).

Beitzell, Edwin Warfield. *The Jesuit Missions of St. Mary's County, Maryland*. Abell, Md.: Privately Printed by the Author, 1959.

Bennett, Lerone Jr. *Before the Mayflower: A History of Black America*. New York: Pelican Books: Fifth Edition, 1982.

Berlin, Ira. *Slaves Without Masters: The Free Negro in the Antebellum South*. New York: The New Press, 1974.

Bermejo, Luis M. *Infallibility on Trial: Church, Conciliarity and Communion*. Westminster, Md.: Christian Classics, 1992.

Billington, Ray Allen. *The Protestant Crusade, 1800–1860: A Study of the Origins of American Nativism*. New York: Macmillan, 1938.

"Biographical Sketches of Louisiana's Governors, from D'Iberville to Foster, by a Louisianese, as a Contribution to the Exhibit of Woman's Work, in the Louisiana State Department, at the World's Industrial and Cotton Centennial Exposition, New Orleans, La, 1884–1885." Baton Rouge, La.: The Advocate, Book and Job Office, 1893.

Blackburn, Robin. *The Making of New World Slavery: From the Baroque to the Modern, 1492–1800*. New York: Verso, 1997.

Blackwell, Richard J. *Galileo, Bellarmine and the Bible*. Notre Dame, Ind.: University of Notre Dame Press, 1991.

Bokenkotter, Thomas. *A Concise History of the Catholic Church*. New York: Doubleday Image Books, 1990 Edition.

Bossy, John. *The English Catholic Community, 1570–1850*. New York: Oxford University Press, 1976.

———. "Reluctant Colonists: The English Catholics Confront the Atlantic," in Quinn, David B., editor. *Early Maryland in a Wider World*. Detroit: Wayne State University Press, 1982.

Bosworth, Timothy W. "Anti-Catholicism as a Political Tool in Mid-Eighteenth Century Maryland." *The Catholic Historical Review*, LXI, no. 4 (October,

1975), pp. 539–563.

Bouwsma, William J. *John Calvin: A Sixteenth Century Portrait.* New York: Oxford University Press, 1988.

Brett, Stephen F. *Slavery and the Catholic Tradition: Rights in the Balance.* New York: Peter Lang, 1994.

Broderick, James. *Robert Bellarmine: Saint and Scholar.* Westminster, Md.: The Newman Press, 1961.

Brown, Raymond E. *A Crucified Christ in Holy Week: Essays on the Four Gospel Passion Narratives.* Collegeville, Minn.: Liturgical Press, 1986.

Cahill, Thomas. *How the Irish Saved Civilization: The Untold Story of Ireland's Heroic Role from the Fall of Rome to the Rise of Medieval Europe.* New York: Doubleday Anchor Books, 1995.

Carr, Lois Green, and Menard, Russell. "Immigration and Opportunity: The Freedman in Early Colonial Maryland," in Tate, Thad W., and Ammerman, David L. *The Chesapeake in the Seventeenth Century: Essays on Anglo-American Society.* New York: W. W. Norton, 1979.

Carr, Lois Green, Morgan, Philip D., and Russo, Jean B., editors. *Colonial Chesapeake Society.* Chapel Hil: University of North Carolina Press, 1988.

Childress, James F., and Macquarrie, John, editors. *The Westminster Dictionary of Christian Ethics.* Philadelphia: The Westminster Press, 1986.

Clancy, Thomas H., S.J. *An Introduction to Jesuit Life: The Constitutions and History Through 435 Years.* St. Louis: The Institute of Jesuit Sources, 1976.

Conrad, Alfred H., and Meyer, John R. *The Economics of Slavery and Other Studies in Econometric History.* Chicago: Aldine, 1964.

Curran, Robert Emmett, S.J. *The Bicentennial History of Georgetown University, I: From Academy to University, 1789–1889.* Washington, D.C.: Georgetown University Press, 1993.

———. " 'Splendid Poverty': Jesuit Slaveholding in Maryland, 1805–1838," in Miller, Randall M., and Wakelyn, Jon L., editors. *Catholics in the Old South: Essays on Church and Culture.* Macon, Ga.: Mercer University Press, 1983.

Davis, Cyprian. *The History of Black Catholics in the United States.* New York: Crossroad, 1990.

Davis, David Brion. *The Problem of Slavery in Western Culture.* New York: Oxford University Press, 1966.

de Guibert, Joseph. *The Jesuits: Their Spiritual Doctrine and Practice: A Historical Study.* Chicago: Loyola University Press, 1964.

Dolan, Jay P. *The American Catholic Experience: A History from Colonial Times to the Present.* Notre Dame, Ind.: University of Notre Dame Press, 1985.

Duffy, Eamon. "Richard Challoner, 1691–1781: A Memoir," in Duffy, Eamon, editor. *Challoner and His Church: A Catholic Bishop in Georgian*

England. London: Dartman, Longman and Todd, 1981.

Duffy, Eamon, editor. *Challoner and His Church: A Catholic Bishop in Georgian England*. London: Darton, Longman and Todd, 1981.

Edwards, Francis, S.J. *The Jesuits in England: From 1580 to the Present Day*. London: Burns and Oates, 1985.

Elkins, Stanley M. *Slavery: A Problem in American Institutional and Intellectual Life*. Chicago: The University of Chicago Press, Third Edition, 1976.

Ellis, John Tracy. *American Catholic Bishops: A Memoir*. Wilmington, Del.: Michael Glazier, 1983.

———. *American Catholicism*. Chicago: The University of Chicago Press, Second Edition Revised, 1969.

Faust, Drew Gilpin. *A Sacred Circle: The Dilemma of the Intellectual in the Old South, 1840–1860*. Baltimore: The Johns Hopkins University Press, 1977.

———. *Southern Stories: Slaveholders in Peace and War*. Columbia: University of Missouri Press, 1992.

Fields, Barbara Jeanne. *Slavery and Freedom on the Middle Ground: Maryland during the Nineteenth Century*. New Haven: Yale University Press, 1985.

Fischer, David Hackett. *Albion's Seed: Four British Folkways in North America*. New York: Oxford University Press, 1989.

Fogarty, Gerald, S.J. "Property and Religious Thought in Colonial Maryland Catholic Thought." *Catholic Historical Review* 71 (1986), pp. 573–600.

Fogarty, Gerald, S.J., Durkin, Joseph T., S.J. and Curran, Robert Emmett, S.J., editors. *The Maryland Jesuits, 1634–1833*. Baltimore: Maryland Province of the Society of Jesus, 1976.

Fogel, Robert William. *Without Consent or Contract: The Rise and Fall of American Slavery*. New York: W. W. Norton, 1989.

Fogel, Robert William, and Engerman, Stanley L. *Time on the Cross: The Economics of American Negro Slavery*. New York: W. W. Norton, Revised Edition 1989.

Foner, Eric. "Slavery, the Civil War, and Reconstruction," in Foner, Eric, editor. *The New American History*. Philadelphia: Temple University Press, 1990.

Foner, Eric, editor. *The New American History*. Philadelphia: Temple University Press, 1990.

Garraghan, Gilbert J., S.J. *The Jesuits of the Middle United States*. Four Volumes. New York: America Press, 1938; Impression Reprinted in Chicago: Loyola University Press, 1983.

Genovese, Eugene. *Roll, Jordan, Roll: The World the Slaves Made*. New York: Random House Vintage Books, 1976 Imprint.

———. *The Slaveholders' Dilemma: Freedom and Progress in Southern Conservative Thought, 1820–1860*. Columbia: University of South

Carolina Press, 1992.

Goodheart, Lawrence B., Brown, Richard D., and Rabe, Stephen G. *Slavery in American Society*. Lexington, Mass.: D. C. Heath, Third Edition 1993.

Graham, Michael, S.J. "Meetinghouse and Chapel: Religion and Community in Seventeenth Century Maryland," in Carr, Lois Green, Morgan, Philip D., and Russo, Jean B.,editors. *Colonial Chesapeake Society*. Chapel Hill: The University of North Carolina Press, 1988.

Gula, Richard M., S.S. *Reason Informed by Faith: Foundations of Catholic Morality*. Mahwah, N.J.: Paulist Press, 1989.

Gutierrez, Gustavo. *Las Casas: In Search of the Poor of Jesus Christ*. Maryknoll, N.J.: Orbis, 1993.

Gutman, Herbert G. *The Black Family in Slavery and Freedom, 1750–1925*. New York: Random House, Vintage Books Edition, 1976.

Hanley, Thomas O'Brien S.J. *Their Rights and Liberties: The Beginnings of Religious and Political Freedom in Maryland*. Chicago: Loyola University Press, 1984.

Harris, Seymour E. *Economics of Harvard*. New York: McGraw Hill, 1970.

Hayes, Zachary, O.F.M. "Purgatory," in Komonchak, Joseph A., Collins, Mary, and Lane, Dermot A., editors. *The New Dictionary of Theology*. Wilmington, Del.: Michael Glazier, 1987.

Henderson, Ian. "Original Sin," in Childress, James F. and Macquarrie, John, editors, *The Westminster Dictionary of Christian Ethics*. Philadelphia: The Westminster Press, 1986.

Hennesey, James, S.J. *American Catholics: A History of the Roman Catholic Community in the United States*. New York: Oxford University Press, 1981.

———. "Roman Catholicism: The Maryland Tradition." *Thought* 51, no. 202 (September, 1976), pp. 282–295.

———. "The Vision of John Carroll." *Thought* 54, no. 214 (September, 1979), pp. 322–333.

Holt, Geoffrey. *St. Omer's and Bruge's Colleges: A Biographical Dictionary*.

Horn, James. "Servant Emigration to the Chesapeake in the Seventeenth Century," in Tate, Thad W., and Ammerman, editors. *The Chesapeake in the Seventeenth Century*. New York: W. W. Norton, 1979.

Howe, Daniel Walker. *The Political Culture of the American Whigs*. Chicago: University of Chicago Press, 1979.

Ignatiev, Noel. *How the Irish Became White*. New York: Routledge, 1995.

"Introduction to Paul." *The New Jerusalem Bible*. Garden City, N.Y.: Doubleday, 1985.

Jones, Cheslyn, Wainwright, Geoffrey, Yarnold, Edward, S.J. and Bradshaw, Paul, editors. *The Study of Liturgy*. New York: Oxford University Press, Revised Edition, 1992.

Jones, Jaqueline. *Labor of Love, Labor of Sorrow: Black Women, Work and the Family, from Slavery to the Present*. New York: Random House, Vintage Books Edition, 1986.

Jordan, David W. *The Foundations of Representative Government in Maryland, 1632–1715*. Cambridge: Cambridge University Press, 1987.

Jordan, Winthrop D. *White over Black: American Attitudes toward the Negro, 1550–1812*. Chapel Hill: University of North Carolina Press, 1968.

Judge, Robert K. "Foundation and First Administration of the Maryland Province." *Woodstock Letters* 88 (November, 1959).

Katz, Stanley N., and Murrin, John M., editors. *Colonial America: Essays in Political and Social Development*. New York: Alfred A. Knopf, 1983.

Kelly, J. N. D. *Early Christian Doctrines*. London: Adam and Charles Black, 1965.

Kolchin, Peter. *American Slavery, 1619–1877*. New York: Hill and Wang, 1993.

———. *Unfree Labor: American Slavery and Russian Serfdom*. Cambridge: The Belknap Press of Harvard University Press, 1987.

Komonchak, Joseph A., Collins, Mary, and Lane, Dermot A., editors. *The New Dictionary of Theology*. Wilmington, Del.: Michael Glazier, Inc., 1987.

Krugler, John D. "Lord Baltimore, Roman Catholics, and Toleration: Religious Policy in Maryland During the Early Catholic Years, 1634–1649." *Catholic Historical Review* LXV (January, 1979), pp. 49–74.

———. "'With Promise of Liberty in Religion:' The Catholic Lords Baltimore and Toleration in Seventeenth Century Maryland, 1634–1692." *Maryland Historical Magazine* 79, no. 1 (Spring, 1984), pp. 21–43.

Kulikoff, Allan. *Tobacco and Slaves: The Development of Southern Cultures in the Chesapeake, 1680–1800*. Chapel Hill: University of North Carolina Press, 1986.

Kupke, Raymond J. "Dearest Christians: Study of Eighteenth Century Anglo-American Catholic Ecclesiology, " in Kupke, Raymond J., editor. *American Catholic Preaching and Piety in the Age of John Carroll*. Lanham, Md.: University Press of America, 1991.

Kupke, Raymond J., editor. *American Catholic Preaching and Piety in the Time of John Carroll*. Melville Studies in Church History, II. Lanham, Md.: University Press of America, 1991.

Kupperman, Karen Ordahl. *Settling with the Indians: The Meeting of English and Indian Cultures in North America, 1580–1640*. Totowa, N.J.: Rowman and Littlefield, 1980.

Lafarge, John, S.J. "Survival of the Catholic Faith in Southern Maryland." *The Catholic Historical Review* XXI, no. 1 (April, 1935).

Land, Aubrey C. *Colonial Maryland: A History*. Millwood, N.J.: KTO Press, 1981.

Lee, Jean B. *The Price of Nationhood: The American Revolution in Charles County*. New York: W.W. Norton, 1994.

Leonard, Ira M., aand Parmet, Robert D. *American Nativism, 1830–1860*. New York: Van Nostrand Reinhold, 1971.

Linck, Joseph C. "The Eucharist as Presented in the Corpus Christi Sermons of Colonial Anglo-America," in Kupke, Raymond J., editor. *American Catholic Preaching and Piety in the Time of John Carroll*. Lanham, Md.: University Press of America, 1991.

Martin, A. Lynn. *The Jesuit Mind: The Mentality of an Elite in Early Modern France*. Ithaca: Cornell University Press, 1988.

Marty, Martin E. *A Short History of American Catholicism*. Allen, Tex.: Thomas More, 1995.

Matthew, David. *Catholicism in England: The Portrait of a Minority, Its Culture and Tradition*. London: Eyre and Spottiswoode, 1955.

McBrien, Richard. *Catholicism*. San Francisco: Harper Collins, 1994 Edition.

McCarthy, Donal, editor. *The World of Daniel O'Connell*. Dublin, Ireland: Mercer Press, 1980.

McConville, Mary. *Political Nativism in the State of Maryland,1820–1860*. Washington, D.C.: Catholic University of America Press, 1928.

McNeill, John, S.J. *The Church and the Homosexual*. New York: Next Year Publications, 1985 Edition.

Meiners, Roger E. "The Evolution of American Higher Education," in Sommer, John W., editor. *The Academy in Crisis: The Political Economy of Higher Education*. New Brunswick, N.J.: Transactions Publishers, 1995.

Menard, Russell R. "The Maryland Slave Population, 1658–1730: A Demographic Profile of Blacks in Four Counties,"in Katz, Stanley N. and Murrin, John M., editors.*Colonial America: Essays in Politics and Social Development*. New York: Alfred A. Knopf, Third Edition, 1983.

Miller, John Chester. *The Wolf by the Ears: Thomas Jefferson and American Slavery*. Charlottesville: University Press of Virginia, 1991.

Miller, Randall M., and Smith, John David, editors. *Dictionary of African American Slavery: Updated, with a New Introduction and Bibliography*. Westport, Conn.: Praeger, 1997.

Miller, Randall M., and Wakelyn, Jon L., editors. *Catholics in the Old South: Essays on Church and Culture*. Macon, Ga.: Mercer University Press, 1983.

Miller, William Lee. *Arguing about Slavery: The Great Battle in the United States Congress*. New York: Alfred A. Knopf, 1995.

Morgan, Edmund S. *American Slavery, American Freedom: The Ordeal of Colonial Virginia*. New York: W. W. Norton, 1975.

Morris, Charles R. *American Catholic: The Saints and Sinners Who Built America's Most Powerful Church*. New York: Times Books, 1997.

Nash, Gary B. *Red, White and Black: The People of Early North America*. Englewood Cliffs, N.J.: Prentice Hall, Third Edition 1992.

Noonan, John T., Jr. "Development in Moral Doctrine." Tulsa, Okla.: Warren Lecture Series on American Catholicism, 1993.

Nord, Warren A. *Religion and American Education: Rethinking a National Dilemma*. Chapel Hill: University of North Carolina Press, 1995.

Normin, Marion. "John Gother and the English Way of Spirituality." *Recusant History* 11. London: The Catholic Record Society, 1972.

O'Brien, David J. *Public Catholicism*. Maryknoll, New York: Orbis, 1996.

O'Connell, Maurice R. *Daniel O'Connell: The Man and his Politics*. Dublin, Ireland: Irish Academic Press, 1990.

O'Malley, John, S.J. *The First Jesuits*. Cambridge: Harvard University Press, 1993.

O'Neill, Charles Edwards. "John Carroll, the Catholic Enlightenment, and Rome," in Kupke, Raymond J.,editor. *American Catholic Preaching and Piety in the Time of John Carroll*. Lanham, Md.: University Press of America, 1991.

Osofsky, Gilbert. "Abolitionists, Irish Immigrants and the Dilemmas of Romantic Nationalism." *The American Historical Review* 80, no. 4 (October, 1975).

Orsy, Ladislas, S.J. "The Meaning of *Novus Habitus Mentis*: The Search for New Horizons." *The Jurist* 48, no. 2 (1988).

Ozment, Steven. *Protestants: The Birth of a Revolution*. New York: Doubleday Image Books, 1991.

Parish, Peter J. *Slavery: History and Historians*. New York: Harper and Row, 1989.

Patterson, Orlando. *Slavery and Social Death: A Comparative Study*. Cambridge: Harvard University Press, 1982.

Pelikan, Jaroslav. *Jesus Through the Centuries: His Place in the History of Culture*. New York: Harper and Row, 1985.

Phillips, Ulrich B. *American Negro Slavery: A Survey of the Supply, Employment and Control of Negro Labor as Determined by the Plantation Regime*. Baton Rouge: Louisiana State University Press, 1966 Reprint.

Porter, H.C. *The Inconstant Savage: England and the North American Indian, 1500–1660*. London: Duckworth, 1979.

Quinn, David B., editor. *Early Maryland in a Wider World*. Detroit: Wayne State University Press, 1982.

Raboteau, Albert J. *A Fire in the Bones: Reflections on African-American Religious History*. Boston: Beacon Press, 1995.

———. *Slave Religion: The "Invisible Institution" in the Antebellum South*. New York: Oxford University Press, 1978.

Randall, Willard Sterne. *Thomas Jefferson: A Life*. New York: Harper Perennial, 1993.

Remini, Robert V. *Henry Clay: Statesman of the Union*. New York: W. W.

Norton, 1991.

Riach, Douglas C. "Daniel O'Connell and American Anti-Slavery." *Irish Historical Studies* XX, no. 77 (March, 1976).

———. "O'Connell and Slavery," in McCarthy, Donal, editor. *The World of Daniel O'Connell*. Dublin, Ireland: Mercer Press, 1980.

Rice, Madeline Hooke. *American Catholic Opinion in the Slavery Controversy*. New York: Columbia University Studies in History, Economics and Public Law no. 508, 1944.

Rivera, Luis N. *A Violent Evangelism: The Political and Religious Conquest of the Americas*. Louisville, Ky.: John Knox/Westminster Press, 1992.

Sellers, Charles. *The Market Revolution: Jacksonian America, 1815–1846*. New York: Oxford University Press, 1991.

"Slavery." *New Catholic Encyclopedia*. New York: McGraw Hill, 1967.

Sleeman, John F. "Usury and Interest," in Childress, James F., and Macquarrie, John, editors. *The Westminster Dictionary of Christian Ethics*. Philadelphia: The Westminster Press, 1986.

Sommer, John W., editor. *The Academy in Crisis: The Political Economy of Higher Education*. New Brunswick, N.J.: Transaction Publishers, 1995.

Spalding, Thomas W. *The Premier See: A History of the Archdiocese of Baltimore*. Baltimore: The Johns Hopkins University Press, 1989.

Stampp, Kenneth M. *The Peculiar Institution: Slavery in the Antebellum South*. New York: Random House Vintage Books, 1989 Imprint.

Staudenraus, P. J. *The African Colonization Movement, 1816–1865*. New York: Columbia University Press, 1961.

Stewart, James Brewer. *William Lloyd Garrison and the Challenge of Emancipation*. Arlington Heights, Ill.: Harlan Davidson, 1992.

Stout, Harry S. *The New England Soul: Preaching and Religious Culture in Colonial New England*. New York: Oxford University Press, 1986.

Tate, Thad W. and Ammerman, David L., editors. *The Chesapeake in the Seventeenth Century: Essays on Anglo-American Society*. New York: W. W. Norton, 1979.

Tylenda, Joseph N., S.J. *Jesuit Saints and Martyrs: Short Biographies of the Saints, Blessed, Venerables and Servants of God of the Society of Jesus*. Chicago, Illinois: Loyola University Press, 1984.

Wainwright, Geoffrey. "The Language of Worship, " in Jones, Cheslyn, Wainwright, Geoffrey, Yarnold, Edward, S.J., and Bradshaw, Paul, editors. *The Study of Liturgy*. New York: Oxford University Press, 1992.

Waugh, Evelyn. *Edmund Campion*. London: Longmans, Green and Company, 1935.

White, Deborah Gray. *Ar'nt I a Woman?: Female Slaves in the Plantation South*. New York: W. W. Norton, 1985.

Whitney, David C., and Whitney, Robin Vaughan. *The American Presidents*. Garden City, N.Y.: Guild America Books, Eighth Edition, 1993.

Wood, Betty. *The Origins of American Slavery: Freedom and Bondage in the English Colonies*. New York: Hill and Wang, 1997.

Yarnold, Edward, S.J. *The Theology of Original Sin*. Notre Dame, Ind.: Fides, 1971.

Zwinge, Joseph, S.J. "The Jesuit Farms in Maryland: Facts and Anecdotes." *Woodstock Letters*, XLI (1912).

III. Unpublished Secondary Sources

Boroughs, Philip L., S.J. "John Woolman (1770–1772): Spirituality and Social Transformation in Colonial America." Ph.D. dissertation, University of California, Berkeley, 1989.

Bretzke, James T., S.J. "New Trends in Moral Theology." Lecture Delivered at the Jesuit School of Theology at Berkeley, Berkeley, California, October 10, 1995.

———. "A Taxonomy of Contemporary Christian Ethics and Moral Theology." Unpublished lecture notes, Jesuit School of Theology at Berkeley, Berkeley, California, 1995.

Finn, Peter C., S.J. "The Slaves of the Jesuits in Maryland." Masters dissertation, Georgetown University, 1974.

Lafarge, John, S.J. "The Jesuit-Baltimore Controversy." Unpublished Manuscript , The John LaFarge, S.J.Papers, Special Collections Division, Lauinger Library, Georgetown University, Washington, D.C.

Index

A

E

G

H

I

J

P

Q

R

Y